TOM PATEY

First published in 2022 by
Scottish Mountaineering Press.

Copyright © Mike Dixon and individual
authors 2022.

All photos © as credited.

The author and contributors have asserted
their rights under the Copyright, Design and
Patents Act 1988 to be identified as the authors
of this work.

A catalogue record of this book is available
from the British Library.

ISBN: 978-1-907233-46-3

All rights reserved. No part of this publication
may be reproduced, stored in or introduced
into a retrieval system, or transmitted in any
form or by any means (electronic, mechanical,
photocopying, recording or otherwise), without
the prior written permission of the publisher.

Every effort has been made to obtain the
necessary permissions with reference to
copyright material. We apologise for any
omission in this respect and will be pleased
to make the appropriate acknowledgements
in any future edition.

Edited by Deziree Wilson.
Designed by Gino Di Meo Studio.
Map graphics by Christopher Smith-Duque.

Maps are derived from Ordnance Survey
OpenData™

© Crown copyright and database right 2022

Printed & bound in Europe by LF Book
Services Ltd on PEFC Accredited Paper.

MIKE DIXON

TOM PATEY

ONE MAN'S LEGACY

Contents

	Foreword	8
	Introduction	12
CHAPTER 1	Minister's Son	18
CHAPTER 2	Aiguilles des Cairngorms	36
CHAPTER 3	The Scorpion and the Eagle	58
CHAPTER 4	Student of Medicine and Mountaineering	80
CHAPTER 5	Land of the Gauloises	104
CHAPTER 6	Dreams are for Action	128
CHAPTER 7	Zero Hour	154
CHAPTER 8	Establishment Mavericks	168
CHAPTER 9	After You, Mike	192
CHAPTER 10	No Ordinary Skier	210
CHAPTER 11	An Admiral and a Christian	224
CHAPTER 12	Locum in Limbo	242
CHAPTER 13	3 West Terrace	262
CHAPTER 14	The Bothy	280
CHAPTER 15	Third Time Lucky	292
CHAPTER 16	Lights, Camera, Sea Stacks	308
CHAPTER 17	With Joe, Don and Bonington	332
CHAPTER 18	The Hare and the Crab	358
CHAPTER 19	Burning the Candle	380
CHAPTER 20	Shades of Black	400
CHAPTER 21	Death and the Maiden	418
	Ian Patey's Memories	432
	One Man's Legacy	434
	Acknowledgements	444
	Bibliography	448
	Index	456

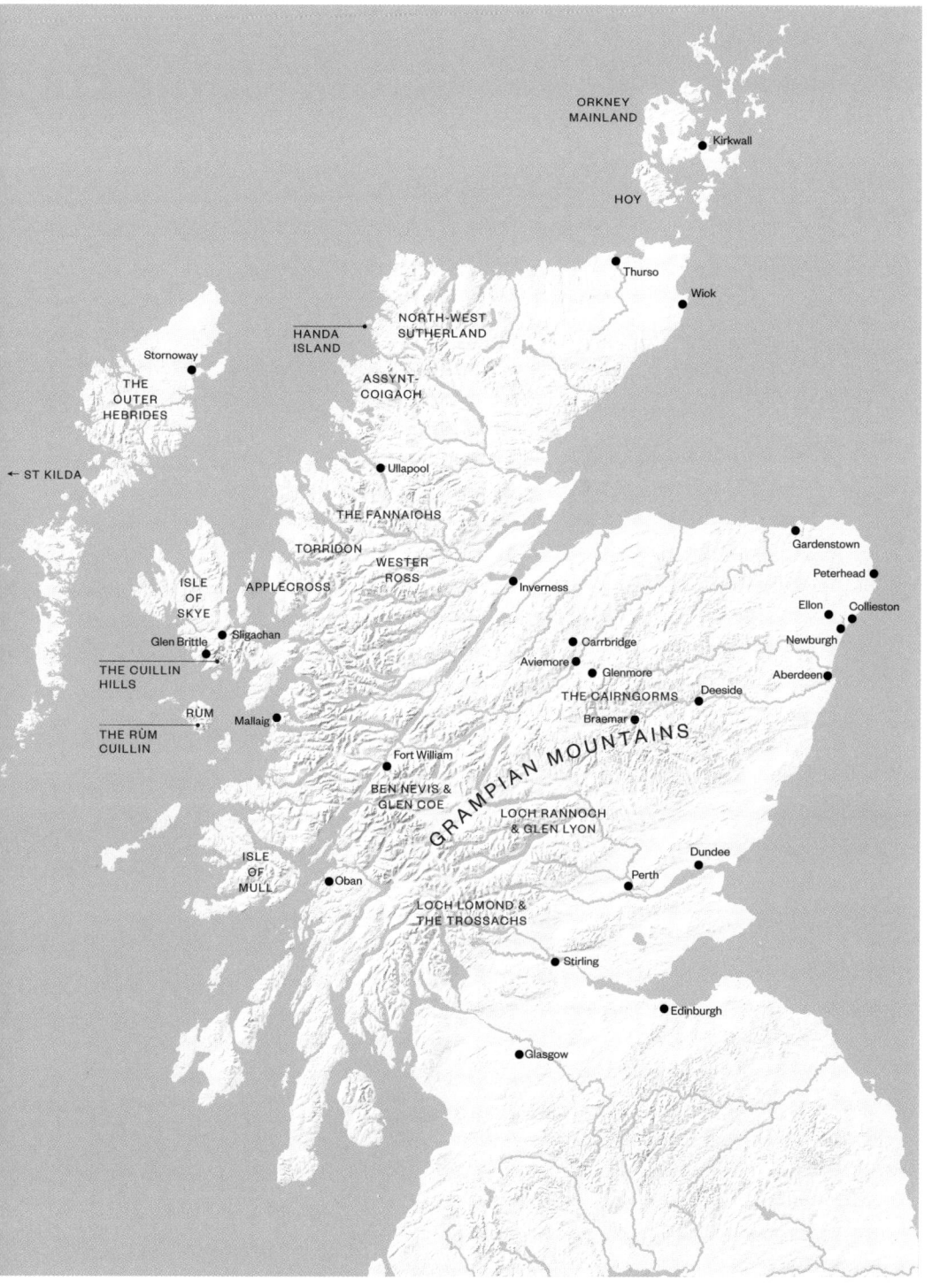

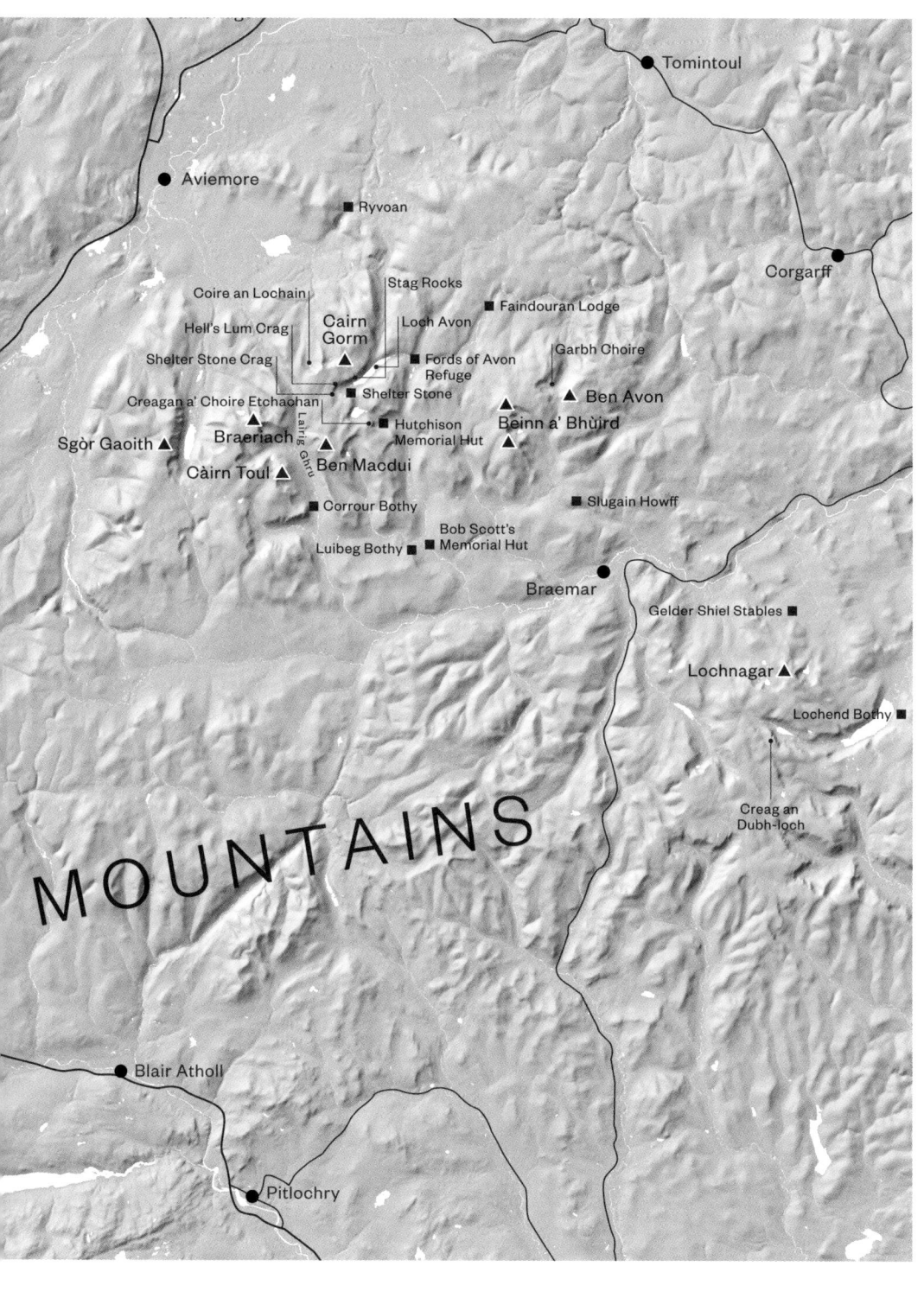

Foreword

When I introduced my son to the joys of Scottish rock climbing, I was keen to show him some of the most iconic and memorable outings on offer. It was only after a wonderful couple of days on the Old Man of Stoer and the Cioch Nose in the North-West Highlands that I was reminded that these eye-catching, top-quality routes are the work of Tom Patey. And as my mind drifted to other Patey classics in this part of the world, I was taken back to my youth when my friends and I started out climbing.

We had a set of heroes that stood out from the crowd and inspired us to follow in their footsteps. We felt an affinity with these people who led us to refer to them by their full Christian names, always prefaced by 'hero'. The list was short and select. There were, to name a few, hero Joseph (Brown), hero Christian (Bonington), hero Douglas (Scott), hero Patrick (Littlejohn) and, of course, hero Thomas (Patey).

Each of our heroes inspired us for different reasons. For many climbers the pursuit of technical competence is key, but for us the appeal was broader; it was exploring, climbing and having a good time that was at the core of what we aspired to. Tom Patey was a legendary man in that respect. We knew of his first ascents in Devon, the Alps, Norway and the Himalaya, but to us he was Mr North-West Scotland, the roving GP from Ullapool who ventured far and wide to climb in summer and winter, put folks up in a bothy in his garden, sang songs while playing his accordion and had a reputation of being the life and soul of any gathering.

In those days, in the late 1970s, the guidebooks to the North-West were very brief and factual, access was difficult, few climbers visited and a significant number of people disapproved of routes there being recorded. It took a very special person to make a mark in such an environment, and Tom's activities were the stuff of folklore. Stories abounded of exploratory adventures and endless drives along single-track roads to make house visits to patients who happened to live close to interesting climbing objectives.

I never met him personally but was attracted to his obvious love of the remote tracts of Scotland and his carefree attitude. He appeared to have a total disregard for convention. He shunned technical equipment and seemed most at home on exploits such as tackling unclimbed sea stacks or soloing remote mixed climbs. Weather conditions didn't appear to bother him, and he was often pictured winter climbing in a snow-blasted woolly jumper. He was clearly one of a kind, and much as I wasn't so keen on the soloing or poor choice of clothing, his approach, the areas he chose and the kind of climbs that he established were inspiring to me.

Despite his iconic status there has, until now, never been a biography delving into the man behind the myths. A collection of his articles and verses was published shortly after his death, but although *One Man's Mountains* gave an insight into his world, we have had to wait 50 years for this long-overdue biography. And what a thorough profile it is. Mike Dixon has researched extensively over many years and interviewed numerous people who knew Tom well. The result is a comprehensive, warts-and-all walk through the many facets of Dr Tom Patey's life, from his childhood as the son of an Episcopalian Minister through to that tragic day in May 1970 when, at the age of only 38, he fell to his death while abseiling after the first ascent of the Maiden sea stack off the north coast of Scotland.

This book is essential reading for anyone even vaguely interested in the climbing scene in the '50s and '60s, the geography and exploration of North-West Scotland and the lasting impact of this remarkable man. I was a little worried that the level of detail would be such that things might come out which would diminish his heroic status. Some incidents and quotes from contemporaries certainly surprised me and do reveal aspects of his personality that did not go down well with everyone. Overall, though, we are left with a picture of a driven man who was fired by an irrepressible desire to explore, climb and serve his patients well. In doing so he had an enormously positive effect on the lives of many and left a legacy that few can aspire to.

The only real wonder is that it has taken so long for a full biography of such a special man to be published.

And Mike need not worry. Much as the detail makes for absorbing reading, there is nothing here that has changed my long-held view. 'Hero Thomas' he will always be.

Mick Fowler

Introduction

Anyone visiting North-West Scotland cannot fail to be impressed by the magical combination of sea and mountains. By world comparisons, the heights of the mountains may be trivial, but elevation is not the sole determinant of quality. The individualistic and shapely peaks, ice-gouged corries and dramatic cliffs afford adventures on some of the world's oldest rocks. It is an area that has resisted the development and commercialism that have swamped ranges such as the Western Alps.

Clustered by the side of Loch Broom, the village of Ullapool is a popular tourist base for exploring the region. It is an attractive, unobtrusive place with the occasional book and music festival and other low-key cultural events.

Should you fall ill in Ullapool, you will be directed to the modern Medical Practice building. In the waiting room is a photograph of a doctor who served the area in the 1960s. It is a famous study of him winter climbing; his equipment and clothing look dated and inadequate by modern high-tech standards. Many will be surprised to note that he is not wearing a helmet or even a warm hat or balaclava. His pallor suggests someone out of his comfort zone, yet this man excelled in this environment and revelled in its physical demands.

Next to the photograph is a citation from Chris Bonington, one of Britain's most famous mountaineers. The subject of his tribute, Dr Tom Patey, is still remembered by a dwindling number of local patients. At the time, few of them would have been aware of the true extent of Patey's fame outside his day job. But when he died in 1970, he was renowned in

British climbing circles, and not just for his tally of first ascents across Scotland, Norway, the Alps and the Karakoram. For Patey, a good day in the mountains was not complete without a late session in the pub. There, he would entertain on the accordion, performing his self-penned songs, poking fun at the climbing world and its key players. Alongside his mountaineering and musical talents, Patey wrote articles about his many adventures. A master of comic deflation and benign satire, he is one of the funniest writers in the history of mountaineering literature, and he stands out in a genre permeated by introspection and seriousness.

Patey is by no means the only one to enhance the sport and contribute to its progression. Several leading Scottish mountaineers of the last century, including W.H. Murray, Dougal Haston, Robin Smith and John Cunningham, have been subjects of biographies. Works about famous English mountaineers are also plentiful, ranging from George Mallory to a recent study of Alex McIntyre. From Patey's own era, Don Whillans's life has been appraised, Joe Brown's story has been chronicled up to the mid-60s, and Martin Boysen and Bonington have written autobiographies. Tom Patey's unique achievements are as noteworthy as those of the illustrious names above; few mountaineers have been as multi-talented.

When I began to consider this book as a potential project, over 40 years had elapsed since Patey's death, and there was general agreement that a biography about the man was long overdue. His friends Bill Brooker, Mike Banks, Don Whillans and Paul Nunn had already died. But such was Patey's wide social network (many unknown to me initially) that there was no shortage of willing contributors. Patey's attitude to life, packing as much as possible into 24 hours, fascinated me. Ordinary mortals look on reverentially and perhaps enviously at individuals who can burn the candle at both ends and still excel in various spheres: we wonder what drives them. There is sometimes an air of pathos about these people, and they are not always easy to live with. In their often shorter-than-average lifespans, they manage to compress more than the accumulated lives of several individuals. In this respect, Patey has more in common with certain luminaries in the entertainment industry, such as Bob Fosse, the celebrated dancer, choreographer and film director of *Cabaret* and *All That Jazz*. Patey's life burned fast and bright until it ended prematurely and brutally during another outing of adventurous new-routing.

Patey's appetite for climbing and socialising has become mythological over time, and part of my task has been to examine the evidence rather than relying on hearsay and folklore. One interviewee suggested that the reluctance of some to discuss Patey is because they 'don't want the myth to be pierced'. In this book, I have attempted to write a balanced account of his life rather than embark on a hagiographic nostalgia trip. Like all humans, Patey had his flaws. Excelling at anything often involves selfishness. Until I started this project, I did not realise how much of a mountaineering 'hero' Patey was to so many. American journalist Lester Bangs's take on such individuals is that 'They wouldn't be heroes if they were infallible.'

Tom Patey's eldest son, Ian, has assembled a remarkable archive about his father, and he generously made much of this available to me. My research was enlivened by contact with the colourful supporting cast in Patey's life, many of significant interest in themselves: a pageant of climbers, mountain writers and musicians alive during a time of great social change from 1932–1970. The Second World War, the advent of the National Health Service (NHS), post-war austerity, musical diversity, the liberalism of the sixties and the satire movement all leave their mark on Patey's story. According to his friends, time spent with Patey was never dull, and my experience writing this biography reflects that sentiment.

It would be disingenuous to say that the journey has always been smooth. Trying to fathom the behaviour, motivations and inner world of someone so complex can be difficult when that person is no longer alive to question directly. But subjects like Tom Patey are a rarity, and despite the challenges, studying him and charting his full and varied life has been a considerable privilege.

Mike Dixon

Patey at Creag Meagaidh in March 1969
before embarking on The Crab Crawl
© John Cleare

01

Patey age three at the
rectory, Ellon, 1935
© Ian Patey collection

Minister's Son

Famam Extendite Factis (Extend your Reputation by Deed).
Ellon Academy motto

Most people who live on or travel along Patey Road in the Aberdeenshire town of Ellon have no awareness of the person it is named after. There is no memorial plaque. In the graveyard of one of the local churches is a gravestone dedicated to the Patey family, but with no obvious path to it. The grave holds five family members, and from it, you glean that one of them was a minister, another a doctor. Underneath the doctor's name is a famous line from the 121st Psalm: 'I will lift up mine eyes unto the hills from whence cometh my help.' This is the only clue as to how Tom Patey earned his fame.

Any biographer will trace the adult interests, behaviour and personality of his subject back to aspects of his upbringing and key events in his childhood. Tom Patey is no different, and his love of music and passion for the outdoors can be attributed to the respective interests of his mother and father.

The Reverend Thomas Maurice Patey (1880–1955) was a minister of the Scottish Episcopalian Church at St Mary's on the Rock in Ellon, a rural community on the River Ythan a few miles north of Aberdeen.[1] During his earlier ministry, the Reverend worked in Burton-on-Trent in East Staffordshire, where he met Audrey Amy Walton (1902–1978), a member of the congregation 21 years his junior who became his second wife on 16 April 1931. Their son, Tom, was born on 20 February 1932 in Ellon and was baptised with his father's Christian and mother's maiden names.

People often refer to Tom Patey's family links as a reason for his

'Irishness'. This concept of Irishness, however, is somewhat nebulous and can encompass anything from W.B. Yeats and James Joyce to leprechauns and Guinness. When people attribute the term to Patey, they are usually referring to his musicality, love of verse and socialising and entertaining skills. Examination of his father's side of the family reveals the Irish connection, but a strong vocational thread is also discernible before this.

When George Patey (1729–1810) ran away from home to join the Navy as a gunner, it defined a career path for the next two generations of Pateys. His son, William, became a Lieutenant in the Navy and William's son, George Edward, rose to the rank of Captain after serving as a midshipman at the Battle of Trafalgar (1805). George Edward was Patey's great-grandfather, and he created an Irish branch of the family by marrying the daughter of Thomas MacNamara Russell, a distinguished Irish sailor who became Admiral in charge of the North

The earliest picture of Patey, age one at Newburgh beach with his mother and half-brother Maurice, 1933 © Ian Patey collection

Patey, second from right, at the Bullers of Buchan with his father and mother (centre) and unknown others, 1938 © Ian Patey collection

Sea Fleet at the time of Trafalgar. When Tom Patey himself chose to enter the Royal Navy for his National Service, he was not setting a family precedent, although by being seconded to the Royal Marines in his medical role, his real preference was for elevated terrain rather than water. The Irish family connection continued to Patey's own father, grandson of the Reverend Edward Hughes from Wexford.

Reverend Patey was a kind, friendly gentleman, popular with his congregation and residents outside of the parish. He did not have a car, but he travelled widely in the area on his bicycle. Ministers received a meagre salary for their duties, and the Reverend once said he could only afford a week away with his family in the school summer holidays as accommodation was so expensive. On hearing this, one member of his congregation said, 'That's ridiculous, you must go for two weeks. We shan't get to hell in a fortnight!' Reverend Patey spent a lot of time outdoors and, when confined inside, was an avid reader. He was also remembered for his keen sense of humour.

Patey's mother was a great talker. Sociable and very musical, she played the organ at both services on Sunday. Audrey also enjoyed attending classical music concerts at Haddo House, a stately home near Ellon now owned by the National Trust for Scotland. On one occasion, during the interval, she remarked to her husband, 'Don't you think the music is wonderful?' to which Reverend Patey replied, 'I'm just listening to that blackbird, isn't it lovely?' (Forbes, 2014). Given a choice, he always preferred to be outside among nature.

Maurice, Patey's quieter half-brother, 16 years his senior, had a love of things mechanical, particularly motorbikes. Later on, Patey would prove himself inept with any electrical or mechanical device, and even climbing equipment did not really interest him. As an adult, he was not in the least bit materialistic.

One of the Reverend's church patrons was Robert Wolrige-Gordon of nearby Esslemont House, a rather grand and dictatorial man. He had been a Captain in the Guards, was a recipient of the Military Cross and read the lesson on a Sunday. His family had settled the lands around

Esslemont Castle since 1728, and their motto was Firm and Strong.²

Wolrige-Gordon wanted to renovate and extend the rectory and envisioned a huge room facing south with a fire at each end. Reverend Patey asked the verger to accompany him to a meeting to talk sense into Wolrige-Gordon as the minister couldn't afford coal for both fires in the room. 'He who pays the piper calls the tune,' was Robert's response (ibid.). So the room was built, but it was hardly used, and it eventually became an extravagant storage space for Maurice's motorbike.

At Robert's insistence, the Patey family lived in Esslemont House during the building work, despite Audrey's misgivings. Patey was pre-school age at the time, and Audrey asked if he could attend nursery with the three Wolrige-Gordon children, but Robert said he did not want to burden his staff with the extra responsibility. Robert, whose three sons would later go on to Eton, was likely aware of the relative status of the two families and reluctant to effect a mix. Dick Hardie, one of Patey's younger friends, recalls having the impression that the Wolrige-Gordons did not want their boys socialising too closely with the local children (Hardie, 2016). This was perhaps Patey's first experience of the kind of snobbery he would later gleefully lampoon.

However, during their stay at Esslemont House, the Pateys ate meals with their host family. Patey, like other young children, was often oblivious to social graces and was never short of something to say. Conversing with the lady of the house in the palatial dining room one evening, he began gesturing with his fork as he recounted a story. 'I must tell you, Mrs Wolrige-Gordon …' Suddenly, the potato on the end of his fork flew off and landed on the opposite side of the room. Patey's parents looked on in silent horror as the butler discreetly retrieved the errant vegetable while their son continued his tale, unaware that he had done anything untoward (Forbes, 2014).

Audrey was very possessive of her only child (ibid.), and Patey did not go to school at the usual age of five but was home-schooled as part of a distance learning programme. Later, however, he attended the local Ellon state school, where most of his friends had connections

Patey at Loch Avon in 1939 during a visit to the Shelter Stone © Ian Patey collection

with the land through farming.

The only surviving schoolwork from Patey's primary years is an illustrated story about a dog called 'Douglas in the Puddles', 'composed by T. Patey and D. Macauley' with two characters called Ma and Pa Smuts. It suggests the boys read *The Broons*, a popular comic strip from the Scottish newspaper *The Sunday Post* about a family who lived in a tenement in the fictional town of Auchenshoogle.

Patey was encouraged to take up the piano and, as well as having lessons locally, he would play duets with his mother on the family piano in the rectory. There may not have been much money in the household, but there were books, music and talk in abundance, and encouragement to experience the outdoors.

Throughout his school days, Patey attended Sunday school up to his confirmation in June 1946, and the main service thereafter, where he sang in the choir with his half-brother.

Family photo albums from Patey's early years depict visits to Newburgh beach on the Ythan estuary and, closer to home, picnics in the Esslemont Estate, at the Bullers of Buchan and Gardenstown.

They also visited the Moray coastal village of Burghead and the Culbin Sands near Nairn.

In 1939, the family holidayed on the west coast at Mallaig, Kyleakin and Kyle of Lochalsh. That same year, Patey and his father visited the Shelter Stone at the head of Loch Avon in the Cairngorms. Even assuming they approached from Deeside and secured transport to Derry Lodge, this is some distance to cover for a seven-year-old.

While Patey was being introduced to his local mountain massif and one of its most spectacular niches, Britain was on the cusp of entering a world war for the second time that century. Close to Ellon, the village of Newburgh became a target, and in January 1942, several bombs fell in the estuary during an attack on the buildings on the quay. The mountains were a safe refuge, and at the age of ten, Patey climbed Ben Macdui, the highest peak in the Cairngorms, while the family were staying in Aviemore. It was September and fresh snow lay on the summit. Around that time, he is also pictured shivering on the summit of Cairn Gorm after a hail shower. That same year, he completed the classic trek

Patey at Ben Macdui summit, 1942 © Ian Patey collection

through the Lairig Ghru, connecting Speyside to Deeside.

A few miles to the east, Aberdeen was the locus of the Nazi bombardments in North-East Scotland and suffered its worst attack on 21 April 1943 when 30 Dornier 217Es dropped 127 bombs, damaging almost a thousand houses and killing 98 civilians and 27 servicemen at the Gordon Barracks in Bridge of Don. A further 93 people were left with serious injuries (Doric Columns, 2021). Thankfully, it was the last German raid on a Scottish city during the war.

After the war, Reverend Patey established a Scout troop in Ellon, the first in the town. Dick Hardie, who was born in Ellon but lived in Orkney, where his father was contracted by the Ministry of Defence, returned to Ellon after the war for his last year at primary school. According to Hardie (2016), the Scout weekend camping trips were not about climbing mountains, despite the Pateys' experience and personal interests. Although the Scouts undertook gentle walks in the foothills of the Cairngorms, they mainly played wide games and learned camp skills and teamwork through initiative tasks and patrol competitions. The Ellon Troop was tutored well, and on several occasions they won the County Flag in a competition between all the Aberdeenshire Scout troops.

Patey was Hardie's Patrol Leader, and the latter noticed that he could be a bit pushy and impatient when given a task and 'wanted to get it done yesterday'. Patey's father, conscious of how a minister's son should behave, tried to 'hold him down a bit'. Patey could be rowdy and 'would be heard,' and 'old Tom slightly objected to that' (ibid.).

Despite this, Patey's parents were fairly easygoing with him in most respects, and they did not seem to mind their untidy son's complete disregard for appearances.

Hardie recalls cycling out to Bennachie, a distinctive local landmark whose relative isolation and rocky tors contrast with the rolling farmland surroundings. On that trip, the boys camped overnight and climbed the hilltops the following day. Patey soon realised the tors were worth exploring, and on their next visit, the boys undertook some scrambling and simple climbing, safeguarded by Audrey's clothesline, an illusory form of security which many well-known climbers of the era also employed on their early outings. (Astonishingly, most of them never came to grief.) In all likelihood, this was Patey's first outing on rock. Afterwards, he bought a pair of South African field boots and asked a local cobbler to put tricouni nails (metal edges) in the soles of them. Tricounis saved wear on the leather and enabled the would-be climber to stand on small edges even in the wet, but they weren't much good for friction moves on rock. When Patey started climbing in earnest as an undergraduate, these nailed boots were the standard footwear for climbers in North-East Scotland throughout the seasons, even when climbers elsewhere began donning crampons in winter. Eventually, the Aberdonians also converted to crampons but not before some significant routes were climbed in winter in 'nails'.

After Scouts, the boys would return to the rectory, where they would gather around the piano to sing traditional songs and be entertained by Patey, who soon began penning his own ditties. He was already

Patey with his harmonica on the summit of Tap o' Noth, Rhynie, 1946.
Other person unknown © Ian Patey collection

extremely articulate, intelligent and a highly talented musician (ibid.). His instrument of choice at the time was the piano, but he also played the harmonica as it was handy for taking on trips. Fellow school pupil and Scout member Charlie Morrison (nicknamed 'Goudie'), whose father worked as a cattleman, also accompanied Patey to the mountains. As well as excursions in the nearby Cairngorms, they explored the west coast, and in 1947, aged 15, they climbed Buachaille Etive Mòr in Glen Coe. On the same trip, they summited Stob Coire nan Lochain, a satellite peak of Bidean nam Bian, the highest mountain in Argyll. Maurice Coutts, another local lad from the Ellon Scouts, would also join Patey on his early rock climbs when the latter matriculated at Aberdeen University. Neither Coutts nor Morrison went to university, but Patey maintained his friendships with them.

All the Patey family exemplified the values of the Scottish Episcopal Church (2021), namely that it is 'diverse in tradition, outlook and culture ... and is expressed in warm relationships of mutual respect for one another.'[3] When it came to mountaineering goals, Patey himself could be somewhat selfish. Socially, however, his inclusiveness was one of his most appealing features as an adult.

By the age of 16, Patey had achieved the necessary school leaving certificates to gain a place at university. In 1947, aged 15, he had gained Lower Level in Maths and the following year Higher Level in English, Chemistry, Physics, Latin and Greek, Lower Level in History and a Pass in Arithmetic.

For his final year of schooling, Patey attended Robert Gordon's College (RGC) in Aberdeen, although it is unclear why he switched to this private, fee-paying school and how it was paid for.[4] The school had a reputation for preparing pupils for competitive examinations for scholarships and bursaries for Aberdeen University, which is probably why Patey attended. It was also a kind of finishing school, and it would have widened his social horizons and put him in contact with more able pupils with ambitions to enter higher education.

At RGC, Patey met red-haired Gordon 'Goggs' Leslie, the son of an Aberdeen slater. Goggs and Patey studied medicine and climbed together in their early student years. At that time, Scotland was proud of its generalist rather than specialised secondary education, and Patey flourished through exposure to a range of subjects. In his leisure pursuits of climbing, writing and music, he developed skills alongside those he deployed in his medical career and exemplified the able all-rounder.

The college also had a mountaineering club, and Patey now had another group he could explore the hills with. He dropped out of the Ellon Scouts but continued to visit the countryside with his family.

New Year 1949 precipitated a radical change in Patey's attitude to mountains. It put him in contact with men who would have a significant influence on him and with whom he would subsequently establish lifelong friendships.

The Cairngorms were in full winter condition and blanketed under a substantial depth of snow. Patey and some fellow final year RGC pupils had based themselves at Bob Scott's bothy at Luibeg for some 'hill bashing', although hillwalking in Scotland in winter is arguably a branch of mountaineering and not to be underestimated. From photographs of the trip and Patey's account in his essay 'Cairngorm Commentary' (*Scottish Mountaineering Club Journal [SMCJ]*, 1962), we know they climbed Beinn Bhreac and ventured onto the Moine Mhòr, where they added to the cairn marking an obscure Munro Top. The school group's activities were driven by Sir Hugh's Munro's list of Scottish peaks over 3,000ft and their subsidiary Tops, which was published in 1891.

The bothy was a popular destination for Hogmanay, and as many as 40 climbers were housed in the main room and various outbuildings. Patey's group had been confined to one of the latter. Bob Scott, the keeper at Luibeg, lived in the adjacent cottage with his wife from 1947 to 1973. He had worked for the Mar Estate since leaving school at the age of 12 and was considered one of the quintessential characters of the Cairngorms in the '50s and '60s. The charge at the bothy was one shilling a night, which helped supplement the stalker's meagre agricultural wage. Firewood was free as long as guests helped with the sawing and chopping.

The Horrible Hielanders at Luibeg Bothy on 7 Jan 1949. According to Patey: 'Left to right I. Rettie (complete in kilt), D. Haston, A. Gill, B. Falconer and Me! I had not washed for six days. The picture was taken in the pouring rain on the day of departure. The owner of the sullen face protruding through from the bothy door is Bill Brooker, one of the best young rock climbers in Aberdeen (17 years old). Next door is the stick shed where we slept on Sunday night.' © Ian Patey collection

If Scott entered the bothy to see who was staying, he would often give the occupants an entertaining natural history lesson. He had an infectious laugh and a great sense of humour, and he was a master storyteller, particularly about his war experiences. Woe betide anybody who disrupted stalking or abused the land around the bothy, however. Scott once warned a group of English Scouts about the necessity of digging latrines. When they continued to ignore his request and foul the grass around their campsite, he exploded and bluntly told the quivering boys and their leader to 'Get doon that bloody glen an' tak' yer bloody shite wi' ye' (Watson, 2011). He could deflate anybody with pretensions or self-importance with a cutting phrase delivered in his sonorous North-East accent with its distinctive rolled Rs. Patey, who also rolled his Rs, would have noted Scott's style, but he took a gentler approach when it came to pricking pomposity or highlighting folly and error in his own speech, verse and prose.

Bill Brooker (1971) remembers that during that New Year:

> *The temperature was right down into the bulb ... [even the] eggs were frozen hard. We were ensconced in the bothy in fair comfort among the straw and so on. That night, a group of young lads — one or two clad in kilts no less — came off the mountains, having spent the night on Ben Macdui, and were ignominiously shoved into Bob Scott's stick shed, which had open wooden slatted sides and was not at all snug. I later discovered one of them had been Tom.*

Scott found the group amusing, particularly since their discomfort was mostly self-inflicted, and he called them the 'Horrible Hielanders'. Patey described the temperature inside the accommodation by quoting Keats: 'Ah bitter chill it was.' Since his early teens, he had built up a wide repertoire of classic literary quotations, which he would reference in articles and picture captions.

A hole in the iced-over burn had to be opened each day to access the water below. Later, the youngsters were allowed into the main bothy where Patey's eyes were opened to another way of experiencing mountains, so much more vibrant and exciting than the one he and his school peers were living.

The bothy had a pecking order, and those of importance sat closer to the comfort of the fire. In two reserved armchairs were Malcolm (Mac) Smith and Brooker, while Patey and his group were confined to the chillier recesses of the room.

Smith, in his late 20s, was at the time the authority on Cairngorm crags and corries. A member of the Etchachan Club, he became a ringmaster and mentor to a younger generation, including Patey, whose lives revolved around escaping to the hills. Smith was a polymath with a keen interest in insects, plants, photography, jazz, literature and debate, and someone very different from the callow youths and stuffy adults that Patey knew.

At 17, Brooker was just a little older than Patey and a pupil at Aberdeen Grammar School, but he associated himself with Smith and other ex-servicemen of the Etchachan Club. Brooker had the social skills and personality to assimilate with any group, a feature that endeared him to many throughout his life. Born in Calcutta in 1931, he moved to Aberdeen at an early age, and he exhibited a bold streak, engaging in street sledging, hands-free bike races and exploring underground waterways. Rugby was displaced by more exciting pursuits, and at 14, he cycled to Skye with a fellow Scout. After being told by the Glen Brittle Youth Hostel warden that the Inaccessible Pinnacle was beyond his experience, Brooker soloed it the next day.

When Patey arrived in the bothy just after New Year, Brooker's star was rising on the Cairngorm climbing scene. While Smith was the Chieftain of the Luibeg Clan, Patey (SMCJ, 1962) characterised Brooker as the 'young Lochinvar' who 'cut a more dashing figure, the complete counterpart to Mac's slightly reserved manner. To all outward appearances, he was merely another pimply-faced schoolboy like ourselves, full of wild talk.' In describing the meeting in 'Cairngorm Commentary', Patey notes that Brooker had 'recently burst into the climbing arena with a series of routes which had defied the best efforts of preceding generations.' In fact, this spurt did not occur until later in the year (often with Johnny Morgan and Doug Sutherland), but Brooker's potential was already noticeable.

The next day, Brooker and Smith made the first winter ascent of Crystal Ridge in Coire Sputan Dearg, returning late with evident signs of having engaged in a tussle but beaming and elated by the climb. Visiting some obscure Munro Top seemed anodyne by comparison. Patey had glimpsed a vitality in these 'real mountaineers' and the exhilarating activity they pursued, which caused him to take stock:

> *'These men spoke of icy vigils and gigantic ice-falls; routes that finished long after dark; remote bivouacs in faraway corries; riotous nights in bothies; late-night dances in Braemar and brimming tankards in the Fife Arms. Adventure, unconventionality, exuberance—these were the very elements missing from our scholarly conception of mountaineering which had led us with mathematical precision up and down the weary lists of Munro's Tables'* (ibid.).

In time, Patey would become the chief prophet of the holy trinity of adventure, unconventionality and exuberance.

There were more hillwalking trips in Scotland before he fully converted to climbing. In 1949, he embarked on another Glen Coe expedition and a pictorial study of Cairngorm lochs and bothies. Reverend Patey also wrote to Bob Scott to see if Patey and some of his friends could spend a few days at Luibeg Bothy in the main room, and he asked the stalker to keep an eye on the group. Scott gave them hay to sleep on but was disappointed to note that one lad had lost his knife and fork, and butter and jam were sticking to all their stuff. Patey showed his naivety by drying his wet boots over a primus stove, and one of them became so malformed and hardened that he could not get it on his foot the next day. Upon telling them off for swearing, Scott (1971) received the reply: 'We can't get harmed with the minister's son here,' as if they had some sort of diplomatic immunity. Scott's retort quickly rectified this assumption, and from then on, profanities were uttered well out of earshot of the bothy's guardian.

In September 1949, Aberdeen University zoology undergraduate Adam Watson (2011) recalled meeting Patey and a friend at Luibeg after the Braemar Games. A noxious smell pervaded the bothy, and an unimpressed Watson later recorded in his diary: 'Two young bodies, one Patey of Ellon and another of Aberdeen, wandered in and created a hell of a mess of spilt oatmeal, porridge and paraffin.'

Watson would not be the only person to form an unfavourable impression of Patey on initial acquaintance.

Tom Patey could have pursued a career in music but eventually opted for medicine at Aberdeen University. Thanks to the influence of his parents and exposure to a more adventurous way of life in the mountains, he would flourish as an undergraduate. He was about to enter the most formative period of his life.

1   The Reverend's first wife, Mabel Vernon Parker, died in 1928, but they had a son, Maurice, born in 1916, and an elder son, Russell George, who died aged five.

2   Robert's wife, Joan, was the daughter of Dame Flora MacLeod, the 28th Chief of the Clan MacLeod. Joan's elder twin son changed his name to John MacLeod of MacLeod to take up the role of 29th Clan Chieftain, which he inherited from his grandmother. In 2000, faced with the high cost of repairs to Dunvegan Castle on Skye, the clan seat for more than 800 years, he put the Black Cuillin mountains up for sale for £10 million. With the sale proceeds, he also planned to build an 80-bedroom hotel on his Skye estate, but after a public outcry the plans were abandoned. Patey would later face a very different battle with this famous mountain range.

3   Dick Hardie's mother had multiple sclerosis, and Patey's mother would attend her with great compassion (Hardie, 2016). Chris Bonington (2017) later acknowledged a similar trait in Patey, which perhaps explained why Patey was never malicious in his prose or songs.

4   Graeme Nicol, who began studying medicine at Aberdeen three years after Patey, thought the former may have received a bursary as his parents did not have the money to fund the year.

02

Patey on his own route,
Alligator Crawl, at
Longhaven © Adam Watson

Aiguilles des Cairngorms

> Those who do not love them don't go up, and those that do can never have enough of it. It is an appetite that grows in feeding. Like drink and passion, it intensifies life to the point of glory.
>
> Nan Shepherd, *The Living Mountain*

In 1949, Aberdeen, like the rest of the UK, was still smarting from the costs of participating in a world war of six years duration. Food, petrol and even sweet rationing was still in place, austerity prevailed and Britain's sense of importance was being eroded by the dissolution of its empire.

Aged 17, Tom Patey entered medical school during a time of momentous change in the delivery of healthcare in the UK. The establishment of the NHS in 1948 promised cradle to grave care funded entirely by taxation.

Scotland, pre-1948, already had a distinctive health care service and was leaning towards this aim. The war years had seen a state-financed hospital building programme in Scotland on a scale unknown in the rest of Europe, and this would be incorporated into the new NHS. Aberdeen led the way in this respect, and by the start of the Second World War, Foresterhill Hospital, where Patey would undertake his training, already had a new infirmary, children's and maternity wards and a medical school.

The concept behind the NHS would have resonated with Patey's own values and political leanings, which were essentially socialist, although he was not vociferous in this respect. He dealt with toffs in a fairly polite, if mocking, way, and his left-leaning attitude could occasionally manifest in displays of inverted snobbery (Nicol, 2014).

Patey's access to higher education was facilitated by his fees being paid by the state. Money would have been fairly tight, but thanks in part to a small maintenance grant and the Knox Bursary (£16), which he received in 1951 for three years, he managed to climb during his holidays and even visit the Alps.

Despite continuing to live at home, studying in Aberdeen meant that Patey could now enjoy the freedoms of a young adult. From the city centre where the River Dee enters the sea, it was not too far to reach the mountains and the source of that river. Deeside was the gateway to the university of open spaces, where immersion in the environment had as much of an impact as any traditional seat of learning. Life in the Cairngorms offered adventure, natural beauty and friendships quite different from urban life.

In the first of his seminal two-volume *Climbers' Guide to the Cairngorms* (1961), Mac Smith elegantly described this unique mountain range:

> *The charm which the Cairngorms exert is of a puzzling nature, for they lack the picturesque form of the peaks of Skye and the West Coast. Perhaps the secret lies in their vastness; the limitless plateaux, the great pine forests of their glens and foothills ... Ideally, they are mountains to be explored, for one can never know them wholly, and every visit brings to light some hitherto unknown feature.*

Despite an absence of jagged skylines and crests, Patey (1954) ironically referred to them as the 'Aiguilles des Cairngorms' in his song of the same name. Today, they are known to possess an incredible variety of summer and winter climbs at all grades, but until the early '60s they were primarily considered a hillwalking venue, and Smith's were the first pure climbing guides for the area to be published.

Bill Brooker used the term 'dignity of solitude' to describe the quality afforded by these elevated, uncluttered spaces (Robertson and Crofton, 2014). Although a benign habitat in good summer weather, this sub-Arctic tundra can quickly become hazardous when fully exposed to the elements. The aesthetic qualities of the Cairngorms tend to take a back seat when one is partway up a route in winter with a storm brewing, and 'what [the climber] values is a task that, demanding of him all he has and is, absorbs and so releases him entirely' (Shepherd, 1977). The gift of solitude requires participants to be self-sufficient if things go astray, and the crux of the route may be navigating the long distance back to safety. Many have been humbled by this test, and some haven't lived to learn the lesson.

When Patey entered Aberdeen University Medical School in autumn 1949, he had hillwalked extensively in Scotland, especially in the Cairngorms, but aside from messing around on the tors of Bennachie with Dick Hardie, he had yet to undertake any technical climbing. After matriculating, he met Mike Taylor, a fellow medical student from Peterhead who would become a close, lifelong friend and, in the early days, participate in some major Cairngorm first ascents.

Patey and Mike Taylor on Lochnagar. Picture on the wall at the Ullapool Bothy
© Ian Patey collection

Like Patey, Taylor travelled by bus to medical school in the city, and one October day during their first term as freshmen, they got talking about climbing. This led to the joint purchase of a rope and, with Patey's Ellon friends Charlie Morrison and Maurice Coutts, they began to explore the sea cliffs on the coastline north of Aberdeen between Collieston and Peterhead.

Patey's intention at the time was to acquire enough climbing skills to summit the main peaks in Scotland. Only a few of these require scrambling or climbing by their easiest routes, and even then, nothing is above Moderate (one notch above the lowest grade of Easy). Patey soon adjusted his target upwards to the grade of Severe but quickly surpassed this too.

By now, climbing had become an end in itself and hillwalking no longer had the same allure. After cycling out from Ellon to Collieston in autumn 1949, he soloed his first new route, a 9m Difficult he called Crab's Wall,[1] and between 1949 and 1952, Patey, Taylor, Morrison and Coutts contributed to 50 new routes on the north-east coastline, mostly in nailed boots. Despite extensive quarrying in the area, the pink granite walls, corners and slabs had a magnetic appeal and were good training ground for the great mountain crags in the Cairngorms and elsewhere in Scotland. In places, several arêtes jut out into the sea, lending the climbs a mini-Alpine ambience. They may have been short in comparison to their mountain counterparts, but there was adventure in abundance on routes accessible at low tide or by abseil, where an inability to top out could have serious consequences. Equipment was primitive, and Morrison, now an apprentice engineer, added some homemade pitons to the quartet's collection of slings and ex-war department (WD) karabiners. Later, Patey augmented the gear pool with an unwieldy nylon rope and would get the blacksmith in Ellon to make snaplink karabiners.

Thoughts soon turned to adventures on a grander scale. At the time, there were two options for gaining access to the mountains from Aberdeen: the public bus service up Deeside or through the university Lairig Club mountaineering meets. Saturday morning was part of the working week, so the majority of hillgoers took the afternoon bus from Bon Accord Square in the centre of Aberdeen to Braemar.

From Braemar, it was a 10-mile walk up to Derry Lodge and nearby Luibeg Bothy with the ever-watchful Bob Scott next door. Climbing on Creagan a' Choire Etchachan entailed a 12-mile return trip with a further 10 miles back to Braemar. Regular Cairngorm climbers were very fit with superb reserves of stamina. Sometimes, though, they would hire a taxi or even the local ambulance in Braemar to reach the Derry Gates. By acquiring the key to a locked gate, they could get all the way to Derry Lodge and Luibeg.

Strachan's was the most popular bus company amongst the outdoor fraternity as the drivers tolerated climbing gear, bulging rucksacks, sharp ice axes and the pungent smell of bodies who had spent the weekend in a tent or bothy. The last bus back to Aberdeen on a Sunday was usually packed, and on one occasion an intrepid passenger climbed up onto one of the wings, sat down and secured himself into position with his rope round a headlight (Hay, 2016).

Patey also acquired an old motorbike for a while and would take Dick Hardie, who was still at school in Ellon, into Aberdeen to catch the Lairig Club bus for day meets, mostly to Lochnagar. It 'certainly wasn't the Rolls Royce of bikes' (Hardie, 2016), and Hardie would perch precariously behind as Patey's bulging rucksack threatened to dislodge him.

By now, Patey was well and truly bitten by the climbing bug and spent as much of his free time as possible pursuing his hobby. The first of his climbs to draw the attention of the wider Aberdeen climbing community was Mitre Ridge (Hard Severe), first climbed by Pat Baird, Jock Leslie and Sandy Wedderburn of Cambridge University in 1933. Thrusting out dramatically in the remote Garbh Corrie of Beinn a' Bhùird, Mitre Ridge is one of the most majestic rock features in the Cairngorms, and Patey's repeat ascent with 'Horrible Hielander' Ian Rettie and Goggs Leslie in 1950 marked a significant change in gear.[2] The first pitch of Mitre Ridge, a long and insecure groove, is the crux, and Patey's success on this, with minimal gear, impressed the local

Patey in his early days as an undergraduate, 1949 © Ian Patey collection cognoscenti. Thereafter, he extended his forays to one of the UK's most famous climbing destinations, the Cuillin of Skye, where he climbed the main peaks and some easy classic routes.

In the winter of 1949-50, Patey made forays into the type of climbing which would ultimately make him famous. With Goggs and Taylor, he made an ascent of Raeburn's Gully (II) on Lochnagar, which usually holds one ice pitch but, apart from a large cornice that requires circumvention, is fairly straightforward.[3] This added to Patey's tally of Crumbling Cranny (II), also on Lochnagar, a winter climb in Coire Kander with the Lairig Club and, with Taylor, the Face Route (I) on the Devil's Point.

At Easter in 1950, he then successfully tackled Tower Ridge (IV,3), a Scottish mixed classic of Alpine proportions on Ben Nevis, with Glasgow University student Jock Pirrit.[4] The scale of this venue is of a greater magnitude than Lochnagar, but they also dispatched Castle Ridge, North Castle Gully and Gardyloo Gully with little fuss.

Beforehand, they had encountered a party from Oxford and Cambridge Universities in the Charles Inglis Clark (CIC) Hut. The group included George Band, who would become a member of the successful British Everest expedition in 1953. Band was an affable, modest man, but one of his party had gleaned that Patey and Pirrit intended to climb Tower Ridge the following day and condescendingly advised them that they would need to start very early as a well-known Everest climber had encountered difficult conditions the day before and had taken 12 hours. With a cut-glass accent, the student from the Home Counties asked what time Patey intended setting off, to which the latter replied breezily: 'About 2 o'clock or so, after we have had our lunch.' Patey was already proficient at moving quickly up mixed ground in any snow conditions, and they were back at the hut well before dark.

This, then, was Patey's respectable but relatively limited winter experience when he approached the base of Douglas-Gibson Gully on Lochnagar on 28 December 1950, with Goggs Leslie.

Douglas-Gibson Gully lies between Shadow Buttress B and Eagle

Ridge in the great North-East Corrie of Lochnagar. It is named after John Gibson and William Douglas from Edinburgh, two original members of the Scottish Mountaineering Club (SMC) who made the first attempt in 1893. A difficult final section put paid to early forays, including one by the brilliant all-round mountaineer Harold Raeburn, who had to make do with his eponymous gully instead.[5]

In September 1933, Aberdeen student Charlie Ludwig, a prodigious climbing talent, finally made the first summer ascent of Douglas-Gibson Gully in just over one hour in gym shoes, according it the modest grade of Severe. In testament to his boldness and skill, Ludwig soloed it with no previous knowledge of the route. Today it is graded Very Severe (VS) in summer, but the formidable headwall, replete with damp, loose rock, deters most mortals. Even Ludwig conceded it was 'quite unjustifiable' (*SMCJ*, 1933). However, such routes are often transformed into perfect specimens for winter climbers.

Before Douglas-Gibson was finally vanquished, George Macleod, Alan Will and Jim Hardie made an attempt a few days earlier when the corrie was plastered with unconsolidated snow. The lower section is normally straightforward, but the final headwall, topped by a menacing cornice, was to be the real test. There was premature excitement when Will was avalanched at the narrows by snow falling from below the cornice. He was deposited onto Macleod's head, but this did not deter the trio. In the lead, Will avoided the summer crux and climbed a groove to reach a convenient rock recess that afforded a cave-like stance. The only belay was a homemade piton driven optimistically into the loose rock of the cave roof. With Macleod brought up to the stance, Will inspected the terrain above and got to a few metres below the cornice when his awareness of water running between the snow and rock and the memory of his earlier avalanche signalled a retreat. Reversing back to the cave was tricky but abseiling off the dodgy peg at the stance was even less appealing, so they elected to untie from their ropes, link them and thread them through a karabiner attached to the piton. Avoiding putting their full weight on the dubious-looking piton, they downclimbed using the doubled rope as a handrail. Macleod was by now seriously fatigued by the day's efforts and struggling to hold on to the rope when he lost his footing and went 'rocketing off ... like a small shooting star' (Patey, 1962), careering down the whole length of the gully and beyond, almost to the loch. Incredibly, his only injuries were a gashed knee and cheek and a broken thumb, the unconsolidated snow having blanketed his fall. Will was left with a panicked and inexperienced 15-year-old Hardie, and they made a slow and nervous descent. Thinking that Macleod was dead, they were astonished to see him emerge from the mists. As if they had not had enough drama for one day, on the way back to Gelder Shiel, Will fell into the loch when the ice fractured around him. The proceedings ended with the group breaking into Will's parents' hut in Ballater.

On the day of Patey and Goggs's ascent of the by now notorious gully, they arrived in the corrie with the advantage that snow conditions were favourable. Patey's description in *The Cairngorm Club Journal*

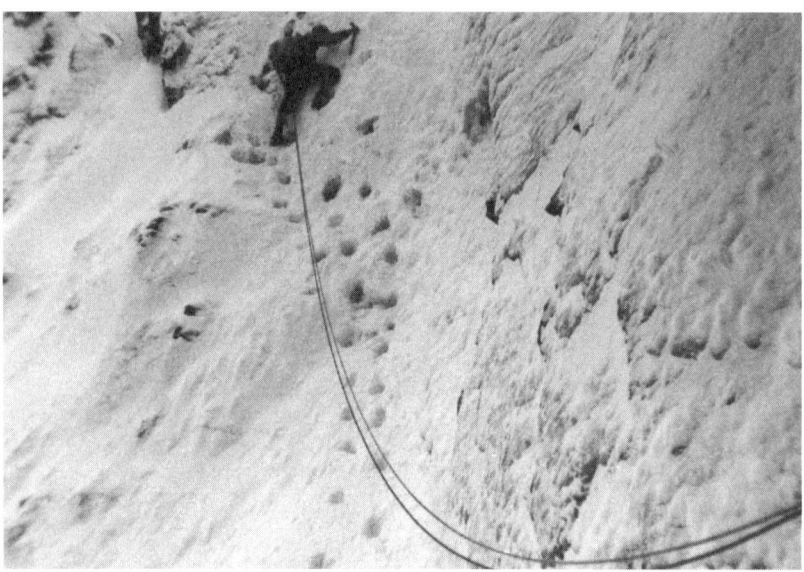

A step-cutting ascent of Douglas-Gibson Gully in the '60s © Allen Fyffe

(1950–51) is surprisingly detailed, especially for a gully and even for a first ascent. It offers an insight into the technicalities more suggestive of a mixed climb than a pure snow and ice route:

> *The upper 200ft occupied seven hours and were continuously hard and exposed. An awkward traverse on the left wall, along a shelf of hard snow, led to ... a steep 15-foot pitch from which fragile snow was removed to permit an ascent on the ice-covered rocks below. At the top, excavation revealed a stance on a small ledge below the crux of the summer route. Here, however, the snow was extremely steep and the party diverged upwards and to the right, across the upper edge of the prominent slab on the wall of the gully. This was covered by several feet of hard snow set at a high angle. A run out of 90ft led to a small cave above and to the right of the slab. Following an unsuccessful attempt on the chimney above the cave, the party traversed ... to the left onto the back of a steep rib, which runs parallel to the summer route. The climbing at this point was critical as only about a foot of hard snow covered the slabs. 60ft of climbing on the rib led to deeper snow where a stance was necessary to safeguard the leader on the final [pitch] to the cornice. This proved to be one of the hardest sections of the climb as the snow steepened almost to the vertical, and an ice axe was used as a foothold to attain a large snow cave below the cornice. The second belayed at the back of the cave while the leader, after much hard work, fashioned a tunnel ... in the roof of the cave, through which the party climbed to the welcome security of the summit plateau.*

After 57 years of attempts, a ghost could finally be laid to rest. The route took nine hours in total, and for Patey, it was a personal epiphany and an important moment in the development of his mountaineering psychology. He had learned several important lessons: 'I cannot recall ever again suffering the agonies of apprehension on a climb,' he said later (SMCJ, 1962). Goggs (2014), who had led alternate pitches until the problematic upper barrier, recalls that Patey had looked:

> *... so happy on the plateau. He was never a screamer. We shook hands. I was very proud. It was so beautiful with a bright moon shining. We had done something that a lot of people had said was going to be hellish difficult ... he knew he had really done something.*

On 30 December, they were off to Luibeg for Hogmanay, from where news of their ascent would soon run throughout the north-east climbing community. Graded VS, Douglas-Gibson was the hardest known gully in Scotland at the time.[6] What Patey and Goggs lacked in experience, they had made up for with grit, determination and youthful ignorance of the seriousness of the enterprise. It represented a breakthrough in the Cairngorms in terms of the commitment required, and their success emphatically announced the arrival of new climbing talent on the scene.[7]

In his early student days, Patey was shy and introverted, and he avoided boisterous gatherings in the Student Union or dances on a Saturday night. Although he had been confident during his school days, he took time finding his feet in a university environment where there were other clever and confident individuals. After succeeding on Douglas-Gibson, however, Patey's rising star rivalled that of Brooker's, and the confidence he gained from this ascent increased his assurance in social settings outside of the mountain environment.[8]

Patey's social status was promoted not only by his growing climbing prowess but his musical ability on the piano and harmonica and his wide repertoire of Scottish, folk, blues, classical and country and western music. He also liked the kazoo, whose 'buzzing' timbral quality was a common feature of the bands that played at the Fife Arms in Braemar at weekends. Patey was often the instigator of social occasions involving music, and when he started performing his own songs his undeniable charisma could dominate a room, but never in a brash or self-aggrandising way.

One of Patey's earliest compositions, influenced by Goggs, was 'Two Tiny Figures', a dark piece about climbers coming to grief on the North Wall of the Eiger that contains some memorable imagery:

Patey on his local sea cliffs at Longhaven, 1950 © Ian Patey collection

With fingers all crippled and cramped with the ice,
He scraped at the knot clamped tight like a vice.
A cold perspiration broke out on his face,
As the ghastly cadaver came ripping through space.

   Goggs had a Teutonic style of humour, and his imagination was fired by Gotz von Berlichingen, a 15th century German imperial knight and mercenary famed for his artificial arm. The rather sinister nature of the prosthetic amused Goggs, and he would pretend to have a demonic arm and perform mock attacks on his fellow students while speaking in a shaky German accent.
   Patey and his friends would often greet each other with the phrase 'Heil' and the relevant surname in a faux German accent. The comic, silly voices in the 1951 radio comedy programme *The Goons* also contributed to the banter. Complaints of cold feet while out climbing in winter would receive retorts such as: 'Miserable veakling! Vait until you are stranded at Death bivouac for zree days in a storm. Zen you vill know vot cold is!' (Nicol, 2014). Typical undergraduate nonsense and fodder for Patey's irreverent articles and songs.

Then there were the Austro-Germanic climbers of the pre-war era driven to succeed on the great unclimbed north faces in the Alps, several of whom perished as a result. Expeditions to Nanga Parbat were sponsored by the state, and the fatalities were wrapped in the Swastika. The hardcore Lairig Club found the perceived deadly seriousness of these practitioners highly amusing and, as British standards in the Alps languished, something to mock and revere in equal measure with black humour.

1951 yielded no new climbs of the magnitude of Douglas-Gibson Gully, but it did see Patey establishing new rock routes on the coastal crags, including Diagonal Crack (V. Diff), which is still one of the best of its grade on the coast, and Alligator Crawl (Severe), which was named after a famous Fats Waller composition (SMCJ, 1998). At VS, The Great Diedre and Hallelujah Staircase, which Patey climbed with Morrison, were solid examples of what was a very respectable grade at the time. Indeed, there were no harder climbs either on the coast or in the Cairngorms, and this gave Patey the confidence to push his grade on mountain routes. To add to the challenge, he climbed Hallelujah Staircase barefoot in a snowstorm, a demonstration of his innate toughness in the outdoors. (Patey suffered from Raynaud's Syndrome, a circulatory condition, which can leave the extremities white and painful in the cold, but he refused to let this curtail his later winter climbing ambitions.)

Lochnagar furnished Patey with several important routes during his time as a medical student. Separated by the Dee from the other main Cairngorm climbing areas, it was accessible even without transport, and he and his friends could walk up from the main A93, usually from near the Danzig Bridge. Nearby, two bothies offered welcome, if spartan, lodgings.

W.H. Murray (1947) described the mountain as 'the greatest citadel of vegetatious granite', and in summer there is a dearth of clean rock. But in winter, it is regal and jewelled, a graceful, concentrated arc of winter climbing par excellence. When Patey ventured into other mountain arenas, he had served a valuable apprenticeship here on a multitude of winter routes in all conditions, and he understood the fickle nature of the winter game:

> *Any snow and ice climb is never the same twice; a rock climb usually is, but I mean you may take a completely different line on every different occasion you go up a particular route; it's just dictated by the conditions, by the depth of snow, by the bank up, by the amount of ice there is on the rocks, the rock holds that are showing. I think the main thing in snow and ice climbing is resourcefulness.* (Patey, 1971a)

Lochnagar was in full winter garb on 20 January 1952, when Patey and Donald Aitken tackled the Tough-Brown Traverse (IV,3). First climbed in 1895 and only the second route to be established on the mountain, it is an undistinguished and vegetated passage in summer but transformed by snow and ice into one of the great lower grade winter classics. It is a grand tour, crossing Parallel A and B Gullies and Parallel Buttress before following the feature of the Great Terrace above the steep section of the Tough-Brown Face. Despite its low technical grade, climbers should avoid complacency, since failure to climb the upper section entails a serious and lengthy retreat. Locating the easiest point to leave the terrace is tricky, and Patey used 'combined tactics', standing on Aitken's shoulders to gain height on the short crux wall. They were blessed with good conditions, however, and climbed it in a creditable five hours.

Later in 1952, Patey climbed his first new mountain rock routes of any real quality.[9] The first was the buttress of the Black Tower (Severe) in Ben Macdui's Coire Sputan Dearg with Goggs and Mike Taylor. Perched above lingering snowfields, the high and remote buttress has the profile of an elegant, twisting spire, and is similar in rock type and technical difficulty to the perennial Cairngorm classic, Eagle Ridge, also graded Severe (Strange, 2010).

Taylor also joined Patey and Bill Brooker for The Stack on Lochnagar in October that year. This feature lies between the two branches of

Black Spout and, as the name suggests, hangs proudly over the lower gully. It may have been technically uneven (mostly V. Diff, with the hardest pitch Hard Severe), but its varied climbing on clean rock meant it was only second in popularity to Eagle Ridge for almost two decades. Combined tactics were used at one point, something that Patey and his peers were never ashamed to honestly record in these early years.

Before a substantial rockfall on the Tough-Brown Face in May 2000, the 80m chimney slot of Parallel Gully B was one of the most impressive features of the whole corrie, with some significant pitches. When word got out that Ian Brooker (Bill's elder brother) and Sandy Lyall had retreated from the lower chimney but successfully completed the upper gully after accessing it from the Tough-Brown Traverse, a complete ascent became irresistible for Patey. Brooker and Lyall had, as it turns out, climbed the hardest passage, known as the Contortion Pitch, in the upper gully, but the daunting main chimney lower down had looked too intimidating.

Thus, two weekends later, on a Lairig Club meet, no fewer than eight climbers had Parallel Gully B in their sights. Leading the attack were Patey and Taylor, followed by Brooker and Mike (Christopher Michael) Dixon from Yorkshire,[10] and Donald Aitken and Mike Philip. Bringing up the rear were Ellon loons Charlie Morrison and John Henderson, who had a cine camera with him to record the climb. (Sadly, the whereabouts of the film have never been traced.) The ascent had all the ingredients for comedy: a circus atmosphere of eight people, three of whom were called Mike, strung out on the route and often yelling to each other simultaneously; a cameraman making them self-conscious; and a dream character in the form of Dixon, affectionately described by Harold Drasdo as 'wildly eccentric'.[11]

Patey and Taylor had swapped leads on the lower chimney fault until the tricky overhanging final section, which Patey led. After the rest of the party overcame this, only Patey, Taylor, Brooker and Dixon continued up the upper fault. Taylor 'led off like a bloodhound on the leash' (Patey, 1953). As it turned out, they found the upper section as hard if not harder than anything in the chimney, though it was unusual for a gully to have such clean rock and varied pitches.

The ascent of Parallel Gully B, Patey's first new mountain route at VS, was the subject of his first published article in the 1953 *SMCJ* but, somewhat disappointingly, it was a rather matter-of-fact piece compared to his later work. Patey's signature style: one-liners, farcical action, snappy dialogue and comic characterisation, are noticeable by their absence. However, an auspicious passage in the article describes the playful one-upmanship he relished:

> *I had just extended one groping arm over the top when Brooker, from below, volunteered the information he had heard that there were no holds above for the last move. Not deigning to acknowledge this refreshing piece of news, I struggled breathlessly over the lip and gave tongue to an exuberant yell.*

It was one of the hardest rock routes in the Cairngorms at the time, but hardly compared to the toughest routes in North Wales, The Lakes and Glen Coe, which were into the Extreme Grade.

1952 also marked Patey's first new rock routes on Creag an Dubhloch, which would become one of Scotland's greatest cliffs in both summer and winter. His first creation, False Gully, climbed with Taylor and Brooker, was nothing special, but it was the last main gully to be climbed on the crag and involved the novel technique of lassoing a projection of rock and swinging across on the rope to gain the easier line. This feature forms roughly the right edge of the Central Gully Wall, which, higher up, presents a spectacular piece of rock architecture, arguably one of the most impressive in Britain. All the way up Central Gully, Patey's mind must have been working overtime trying to fathom feasible breaches in the monstrous bulk of rock above him. He could not have failed to notice its potential, but the obvious extreme technical difficulties it would entail were prohibitive, and he settled for a short line on the left extremity. Sabre Edge, 80m long, looks like a trivial afterthought to modern climbers, but it was the first successful probe. Its ascent was not a foregone conclusion, and Patey had to stand on Charlie Morrison's shoulders to breach the gap between a pinnacle and the main arête.

Despite venturing more widely to places such as the North Buttresses and A' Chìoch of Sgùrr a' Chaorachain in Applecross on the west coast of Scotland, the Cairngorms held enduring appeal for Patey. In an oft-quoted passage from 'Cairngorm Commentary' (SMCJ, 1962) he describes the deep-rooted ties that bound him to the area:

> *The Cairngorm climbing fraternity has always been a closely-knit community linked by similar ideals and aspirations. Good climbing and good company often go together: each is essential to the enjoyment of the other. In the Cairngorms, they are inseparable.*

The basis of this fraternity was the bothy culture. In the early days, the dearth of private transport meant that it was prohibitive to go away for just a day, and bothies—estate-owned abandoned houses of gamekeepers or shepherds—were often left open for general use at either no or minimal charge. Luibeg Bothy next to Bob Scott's cottage in Glen Derry was the hub for climbers seeking access to Ben Macdui's Coire Sputan Dearg and Creagan a' Choire Etchachan, as well as the corries of Braeriach, which also harbours Corrour Bothy in the Lairig Ghru. Lochnagar had the cold Gelder Shiel Bothy and, by the shores of Loch Muick, Lochend, which also served Creag an Dubh-loch.

There were even more basic shelters in the form of howffs, natural outcrops or boulder formations adapted to create something reasonably weather tight. Most of these venues required a lengthy walk-in, but this was all part of the Cairngorm experience and, besides, it enhanced fitness. Detailed mountain weather forecasts were unavailable, but people would take to the hills regardless, and if the weather was too bad, tackle easier routes or hillwalks. Some went along with no big mountaineering ambitions, simply enjoying the camaraderie and craic. The collection of characters and personalities always guaranteed entertaining evenings.

Bothy life enabled climbing information, including deeds south of the border and beyond, to be circulated. Joe Brown was already mentioned with hallowed reverence for his sensational new routes on Derbyshire Gritstone and the mountain crags of North Wales. In 'Cairngorm Commentary' (ibid.), Patey paints a delightful picture of some of the 'hairy vagabonds' who frequented the bothies at the time: Sandy-Sandy, Esposito, the Hash Kings and Droopydrawers, whose party trick was to imitate all the instruments in a jazz band.

Round the bothy fire, climbers would relax, discuss the day's ascents, epics and near misses, and embellish them for posterity. While Paleolithic man would gather round fires at night to discuss hazards and survival tactics, the potentially dangerous antics embarked upon by climbers are voluntary. When daily work routines provide virtually nothing of comparable vitality, tussling with the physical challenges afforded by natural features of the peaks and corries confers a satisfying tiredness. Later, in a simple bothy with a fire, good company and alcohol, the day can end in blissful contentment.

Minds and imaginations were expanded by conversations which could include politics, music and natural history, as well as the hatching of climbing plans. Some socially awkward individuals found themselves welcomed into a broad church. For many, it complemented—if not exceeded—any formal education. Bonds were cemented between individuals who shared common values and goals, against the backdrop of an inspiring landscape. Patey later reflected that he was at his happiest in what was an uncomplicated, less materialistic world.

He was also garnering a reputation for scruffiness and untidiness which he would maintain throughout his life, and early associates affectionately referred to him as 'an ugly, scruffy bugger'. Clothes, in particular, were not to be thrown out in haste. Big Stan Long, a lofty Cairngorm presence, once gave his tattered trousers a royal send-off by tying them round the chimney at Gelder Shiel. The following weekend, Patey spotted them and decided they would make a perfect replacement for his own threadbare pair. So off he trotted with them into the corrie.

Towards the end of 1952 and into the following year, Patey and his peers applied their skills and boldness on some of the principal routes of their lives. Patey would establish three winter routes which ranked alongside any in the country at the time and remain highly respected to this day. Although he went on to achieve much more in Scotland and abroad than any of his contemporaries, these routes represented the zenith of technical difficulty in those formative years and a standard of climbing in the Cairngorms that neither he nor anyone else would surpass for over another decade.

During these early forays and in the subsequent rich harvest reaped right up until the last day of his life, Patey was driven by a guiding principle:

> *To my mind, the magic of a great route does not lie in its technical difficulty or even the excellence of its rock, but in something less readily definable*—atmosphere *is the term generally applied. A route should fulfil an honest purpose: it should follow a natural line of weakness up a natural obstacle and reach a natural conclusion. There are many so-called routes whose conception would not tax the mental faculties of an ape ... Such routes portray a complete lack of purpose, imagination or logic on the part of their creators. In the Cairngorms, the climber's mental horizon is fortunately wider.* (SMCJ, 1962)

This *atmosphere* is certainly present in Patey's greatest routes, regardless of their grade.

1   Coincidentally, this would presage one of his most famous winter routes, Crab Crawl (IV,4), on Creag Meagaidh, which he soloed 20 years later.

2   Up to this point, Patey had done just a handful of mountain routes, mostly on Lochnagar, none harder than V. Diff.

3   In his SMC application, submitted in 1954, Patey lists this as a summer ascent too.

4   In his SMC application form, the Nevis classic is dated 1951, but the earlier year is more likely because, according to Mike Taylor, Patey 'was so thrilled by it that it could scarcely have been 1951, by which time he had Douglas-Gibson under his belt and … we were confidently anticipating our trip to Zermatt in the summer'.

5   Raeburn was irresistibly drawn to Douglas-Gibson and, in October 1902, inspected the final barrier by downclimbing most of it, after which he claimed it was doable. The next day he was thwarted by ice and a stream flowing down the first cave pitch. Six years later, he was back for a winter attempt but was rebuffed by mild temperatures and avalanche conditions. Any betting person would have backed Raeburn on eventually climbing the gully, but the right conditions never materialised.

6   Winter routes were often ungraded when descriptions of first ascents were given, but when conditions were similar, the same grading adjectival system was given to both summer and winter routes. This, however, was unsatisfactory as the climbing styles were quite different, and in the 1956 *SMCJ*, new winter routes on Lochnagar were given the roman numerical grade from I to V. The new system was not properly explained or established until the two-volume *Climbers' Guide to the Cairngorms* appeared in 1961. When the Roman numeral winter grading system was introduced, Douglas-Gibson became the first Grade V route in Scotland, and to this day it is respected for its serious nature.

7   Goggs Leslie was the only one of that generation to climb Douglas-Gibson Gully in both summer and winter. In the modern era, Andy Nisbet also climbed it in both seasons.

8   Tall, genial and a keen dancer, Brooker got on with everybody and his arrival in a coffee shop or student bar with enthusiastic observations, the latest climbing gossip and plans for new adventures instantly enlivened his group of friends. He never bore a grudge, but he dismissed all pretensions just like he did scary pitches, with a confidential grin and his catchphrase: 'What a laugh, man!' (*SMCJ*, 2012).

9   In 1951, Patey had climbed the less memorable Shadow Chimney (Severe) with Maurice Coutts and Scarface (Severe) with Goggs Leslie and Mike Taylor in Lochnagar's North-East Corrie.

10   Dixon initiated Patey's Yorkshire connection with the 'Bradford Lads' from which Dennis Gray became his most regular contact, especially when he moved to Edinburgh in the '60s for work.

11   Dixon once turned up at the house of the parents of the Drasdo brothers in Bradford and was sent out to fetch fish and chips for the family. Before handing over the supper to the famished household, he insisted on reciting some of his recently composed poems (Gray, 2016). When he tried to get out of National Service by feigning a mental health condition, the army psychiatrist found him such a fascinating person and interesting conversationalist he concocted a reason not to release him.

03

Approaching Mitre
Ridge from the East
© Greg Strange

The Scorpion and the Eagle

Most Scottish routes have lost something to the vicious peck of the drooped axe, but not Eagle Ridge.

Nick Banks, *Cold Climbs*

Even though he was the most able and focused of a talented group, Patey was not involved in every significant Cairngorm climb in the winter of 1952-53. Realising that strong partners were required for some of the routes he had in mind, he shrewdly observed the big leads others were doing and recognised the time was right to up the stakes and fulfil some personal ambitions.

New talent was also joining the Aberdeen University Lairig Club at the start of every academic year. Graeme Nicol, who at 17 was three years younger than Patey, entered medical school in autumn 1952 and attended a November club meet in Glenmore, where he met Patey for the first time. As a pupil at Aberdeen Grammar School, Nicol had been a 'sulky wee boy who walked along beside the gymnasium hitting his fist against the granite wall' (Craig, 2001), and he and a group of like-minded friends had been nicknamed the Boor Boys due to their coarse, unruly behaviour.

Good early snow cover and ice forming on the higher cliffs heralded a flurry of new route activity during the meet. Several students headed up to Coire an Lochain, but conditions were hellish, and gradually people dropped out. Eventually, only Patey, Nicol and Andy Wedderburn were left. Patey was already an established celebrity in the Cairngorm climbing scene, and Nicol (1971) recalls: 'I'd heard about this great man, so I followed in his footsteps to the foot of a steep gully and I followed him up the gully, and eventually I persuaded him to throw a rope down. And we did the climb.' This was the first ascent of Y Gully

Left Hand Branch (IV,4), whose crux comprised a 20ft icicle. Thereafter, Nicol became the apprentice and *enfant terrible* of the Patey group, an association that continued for several years.

Patey had a messianic zeal for converting people to climbing and encouraging their development. After climbing with a keen novice, he would often bandy around the phrase: 'He will probably be the best climber in Scotland one day.' This enthusiasm sometimes manifested as capriciousness, however, and Patey would 'take a fancy to someone who was new and different at the expense of someone he already knew. This was nice if you were [in favour] but a bit hurtful if [you were] not' (Nicol, 2014). On the way down from their first route together, Nicol mentioned that Polypody Groove on Beinn a' Bhùird would make a good winter climb. Later, Nicol discovered that Patey was thinking of doing it with other people and was somewhat put out as he had instigated the idea. But Patey could be very charming, and when Nicol bumped into him in the student union building, Patey said, 'Oh man, I'm sorry if I offended you. I didn't mean to bypass you. If we ever do that climb, you'll be on it, of course.'

Earlier that year, Patey had met Ken Grassick, another Aberdeen Grammar School pupil and Boor Boy, at Lochend Bothy. Grassick had a nonchalant attitude and a reputation for being accident-prone. He and his peers were traditionally unpleasant to others they met in bothies, but this did not deter Patey from inviting him climbing. Grassick, having heard all about Patey's success on Douglas-Gibson Gully, was flattered, and together they climbed Eagle Ridge and Black Spout Pinnacle via an unspecified route—the hardest routes Grassick had done to date. This was the only time he ever managed to keep up with Patey on an approach to a cliff—Patey usually charged ahead, soloed the initial pitch and was rested and eager to get going before his companions arrived in a breathless lather. Of course, it helped that Patey's rucksack was usually light as it never contained much gear, but he always carried a badly coiled rope, and upon reaching the top of a route, he would frequently walk off, leaving his second to sort out the tangle. This kind of one-upmanship helped confirm Patey's status in the climbing echelons, especially if there was competition about, and it consolidated his reputation for insouciance.

A few weeks after climbing The Stack on Lochnagar with Patey and Bill Brooker, Mike Taylor was back with Goggs Leslie and Leslie Fallowfield for the first winter ascent. Originally graded IV, it is now solid V,6 and was a significant achievement. The next day, Patey was in the corrie with W.H. Murray, one of the most significant figures in the history of Scottish mountaineering, and together they climbed Black Spout Buttress, which afforded a grandstand view of The Stack. Murray commented to Patey that he could scarcely believe that such an outrageously looking steep and bold line could be climbed in winter conditions.[1]

Patey must have felt a little piqued to have missed out on his friends' big ascent, and in the Union a week later, he brandished a copy of the SMC district guide to the Cairngorms at Nicol and jabbed a finger at a small photo of Carn Etchachan and the Shelter Stone Crag: 'Oh man,' he enthused, 'there's supposed to be no climbing at all on the north face of Carn Etchachan. There's got to be some climbing there.'

The following weekend saw Patey and Taylor ensconced at Derry Lodge, to which they were granted access by being Cairngorm Club members. Meanwhile, Nicol and Grassick were at Luibeg Bothy with Mac Smith, whose mysterious lack of enthusiasm about Carn Etchachan's potential was, Patey suspected, because he was saving the plum lines for himself. The crag, lying at the head of Loch Avon, is a triangular configuration of ribs and grooves separated from the Shelter Stone Crag by Castlegates Gully. Shelter Stone Crag, with its continuous sweeps of immaculate granite, dominates like a huge headstone, but for Patey the allure of Carn Etchachan was that it was yet to have a route recorded on it.

It was relatively mild on the four-hour walk-in, with snow on the ground but insects in the air. The climb began chaotically with the two pairs, all moving together, trying to find a way up the lower section

From left: Kenny Grassick, Patey, Bill Brooker and another at Lochend Bothy near Loch Muick © Ian Patey collection

and becoming stuck after barely advancing 100m. Despite Patey's circulatory affliction, he had neglected to bring gloves with him, so Taylor took over the lead and Nicol generously donated his own gloves.

A subterranean chimney eventually proved the key to a blank wall, but a desperate upper gully proved to be the sting in the tail. Patey, now climbing with Nicol, led the crux over a double band of overhangs coated in a mean slick of verglas, on which he deployed the adhesive properties of Nicol's woolly gloves to hold him in balance. Slender nicks in the ice reluctantly admitted the nails on his boots. A one-handed swing and a tentative pull up on a finger hold enabled him to win through—but only just. The drama continued as Grassick, who was hauling himself up a fixed line behind them, fell past Taylor, who was yanked tight against the belay but dutifully arrested the fall. Observing all this, Nicol wryly commented: 'It's alright ... we're not tied onto them anyway.' Luckily, Grassick's 10m fall had terminated in soft snow and he was uninjured.

The potential cul-de-sac of the second overhang was neatly circumvented by a traverse on a foot-wide ledge across the vertical right wall to easy ground. The route had taken seven hours in total, and the two pairs had earned each other's lifelong respect.

With 62 years of hindsight, Nicol reflected that 'The whole thing was just bloody madness,' and could have easily resulted in four inert bodies lying in Castlegates Gully.

Nicol, young and inexperienced, was shattered on his return to Derry Lodge. The next day, they could barely walk, and they took a taxi part of the way to Braemar then Strachan's bus to Aberdeen. Nicol did not comprehend the significance of the route at the time, but Patey, with his commercial, competitive eye, said, 'It's going to be a right royal route, man.'

Patey named the climb Scorpion because of the crux finish, but depending on the build-up, the sting is often a daunting cornice. He also claimed he could see the shape of a scorpion in a photograph of the cliff, with the tail represented by the final gully. Only the second Grade V to be recorded in the Cairngorms, Scorpion has foxed many

Graeme Nicol on the first winter ascent of Scorpion, 1952 © Ian Patey collection

a climber since, and several parties have unwittingly climbed parallel routes, or, after becoming baffled and cragfast, have retreated.

The comparison in the quality of writing between Patey's first published article about the ascent of Parallel Gully B in summer and 'Appointment with Scorpion' six months later is striking. In the latter he is more assured, has an eye for the comical, an ear for sparky dialogue, and he memorably characterises Nicol, who, being younger, was somewhat over-enthusiastic in embracing the group's mock-Teutonic attitude. Patey depicts him as a fanatically driven mountaineer of the pre-war Munich school, whose role models had often perished on those pitiless Alpine north faces in the 1930s: 'Nicol ... was steadily working himself into a frenzy at the prospect of a bivouac on the face—a distinction he had long coveted.' But Patey had only known Nicol for a couple of weeks, and he added to his character sketch over the ensuing years until the article appeared in print four years later in the *Etchachan Club Journal* of 1956. By then, Patey had honed the characteristic style seen in all his classic works.

A thaw at the beginning of January cleared the cliffs of any unstable material, and the freeze that followed ensured optimum conditions of firm snow and ice. On consecutive days of the weekend of the 24th and 25th, two great classics on Lochnagar fell. The first was to Ken Grassick (clearly undeterred by his experience on Scorpion), with Hamish Bates, another Boor Boy. In Polyphemus Gully (V,5), they created the best gully climb on the mountain and a rival to some of the classics on Ben

From left: Brooker, Patey and Taylor, one of the strongest winter climbing teams in the history of Scottish mountaineering at a bothy in Applecross, 1953
© Ian Patey collection

Nevis and Creag Meagaidh.[2] The upper pitch provided the crux; thin ice in a groove avoided a perilous icy overhanging.

Sunday's route quickly usurped Polyphemus's short reign as the winter jewel of the corrie. Since its first summer ascent by SMC stalwart J.H.B. Bell and Nancy Forsyth, Eagle Ridge has remained one of the great Scottish classics and the most popular rock route on Lochnagar. Clean granite with thrilling situations on the soaring crest overlooks Douglas-Gibson Gully. Its edge is enlivened by two harder sections: the tower lower down and the traditional crux higher up, where a short wall is tackled from a knife-edge take-off point. The final pitch often proves equally taxing for those who have unwittingly relaxed their guard. For its grade, it is one of the most outstanding routes in Britain.

Attempting Eagle Ridge in winter would have seemed incredible to most active climbers at the time. From afar, it presents an alluringly beautiful profile of graceful arêtes topped by sculptured snow and interrupted by precipitous buttresses. Not for nothing is it referred to as The Queen of Lochnagar's winter climbs, and it is as emblematic of the mountain as Point Five Gully is of Ben Nevis. Patey, Brooker and Taylor, however, were all prepared for the challenge and had a number of hard, recent ascents under their belts to bolster their confidence. Moreover, they had intimate knowledge of the route in summer—indeed, Patey had done it four times, once in descent. Nevertheless, it was the first bona fide classic summer rock climb they attempted in winter conditions.

After a long walk into the corrie from the Danzig Bridge, the trio were rewarded with iron-hard snow on the slabs and ledges and good ice in the cracks. Patey led all the key pitches using combined tactics to overcome a brittle crucial section on the tower. The ascent time of just four-and-a-half hours is testament to a talented team on top form. In his pocket diary entry for the day, Brooker declared the route HS, using the same grading system as for rock routes. Later this was revised upwards to VS, and for many years Eagle Ridge was given a winter grade of V. Its current claim of VI,6 is more realistic but assumes average conditions, and unconsolidated powder can make it extremely arduous, if not impossible.³

At the time, Eagle Ridge was the hardest mixed route in Scotland. The following month, however, Hamish MacInnes and partners, including a young Chris Bonington, established Agag's Groove (VII,6) and Crowberry Ridge Direct (VII,7) on Buachaille Etive Mòr in Glen Coe. The former was only half the length of Eagle Ridge but the latter a little longer. Back then, MacInnes was Patey's main rival for the crown of best winter mountaineer in Scotland and, like Patey, he had a kernel of toughness and a high threshold for discomfort. Raven's Gully (V,6), which he climbed with Bonington, is more of a mixed climb than a conventional gully and was harder than anything else within this genre in the Cairngorms at the time.

Following their matter-of-fact ascent of Eagle Ridge, Patey and Taylor were back in the same corrie a month later to explore the Black Spout Pinnacle area and a new line to the right of the steepest section known as Black Spout Wall. A major thaw had left the buttresses bare, and the pair encountered good rock climbing conditions until they reached the crux: an exposed traverse which they climbed without their boots on due to an evil glaze of thin ice. Under proper winter conditions, the technicalities of Route 2 are equal to those of Eagle Ridge.

During the Easter holidays, Patey, Taylor and Brooker headed west on motorbikes with their eyes on the Great Buttress of Carn Dearg on Ben Nevis. If the unclimbed gullies of Point Five and Zero occupied the winter dreams of all leading climbers of the day, then the great chimney and corner lines of what would later become Sassenach and Centurion had a similarly magnetic pull for rock climbers. Poor weather thwarted their plans, however, and after an indifferent outing on North Trident Buttress, they decamped to the Applecross peninsula, whose possibilities had been assessed on previous trips.

Back then, the quickest access from the south was via Stromeferry. Missing the last crossing of the day proved unexpectedly fortuitous when friendly forestry workers offered to put the trio up for the night in a bothy. Until then, Patey's musical interests were confined to the piano and the harmonica, which he took with him on trips, but upon hearing one of the bothy occupants playing the accordion, his musical life changed irrevocably. He relished the instrument's sound and had a natural talent for it. Despite its bulk, Patey soon became inseparable from his accordion on most social occasions thereafter and would entertain fellow students with it on the bus during club meets.

Several snowstorms blanketed the mountains at the end of March, and with the extra daylight, Patey and Brooker hatched a plan for a winter attempt of Beinn a' Bhùird's alluring yet intimidating Mitre Ridge, which lies in the deep recesses of the remotest corrie of the mountain and requires considerable commitment, particularly in winter. Its West Wall, just off vertical, is a complex lattice of cracks with some major fault lines; the East Wall is slabbier and more vegetated. Several towers punctuate the crest and it abuts the main mountain mass by a short but narrow spectacular arête.

Their transport from Aberdeen was Brooker's BSA 'Sloper' motorcycle, but they did not embark on the eight-mile walk-in until late morning and only began climbing after midday. They were gladdened by the sight of a good covering of snow on all the ledges and recesses, with fresh powder lying on top of hard snow on the north and west aspects.

They followed the direct line that Patey had climbed in summer three years earlier but avoided the initial groove by taking the Ludwig start. Both men were using a shortened single axe and while Brooker preferred to be tethered to his axe, Patey favoured an ambidextrous approach and the ability to make use of rock holds without a sliding wrist sling getting in the way—a method that was considered cavalier at the time. Normally they would swing leads until things became too technical for Brooker, but as Patey set off on the third pitch—a traverse leading to the first main difficulty—a hold snapped and he fell 5m onto soft snow. (This was the only time Brooker knew Patey to fall and it was indeed rare, with just one more recorded incident in the Alps in the '60s.) Patey was unhurt but shaken, and Brooker took over and led the first crux chimney. The shorter Patey then launched upwards from

Bill Brooker near the top of Mitre Ridge on the first winter ascent
© Ian Patey collection

Brooker's knee to the nape of his neck, and with a final push from his nailed boot, surmounted a steep wall to reach a belay under the first tower in a spectacular position on the buttress crest.

Brooker's next pitch was particularly trying. A delicate traverse led to a splintered chimney where holds had to be dug out and patches of frozen turf exploited:

> *It proved to be the hardest pitch of our climb and demanded concentration to the point where the entire outside world was shut off from my consciousness. There was only me, this steep iced rock, the need for precise and careful placing of tricouni nail edges whenever a move was made, and the dry throat I always developed in such situations.* (Brooker, 2001)

A succession of exhilarating steps led to the col between the two towers and the second was turned on the left. A straightforward but photogenic traverse across a narrow crenellated arête offered a thrilling finale to their four-and-a-half-hour odyssey, which completed a trilogy of major ascents that season.[4]

In the seven years after the significant achievements of Patey and MacInnes, standards on pure ice climbs on Ben Nevis and Creag Meagaidh rose, culminating in Robin Smith and Jimmy Marshall's epic week on Ben Nevis in February 1960. As well as their rapid and stylish ascent of Point Five Gully in a single push, they created the open face climbs of Gardyloo Buttress and Orion Face Direct, which were as hard as any ice routes in Europe at the time. Even today, Orion Face Direct remains one of the country's outstanding outings.

While these are magnificent lines, they also look very intimidating, and it wasn't until the '70s that they began to be climbed regularly. Patey's early mixed classics did not have the same popular appeal, however. One reason for this is that Scorpion was the only one he wrote about and even then his account, published in the *Etchachan Club Journal*, had limited circulation. Only after his death and the publication of *One Man's Mountains* was the significance of the route more widely appreciated. While both Smith and Marshall wrote vivid and inspiring articles and their sensational climbs could be appreciated from the road below, Patey's were neither as accessible nor as visible. Moreover, while the advent of front pointing and inclined axe picks made the classic Grade V ice lines more achievable for the masses, this did not apply to Patey's and MacInnes's mixed routes, which required technical ingenuity: although they offer conventional rock protection, conditions are variable, and jamming axe picks in cracks or hooking them over holds feels more precarious than embedding them in solid snow ice.

Patey's Cairngorm trilogy has not been significantly humbled by modern equipment or diminished by multiple ascents in ridiculously fast times, but its inclusion in the classic *Cold Climbs* (Wilson, Alcock and Barry, 1983) increased the appeal of these climbs among a younger generation of climbers who feel obliged to pit themselves against the testpieces of previous generations. Mixed climbing has been the medium for the modern evolution of the sport, and Patey's routes fall into this category. Despite the technical grade of today's hardest routes being double that of Patey's, his early achievements remain formidable undertakings for most climbers.

It is also worth bearing in mind that, in the '50s, mountaineering clothing and equipment were extremely rudimentary and winter climbing at the highest levels was for a tough breed. Hawser laid ropes, tied round the climbers' waists, were like coils of steel when frozen. Rope slings, ex-WD karabiners and the odd piton (often homemade) meant that ice protection was virtually illusory and serious runouts were common. Wooden shafted axes with straight picks were used to cut steps, a time-consuming and exhausting practice. Patey and his contemporaries wore heavy-duty jackets which were shell-like when frozen, but whose porousness allowed the cold to seep in. Often a beret was a gesture to heat loss from the head, and gaiters and mittens were noticeable by their absence. Despite, or perhaps because of these disadvantages, the rewards for a successful ascent of a hard route were undeniable.

North East Corrie of Lochnagar. Douglas-Gibson Gully is on the left, Eagle Ridge lies to its right. Patey, Brooker and Smith's 1956 Parallel Buttress is to the right of the central Parallel Gully A. Patey and Aitken's Tough-Brown Traverse starts left of that gully, crossing it, Parallel Buttress and Parallel Gully B before taking a rising line across the Tough-Brown Face. Photo on the wall at Ullapool Bothy © Ian Patey collection

With the late winter snows finally melting, attention turned to the creation of a rock route on one of the greatest Cairngorm cliffs: Shelter Stone Crag, adjacent to Carn Etchachan, home of Scorpion.

The showpieces of the crag are the Central Slabs, a 100m sweep of immaculate, if thin, granite, and the 300m Main Bastion, which is topped by some imposing corners. The route Patey and Taylor created, The Sticil Face (HS), was the first on the open aspect of the cliff since Harold Raeburn and F.S. Goggs established Castle Wall (Diff) and Raeburn's Buttress (Severe) in 1907. Breaching the shallow gully between the Central Slabs and Raeburn's Buttress, Taylor led the crux up an edge by the side of the damp main fault. They then traversed above the main slabs and exited via an enclosed chimney left of the Main Bastion. Wandering in nature with much vegetation, it was hardly a satisfactory route—

the true quality of the line is revealed under winter conditions—but it did create another opening in this most impressive cliff.

The pair's next new Cairngorm route satisfied Patey's quest for climbs with atmosphere regardless of technicalities. Squareface's greatest asset was its incredible situation on a rectangular sheet of rock on the side wall of Back Bay Gully high in the Garbh Choire of Beinn a' Bhùird, the home of Mitre Ridge. Mac Smith had enthused about the feature and had already named it, which spurred Patey and Taylor to snatch the prize. Looked at head-on, the feature appears as though any route up the blank-looking face will be of extreme severity, but in reality, the slab is generously furnished with holds, although the easiest line is a little circuitous. At the top, a prominent jam crack provided a fitting finale for the pair, and Smith arrived at the lip to chart their progress. Despite its lowly grade of V. Diff, Squareface is synonymous with Patey and is often climbed with a route on Mitre Ridge to give a tremendously satisfying day out. Late in the day, with the mellow evening sun on it, one can soak in the remote atmosphere of one of the great Cairngorm corries.

In August, the Aberdeen climbing scene was rocked by a death on one of Patey's routes on Lochnagar. Before this, Graeme Nicol had a close shave when he fell before the main chimney pitch on Parallel Gully B: he came taut on the rope just as he skimmed the ground. Lucky to escape with four broken ribs, Nicol, with classic swagger, asked the two climbers who attended to him to turn him over so he could see where he fell. 'It wasn't VS,' he cried bitterly at the ignominy, 'only Hard Severe' (Patey, 1962). He also allegedly said with an air of sangfroid: 'If you take up this game, you've got to know how to fall.'

The line between humour and tragedy is thin, and a week later in the upper gully of the same route, Bill Stewart fell to his death while traversing from the Contortion Groove. Stewart had draped his rope round a spike to act as a running belay, but despite his fall being short, the rope was severed. Ironically, he and his partner, James (Chesty) Bruce, had been on the climb the previous weekend when Nicol had his accident and they had retreated. They had returned to complete the climb in full by ascending the upper section, this time with two women, one of whom was Elizabeth (Betty) Davidson, an attractive, dark-haired girl who worked as a secretary in Aberdeen. Stewart's accident affected the younger contingent in particular, and afterwards they became more circumspect and inclined to confine their activities to hillwalking and skiing.

Out west, Applecross and Skye were now regular ports of call. Here, Patey established new routes on Sgùrr a' Chaorachain and Meall Gorm and, with Mike Taylor, briskly traversed the Cuillin Ridge in eight-and-a-half hours. Disappointment over the Easter trip to Ben Nevis had been festering, however, and in early October Patey, Taylor and Brooker returned to attempt a route on Carn Dearg Buttress, a magnificent piece of rock architecture comprising huge corners, overhangs and overlapping slabs. Robin Smith (1960) compared it to a 'black haystack', and it has a mighty presence above the approach up the Allt a' Mhuilinn.[5]

The plan was to gain access to a great upper chimney from the base of a corner system lower down and to its left. In effect, Patey was linking what would become the classic routes of Centurion with Sassenach. Following the former for a pitch, Patey then led across a series of slabby shelves but, even with the security of a peg runner halfway across, he could not continue—perhaps due to the inferiority of his plimsoll footwear—and was thus denied access to the chimneys.[6] Undeterred by this, they abseiled off, headed to the right edge of the buttress and made an exposed traverse crossing Waterfall Gully. This was followed by a short abseil, then spectacular moves across what is now Titan's Wall. The rounding of the exposed edge of the buttress led to a continuation to the great chimney's base. Today, this approach is known as the Patey Traverse and is graded VS. Luckily, Taylor and Brooker maintained enough composure to follow the pitch: without the rope above them this was equivalent to leading.

About 12m up the main chimney, Patey encountered a large, wobbly chockstone which, if dislodged, would obliterate anyone below.

Fading daylight forced a retreat, but the overhanging terrain meant that their abseil rope did not reach the ground. The only alternative was to reverse the last section of the traverse and then abseil off, leaving behind three pegs and their first rope, which would not pull free. (Being thrifty Aberdonians, they retrieved the rope three days later.) The trio could never have contemplated the direct overhanging approach to the chimney, and it must have been an eye-opener and humbling confirmation of their own skills when Joe Brown and Don Whillans made the first ascent of Sassenach via this entry the following year.[7] At this juncture, Patey had still not climbed a significant new route outside the Cairngorms and indeed would not do so until 1957.

Despite his initial shyness at university, Patey eventually joined in with all manner of undergraduate frivolity, sometimes with a mountaineering flavour. During Student Charities Week, a midnight ascent of Mitchell's Tower spire in the Marischal College was almost mandatory, and in the quadrangle of the same building, an annual 'battle' preceded the election of the university rector. The supporters of the four candidates held two semi-finals where they had to capture the flag of the opposing team while hurling fish oil, rat excrement laced with maggots, rotten tomatoes and pig dung at each other. Naturally, the Lairig Club members used a rope and climbing skills to capture the flag by abseiling from above.

In November 1953, the well-known and popular celebrity Tom Weir was the guest speaker at the annual formal dinner of the Cairngorm Club. Fellow student Adam Watson accompanied Patey to the dinner. Watson studied at Aberdeen for both his undergraduate degree in zoology and his PhD, and he became a highly respected scientist and an authority on everything from wildlife to snow patches in the Cairngorms. Two years older than Patey, he was an admirer of the younger student and climbed and socialised with him frequently during this period.

The day following the dinner event, Patey and Watson, with Mike Taylor and Bill Brooker, took Weir on a tour of Lochnagar, including an ascent of Eagle Ridge, which Patey proclaimed was the best rock route in the corrie. Sleet, wind and wet, slippery rock on this dreich November day did not spoil the enjoyment, and Weir confirmed the quality of the climb. Noting the contrasting styles of Patey and Taylor, Weir (1981) said:

> *Patey was exuberant as he scraped, lunged and grunted, drawing breath only to extol some feature of the elegant route I might be missing. By contrast, Taylor looked meticulously controlled and demanded his right to lead some of the choicest pitches.*

They drove back to Aberdeen via a tour round Balmoral Castle, whose security was significantly more relaxed back then. Patey mooted the idea of a climbing guidebook to the Cairngorms, which Weir agreed was something the SMC should publish. To facilitate this, it would be beneficial if those involved became club members and Weir offered to act as a proposer. Weir would become one of Patey's closer older friends and someone in whom Patey confided on topics he might have shielded from others.

The last significant event of that auspicious year took place the following weekend and involved another ascent of Eagle Ridge, this time under eight inches of fresh powder snow. Tom Bourdillon was in Aberdeen to lecture on the successful British ascent of Everest earlier in the year. With Charles Evans, he had reached the South Summit and thus paved the way for the successful summit bid by Edmund Hilary and Sherpa Tensing. Patey led the vibram-soled Bourdillon up Eagle Ridge in conditions that proved much harder than on the first winter ascent. Bourdillon, a physicist and ex-President of the Oxford University Mountaineering Club, was a leading Alpine climber, one of the founding members of the Alpine Climbing Group (ACG) and its first President at its inaugural meeting in April 1953. Although also a member of the Alpine Club, Bourdillon had become disgruntled at the stagnation in the older organisation. He wanted to raise the standard of Alpine routes tackled by British climbers by demanding far higher standards for admittance and requiring regular achievements at those levels to maintain membership. By 1967 both outfits were reconciled, and the ACG had become part of the Alpine Club, containing in its membership most of the leading British Alpinists. Bourdillon admitted that Eagle Ridge in winter was the hardest climb of his life, and it is no surprise that Patey became a member of the ACG soon after this, and its President in 1969.

1   Murray, who was renowned for his climbs in the '30s and the evocative way he wrote about them, acted as Deputy Leader to Eric Shipton on the Everest Reconnaissance expedition of 1951. Patey was considered for the 1953 expedition but was rejected because of his age (he was only 21 at the time).

2   Polyphemus Gully had been attempted by Brooker, Johnny Morgan and Doug Sutherland three years earlier, but they had been thwarted by impending darkness and difficulties on the icy upper section. Brooker's lead was an advance in technical difficulty and a retreat was successfully executed.

3   Recalling his ascent with Neil Quinn 13 years later, the indomitable Doug Lang (*SMCJ*, 1969) said: 'The sight of Eagle Ridge in full winter garb is awe-inspiring and frightening. I am amazed we ever had the audacity to try and climb it. Whenever I look on those icy towers, my heart still jumps a beat.'

4   Mitre Ridge had to wait 21 years for its second ascent when Greg Strange climbed it with Dennis King in March 1974. Strange was expecting 'a pleasant romp up this old classic,' but got more than he bargained for. Like the original ascent, there was an end-of-season Alpine ambience with a fusion of snow and sun. Having taken about one-and-a-half hours longer than Patey and Brooker, Strange considered the route to be on a par with Eagle Ridge and Parallel Gully B in terms of difficulty and commitment. In Mac Smith's guide it was given Grade IV, the technicalities being too short to warrant the highest grade. It is now a more realistic V,6.

5   The trio had already romantically named the great cliff Wall of the Winds without having set foot on it. Patey later gave this name to another imposing cliff on a sector of the Triple Buttresses of Beinn Eighe.

6   After his Alpine season that year, Patey had bought a pair of rubber moulded-sole boots known universally as Vibrams (though many were copies of the originals invented by Vitale Bramine in the mid '30s), which superseded nailed boots on rock climbs, being lighter and affording greater friction. On wet rock or snow and ice, however, they could not rival nails.

7   Patey did, however, contribute something to the first ascent when he told Whillans about the series of great corner chimneys high on the buttress when the pair met in Chamonix in the summer of 1953.

04

Patey's graduation portrait
© Ian Patey collection

Student of Medicine and Mountaineering

A. P. S. Ltd.      Aberdeen & Edinburgh

To Betty
With Love
from Tom

Who needs a career?
It was never any substitute for a life.

William McIlvanney, 'Waving' in *Walking Wounded*

If the winter of 1952–53 was Patey's high point in terms of the difficulty and significance of his climbs, the following year was one of his most productive in terms of sheer output. Work on the Cairngorm climbing guide also began in earnest. Mac Smith's unrivalled knowledge of the range's corries and cliffs confirmed his authority as overall author and editor, while Patey assessed most of the existing routes, ably assisted by Mike Taylor. Adam Watson confirmed grades, route lengths and descriptions of crags, and other Aberdeen-based climbers offered their services. By now, Patey had become so proficient at soloing that he checked many of the routes alone, keeping a keen eye out for potential new lines.[1]

Their endeavours were supported by Watson's old jeep, which was nicknamed the Roaring Fart and could transport six climbers with rucksacks. This made for swifter access to the hills, and afterwards, the pub.

There were three main mountaineering clubs operating out of Aberdeen at that time: the University Lairig Club, the Etchachan Club and the Cairngorm Club. The latter, founded in 1887, is the longest established club in Scotland, predating the SMC by two years. Patey, Taylor and Bill Brooker were all members of the Cairngorm Club in their early student days, but its members were more interested in hillwalking than climbing and it seemed a rather staid and conservative outfit. Meets were described as 'motor coach excursions' and the regular, lengthy refreshment stops had an air of old-fashioned formality.

The Etchachan Club, established in 1938, was modelled on the

Glasgow-based Lomond Club, whose founders wanted affordable meets and transportation as close to the hills and climbing venues as possible. The Etchachan favoured operating in small pairs or groups rather than embarking on the kind of mass ascents that were common in the Cairngorm Club. Moreover, they insisted on punctuality, and Patey and other Lairig members felt constrained by the half-hour pub stops. While the Etchachan did not have the riotous air of the Lairig, whose protagonists were immensely talented and bold, it nevertheless had some fine climbers in its ranks. Mac Smith was a stalwart, and hardcore members would meet every Friday evening at the same table in the Victoria Restaurant to discuss their plans for the weekend.

Although newcomers were not always welcomed with open arms, the Patey gang inevitably graduated to the Etchachan Club, which was 'never guilty as a club of any leanings toward the pretension which prevails in much that makes up the climbing scene ...' (Smith, M. 1962b).

When Patey and Watson joined this somewhat insular group, they were aware of suspicion towards other climbers based in the city or

Patey, Mike Taylor and the Roaring Fart. Coylumbridge campsite, 1 September 1954
© Adam Watson

those visiting from south of the border. But parochialism was anathema to Patey. He hated staunch exponents of nationalism and narrow, dogmatic viewpoints, and he socialised and climbed freely with everyone. He also welcomed new visitors, recognising the benefits of climbing with some of the UK's leading mountaineers. His 'experience, honesty, classless attitude, and above all enthusiasm for the Cairngorms meant that by 1955 the Aberdeen climbers had become a closer group, largely due to him' (Watson, 2011).

Meanwhile, the Lairig Club was at its zenith, with a high calibre of climbers which included the old guard of Patey, Taylor and Brooker, and 'Young Turks', Nicol and Ken Grassick. Grassick (Patey, 1962) went so far as to boldly assert in the student magazine, *Gaudie* that newcomers would be introduced to 'Qualified climbing instructors, including some of world repute [who] will be glad to show [them] the ropes.' Their growing fame attracted many more members, whose subscriptions enabled the popular bus meets to be organised at minimal cost. The number in attendance could swell to as many as 70 and both sexes were welcome. Some would go along for the hillwalking or the convivial refreshment stops on the way home, and New Year meets (usually at Cairngorm Hotel in Aviemore) saw students mix with the older hierarchy of SMC members from Glasgow, such as Tom Weir and Len Lovat.

In addition to these three climbing clubs, smaller outfits, such as the Kincorth Mountaineering Club, emerged. The key members of this group of seven men were mostly tradesmen or engineers, and Patey respected their working-class backgrounds and abilities and enjoyed climbing with them. Freddie Malcolm and Alex 'Sticker' Thom were a strong partnership from the start, and the subjects of an early Patey song:

Freddie and Sticker
No guys are slicker
Shooting up VSs with plenty to spare
Up in Coire na Ciche

With a new route every week
They're the aristocrats of Bon Accord Square.

The Kincorth Club explored the corries of Beinn a' Bhùird extensively and were so enamoured by them that they constructed a howff when the Slugain Bothy was destroyed. Access to these remote climbing venues involved a considerable walk from the main road at Invercauld, so even basic accommodation en route was welcome.[2] A visitor's book inside documented the official opening and offered a teasing invitation:

This howff was constructed In the Year of Our Lord 1954, by the Kincorth Club, for the Kincorth Club. All climbers please leave names, and location of intended climbs. Female climbers please leave names, addresses, and telephone numbers.

Patey's only notable new winter route of 1954 fell at the end of March, when a team of students including Taylor, Nicol and Goggs Leslie headed to Garbh Choire in Beinn a' Bhùird. After recently climbing Mitre Ridge with Brooker, Patey was keen to tap the potential of the corrie, and with Nicol he attempted the South-East Gully bounding the left-hand side of Mitre Ridge, but was obliged to transfer to an ice couloir on the East Wall (East Wall Original Route, IV) due to thaw conditions.

Meanwhile, Taylor and Goggs climbed the icefall of The Flume. The quartet then scaled two Grade II gullies between Mitre Ridge and the Squareface Buttress, filling in gaps for the forthcoming guidebook. Given the commitment required to reach the venue, it was a commendable day's effort, but it marked the end of Goggs's serious interest in climbing.

As if to compensate for the shortage of winter activity, the pace during the rock climbing season became frenetic. One weekend in June, Patey and Watson were engaged in guidebook work and had retired to the Fife Arms in Braemar, where Patey entertained on the piano and accordion, accompanied by Watson on the harmonica and kazoo. The audience was delighted with the pair's rendition of songs Watson had learned from Swiss friends during a trip to Arctic Canada, and the barman invited them to return, with the offer of free drinks. Patey was on a high from the informal performance and seemingly possessed by a supernatural energy, no doubt enhanced by alcohol. 'Far from [becoming more senseless] with each whisky that he downed, he seemed to burn it like fuel and become mentally sharper' (Watson, 2011). When the pub closed, they decamped to the nearby Brauchdryne Café for food, more music and singing, and the owner's son joined in on his own accordion. Patey described it as the best evening of his life, and afterwards Watson drove them to Luibeg Bothy in his trusty jeep, saving them a ten-mile walk. Patey's raucous exuberance fell away immediately and he became quiet and contained on the journey. This ability to compartmentalise his life and switch into a different mode at the drop of a hat was one of his defining traits, and a feature of his personality that would come more pronounced in the ensuing years (ibid.).

 The next day the trio climbed Crystal Ridge and Hanging Dyke in Coire Sputan Dearg in splendid weather, then Watson and Patey added a few more routes to the tally. Snowfields and strips at the sides of the buttresses conferred an Alpine ambience and provided quick gleeful glissades in between climbs. When Watson finally headed over to Derry Cairngorm to conduct his ptarmigan research, Patey ticked off all the remaining lines in the corrie, and was thus able to compare and grade them for the guidebook under uniformly benign conditions.

 Peering over the edge of Creagan a' Choire Etchachan the following day, Watson spotted Patey, completely dwarfed by the cliff, advancing up the exposed right edge of The Bastion, most likely on the Original Route, graded Severe. Watson himself was extremely fit, but he was in awe of Patey's enthusiasm and energy.

 The weekend was not complete without another visit to the Fife Arms, where Patey played the piano and earned more free drinks, before collecting Malcolm, Sticker and Graeme Nicol (who had been climbing

Patey, just visible as a white dot, soloing Original Route (Severe) on The Bastion in Creagan a' Choire Etchachan, 6 June 1954 © Adam Watson

Patey holding court as an undergraduate © C.M. Dixon

on Beinn a' Bhùird) at Invercauld, and heading to the Inver Inn for more music and refreshments.

Life was good for Patey that year. He was probably the most respected Cairngorm climber at the time, with a catalogue of impressive routes under his belt, and he was enjoying a carefree existence away from the city, with no responsibilities other than keeping abreast of his studies. Socially, he had blossomed and his passion for music was melded into pre and après climbing sessions with appreciative friends.

He had also become more friendly with Betty Davidson, who was part of the gang that took the bus to upper Deeside at weekends. An associate member of the Cairngorm Club, Betty had a love of the hills and often introduced others to the outdoors through her leadership roles with local Cub Scouts and Rangers. A fine singer, she was a trained operatic soprano with Gaelic songs in her repertoire, and she took part in stage productions in Aberdeen. It was hardly surprising that Patey was attracted to someone who shared his interests, and Betty would soon accompany him on frequent bothy trips and climbs on the coast.

In *It's a Fine Day for the Hill* (2011), Watson devotes a chapter to Patey, where he offers a comprehensive portrait of his subject with observations that have not been recorded in print by others. It is an evocative account of a bygone era that complements and dovetails with Patey's 'Cairngorm Commentary'. Both Watson and Patey were talented polymaths and shared a love of the Cairngorms beyond climbing, including music, long walk-ins and the camaraderie of the bothies and howffs. Their discussion of metaphysics, religion, the spiritual world, and old castles reached late into the night at Malcolm and Sticker's howff, and so unnerved Malcolm that he would not stray far from the shelter in the dark. Very few others had these sorts of discussions with Patey during his life.

Watson (ibid.) also observed how in tune Patey was with the mountain environment, and while he could match Patey's pace, he was struck by how quickly his friend could pick the most efficient route through broken ground, almost instinctively and without any reduction in speed:

> *Tom and I shared a deep interest in knowing terrain from even brief acquaintance. We developed this even on fine days with no chance of fog. Neither of us took a map and compass on hills we knew except in snow for some high hills and plateaux. We liked doing without a map when fog rolled in, for it helped us to know terrain and take the best route unaided.*

Nor did Patey see climbing simply in terms of scaling clean, solid rock. Coping with vegetation and rattly holds was all part of the necessary armoury of an efficient mountaineer. In this respect he was like the great Scottish pioneer J.H.B. Bell, who said, 'Any fool can climb good rock, but it takes craft and cunning to get up vegetatious schist and granite' (Murray, 1947).

Watson also noticed other idiosyncrasies in Patey's character. Crossing a bridge over water in a vehicle, for example, unnerved Patey, though he was unconcerned about being on a cliff with waves crashing below him. He was also afraid of adders and detested fleas and ticks, and his extreme reaction to flea bites generated much amusement amongst his friends. Once, at Watson and Smith's flat in Aberdeen, they looked on, racked with convulsions, as Patey knelt in the nude, frantically searching through his vest, shirt, trousers and underpants for a flea which had latched on to him on the bus (Watson, 2005).

During that year, Watson and other climbers were often welcomed to the rectory after climbing at Longhaven. There was conversation and singing and Patey's parents were sociable and hospitable. Reverend Patey commented that being in young company had a positive, energising effect on him, and the younger Patey was radiant and relaxed.

This year also saw Patey's first forays outside Scotland. On a visit to the Lake District, he climbed on Gimmer Crag, Pavey Ark, Raven's Crag and White Ghyll in Langdale, and Pisgah Buttress Direct on Scafell. Technically there was nothing outstanding about his success on these classic routes, but it did broaden his scope.

Towards the end of the summer, Patey visited the Northern

Betty Davidson and Patey © Adam Watson

Cairngorms, assessing routes on the neglected, rambling cliffs of Sgoran Dubh above Loch Einich with Watson, Mike Taylor and Leslie Fallowfield. With Watson, he climbed Aladdin's Buttress in Coire an t-Sneachda and Western Route in Coire an Lochain, no doubt weighing up their viability as winter climbs, although he would have to wait some time before realising these ambitions.

Patey was also enjoying spending time with Betty in the mountains, and together they helped build the Hutchison Memorial Hut below Creagan a' Choire Etchachan, which gave much quicker access to the cliffs surrounding Loch Avon. (Although once it became clear how cold the new hut was in winter, some continued to approach Choire Etchachan from the cosier Luibeg.) But this idyllic period ended when Betty boarded a boat to the USA with the intention of emigrating there. Patey missed her desperately and, unsurprisingly, he attempted to

Patey with Betty and another friend, helping to build the Hutchison Memorial Hut in Creagan a' Choire Etchachan © Ian Patey collection

distract himself from his love-sickness by seeking out more new routes in the Cairngorms.[3] Soon, however, he wrote to her in Vermont (where she was staying with cousins), complaining that he could not study properly and wanted her to come back. After exchanging many letters, Betty was eventually persuaded to return when Patey made it clear he wished to spend the rest of his life with her.

During the September long weekend, Luibeg was full of local activists. On the Saturday, Kincorthers Malcolm and Sticker were approaching the newly built Hutchison Hut when the unmistakable outline of Patey came steaming towards them. Malcolm (2013) recalls: 'He was so persuasive; he didn't fit into *your* plans,' and he and Sticker were ushered onwards to Carn Etchachan, where they followed Patey as he shot off up Scorpion (V. Diff). After his successful first ascent of the route in winter, it must have seemed like a walk in the park for Patey, but he was 'not someone for taking in a view' (ibid.), and Malcolm and Sticker struggled to keep up as they soloed this long, exposed route. Malcolm was fond of Patey and enjoyed climbing with him, but Sticker had reservations:

> I admired Tom in every way. In the hills and the pub he had great talent. [But,] Tom was very much a one-man band, so I did not like climbing with him. He was too serious, too driven for me. [He] took chances.

A descent of The Battlements took them to a hanging crack that Patey had had in his sights for some time. Malcolm remembers Boa, as it became known, as a wonderful climb on solid rock, and afterwards he carried Patey's accordion over to Corrour Bothy for a singalong with Watson, Mac Smith, Mike Taylor and Gordon H. Leslie, who had been exploring on Braeriach.

On the Monday, Watson drove the two teams down to Ballochbuie, where they walked into Lochnagar's North-East Corrie and climbed the chimney crack on the side of Raeburn's Gully (which Patey had already called The Clam), after approaching it from the corrie rim and downclimbing the gully. It was a thrutchy, dirty ascent involving back and footing, strategic knee placements and subterranean sections where chockstones had to be climbed from behind and threaded. Smith had originally intended to spectate, but when a colossal chockstone was dislodged in Raeburn's Gully, he joined the climbers rather than take his chances re-ascending a potential bowling alley. Watson, who had opted to take photographs rather than join them on the route, waited for the others to return by the roadside, where the Queen's equerry and other members of a shooting party were picnicking next to a couple of polished land rovers. The Clam team provided the well-to-do party with an amusing spectacle when they appeared with Patey, who was clad in what had once been a white sweater but was now filthy and covered in slime from the chimney.

The weather improved throughout autumn, and in October, Patey invited Malcolm and Sticker along to Lochend Bothy to scope out a potential new route on the tremendous Central Gully Wall on Creag an Dubh-loch, which still had no major breach in it. At its most formidable section is a colossal maze of bulging walls, hanging slabs, overlaps and corners. Climbing new lines[4] here requires creatively linking up areas of weakness before setting foot on the rock. The exposure is considerable and success requires bold commitment. Higher up the wall are three obvious corners, and Patey calculated that the highest one, which he called Vertigo Wall, was the most likely to provide success.

Alan Will and George Macleod, who had nearly pipped Patey to the first winter ascent of Douglas-Gibson Gully almost four years earlier, were also at the bothy. Patey liked to keep his options open, and would sometimes invite several friends along and then decide who he would climb with nearer the time, after weighing up who was on form. This inevitably led to some wounded feelings, but on this occasion all five of them assembled in Central Gully under one of Britain's most impressive rock faces.

Without warning, Patey tied on the rope, then shot across to the base of the wall and started up the first pitch. Macleod, who was keen

STUDENT OF MEDICINE AND MOUNTAINEERING

The first ascent of The Clam (Patey's handwriting) © Gordon H. Leslie

Elizabeth (Betty) Davidson © John Hay, SMC Image Archive

to be involved in a first ascent, had to half run, half stumble across the scree, quickly grab the rope and try to tie on as it rapidly snaked out. Malcolm and Sticker, disinclined to be tail-end extras even on a major first ascent, were annoyed with Patey and with Macleod for dashing after him, and they left them to it.[5]

Lower down, Vertigo Wall twists around the corner system to reach a damp chimney; an exposed traverse higher up avoids an imposing headwall, from whence it gets its name. Although several pegs were deployed on this first ascent, it was nevertheless a significant breakthrough in terms of the exposure encountered in its upper sections and the psychology required to attempt it. Despite being 'only' VS, the traverse would render any retreat problematic, especially down uncharted rock. It was a serious undertaking for Will, who had done nothing for months during his National Service in the RAF. Macleod, who had taken that 1,000ft fall on Douglas-Gibson Gully, somehow managed to cling on throughout, perhaps galvanised by the fact that the nylon cord round his waist to which the rope was attached had worked its way loose: upon reaching easy ground, it came off altogether.[6]

Proposed by Tom Weir and seconded by Len Lovat, Patey submitted his application for the SMC in September 1954. He was duly accepted along with Mike Taylor and Adam Watson. The SMC had and still has a wide range of abilities across its membership, and one humorous early article in its journal distinguished the *Ultramontanes*, who actively sought out difficult routes up mountains, from the *Salvationists*, who opted for safer lines (Almond, 1893). Patey, Taylor and Brooker, who were in the vanguard of winter climbing at the time, fell into the former category. Even by today's higher standards, Patey would easily gain admittance to the SMC with his impressive and extensive experience in winter over a four-year period. Watson's interests in the mountains were broader, but his contributions were just as significant.

With final medical examinations looming in 1955, Mike Taylor quit guidebook work, but Patey was unfazed by the academic pressure, and he continued to develop the publication with Mac Smith. Initially, Patey and Smith were joint editors, but eventually Smith took over, and a two-volume guidebook was published in 1961 and 1962. By then, Patey had been involved with 80 of the first ascents in it, and it remains highly regarded for the detail and quality of the descriptions and its promotion of a major climbing destination. Smith generously recorded his gratitude to Patey in the acknowledgements section of Volume 1: 'Without the aid of T.W. Patey, the Editor's constant associate in the venture from 1954 to 1956, this guide could not have been written.'

Despite Patey's commitment to his studies, his friend and fellow medic Mike Taylor observed that they rarely discussed medicine: 'Although I was with him for six years as a medical student, [and] we were great pals on a climbing basis ... we never discussed medicine apart from examination results.'

Graeme Nicol offered an explanation of sorts: 'He was a very complex chap, Tom. Really, you were a bit of a bore and a prig ... if you wasted your time speaking about work ... when there were [more] important things to be discussed ... Mountaineering, how to [forge] a new route up such and such a face: this is what he wanted to speak [of] and write songs about.'

Patey, with his socialist leanings, was about to enter one of the classic middle-class professions, and he was acutely conscious of its attendant pretensions. When Betty returned from her GP with a diagnosis of rhinitis, Patey assured her that it was simply a running nose. Neither did he think a diagnosis should prevent one from continuing with normal life. When Tom Weir was diagnosed with flu and ready to cancel a lecture in Aberdeen, Patey contacted him and recommended good company as the best medicine, declaring that: 'Most doctors were fools; that a man like myself shouldn't be stopped by anything so trivial as flu' (Weir, 1981). Weir, who had already observed a tough, callous streak in Patey that led him to have high expectations of his companions, went ahead with the talk and then stayed the night at the rectory in Ellon. Patey enthused about recent and future climbs during a musical nightcap, and the following morning Weir was whisked away to a sea-lashed route on the Longhaven cliffs. What could have been a self-pitying time at home in Glasgow had been transformed into a memorable occasion. 'Patey had a way of expanding you with his presence,' Weir wrote later. Adam Watson (1981), too, remarked, 'I have never met anyone before or since [who was] as persuasive as Patey; [he had an] extraordinary force of personality.'

January 1955 saw Patey, Nicol, Watson and other north-east climbers attend a Royal Scottish Geographical lecture about Nanga Parbat by Austrian Hermann Buhl and Dr Walter Frauenberger. Buhl had made a solo ascent of the 8,000m peak just over a month after the first ascent of Everest. It was only the third of the 14 highest mountains to be scaled, and Buhl, a ruthlessly tough mountaineer who acclimatised by walking through the streets of Innsbruck clutching a snowball, was a real hero to the Aberdeen contingent.

The account of Buhl's epic solo, high-altitude bivouac and exhausting descent attracted a full house. After finishing his talk to much applause, Buhl mingled with the audience and Patey, Nicol and Watson made a beeline for him. When Buhl enquired about the local climbing venues, Watson waxed lyrical about the mighty 300m Creag an Dubh-loch and Shelter Stone crags, as Patey and Nicol nodded proudly. Buhl replied somewhat witheringly, 'Small cleefs, small cleefs', but the Aberdonians did not resent the great man's reaction to their beloved mountain cliffs, and it was a real thrill, especially for Nicol, to meet a mountaineer of such stature and whose achievements they revered.

Although new winter routes were sparse in 1954, and lacking the technical tariffs of the previous year, Patey had become increasingly efficient at moving over mixed ground. This was evidenced by his first ascent of Bell's Route on Shadow Buttress B (V,6) on Lochnagar in January. Admittedly, he had the advantage of superb conditions, prior knowledge from a summer ascent, and a point of aid on the crux, but he led Alan Will up the route in a blistering one-and-a-half hours. No wonder Will could remember little of it later. They even had time to climb The Gutter, an offshoot of Raeburn's Gully. To the post-Patey

Aberdeen climbers, these times remain a harsh reminder of how good their predecessors were. Mac Smith nicknamed Patey 'The Machine' for his no-nonsense approach and efficiency. Two days after his ascent, Patey joined the Etchachan Club, of which Will was already a member.

Will was a champion athlete at Robert Gordon's College and had originally intended to become a PE teacher. He subsequently trained as a journalist, but even at the peak of his fitness he struggled to keep up with Patey on the long walk-ins that are a key feature of Cairngorm climbing.

The following month, Will, Patey, Mac Smith and George Adams made the first ascent of Central Chimney on Creagan a' Choire Etchachan. Heavy snow conditions favoured an approach on skis, and on the way back, Patey accelerated away from the group in typical fashion. Will, just out of the RAF, was determined to keep up with him this time. Patey was not known for his elegance or technique on skis, but he overcame this with his fitness and drive, and soon they were engaged in a silent battle, both struggling to maintain the pace. On reaching their destination, a breathless Will quizzed Patey about where he got his energy from. 'That's the reason,' replied Patey, holding out his palm to reveal three small white pills, possibly amphetamines. It was the only occasion Patey shared this information with Will, who eschewed stimulants personally, but considered taking 'uppers' to be fairly innocent and simply something to keep one going (Will, 2013).

After the successful ascent of Backdoor Route on Lochnagar with Will, MacLeod and Sticker in March, Patey's thoughts turned towards the Dubh-loch and a winter ascent of something with the significance of Vertigo Wall.

It began with Patey and Will travelling to Braemar to stay at the delightfully named 'Vermin Villa' outside the village. Patey's food for the weekend was a round dixie of boiled potatoes, which he had acquired from the cook at the Aberdeen Royal Infirmary residences. He had no cooking equipment, cutlery or any other food. 'He was a hard man,' recalls Will (ibid.).

The 'Villa' was in fact a barn, part of an old farm on the edge of the village as you head south over the Cluanie towards what is now the ski centre at Glen Shee. There was no shortage of mice and rats, so the favoured sleeping area was up in the rafters. The approach up Glen Callater and over Carn Sagairt Mor to the Dubh-loch was a long, familiar one. Two years earlier, they had beaten the same ground during an attempt on what became Sabre Cut (IV,5). This time their sights were on a direct ascent of the major couloir of Labyrinth, set between the Central Slabs and Broad Terrace Wall.

Progress was swift up the lower section, despite poor snow conditions. The Direct Finish continues to a cul-de-sac with intimidating vertical to overhanging ice to exit. It is questionable whether anyone in Britain (or indeed anywhere else) could have climbed such a pitch with the gear available at the time, especially in suboptimal conditions. After a tentative look, the pair retreated via the Hanging Garden and the narrow, exposed ledge of the Broad Terrace to the bottom of South-East Gully. Labyrinth Direct (VII,6) was not climbed until 1972, and even then it was years ahead of its time.

Will considered Patey a congenial companion, and he felt confident with him even in tight situations, where he seemed 'almost immortal'. Nevertheless, Will (2013) recognised that 'The way he climbed he was very much an individual, looking after number one. He virtually always led; he chose the line. Anyone climbing with him was just a supporter.'

Despite the constraints on his time through his studies and climbing activities, Patey continued to nurture his passion for music, and in late March he gave a virtuoso performance on the piano and accordion at a party to celebrate Adam Watson's marriage. Patey's enthusiasm as he sang traditional songs and his own recent compositions had been infectious. 'Had he not been there, the party would not [have been] such an extraordinarily memorable event' (Watson, 1981).

Patey finally graduated from Medical School on 8 July 1955, alongside Mike Taylor, Goggs Leslie and Leslie Fallowfield. His peers considered him to be academically gifted, a judgement borne out by the fact that he was awarded the Gold Medal in Physiology in his second year. Graeme Nicol believed that Patey could have had a career as a consultant or in medical research or even as a full-time musician. However, a senior position in a hospital would require further years of studying and perhaps curtail his activities in the mountains, so he chose general practice instead.

It has been claimed that Patey passed his M.B., Ch.B degree 'without particular effort or distinction' (SMCJ, 1971), and while it may be true that he did not have to exert himself unduly, his achievements were nevertheless noteworthy. Indeed, far from just muddling through, he exceeded the minimum requirements at every stage.

Living at home, Patey had peace and quiet to study when he needed it, and the ability to assimilate complex academic ideas and information. But his fullest form of self-expression would always be mountaineering, through which he could also channel his love of music and prose. Patey's daughter, Rona, who followed in her father's footsteps into medical school, reflected that 'climbing for him was more of a vocation than being a doctor' (Hedgecoe, 2007).

1   Patey also championed the idea of a guidebook to the north-east sea cliffs, which was published by the Etchachan Club in 1960. He was responsible for checking the routes at Longhaven, but he assisted with other areas too.

2   The Slugain glen acquired two similar edifices, one of which became known as the Secret Howff. In 'Cairngorm Commentary' (*SMCJ*, 1962), Patey confuses information about the construction and appearance of both howffs and incorrectly describes the Kincorth's effort as the secret one. The Secret Howff was far more elaborate in its construction and design, an 'eighth wonder of the Cairngorms', requiring clandestine transportation of building materials to avoid detection from the estate. The Kincorth original lasted until the end of the decade but the now not-so-Secret Howff has survived for over 60 years (Brebner, 2017).

3   Perhaps his most important development was on the upper cliff above the Great Terrace on Carn Etchachan. This began in August when Patey and Bill Brooker climbed The Battlements (Moderate), a groove in the upper sector of the main cliff that would eventually form part of the classic winter line: Route Major (IV,5).

4   Malcolm and Sticker returned the following week to repeat it, but when Sticker fell on the crux pitch and Malcolm suffered bad rope burns holding him, they abseiled off. A couple of weeks later they returned to complete it and reaped more enjoyment doing it on their own than they would have bringing up the rear.

5   The original Vertigo Wall was first climbed in winter by Andy Nisbet and Alf Robertson in 1977. Despite a bivouac and multiple aid points, it represented a significant breakthrough. Eight years later, Nisbet returned with Andy Cunningham to climb it free (VII,7). Today, it has the reputation of being one of Scotland's great, truly mixed lines.

6   In his first year (1949–50), he was awarded a First Class Certificate of Merit in Medical Chemistry and a Second Class Certificate of Merit in Biology. In 1950–52 he achieved a First with high distinction in Systematic Anatomy, First in Embryology and Seconds in Practical Anatomy, Histology, Physiology and Biochemistry. In 1952–53 he gained a Second in the Practice of Medicine, and in 1953-54 Seconds in Mental Health, Forensic Medicine, Public Health and Social Medicine. In his final year, 1954–55, he achieved a Second in Obstetrics and Gynaecology.

05

Bill Brooker in a relaxed pose on the Vire à Bicyclette, Charmoz-Grepon Traverse, 1952
© Ian Patey collection

Land of the Gauloises

The bloated aristocrats
sip their champagne
As the corpses come down
in the Montenvers train

Tom Patey, 'Aiguilles des Cairngorms'

Since 1951, Patey had spent two to three weeks in the French and Swiss Alps each summer, and upon graduation he was less concerned about his medical career than the forthcoming Alpine season.[1] After obtaining experience in summer and winter on domestic mountains, Alpinism was considered an integral part of the armoury of skills, and a natural progression for British mountaineers. The ultimate aim would have been to climb in the Himalaya, but the cost and time required to do so made it prohibitive for most.

Patey's first Alpine season was split between Zermatt and Arolla in Switzerland. From the former, he made ascents of the Matterhorn and the Zinalrothorn and was turned back by a blizzard on Monte Rosa. From the latter, he climbed the West Face of the Aiguille de la Tsa and the Grande Dent de Veisivi, and he traversed the Petite Dent de Veisivi. All these climbs were completed without the assistance of local guides. Instead, he was accompanied by fellow medics Mike Taylor, Goggs Leslie and Don Aitken, and Ellon friend Charlie Morrison.

In 1952, Chamonix became the base for the next four years. The previous year's contingent (minus Goggs) was joined by Bill Brooker, Johnny Morgan, Mike Philip and Sandy Imray.

Attention centred on the Chamonix Aiguilles, needles of quality granite that are relatively accessible from Chamonix. Patey climbed seven of these independent summits by their ordinary routes as well as the classic, airy Charmoz-Grépon traverse (D-). He also summitted Mont Blanc and the Aiguille de Bionassay, which by comparison were straightforward snow climbs. The South-East Side of the Grand Dru (AD) completed the tally of ascents that season.

The 1953 Alpine season saw Patey climbing with Mike Taylor for ten days in July. The weather was generally favourable, but the mountains were only just coming into condition.

Their first route was the East Face of the Aiguille de Blaitière (D-), with fine, sustained climbing in its upper reaches. They then breezed up the North-North-East Ridge of the Aiguille de l'M (IV/V-), which had only been climbed five years earlier but was already a popular

Front from left: Patey, Mike Taylor. Back from left: Charlie Morrison, Don Aitken and Goggs Leslie. Switzerland, 1951 © Ian Patey collection

classic rock route. An ascent of the Aiguille des Grands Charmoz via the North-East Arête de la République (TD-) involved a round trip of 14 hours and was Patey's hardest Alpine route to date.

From the Charpoua Hut they traversed the snowy Aiguille Verte by the Arête Sans Nom (D+) in 13 hours, then descended the Whymper Couloir in five hours to reach the Couvercle Hut. The Arête, still considered one of the finest of its class in the Alps, is rarely climbed due to its length, seriousness and the commitment it requires, and their time under such conditions was impressive. To finish the holiday, they made a moonlight ascent of the South-East Face (PD) of The Cardinal, a spectacularly sharp rock spire between the Aiguille du Moine and Aigulle Verte, returning to the hut at 5.30am.

The following year marked the first Alpine season for Graeme Nicol and Kincorthers Freddie Malcolm and Alex 'Sticker' Thom. It was generally uneventful but was enlivened by one significant outing. Patey applied the knowledge he had acquired on the Aiguille Verte the

Patey at a free campsite in the Chamonix valley © Ian Patey collection

The camp below the Aiguilles in 1952. Back left to right: Patey, Mike Taylor, Mike Philip, Johnny Morgan, Charlie Morrison. Front left to right: Don Aitken, Sandy Imray, Bill Brooker © Ian Patey collection

previous year to another long, serious expedition on the Grands Montets Ridge, which occupies a magnificent position between the Nant Blanc and Argentière Glaciers. However, a blizzard thwarted their attempt at a col before the main difficulties.

The Chamonix Aiguilles were plastered too, and options were dwindling. Eventually, they plumped for the Papillons Arête (V) on the Aiguille du Peigne, whose open aspect allowed the snow to clear more quickly.

They stashed gear at the foot of the route, taking only one axe and one pair of crampons between the four of them. Using various points of aid to overcome some of the difficulties, Patey led with Nicol, followed by Malcolm and Sticker. Malcolm was awed by the situations and exposure on the route, which were of a different order of magnitude from those he had experienced in the Cairngorms. Nicol, who was off form, struggled to follow Patey up an overhang and had to return to the belay and let Sticker climb through before finally surmounting it as the last man behind Malcolm.

Most climbers descend from the top of the route, but Patey had other ideas. To his knowledge, no party had ascended the Papillons followed by the upper West-North-West Face (the 'Chamonix Face') to the summit, and he saw an opportunity for a 'first'. Patey's powers of persuasion left little doubt that the other three would accompany him.

It was a completely different style of climbing from the lower airy arête, comprising narrow chimneys and layback cracks. By mid-afternoon, Nicol, Malcolm and Sticker were beginning to wilt from the exertion and the 5.30am start, but Patey was 'showing no visible signs of fatigue' (Malcolm, 1954), and he impressed upon them that they had to keep moving if they did not want to spend the night out.

At only one point did Patey stall: emerging from a chimney and attempting to exit onto a ledge, he slithered back down verglas into the fissure. The hardest technical grade of the routes they regularly ventured onto was V, which equated to about VS back home, and Patey used a piton to reach the ledge above, the end of the main difficulties. The occasional stonefall and roar of avalanches on the flanks confirmed the objective dangers. There was no time to climb the final 100ft to the summit, and they began hurriedly descending the Voie Normale, Patey out in front.

About a third of the way down, they unroped for a while to speed up and try to beat the encroaching darkness. A slip on the snow-covered rocks would probably have been fatal at this point. The Kincorthers lost contact with the others and started abseiling down a steep face, unsure where it would take them. From the sound of pegs being hammered in, they realised that Patey and Nicol were also abseiling parallel to them, and they reunited for the final abseil and easy snow slopes leading to the moraine.

After half an hour of searching for their stashed gear, they admitted defeat. Malcolm, who had carried his own axe and crampons up and down the route, could afford to be smug. Nicol had bought his axe only two days earlier at the princely sum of £4.10 shillings, and 'one becomes sentimentally attached to one's gear at such prices'.

A tortuous descent down steep, vague paths entailed fighting through undergrowth, stumbling over boulders and bumping into trees. At half-past midnight, they finally reached the campsite. Malcolm, whose experience that day was his most exacting to date, gave full credit to Patey for his leadership both on the ascent and descent, recognising that he had successfully transferred skills learnt in Scotland to a bigger arena.

The weather deteriorated soon after, fostering homesickness and a yearning among the group for unclimbed rock back in the Cairngorms, which were sweltering in a heatwave. Nothing they had climbed back home could quite have prepared them for the physical demands of the full-on Alpine experience, which involved testing descents, glacier approaches, avalanches, stonefall and the perils of poor weather. In this environment, fatigue and flagging concentration can be lethal.

Although the season produced only one significant ascent, it did inspire a great Patey song. The ironically titled 'Aiguilles des Cairngorms' is full of nostalgia for his local mountains and wittily compares Chamonix with Deeside. The third verse memorably lampoons the great Chamonix guide Armand Charlet:

> *I met Armand Charlet, he said with a frown*
> *'I think if you're British you climb with Joe Brown?*
> *So tell me how many North Faces you've done?'*
> *He sighed with dismay when I answered him 'None.*
> *I climb in the Cairngorms you'll know of their fame?'*
> *He said: 'I-have-not-even-heard-of-the-name.'*
> *Back home in the Cairngorms they all would agree*
> *What an ignorant bastard old Charlet must be.*

But the lauded French mountaineer almost had the last laugh during the 1955 Alpine season. Patey had arranged to climb with Malcolm again, his sights on an ascent of a prestigious North Face of the Aiguille du Plan (TD-), which had been first ascended by Charlet in 1929 with Jules Simond and Paul Dillemann.[2] Malcolm hitched from Aberdeen down to Southampton, where he met Patey on the ferry. At Paris, they caught a packed train to Chamonix, sharing a bottle of wine to dull the discomfort of propping themselves up in the corridor. Somewhat inebriated, they snuck into the First Class compartment and fell asleep in the overhead racks before a couple of policemen tried to throw them off at Dijon. In fractured French, Patey argued that, even though they were in a First Class carriage, they were not occupying First Class seats. Unable to counter this logic, the policemen allowed them back on the train with a warning.

The real meat of the North Face of the Aiguille du Plan is a hanging glacier in the upper half of the face, through which a route must be threaded. The danger of icefall and serac collapse is ever-present, and the route frequently changes as climbers seek out the safest line across the shifting glacier. Access to the hanging glacier is via a rock ridge about 800m long, whose steep sections include one technical pitch at Grade IV. In typical fashion, Patey set off at a furious pace and Malcolm had no option but to follow, unroped. Soon, they were confronted by a huge groove in the glacier caused by falling seracs. They literally ran across this together then kept to the right of the glacier to reach a steep rock step leading to a ledge, where Patey banged in a peg and they took a breather.

Later, Patey told W.H. Murray that he had sensed conditions were 'ripe' and had thus diverted to the iced rocks of the Aiguilles des Deux Aigles. Suddenly there was a thunderous roar, and a huge serac collapsed straight down the channel they had crossed not ten minutes before, smothering them in lateral ice debris. They escaped without injury but were shaken by the close shave. Regaining the glacier, Patey lost his ice axe so he commandeered Malcolm's and cut steps through the serac zone as they moved together. (Back then, it was the norm to carry one axe and a peg hammer each.) Once they had navigated through the seracs, they kicked steps up the glacier's easier-angled upper section.

After nine hours of almost non-stop activity, they reached the summit. Malcolm (2013) summarised his companion's relentless drive to attain his goal: 'Patey never eats, drinks [or] shits till he gets to the top.' In arenas such as the Alps, cautious speed, expert route-finding and mental composure are crucial factors for success and survival. In his famous article 'Apes or Ballerinas?' (1969), Patey, who exemplified all these traits, summarised it thus:

> *An efficient mountaineer ... need fulfil only three criteria. He must not fall off. He must not lose the route. He must not waste time. Time may be endless on an English outcrop; in the Alps it can mean the difference between life and death.*

At the summit, they sat for half an hour enjoying simple fare: water, Swiss cheese and a baguette, soaking up the sun and views with the satisfaction that they had completed the first British ascent of a major Alpine route.

Malcolm (2013) liked Patey immensely but had one reservation: 'He was a wonderful companion on the hill—if you could keep up with him.' Things were no different on the descent across the Envers du Plan Glacier. On easy ground but roped up because of the crevasses, Patey shot ahead, and every so often Malcolm would be yanked forward—hardly the safest practice for glacier passage.

Malcolm's enthusiasm waned when the weather turned for the worse, and he returned home. Patey, however, was keen to eke one more route out of the season and he teamed up with Len Lovat from Glasgow, who had seconded his application for the SMC the previous year. Lovat, having just arrived, wanted to acclimatise on something relatively straightforward, but it was Patey's last opportunity before heading home. As a compromise, they chose the North Face of the Pain de Sucre (D), a subsidiary peak between the Aiguille du Plan and the Dent du Requin. The route was one of the ice classics in the Aiguilles, and Patey was fascinated by the face's history, having read an account

North Face of the Aiguille du Plan
© John Cleare

of the second ascent in Andre Roch's *Climbs of my Youth* (1949).

Patey and Lovat trudged in the rain up to the Envers Hut, where they encountered Ron Moseley, one of the leading lights of the esteemed Rock and Ice Club, whose members Joe Brown and Don Whillans were at the forefront of British climbing at the time. Moseley had completed Grade VI pitches that season, and Patey was now coming into contact with people who could climb rock at a much higher grade than him and his peers on the Aberdeen scene.

The next morning looked promising, and Patey and Lovat set off under a starry sky. Ahead of them was another English pair, and in his 1955 *Etchachan Club Journal* article, Patey refers to them simply as 'J' and 'A'. The 'A' was John 'Ram' Ramsden, one of the Bradford Lads. 'J' (name unknown) was an inexperienced climber from Derby. They were heading for the Ryan-Lochmatter route on the Aiguille du Plan, an ambitious target for their first Alpine route together, which Ramsden was advised against tackling. Both routes are approached via the Envers de Blaitière Glacier and are then roughly parallel. Patey and Lovat's line follows an icy slope then crosses snow-covered slabs to the upper snows and the summit. With an average angle of 56°, it was straightforward compared to many of the technical routes Patey had tackled in Scotland, but it was nevertheless a protracted outing.

The Scots caught up with the others just before the 1,000m ice slope and wove a route through a zone of seracs. Patey, who was hardly a champion of best practice, was nevertheless alarmed to see that the English climbers had not even roped up, and he voiced his concern. Soon after, Ramsden took a 30ft fall on an ice wall in the serac barrier after attacking it in a cavalier manner. The Scots found an easier alternative and began step-cutting up the initial ice slope, but they were eager to get off the avalanche-scoured ground before the sun warmed the menacing cornices above. Meanwhile, Ramsden and J, who had missed the traverse to their own route, were attempting to reach another access point higher up.

Patey and Lovat were on the final section of the tricky, rocky traverse before the easier upper slopes and a clear run to the summit when disaster struck. A few hundred metres below them, Ramsden and J were falling, desperately trying to brake with their axes, to no avail. They careered headfirst over a 100m ice wall and continued for a further 1,000m before plunging into a crevasse at the foot of the initial slope. Patey and Lovat immediately began downclimbing towards them on rapidly melting snow, prepared for the worst. 'My mind was filled with gory pictures of disarticulation or decapitation,' recalled Patey later (*Etchachan Club Journal*, 1955). Halfway down, they were shocked to see one of the men emerge from the abyss shouting for help. This spurred them on to descend at a speed that would have been considered reckless in normal circumstances, pausing briefly to retrieve the franc and pound notes, rucksack, ice axe and crushed aluminium water bottle that had scattered during the fall.

On reaching the casualties—Patey's first proper patients as a newly qualified doctor—he recognised that Ramsden was in the worst state, with a probable fractured skull and minus much of the skin on his face. In his semi-delirious state, Ramsden was more concerned that he had lost his axe down the crevasse. Despite the severity of the incident, Patey (ibid.) later recalled, with black humour: 'Both men had badly swollen eyelids so they could not see each other. This was perhaps just as well.' They anchored the men to ice axes then Lovat descended to the Envers Hut to initiate a rescue.[3]

Patey and the Englishmen were now marooned on a small island between two crevasses, directly in the path of any snow or ice debris that might sweep down. 'Three thousand feet above, the grandfather of all cornices leered down malignantly' (ibid.). Below them was an enormous crevasse into which they would inevitably be deposited should any snow be unleashed from above. With the solar glare reflecting off the snow, it was now stiflingly hot, and Patey wrapped up both casualties to protect them from the searing exposure.

Beyond that, there was little he could do but wait helplessly as the unstable glacier he was trapped on literally fell apart. Small avalanches swept by, snow bridges collapsed and seracs disintegrated at regular intervals. Meanwhile, their meagre island was diminishing rapidly: 'The sensation was oddly akin to being marooned on an iceberg in the Gulf Stream' (ibid.). The rescue party was only ten minutes away when the cornice looming above the helpless trio collapsed and thousands of tons of debris tumbled down towards them. Miraculously, it came to a stop a mere 100ft above. Two British climbers whom they had met in the hut, known only as Doug and Dave, reached Patey first and set about moving Ramsden and J to a safer spot. When the hut guardian arrived, it was agreed that Doug would stay with the more seriously injured Ramsden while Patey, Dave and the guardian escorted J down.

Despite a 3:1 ratio for those assisting J, it was a complicated descent. The casualty was virtually blind from his swollen face and the glare of the snow, and he constantly slipped and stumbled through the crevassed section of the glacier. A contingent of Chamonix guides and Chasseurs Alpins (French mountain infantry) passed them on their way to the upper casualty. Forty guides working in small relay teams eventually evacuated Ramsden down to the hut after six hours of effort. J was discharged from hospital the next day, but Ramsden had fractured his skull in three places, necessitating a longer stay and a large medical bill to add to the cost of his rescue. Unfortunately, he was not insured.

After this drama, Patey returned to Aberdeen to exercise his medical skills in more conventional settings, serving his pre-registration year at hospitals in Inverurie, Stracathro and Foresterhill in Aberdeen. It was still summer and he was keen to pursue new rock routes in the Cairngorms before the weather deteriorated later in the year. His activity focussed on the Loch Avon Basin and Carn Etchachan, where he added three further routes to the four he had reaped the previous year. The best of these, Crevasse Route (Severe), was climbed with Mac Smith and Bert Duguid on the first main buttress at the left end of the Upper Cliff, and linked a couple of rock crevasses with enjoyable, varied pitches.

Still in August, Patey turned his attention to the series of crags on the north side of Loch Avon known collectively as Stag Rocks. Diagonal

Gully separates the two main sectors; the right section is divided in two by Amphitheatre Gully, and to the right of this is Longbow Crag, named after the large roof about halfway up. Others, including Patey, had attempted it roped, but while the upper and lower sections had already been accounted for, the middle section was problematic and had thus far thwarted a continuous ascent. Returning solo, Patey managed to circumvent the overhang by a rightwards traverse to make committing moves into a groove. Graded VS in Mac Smith's guide (now HS) and 600ft long, Relay Climb was one of the more difficult free-climbed pitches in the Cairngorms at the time, and one of Patey's hardest and boldest solo ascents to date.

For his next significant outing, in September Patey partnered up with John Hay, an ex-Aberdeen Grammar School pupil who was about to start a law degree at Aberdeen University.

On the right side of Creagan a' Choire Etchachan lay a magnificent sweep of clean, crimson slabs 100m wide and up to 150m in height with not a single route recorded on them, and Patey was drawn to the rightmost of two great corners that break the continuity. The key pitch was the clean-cut slabby section, which was damp and prompted an ascent in stocking soles. There was copious vegetation in the corner crack, and Patey, who was leading, tried to rely on friction as little as possible and instead utilise small incut holds on the slabs for his feet while laying off the corner crack with his hands. At the crux, where the crack narrows, he deployed two pegs for direct aid. The pitch was sustained thereafter until a large spike at its top afforded a belay. An intimidating bulge above was passed on the left with another point of aid. The pitches before and after this were an anti-climax, but despite a total of four points of aid, they had created the most sustained VS in the range. Subsequent dry ascents used the pitons more for protection until it was climbed free as the norm. Its original name, Crimson Slabs, was later given to the entire expanse of rock on this part of the crag, and the route was renamed The Dagger.[4]

On the same day that The Dagger was established, Jerry Smith,

The Dagger on Crimson Slabs, late '50s style. Note the use of Vibrams instead of nails © John Hay

an Englishman who had been quietly climbing on the fringes of the Aberdeen scene, emphatically announced his presence. Modest and self-effacing, Smith had been working as a soil scientist at the Macaulay Institute since the early '50s, but he did not mix with members of the vibrant, developing Aberdeen scene. Instead, he discreetly applied himself on the hardest rock routes in the area (including Parallel Gully B), some of which he soloed. In early September, he climbed both Patey routes on Creag an Dubh-loch, but in better style. With J. Dennis he freed Sabre Edge (HS) and cut the number of aid points on Vertigo Wall (VS) to one. The next day he went to Lochnagar, again with Dennis, and created an original and futuristic route on the Pinnacle Face of Black Spout Pinnacle, which followed a sustained open slabby face with no obvious natural feature. Although somewhat vegetated, it was the prototype for the modern Cairngorm face climb, a genre for which the range would later become famous.

Smith had broken a psychological barrier. In the space of two days, he had become one of the leading climbers operating out of the city. Any notion that he was merely a rock climber, however, would be unequivocally quashed during the forthcoming winter season.

On the domestic front, Patey was much happier now that Betty had returned to Aberdeen from the USA. At the end of September 1955, she accompanied Patey and Graeme Nicol on the first ascent of the modest but pleasant Escalator on Hell's Lum, a line which really comes into its own in winter.

Patey benefited from Betty's support in December that year when his father died. Reverend Patey, who worked full-time as a minister in Ellon until his death at the age of 75, had been instrumental in fostering his son's lifelong love of the mountains.[5]

Mountains and friendships helped Patey through the grieving process, and at New Year he and Betty celebrated at the Cairngorm Hotel in Aviemore with John Hay and Bill Brooker. To save money, Patey and Hay walked to Aviemore from the Linn of Dee, contending with snow and a headwind at the highpoint of the Lairig Ghru. Patey was wearing a golf jacket with no hood and an open neck collar shirt; he had no hat. Eventually, exhausted, he turned to Hay and announced he could not go on. This was neither the first nor last time that Patey would suffer from his cavalier approach to preparation for the mountain environment. Luckily, Hay had a scarf and old hat in his rucksack, and a liner from a lady's jacket which he used to wrap his primus stove in. With this additional, if flimsy, protection from the elements, Patey recovered enough to complete the trek to the New Year festivities.

Patey on accordion, Tom Weir on the drum. Cairngorm Hotel, Aviemore, New Year 1956 © John Hay

Soon, the party was in full swing. Bradford Lads Duncan Boston and Alf Beanland were in attendance, as well as Len Lovat and Tom Weir from Glasgow, and there was no shortage of musicians: Patey on the accordion, Hay on the fiddle and Weir on the drums. Weir played in various dance bands in his home city, and although he had never been a lover of big parties, he admitted that this one was unforgettable. There was a potent concoction of spirits, and as Patey took liberal swigs between dance numbers, his nimble fingers became increasingly livelier on the accordion. 'He was still playing when most of the dancers had collapsed' (Weir, 1981), and long after Weir had retired to bed.

Despite this, the temptation of bagging a new route was simply too great, and Patey joined Weir the following morning to go climbing:

> *True, he looked terrible, as pale as a ghost and racked by a cough. But this was not abnormal. The cough came from smoking; the face belied a man with so much stamina that when alone in the Cairngorms, he frequently ran to the crags, punched a few hard routes and jogged back again.* (Weir, 1981)

On 2 January, Patey, Betty, Beanland, Hay and Lovat climbed No 5 Buttress Gully on Sgòr Gaoith in Glen Einich. Though straightforward at Grade II, the approach was long and daylight hours short, though for once, they had had a decent sleep the night before.

March 1956 produced a winter first ascent of a major feature on Lochnagar: Parallel Buttress. W.H. Murray and J.H.B. Bell had made the first summer ascent in May 1939. However, Bell had used two pegs on the

Patey below The Tower, Parallel Buttress © Bill Brooker

crux Tower—the first time metal had been hammered into Cairngorm rock—and Murray in particular felt guilty about this.

Patey and many others had considered the buttress's winter potential, and the weekend before the successful ascent, he and Allan Will had retreated, leaving a peg at their high point. Patey recruited the formidable team of Brooker and Jerry Smith for the return match. In 'Sestogradists in Scotland', a classic article featured in the *Climbers' Club Journal* in 1957, Smith details the nature and hardships of winter climbing and paints an insightful picture of Patey, from his inadequate clothing, speed 'racing towards the rocks like a sheepdog recalled by its master' and his scheming to hog the lead: 'He pronounced the stance unsafe for three, and he must move on before Bill could start.' Brooker photographed the ascent, and his famous image of a frozen Patey could be from a textbook on hypothermia; one almost shivers in sympathy. Smith has a balaclava, Patey a mantle of snow over his hair. Unsmiling, his face has not the usual ghostly pallor but is coloured in 'shades of mauve and green ... he had left most of his kit at home and had borrowed the clothes that he had stood in, which were inadequate' (ibid.). The powder snow has frozen on Patey's short anorak, and he has no gaiters over his socks and boots. He is not even carrying a rucksack. By comparison, Smith is wrapped up in several layers of windproof clothing and, for 1956, is well equipped. No one looking at these images can be in any doubt as to Patey's toughness, nor his woeful negligence.

After soloing up the start of Parallel A Gully, they climbed the right-hand side of the buttress to the peg from which Patey had retreated the previous weekend, using it to gain a difficult groove. Smith's account is a vivid description of the guile and skills required to climb mixed pitches back then, and of the physical discomforts endured. Seconding, he used nicks Patey had cut in the ice as handholds for his leather-gloved hands. Both Patey and Smith were 'slingless wonders' and used no loop or sling to attach to their axe. Smith would, however, clip his axe into his waistline when he needed to use both hands, and at one point he pulled up on 'a snowball squashed against a slab' before pressing a glove against the ice for adhesion.

Patey was unfamiliar with the route and, with time marching on, they opted to climb the middle section of Parallel Gully B and regain the buttress via a ledge girdling it, known as The Necklace. The gully turned out to be full of unconsolidated powder. Spindrift penetrated their clothing and frozen mist crystallised onto clothes, hair and eyebrows. Brooker was disgruntled by the detour as the pitches he wanted to lead had been bypassed. Patey resumed the lead on the traverse pitch, which was insecure due to the soft powder, and fashioned a belay using an axe pick driven a couple of inches into confetti-like snow—it was totally inadequate and of psychological value only. The other two later improved this with a peg, but by this time Patey had led the next pitch.

One more pitch took them to the base of the crux Tower, a feature memorably described by Smith (1957) as 'sepulchral walls of rock, suppurating verglas'. Smith, leading, used the continental aid tactic of two etriers, a kind of mini stepladder which he attached to pitons. As with Bell and Murray's use of pegs, this was a fairly controversial approach, and Smith knew there would be mutterings from the general climbing community. Brooker assured him that there was a good flake over which he could hook his axe, and once committed he was soon on a cosy bank of steep snow, which crossed usually impassable smooth slabs and thus avoided the upper part of the tower. Patey led to the neck behind the tower, enthusing about how winter often makes feasible pitches that are impossible in summer. A short wall of snow took them to an exquisitely sculpted snow ridge, which Brooker pronounced the finest he had seen in the Cairngorms.

A mad dash down to the Spittal of Glen Muick in under an hour was followed by a two-mile stomp along the road, where a taxi was already waiting for them. On the bus home, they regaled the rapt audience with every detail, even though, objectively, it had been a flawed ascent: they had not followed the buttress continuously and had used several points of aid. Nevertheless, it had been a mighty effort, given the conditions and their rudimentary gear.

Patey below the Tower on Parallel
Buttres © Bill Brooker

In 'Sestogradists in Scotland', Smith comes across as perhaps the weakest of the trio, but the following weekend with Brooker he performed outstandingly. The glittering prize was an ascent of the only unclimbed buttress in winter on Lochnagar: Black Spout Pinnacle. In one week, conditions had changed dramatically and were now perfect. The snow was firm and frozen, the cracks were icy and the rock bare and dry. On the ascent of Route 1, Smith led the initial crux pitch on steep, iced slabs with one point of aid, which enabled him to cut steps for the next section. All in all, it was a more satisfactory style of ascent than that of Parallel Buttress, with superb situations in the upper reaches. Eventually, it became the sixth route in the Cairngorms to be given Grade V in the new grading system for winter routes. Emphasising the breadth of talent operating in the Cairngorms at the time, Brooker completed a fine personal Lochnagar trilogy that month when he climbed Eagle Buttress (IV,3) with Mike Taylor.

Patey was now in the pre-registration year of his medical career, but he was not going to let that interfere with his leisure pursuits:

> *Once, for instance, he left Stracathro Hospital at 6.00pm, cycled the twenty or so miles to Clova, walked the five-mile Capel Mounth path (with accordion) to Loch Muick and caroused with song and story far into the night at Lochend Bothy. Next day, he [made] the return trip to Lochnagar (fifteen miles), climbing three routes and returning to Clova, his bicycle and Stracathro, ready to commence night duty at the hospital.* (SMCJ, 1971)

Courting Betty also occupied his time, and photographs taken of the couple in the Cairngorms show them very much in love, smiling and fooling around for the camera. With Alan Will and his girlfriend Joan (whom he would later marry), the quartet paint a picture of carefree, happy young adults. Soon, however, Patey and Betty would be separated, and his reputation as an outstanding mountaineer would be sealed on a monumental peak in one of the highest mountain ranges on Earth.

1   Perhaps as a result of feeling some personal responsibility towards Sandy Imray, who was the least experienced of the group, Patey missed out on an ascent by Brooker, Taylor, Philip and Morgan of the Innominata Ridge (D/D+) of Mont Blanc from a bivouac at the Eccles Hut. This is a magnificent high-altitude mixed route between the wild and remote Freney and Brouillard faces.

2   Chamonix Guide Jean-Franck Charlet, grandson of the first ascensionist of the North Face of the Aiguille du Plan, would in 1979 forsake 'the gauloises and garlic and wine' of his native land, and as part of an invited team of six French hot shots, climb classic routes on Lochnagar, Creag an Dubh-loch, Ben Nevis and Creag Meagaidh. By then, Scottish winter climbing had garnered a world reputation for its unique quality and rich history.

3   In contrast with Patey's selective account, Duncan Boston (2021) recalls that he and Ron Moseley were on the route with Patey and Lovat and assisted with the rescue from the start.

4   Hay returned the following year (1956) to make the first ascent of the parallel corner, an easier but finer climb he named Djibangi, also graded VS. In fact, the cliff was home to some of Hay's finest routes: in winter he made first ascents of Quartzvein Edge and the Red Chimney by its original line.

5   Following his death, Reverend Patey's widow and eldest son Maurice moved back down to the Derby area. In the 1970s, Maurice eventually converted his love of motorbikes into a career when he teamed up with George Silk to form Silk Engineering, which provided a spares and repairs service for Scott motorcycle owners. At Darley Abbey in Derbyshire, they produced the Silk 700S two-stroke motorcycle until 1979.

06

The classic profile of the Muztagh Tower from the south-east with the Baltoro Glacier in the foreground © John Cleare

Dreams are for Action

It's stunningly impressive, but not impossible – the perfect mountain.

Andrew Greig, *Summit Fever*

The first ascent of the Muztagh Tower (7,276m) by a British party in 1956 would never have happened were it not for John Hartog. On paper he was the weakest of the four-man team and he led no key sections on the climb. But success on such a big, remote mountain depends on many factors other than just mountaineering skills. Hartog must also take some credit for the second ascent, which occurred shortly after.

For a small team to attempt an unclimbed peak with no obvious or straightforward-looking route was a bold venture at the time. Small-scale British expeditions operating in the Greater Ranges were not new, however, and sat alongside the larger enterprises intent on climbing Everest and the other Himalayan giants. Before the First World War, Alexander Kellas and Tom Longstaff were exponents of lightweight expeditions on peaks over 7,000m. In 1933, the first ascent by Colin Kirkus and Charles Warren of Bhagirathi III (6,454m) in the Indian Himalaya used no fixed ropes or support above Advanced Base Camp, a strategy that would be deemed 'Alpine style' today. On the highest peaks, a larger team was no guarantee against failure and tragedy. Nine perished on the German Nanga Parbat expedition of 1934.

For climbers who dislike the strictures and mass assault tactics of large expeditions, the small-scale approach has a strong aesthetic appeal. Shipton and Tilman were perhaps the doyens of this. Although they took part in larger expeditions, they preferred cheap, exploratory affairs with few personnel. Self-reliance was key, and gear was kept to a minimum. 'Get most of little' became the mantra and the blueprint for the Alpine style favoured later in the century by talented mountaineers from around the globe.

After the Second World War, the big expeditions had a strong nationalist component, which attracted funding. Conquering the highest peaks was a way for defeated nations to regain their self-esteem. Nanga Parbat became linked with Germany and Austria, K2 with the Italians. For the British, the obsession with the prize of Everest had been about maintaining some status and importance in the world as the Empire dwindled. With Everest now vanquished, the impetus to climb a peak like the Muztagh Tower was not tainted with nationalism but there was friendly competitiveness as the French had the same goal.

The Karakoram spans Pakistan, India and China and is generally considered a separate range from the Himalaya. Its name derives from the Turkic words meaning 'black' and 'gravel' or 'rock' and was applied to the Karakoram Pass, the highest point on what used to be the main trading route between China and India. It is one of the highest mountain ranges in the world with an average elevation of 6,000m along its 300-mile length and four 8,000m peaks, although many of the impressive lower peaks vie for attention. A constellation of granite and ice towers, spires and citadels lord over a sterile, arid landscape, laced with the largest glaciers in the world outside the polar regions.

The Muztagh Tower was first discovered and named by Sir Martin Conway in his Karakoram survey expedition of 1892. It was described as 'impregnable', and in Vittorio Sella's iconic telephoto of the peak, taken on the Duke of Abruzzi's 1909 K2 expedition, the Tower appears as a mighty ice-sheathed, rectangular obelisk, tapering to a chisel-edged summit slicing the sky. Sella's photo swamped the collective consciousness of aspirants, despite the fact that another published image from 1909 depicted a far more benign aspect with two reasonably-angled ridges. On his original expedition, Conway was aware of the Tower's deceptive appearance and deemed the south-east arête quite climbable.

John Hartog had read Chemistry at Oxford, where he had been president of the university mountaineering club. A competent climber with experience of climbing in Britain in all seasons as well as in Norway and the Alps, he had shown organisational and logistic skills in his leadership of the 1949 Oxford expedition to Spitzbergen and was proposed for the Alpine Club in 1951 by John Hunt, who would go on to lead the successful 1953 Everest expedition.

As a Jewish schoolboy living in London in the '30s, Hartog had contacted W.H. Murray about the possibility of joining the newly established Junior Mountaineering Club of Scotland. Murray was flabbergasted when the 17-year-old asked whether his religion would be a barrier to membership, a reference to the increasingly appalling treatment of the Jews at the hands of the Nazis in Germany since 1933.

Murray visited Hartog at his home, where Sella's classic image hung on the bedroom wall. Hartog told Murray it had been his ambition to climb the Muztagh Tower since the age of 14, after reading R.L.G. Irving's recently published *The Romance of Mountaineering* (1935), which described the Tower as 'Nature's last stronghold—probably the most inaccessible of all great peaks, for its immense precipices show no weakness in its defences.' Six months after reading Irving's gushing assessment of the peak, Hartog perused Conway's description, which subsequently established the south-east arête as a realistic objective. Hartog was thinking seriously about climbing the mountain 20 years before he set foot on it.

Murray was too polite to deride the schoolboy's dream, even though he thought the Tower looked much harder than the recently scaled North Face of the Eiger.

In early 1955, Hartog pencilled in the trip for the following summer and began to assemble a team. However, his usual companions could neither obtain the necessary three months leave from their work nor meet the financial obligations. In May that year, Ian McNaught-Davis (universally known as Mac), who was then working as a geophysicist for British Petroleum in East Africa, offered to share the leadership and financial responsibilities of the expedition. A Yorkshireman, Mac had read Maths at Manchester University and had then done various manual jobs in exotic locations and some teaching before moving into industry. He had a fine Alpine record, with first British ascents of the Peuterey Ridge (via the Dames Anglaises Arête) in the Mont Blanc massif and the Comici Route on the Cima Grande in the Dolomites, one of the classic six Alpine north faces. He had also been on an expedition to Ruwenzori in Africa. Highly sociable and loquacious with an ebullient sense of humour, Mac was very different from Hartog. Like Patey, he lived life to the full.

Shortly after Mac came onboard, permission was sought from the Government of Pakistan and granted. But as Mac was out of the country until February 1956, it was left to Hartog to plan the trip and order the necessary equipment. By now, Hartog had read everything about the peak and studied every photograph, and he was an expert in the area without ever having been there. Ardito Desio, leader of the Italian expedition that made the first ascent of K2, corresponded with Hartog upon his return and provided him with aerial photographs taken during the reconnaissance of K2. With these, Hartog was able to square the ground photos with the true topography of the peak and assess the two main ridges offering the likely lines of ascent.

Less than three weeks before sailing out, Joe Brown and Patey were recruited. After being recommended to Mike Banks by Ross Higgins, secretary of the SMC, Patey was supposed to go on an expedition to the same mountain led by Banks with fellow Scot, Hamish MacInnes. However, being a junior doctor at the time, Patey could not raise the necessary funds.[1] Hartog rang Patey, who was at a loose end after pulling out of Banks's trip. Mac, who knew Brown and Patey from the Alpine Climbing Group (ACG), although only on a superficial level, knew the value of having a doctor in the team. Not only could Brown and Patey go at short notice, crucially, they could also raise the necessary £100—a fifth of the amount that Patey had been asked to contribute to Banks's expedition.

In the 1987 *Alpine Journal*, Roger Chorley, the Alpine Club President from 1983–85, describes Hartog's personality:

His complex character meant he was not an easy person to know. He ... could be engagingly good company and could show great thoughtfulness and generosity. But equally ... he could be unnecessarily stubborn with irritatingly strong opinions ... and I don't think he made any close friends.

These were less than ideal traits in an expedition member but, for Joe Brown at least, 'John was a lovable character, such a bumbly person.' Moreover, Hartog had an analytical mind, which he applied assiduously to the forthcoming trip, the whole point of which was to tackle a challenging peak, with height being a secondary consideration. The Muztagh Tower was an exemplar of this, and the range has provided a galaxy of objectives right up to the present day.

Patey's attitude was: 'No peak is impossible until it has been attempted.' He flew out three weeks after the others (who travelled by boat) as he had work commitments to honour in Scotland. The team met in Rawalpindi before taking an internal flight to Skardu, the starting point for most Karakoram expeditions. Luxury purchases were deferred until they reached Pakistan, with the result that they had no luxuries and had to make do with repetitive rations from home.

One hundred Balti porters were hired for the 11-day trek up the Shirgar Valley to the Baltoro Glacier. In his autobiography, *The Hard Years* (1967), Brown includes several details of the approach journey, including train journeys blasted by sand, bartering and haggling with the locals, a gripping flight through narrow ravines, insecure river crossings and villagers demanding medical attention. Then there was trouble with the porters, who had been handsomely rewarded for their work on the K2 expedition two years earlier. The British were operating on a tight budget, and although they were paying a fair rate, the porters expected extra payment and equipment. Beating the recalcitrants into action—a task carried out by the native Sirdar—proved an effective technique and, unsurprisingly, there were no further strikes. Just four porters were selected for duties on the actual mountain.

Never one to get overly lyrical about landscapes, and perhaps constrained by space, Patey's article in the 1957 *SMCJ* contains none of this colourful detail. One wonders whether the approach and all its bureaucratic diversions were simply an inconvenience to him. From the plane, he was impressed by the sight of Nanga Parbat, which was soloed by the great Austrian climber Herman Buhl in 1953, but that was the only thing he recorded until the climbing began in earnest. Although this was his first time out of Europe, the journey, exploration and engagement with a new culture was of little significance for him when set against the real motivation for the trip: the climbing objective.

It was the first time Brown had met Patey and his initial impression was not favourable. At the last oasis at Urdukas, they tossed a coin to see who would go and collect water. Patey lost but then refused to honour the bet. Moreover, his maintenance of the medical equipment was haphazard, to say the least—Brown recalls discovering several syringes full of sand.

Patey was perhaps unsure how to take Brown, who was already renowned in the British climbing world. News of Brown's achievements had reached Luibeg Bothy and details of his Alpine exploits had appeared in the *Alpine Journal*. In 1953, Brown, with the equally talented fellow Rock and Ice Club member, Don Whillans, had made a rapid repeat of the West Face of the Dru, reckoned to be the hardest rock route in the Western Alps at the time. In 1955, he had made the first ascent of Kanchenjunga (8,586m) with George Band. Brown was in a different class, excelling at every aspect of the sport and establishing new standards on gritstone outcrops and the Welsh mountain crags. He was succeeding on routes that others had deemed impossible, and many climbers were tongue-tied when they first met him. Some, including Chris Bonington, felt under self-imposed pressure to climb well with him and subsequently found themselves under-performing.

On Ben Nevis's Carn Dearg Buttress, Brown had established Sassenach (E1 5b) with Whillans, which the Scots had made no serious impression on. Patey and other Aberdonians had attempted it via

Mac topping up his tan en route to the Muztagh Tower © Joe Brown

a circuitous approach but had failed in the huge upper chimneys, the main feature of the route. Patey later revisited it with Bill Brooker, armed with Brown's handwritten description of the route. They climbed up to the key, overhanging second pitch, took one look and abseiled off. The closeted Aberdeen climbing scene had had a rude awakening. Patey had a theory that the new super climbers of the future would be of the build of Brown and Whillans. He returned once more to Sassenach with George Macleod, whose physique was more like the Englishmen's, but was again defeated.

But while Brown was consistently climbing three technical grades harder than Patey on rock, in winter Patey could hold his own against anyone in Britain.[2] Brown had less experience of snow and ice, purely due to the more reliable, lengthier winter conditions on the Scottish mountains. Nevertheless, his ascent of Western Gully on The Black Ladders with Ron Moseley, was probably the first. (Early Welsh winter routes were not as carefully recorded as those in Scotland.) Long considered Grade IV, Western Gully is now realistically graded V with technical sections of 6.

Embarking on a trip with virtually unknown companions is always a risk, especially given the length of time they would be together. In a candid diary Mac kept for the duration of the Muztagh Tower expedition, he offered his opinions of his three team members. The published accounts of the other expedition members were polite and matter-of-fact, but Mac recorded in detail the occasions he was annoyed and the reasons why. At the same time, he had enough insight to acknowledge that his judgements were affected by his own nature, bouts of illness, the effects of altitude and periods of bad weather when they were forced to live in close contact with one another in tents.

It is clear that he did not hit it off with John:

Should have realised by now that a consultation is a mere formality and he is going to have his own way whatever is said ... John is so self-opinionated and so sure he is right that although most of the time he is, he's so irritating about it that he incites a certain amount of rebellion. From our brief chat today RISK *is something that he is not prepared to consider. What will happen if we come across physical difficulty on the peak I don't dare wonder. All I have to hear now is the word* UNJUSTIFIABLE. *Is this book an outlet for venting spite? (Saturday 12 May)*

It also rankled Mac that Patey did little on the walk-in except deliver basic medical care and check-ups to the locals. 'Tom seems to pride himself in shooting ahead and arriving in camp first,' he noted. At camp:

Tom ... escaped all the boring work by pushing off for a walk, returning only after all the rations had been given out and the meal was almost ready. Tom returns and says what wonderful views there are around having climbed about 4,000 feet above the camp. He has a few patients in the morning and a few in the evening so apparently doesn't intend to do anything else. At the moment I feel that it is rather a poor showing. If he expects to be carried to and from the Tower putting as little into it as he is at the moment then he will get a reasonably unpleasant surprise. (Monday 21 May)

On the approach, there was a certain amount of ribaldry amongst the team, which facilitated the bonding process: 'Tom listened to a fart in a stethoscope and described it, amid peals of laughter, as a cross between Harry James on the trumpet and the guns at Edinburgh Castle.'

Conversations amongst three intelligent people were not always erudite:

Mac: I don't want to see your hairy arse.
Joe: I've got alopecia of the arsehole.
Tom: That's a bloody weird complaint. (Wednesday 23 May)

It seems that Hartog was not an active participant in this badinage.

Muztagh Tower from the Muztagh Glacier. The NW Ridge is the left-hand skyline. From the Left: Mac, Brown, Hartog © Ian Patey collection

On reaching the snout of the Baltoro Glacier, they began to appreciate the sheer scale of the Karakoram glaciers. Crossing the Baltoro was a slow, meandering journey for five miles across chaotic waves of ice, gravel and boulders. Leaving the upper Baltoro Glacier and the classic view of the Tower, the prospect from the Muztagh Glacier to the west face of the peak generated optimism among the party. But establishing Base Camp at 4,282m on the Muztagh Glacier involved tortuous route finding over tedious ground, despite it being only a mile and a half from the junction with the Baltoro.

The saving grace was that the angle of the two main ridges had dropped dramatically, and the Tower now looked far more benign than when viewed head-on. Hartog, who had carefully studied all the photographs, suggested that the North-West Ridge offered the most promising line, being a shorter and safer, if steeper, alternative to the opposing South-East Ridge.

When bad weather prevented progress establishing the lower camps, Patey tended towards solitude and went off for solo walks. Hartog noted that Patey was consistently the quickest of the four at climbing uphill.

Brown and Mac would pass the time boulder trundling and having mock toboggan races on air beds, steering with their ice axes. (By the end of the expedition, most were in shreds, and only one axe shaft remained intact. Hartog disapproved of their diversions.) In fact, Brown was the only one Mac felt a bond of friendship with. He despaired at Patey's laziness at camp and wondered if Hartog was out of his depth with the management of his fellow team members. Mac also worried about Hartog's 'slow-moving [sic] and his unwillingness to attempt difficulties', and was concerned about being paired with him for a summit assault.

When Hartog descended to Urdukas for supplies with three porters, Mac felt either Brown or Patey should have gone with him:

> *Tom was of the opinion that he had nothing to thank John for, and rather the reverse was the case. This was [so] obviously stupid that I could no longer trust myself to reply ... Tom, who has put the barest minimum into the expedition, dares to accuse John, without whom the expedition would never have been formed and certainly Tom would never have been invited. He is almost juvenile in his enthusiasm, rushing ahead like a puppy dog at any opportunity. It is very difficult to get Tom to do anything around camp other than make porridge in the morning. Accused Tom of faulty judgement, mainly, I confess, out of my own irritability. (Monday 11 June)*

Mac was ambitious too, but as a climber he was hardly in the same class as Brown and Patey, and it must have been disheartening for him to see Patey so at home in this hostile, oxygen-starved environment. Something else was grating, too:

> *More disappointed with Tom every day. He is obviously out to make a name for himself by climbing as many points as possible. Looking round the party, he realises his best chance of achieving this is by latching onto Joe. His talk is mainly planning which routes he intends doing*

Patey and Brown at Base Camp © Ian Patey collection

with Joe and what they are going to do together after the Tower has been climbed. They form a plan together of what they intend to climb then throw out a casual invitation, making it clear that Tom at least would be pleased if everyone refused. (Tuesday 12 June)

The next climbing objective was the col at the base of the North-West Ridge, where Camp III would be established at 6,355m before the real meat of the ascent began. The 600m ice wall leading to it presented a considerable challenge due to the poor quality of the snow, which lay over a bed of ice. Brown and Hartog succeeded on the initial section but had to retreat a couple of hundred metres short of their objective.

Patey and Mac took around six hours to climb the upper section. Security was poor on the upper slopes, so they transferred to the snowy rocks on one side. The final obstacle was a rocky cliff on which a chimney

Camp II. Two of the peaks behind were climbed during the expedition for acclimatisation © Ian McNaught-Davis

unlocked the key to the col, which Patey graded as VS. Brown was unnerved by the snow up to the col. None of the team had front points on their crampons, so steps had to be cut the whole way, sometimes requiring as many as 20 blows to create something which could realistically be stood in. But Patey was in his element—his winter climbing experience in Scotland alone meant he was by far the most versed in the vagaries of snow conditions. As Brown noted, 'It was a conclusive demonstration why he was fêted as the best snow and ice man in Scotland.'

Mac, now fully occupied in the task he came for, was much happier: 'The best day's climbing since arriving in Pakistan. Only spoilt by the thought we will have to do it at least twice more.'

Bad weather foiled their desire to fix ropes at the col and establish tents at Camp III, and an inevitable descent to Base Camp ensued. Talk again centred on summit bids. According to Mac: 'No one is very keen on climbing with [John], and above the col it is not going to be a holiday.'

News had travelled of the French Expedition also intent on making the first ascent of the Tower. Although the French had little knowledge of the mountain and feasible lines, they were an all-star team comprising Guido Magnone, Robert Paragot, André Contamine and Paul Keller, with plenty of funds and food that was gourmet compared to the Brits' monotonous rations.

When two of the French paid them a visit, Hartog suggested the South-East Ridge and a way of dealing with the problematic access to it. Relations between the teams were cordial, and it was a genial and relaxing interlude.

Back on the mountain when the weather improved, the final section to the col was equipped with fixed ropes. A pool under the ice provided a useful water source. Brown was impressed by Patey's selfless attitude when the latter returned to Base Camp from Camp III to fetch a crucial item for the final stages of the climb. The round trip would normally take five days: two down and three back up. Patey, whose strength and fitness at altitude were second to none, cut a day off each leg. However, his attitude to domestic duties remained woeful, the only exception being his willingness to make porridge, his signature dish.

The sight of the North-West Ridge from the col dispelled any concerns that it might be an easy snow plod. Patey compared it to the lower part of Observatory Ridge, which is held to be the most difficult of the Ben Nevis ridges in winter and has been upgraded in recent years from Grade III to V. It was another indicator of the kind of technical difficulties they were up against. Indeed, Brown acknowledged that it would be his hardest climb to date and it might be too difficult for him, but the challenge had the effect of raising morale rather than crushing it. They were invigorated by what was on offer.

Mac and Hartog made the first sortie but did not get far. Hartog compared the rise between Camps III and IV to the technical difficulties of the great routes on the Brenva Face of Mont Blanc, but with over 3,000m of additional altitude to contend with. The West Face was unrelentingly steep and rocky, whereas the North Face was plastered in snow and ice at an extreme angle. They adhered to the North-West

Patey and Hartog on initial slopes of the North-West Ridge above Camp III
© Joe Brown

Arête as closely as possible but made several necessary deviations onto the adjacent faces. Brown judged sections to be Alpine Grade V, and Patey was impressed by its sustained nature, which never dropped below British Severe.[3] With powder snow and verglassed rock, much of it fell into the category of mixed climbing, something Patey excelled at. He compared the difficulties to the Lochnagar buttresses in winter, and in his song 'Praise of the 'Gar', he proudly refers to the technical standards of the climbs on his local mountain:

Lhotse and Nuptse and Distaghil Sar
Are excellent training for dark Lochnagar

Brown and Patey were still short of a suitable site for Camp IV when they decided to retreat after a successful foray requiring three days' effort.

In photographs of the ascent, Patey's clothing seems inadequate for winter hillwalking in the Lake District, never mind the Karakoram. Remarkably, he did not have a decent sleeping bag or ice axe prior to the expedition, and he had had to borrow these from John Hay.[4] As to equipment, the team had no harnesses or helmets, just some rope slings, rock pegs and rudimentary ice pegs. With stiff hawser ropes, straight-pick axes and heavy metal karabiners, none of the technical gear was lightweight.

From then on, as Brown noted, 'more by personal inclination than design', the party split into two pairs: Brown and Mac, Patey and Hartog. Brown led the key passage up the 30m cliff just below Camp IV, which involved a remarkably exposed traverse onto the West Face topped by an overhang, on which Brown ripped his down trousers. The site was not ideal, but the terrain above looked worse, so they established this highest camp in the narrow, confined spot.

Except for the final tricky section, the ground between Camps III and IV was strewn with fixed ropes which eventually afforded rapid descents. After settling into their highest tent, Brown and Mac decided to make their summit bid the following day.

The ridge was now blocked by overhangs on which Brown's feet dangled free as he hauled himself up. When he could not force a line through these, he traversed onto the North Face, following a couloir comprising three feet of loose powder on a bed of ice. Despite being only 60m long, the three pitches up this (with no belays) were particularly trying for Brown, who was doing all the leading. Recalling the intense exposure and zero security, Brown recorded it as one of the most harrowing experiences in all his mountaineering career: 'The adrenaline knackers you so you're losing energy at a phenomenal rate.' They talked about retreating, but this would have been just as dangerous, and Mac followed this unprotected section with delicate care. Eventually, at the top of the third pitch, Brown discovered a crack for a piton and the pressure eased.

The suicidal snow could be exchanged for a tower of good quality rock furnished with large holds. It was, however, a false summit, so they continued, exhausted. On top of the next rise, they realised for the first time that the Muztagh Tower had twin summits and that the true top was beyond them yet.

It was now 6.00pm, and a bivouac was inevitable. Now seriously fatigued, they descended to the col between the tops, where Brown fell through a cornice. Instinctively, he threw his arms wide to prevent himself from plunging down the hole, savouring the 2,000m drop down the North Face to the glacier. Despite being so close to their goal, they decided to retreat, but even returning the short distance to the west top required great effort. They bivouacked just below this, leaving their boots on but untying the laces. Brown sat on his gloves, which provided some rudimentary insulation.

It snowed briefly during the night, adding to their anxiety about the return to Camp III the following morning. Fortunately, the weather the following day was benign, but Brown's gloves were frozen stiff and unusable. Whenever he touched rock, his skin instantly froze to it, and if Mac had not unearthed a spare pair of socks from his sack for Brown to use as substitute gloves, frostbite would have been guaranteed. Both

Patey on the final few metres to the East Summit. K2 behind © John Hartog

were unable to get any food down and their only liquid was the lumps of snow they sucked. But the unconsolidated snow in the couloir had now frozen, and they descended safely using the now stable, generous steps.

Here, they met Hartog and Patey, who, having been unable to get their primus stove going earlier, had no spare water to offer the descending pair. Patey declined an offer of duvet trousers as the favourable conditions meant he and Hartog could be up to the true summit and back to Camp IV in a day. He did not even have a windproof jacket with him.

Patey and Hartog reached the true, east summit (just 3m higher than the west) after negotiating a short step of Alpine Grade V. A classically narrow snow arête completed the ascent with the majesty of K2 on full display in the background. Patey graciously allowed Hartog to lead the final steps to the top. The dream that originated 20 years earlier in the mind of a 14-year-old schoolboy was finally realised. Patey could not resist puncturing their unarguably great achievement with humour, and commented that:

> *The usual summit rites were restricted to photography, as we had forgotten to bring a flag along with us on the expedition. Bill Brooker had promised to present me with a Scottish Lion Rampant before I left Aberdeen, but unfortunately all the flags he had inspected in the shops were too expensive.*

Patey was in a 'regular fever of impatience' to get down to the upper camp, but Hartog was always slower on descents. Tiredness led to carelessness, and at one point, the bowline around Patey's waist became undone.

At the inevitable bivouac, about an hour from Camp IV, Patey admitted that he was concerned about frostbite, so Hartog generously rubbed Patey's feet, legs and thighs throughout the sleepless night. Unfortunately, Hartog neglected his own welfare and, not wishing to deal with frozen laces caked in ice, made the serious error of leaving his boots on.

The next morning, Patey was shivering so violently that Hartog had to lead the descent, and when they reached Camp IV, Patey collapsed into his sleeping bag. (He attributed this to a drug he had taken during the night, which was supposedly effective against frostbite.) A few hours later, Hartog descended several hundred feet on his own and hailed Mac at Camp III, yelling that they would continue their descent in the afternoon. Patey dismissed this idea, however, as he was in no state to move, so Hartog prepared to get in his sleeping bag for a full day of rest.

The damage to Hartog's feet was clear when he removed his boots, and Patey confirmed frostbite. Despite massaging his feet, Hartog's toes remained an ominous dirty white colour. The following morning, although Hartog was clearly unwell, he had a rejuvenated Patey to guide him. Unfortunately, they now had the extra weight of a tent, stove and sleeping bags on their backs. Amid bouts of vomiting and incontinence, Hartog suffered bad rope burns on the first abseil, so Patey belayed him down the long stretch of fixed ropes, checking a fall when Hartog lost a foothold. Not far from the camp, Brown and Mac came up to relieve Hartog of his pack and assist him down the final section. Despite looking 'sick, semi-insane and very weak', Hartog was talking excitedly, as if drunk. 'Intoxicated with happiness' about their success, endorphins had no doubt helped him stay alert and survive the discomforts.

The next day, however, Hartog was tent-bound, semi-delirious and hardly able to walk, puking into a biscuit tin as his feet were massaged.

Hartog required considerable assistance from Mac on the descent. On the ice slope below Camp III, a dramatic stonefall enveloped them, ripping their rucksacks off. They were catapulted down the slope and only came to a stop when their waist karabiners butted up against the pitons securing the fixed ropes. They continued the tortuous descent, and it took Hartog a week to reach Base Camp. By now, his toes were black and he could not walk. Surgical intervention and a prompt return to the valley were necessary.

Down in Urdukas, where Patey was giving treatment to a porter, Mac recorded that:

> *Tom's feet are not so good, one little toe having lost all the skin and nail (preserved by Tom in a matchbox) and is now septic ... With Tom hardly walking we have two invalids and soon John will arrive making three and more tedious.*

With the assistance of two mail runners, Hartog finally arrived at camp, along with news of the French team's success on the peak.[5] Their party included Dr Francois Florence, a frostbite expert, and when they visited the Brits the following day, Florence:

> *Immediately set about John's feet and, as a red rim was forming round the bad small toe, he put him on penicillin streptomycin injections. A beautiful case and first aid kit made Tom look the beginner he is. Tom even refused to give John the injection, saying that John objected.*

Florence advised that Patey should descend with Hartog, and porters (including those with the French Expedition) carried him in stages on an improvised chair, which Patey, with typical black humour, referred to as a 'funeral pyre'. Hartog was forever grateful for the assistance of the French and their warm attitude to the British team:

> *The kindness of the French remains for me one of the noblest deeds in the history of international mountaineering—the conversion of rivalry to great kindness and affection.*

Mac's diary ends with a far-from-fond farewell to his teammates:

> *Glad to be rid of them both. Tom had three books from the French, but when asked to leave one he refused, which we all thought as bad as when he tossed for who should go for water with Joe.*

Patey tried to get Mac to give him his boots, complaining he could not get his own on due to a swollen foot, but Mac refused, suggesting he

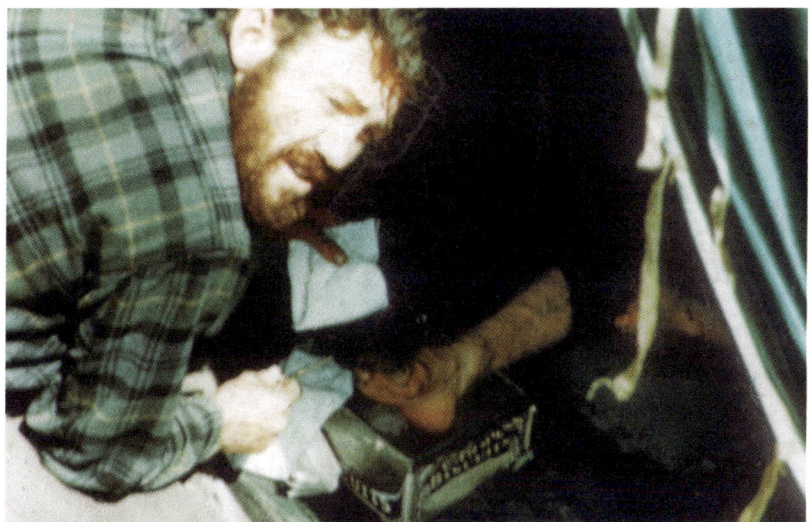
Patey treating Hartog's feet © Ian Patey collection

remove the insole and the bandage he had on. Patey limped away, and when Mac saw him on the glacier he was shooting off at his usual speed.

After the amputation of the two smallest toes on one foot and the ends of all his toes on another, it was the end of any serious mountaineering for Hartog. However, he remained an enthusiastic attendee at SMC meets and continued his long friendship with W.H. Murray, who wrote Hartog's obituary in the *SMCJ* (1987). Unlike that penned by Roger Chorley in the *Alpine Journal* (1987), Murray makes no mention of Hartog's waspish and somewhat cold personality, concluding with a heartfelt sentiment:

> *The Muztagh story had begun with a schoolboy's dream. John was so unassuming that I forbore to scoff, but I confess I had thought his dream impractical. This is an old, old story, which we all have to keep in mind—that dreams are more potent than reason; that if you can dream a thing, you can attain it too, as often or not. Dreams are for action.*

Despite Mac's dislike of some aspects of Patey's character, they became lifelong friends. Although they did not climb seriously together again, Mac discovered Patey's sociable and entertaining side and they bonded very well on this level.

After Brown's initial wariness of Patey, they too developed a closeness and subsequently climbed together in the Alps, Scotland and Norway, often establishing new routes. Many years later, Brown (2013) reflected:

The thing with all of my friends that has kept us all together, kept us all climbing, is the enthusiasm. Tom's enthusiasm was second to none, and I know he felt the same way about me.

Patey had proved his worth at altitude in terms of technical skill and a capacity for hard work at key moments. He must also take credit for getting the weakest member of the team to the summit and down again. On mixed terrain, he was the equal of some of the greatest climbers of the time. Two years later he would return to the Karakoram, where his mountaineering skills, tenacity and hardiness would be applied on a far more traditional expedition.

1   Banks had presumptuously given an interview to the BBC about the impregnable peak they were going to attempt, and this prompted an invite from Hartog to discuss objectives. Like W.H. Murray 16 years earlier, Banks was struck by the famous Sella picture on the drawing-room wall in Hartog's Earl's Court flat, now an enormous version of the one hanging in his bedroom. Hartog revealed he had already obtained official permission to climb the peak, as had a French team. Banks, conceding that he was too late and that there could not be three teams on the mountain, abandoned the Tower and chose Rakaposhi instead.

2   Much was made of Brown's failure to climb Point Five Gully in January 1956, when he fell off the second pitch after an ice bulge collapsed. The Scots were relieved that another major line hadn't fallen to Brown and his associates, but their pride was dealt a second blow when, later in the year, Whillans and Bob Downes climbed Centurion (HVS 5a).

3   It should be noted that the three written accounts of the climb by Hartog, Patey and Brown all differ somewhat, and it is not always easy to match the three viewpoints or sequence of events. The vagaries of memory when combined with altitude obviously play some part here. Patey remarked that the snow lay on a steeper angle than Scotland or the Alps but was generally more stable, though Brown and Mac later disagreed with this.

4   The returned bag was well used, while the axe remained forever somewhere in the Greater Ranges. Patey at least paid Hay for a replacement, which resides in his home in Torridon.

5   The French had reached the summit six days after the English team. They were effusive about the ascent of the South-East Ridge, giving it ED, the hardest Alpine grade at the time. Both routes were similar in technical difficulty. In less than a week, the Muztagh Tower possessed two of the hardest routes in the Greater Ranges.

07

Zero Gully lies between the broad North-East Buttress on the left and the slender Observatory Ridge, on the North Face of Ben Nevis
© Hamish MacInnes

Zero Hour

No modern winter climb excites the same awe, and what was involved in those early ascents is easily forgotten.

Allen Fyffe, *Cold Climbs*

Returning to Aberdeen after his successful ascent of the Muztagh Tower, Patey had work at Inverurie Hospital and a girlfriend to think of. In December, he proposed to Betty during an ascent of Ben Vorlich above Loch Lomond, and she duly accepted. Arrangements were made for a wedding the following year, but in the meantime, climbing was never far from his thoughts. A cold mid-January in 1957 saw Patey at Creag an Dubh-loch with Kincorthers Freddie Malcolm and Alex 'Sticker' Thom, who were on leave from the Paratroopers. In good conditions, they climbed the first major winter route on this imposing cliff: the gully breaking the right wall of Central Gully below Sabre Edge, which starts high up in that obvious fault. This might be viewed as something of an afterthought route when compared with the longer, more awe-inspiring lines further down the gully wall. But despite its brevity, Sabre Cut (IV,5) was no pushover, and over the course of three hours they utilised a couple of icicle belays and took in a steep 40ft ice pitch. Unusually, Patey asked Malcolm to lead the crux as he did not feel up to it, but the latter declined the offer.

The following month, Patey headed to Carn Etchachan with Mac Smith, who was still working on his two-volume *Climbers' Guide to the Cairngorms*. Climbing the full height of the main face and taking advantage of Patey's prior acquaintance with the cliff, they created one of the longest routes in the Cairngorms and a great mixed classic. Route Major (IV,5) weaves around to exploit the weaknesses in the face and is a mountaineering route par excellence, with a magnificent outlook from above the head of Loch Avon. Snow conditions were superb, 'the axe required for every step' (Smith, 1961), and the climbing time of three-and-a-half hours testament to their skills as much as the conditions. That day, they found the crux to be the upper Battlements groove, but most believe it to be the lower tapered chimney. Patey was no doubt in his element on a climb with a bit of every type of winter climbing thrown into the mix.

The North-East Face of Ben Nevis is a premier mountaineering venue of world renown with a rich and fascinating history. It has an Alpine ambience due to the length of the routes and the lingering presence of snow: spring can be well underway by the banks of Loch Linnhe while winter still dominates on the peak. Its position means that it is open to the onslaught of the prevalent south-westerly fronts which batter the coast. The mild interludes and periods of freeze/thaw produce a superb medium for climbing: snow ice that is easy for a pick to penetrate and reliable enough to hang from.

By February 1957, the two unclimbed but named gullies of Point

Patey and Betty after the Muztagh Tower © Ian Patey collection

Five and Zero were the most sought-after objectives in the country, in the sights of all the top Scottish climbers and, more worryingly for the Scots, many of the leading performers south of the border. The problem was finding the gullies in climbable condition: unconsolidated powder on the plateau can blow down the two chutes, enveloping climbers in hissing spindrift and making progress almost impossible. Nowadays, thanks to the tag, 'Probably the most famous ice gully in the world' (SMC, 2008), Point Five attracts climbers from all over the globe, and there can be a continuous line of ropes from bottom to top on a busy day.

Zero, although technically easier, has a reputation for being more serious due to its poorer belays. For both gullies, early ascensionists would have to cut steps in stretches of very steep ice, with all the trepidation and insecurity that entailed.

Ben Nevis can be an intimidating venue in winter, the scale and height of the north-east cliffs way beyond anything else in Britain. Allen Fyffe, who climbed several of the hardest winter climbs in Scotland in the '60s and '70s, noted that:

> Our experience of Grade V routes was limited to the 'Gorms', home territory for Aberdeen climbers such as ourselves. But The Ben was bigger and badder than anywhere else, and we knew little about it.

The weekend after his ascent of Route Major with Smith, Patey hitched over from the east with Graeme Nicol and arrived at the CIC Hut before the main weekend throng.

They were later joined by SMC stalwarts Len Lovat, Malcolm Slesser, Donald Bennet, Douglas Scott and non-member Norman Tennent: a group of competent all-round mountaineers, though none in Patey's class in terms of winter climbing ability.

Debilitating spindrift on Saturday ruled out any gully ascents, so Slesser, Bennet, Scott and Tennent headed for the classic North-East Buttress, while Patey, Nicol and Lovat made for the virgin face in Coire Leis, later christened the Little Brenva Face. According to Nicol, tackling

Cresta (III) on that face was Patey's idea, but it had been suggested to him by W.H. Murray. Little Brenva is a classic example of terrain which is of no interest to the summer climber but can produce quality lines in winter, and Patey, with his creative mind, 'was brilliant at seeing lines' (Nicol, 2014). The trio were pleased with their success on Cresta, which they completed in three hours, but it did not sate Patey's and Nicol's ambitions.

Any notion that there would be no competition that weekend for the two glittering prize gullies was shattered upon their return to the hut, where Creagh Dhu Club members Mick Noon and John Cunningham—one of the most outstanding rock climbers in Scotland at the time—were ensconced. Cunningham had been on key ascents on the steep walls in Glen Coe, although he had not made the same impact in winter climbing.[1]

It was an eclectic mix of personalities in the CIC Hut that weekend: shipyard workers Cunningham and Noon, academics Slesser and Bennet, ex-submarine commander Tennent, lawyer Lovat, photographer Scott and medics Patey and Nicol. Of course, just because certain people are members of the same club does not necessarily mean they like each other. There was a dramatic entrance late on Saturday evening by Hamish MacInnes, who had rushed over from the Steall Hut in Glen Nevis when he heard of the personnel gathered and the goals they had in mind.

Born in 1930, MacInnes had been introduced to climbing after the Second World War by a neighbour when he was living with his parents in Greenock. He founded the Greenock Climbing Club and climbed regularly with the Creagh Dhu Club while never actually becoming a member. MacInnes's experience stretched from Scotland to the Alps, New Zealand and the Himalaya. He made a living from instructing and, later in his career, from the design of climbing and mountain rescue equipment and film safety work. That weekend he had with him The Message, the first all-metal shafted ice hammer, which he had recently invented.

In 1953, MacInnes had made a similar breakthrough in winter climbing to that achieved by Patey in the Cairngorms, and by 1957 they were two of the leading Scottish winter protagonists, with similar drives and often the same routes on their respective hit lists.

Sunday morning heralded poor conditions, but Noon, Cunningham and MacInnes left early for Zero, returning later, disappointed. Despite the likelihood of avalanches, Patey and Nicol risked Comb Gully (IV), which they climbed in just over an hour in a blizzard and suffocating spindrift, albeit with excellent snow ice in which they could cut steps.

According to Nicol, when they reached the top, Patey vanished without warning to descend Number Three Gully, leaving his companion stranded.[2] Nicol, who had limited knowledge of the mountain's topography, was afraid after being abandoned in such poor weather. He eventually descended near the Red Burn and took the traverse path back to the CIC Hut from the halfway lochan, reuniting with Patey hours later. Despite his compassion and consideration in other situations,

Jim McArtney step-cutting up Zero Gully in February 1967, ten years after the first ascent © Allen Fyffe

'That was very much Tom; once he'd done the climb, he'd be off, not really bothered if you were with him or not' (Nicol, 2014).

On Monday, conditions in Zero Gully were superb, with neither spindrift nor avalanche debris to contend with. MacInnes and Patey set off with Nicol, who was 'the young guy with the big boys' and therefore sanguine about the undertaking.

Zero Gully takes the depression between the Orion Face and Observatory Ridge and is more an open, shallow groove than an enclosed slot typical of a traditional Scottish gully. In April 1936, J.H.B. Bell and Colin Allan had made a partial winter ascent but had avoided the lower difficulties by taking to the rocks of Slav Route (VI) on the left-hand side, rejoining the gully for the easier, upper section.

This was now MacInnes's seventh attempt on Zero—frustratingly, he had already climbed the major difficulties in the lower section before an avalanche had necessitated a retreat. He had become obsessive about it and had even soloed the adjacent Observatory Ridge in winter to inspect it.

Patey was pointed at the first long chute pitch leading up to an overhang. As he progressed, MacInnes drily recounted the various mishaps incurred by previous suitors. This gentle one-upmanship was a common feature of their relationship, and is memorably described in Patey's humorous account of their first winter traverse of the Cuillin Ridge. At least MacInnes could furnish Patey with useful information about belays: at the top of the first pitch was a piece of nylon cord attached to an ice axe embedded in the snow, which MacInnes and Bob Hope had abseiled off the previous month.

Patey led the precipitous 20-foot section above by taking tension from rudimentary ice screws in order to cut steps, as it was simply too steep to remain in balance without some aid. Above this, Patey failed to uncover MacInnes's abandoned ice piton and had to make do with an axe belay.

A traverse back into the main bed of the gully on less steep but very exposed ground led to what was clearly one of the hardest sections on the route. It had been from below this section that MacInnes and Hope had abandoned their attempt in the face of spindrift avalanches. MacInnes, unlike the tricouni-clad Aberdonians, was wearing crampons but still took two hours to lead the formidable 100m pitch, which gave his belayers an opportunity to taunt him, Nicol singing the 'New Orleans Funeral March'. Patey was forced to acknowledge MacInnes's lead, however, when he required a tight rope for much of it.

Above this, the ground eased and, moving together, they set a furious pace as they continued to cut steps, reaching the top in 50 minutes. After a total of five hours, the first Grade V climb on Ben Nevis had been established. It was a milestone in the mountain's history and remains legendary, not so much for the quality of the climbing but for the history associated with it and the breakthrough it represented at the time. Despite its simple name, it evoked a powerful emotional response in those who aspired to climb it. Jimmy Cruickshank (2006) wrote of the first ascent: 'Their efforts did little to dissipate the feeling of awe its nihilistic name tended to inspire.'

Zero Gully was quite unlike Patey's great trilogy of winter routes in the Cairngorms, and his fame would now spread beyond the northeast of Scotland.

After the elation of the climb, Nicol recalls that the attitude of some of the SMC members back at the CIC Hut cast something of a shadow over the occasion. He got the impression that the ascent was the cause of, not annoyance, but disappointment among some of the older chaps who perhaps fancied doing the climb themselves. Patey took up an offer of a lift back east with Norman Tennent, abandoned his hut cleaning duties and shot off down the Allt a' Mhuilinn, leaving Nicol to fulfil the responsibilities at the insistence of Bennet and Slesser.

In April, Patey linked up with Jimmy Marshall, an Edinburgh architect by profession and a skilled all-round mountaineer who stood out amongst his fellow SMC members but needed the company of equally able, ambitious partners to realise his potential.

The day after Marshall delivered a slide show to the Etchachan

The first ascent of Zero Gully. Patey, Nicol and MacInnes are visible as dots on the initial pitches © Douglas Scott

Club in Aberdeen, Patey gave him a tour of Lochnagar. They made rapid ascents of Polyphemus Gully and Route 2, both graded Severe, and finished the day off with the first ascent of Shylock's Chimney, a back-and-foot VS to the right of West Gully. On his local territory, Patey led everything, but the wily Marshall must have been weighing up the possibilities for future ascents: the following winter he would leave the Aberdeen cognoscenti speechless when he poached Parallel Gully B from their local crag. Marshall had been inspired by Patey's early routes and writings, which expanded the horizons of what could be achieved in winter.

Patey took advantage of the Cairngorm crags with a southern aspect being clear of snow early that year. He stayed at the Etchachan Hut with Betty on 18 April, and the entry in the hut logbook records his continuing boldness. Djibangi was, 'A very pleasant route, medium VS Standard. Solo, one hour. No piton for the top pitch so jammed ice axe used!' (1957). He then went over to the Shelter Stone Crag and attempted to solo a direct route up the Main Bastion, turning back 'above several severe pitches. Rocks very greasy' after 150m of climbing.[3]

Creag an Dubh-loch was now becoming a magnet for all the talented Aberdeen-based climbers for two reasons. First, the phenomenal Central Gully Wall all the way round to its frontal face still had only two routes on it. Patey's Vertigo Wall and Sabre Edge were side orders compared to what was potentially on offer here. It was also one of the most sensational and inspiring stretches of rock in Britain and, with National Service approaching, an irresistible draw for Patey. Below Vertigo Wall was a major corner system (later named The Giant), and many thought (falsely) that this was the key to the breach of this section of the cliff.

Instead of using the obvious ramp to access this great corner, which looked prohibitively difficult, Patey, with his eye for a plum line, started higher up the gully and used tension to traverse a rock-scarred slab to a stance 60ft above a massive, wedged block.

Above, a steep corner led to further slabs, but Patey ventured no further that day. Nevertheless, he had now pieced together the route and he intended to return, climb the steep corner, then cross the huge corner and reach easier ground via a notch in the skyline. He never came back to complete it, however, and it was not realised for over a decade, and even then not quite by the line in the upper section that Patey had envisaged.

Two bold attempts by other parties nearly succeeded before the route was eventually climbed by Mike Rennie and Brian Findlay in 1969. Above the steep corner they continued direct, discovering an elegant, exposed line weaving up cracks in a slab but at an amenable grade. Their route, Goliath (HVS), became an instant classic and features in Ken Wilson's *Hard Rock*, a celebration of some of Britain's greatest rock climbs.

It had now been eight years since Patey had entered university, and in that time Britain's fortunes had transformed. A boom in the post-war global economy had led to a dramatic rise in living standards. For young people, rock and roll music was shining a searchlight across the Atlantic, and the whole landscape seemed brighter than the 'biblical bleak' of the immediate post-war years.

On 29 July 1957, Patey married Betty at St Andrew's Cathedral in Aberdeen. The reception was held at the Royal Athenaeum Hotel, with a pianist and their own records providing the music for dancing. In attendance was a guard of honour of Cub Scouts and Bill Brooker as best man, after Patey's shy half-brother Maurice declined the offer. In complete contrast to his usual disregard for his appearance, Patey looked immaculate in his suit. Now aged 25, had he reached a turning point in his life? People might have expected this smartness to continue during his National Service. They might have expected his climbing activities to be curtailed on account of his career, matrimonial and subsequent family responsibilities. On each account, they would be proved wrong. Even the four years serving his Queen and Country in the Royal Marines were used to advance Patey's mountaineering ambitions.

Patey in a different kind of blizzard. Bill Brooker behind © Ian Patey collection

1   The following year the pair would climb Carnivore (E2 5c), considered one of the hardest routes in Glen Coe and a classic to this day.

2   In 'The Zero Gully Affair' (*SMCJ*, 1958), Patey contradicts Nicol's account, and claims that they cut steps down North Gully together.

3   Postern was climbed later that summer and The Citadel the following year.

08

Establishment Mavericks

Patey and John 'Zeke' Deacon on a Cairngorm Royal Marines training course © John Deacon collection

The camaraderie is very deep. It really is a band of brothers.

John 'Zeke' Deacon

Following the National Service Act of 1948, males aged between 17 and 21 who passed the fitness criteria were expected to join a military service for 18 months and then remain on the reserve list for four years. After the British involvement in the Korean War in 1950, the initial period was extended to two years, and the reserve list was reduced by six months. Because of Patey's medical degree, his National Service was deferred until after his graduation and training as a house and junior doctor. By entering as an officer and volunteering for three years, he would have more interesting work and be afforded more privileges.

Despite Patey's family connection with the Navy, it is perhaps strange that, with his interest in mountaineering, he selected this form of military service, especially with the prospect of spending long periods at sea. In his book *Rakaposhi* (1959), Mike Banks hints at his influence on Patey's decision to join the Navy and, subsequently, the Royal Marines. In a 1987 article in *Climber*, Banks candidly admits that he worked a great fiddle to get Patey attached to the Commando climbing unit (part of 42 Commando at Bickleigh in Devon) of the Royal Marines. Banks, who was running the unit, had wanted Patey for his own 1956 expedition to the Muztagh Tower, but he had had to alter his goal when he realised two other teams had the same plans. With a military expedition to the Greater Ranges in the pipeline, he was determined to have Patey on board. Like Patey, Banks was driven, adventurous and single-minded, with strong organisational skills. Unlike Patey, however, Banks dressed smartly and spoke in received pronunciation, even though he was considered an 'establishment renegade' (Goodwin, 2013).

Patey dotted around several Navy bases until he settled down with the Royal Marines. He spent time at Royal Navy hospitals at Portsmouth and Gosport, and did basic training on saluting and marching. He then undertook commando training at Bickleigh, which entailed no medical duties but included some cliff assault exercises.

Being stationed in the south-west of England meant that, for the first time in his life, Patey would be a considerable distance from any mountains. Although there was a wide selection of outcrop climbing on offer, this was never Patey's forte. However, the prospect of an expedition at no personal cost was a huge incentive. Moreover, being attached to the climbing unit meant he would attend the winter warfare courses in the Cairngorms and Norway. In both postings there would be time off to pursue his personal climbing.

The Royal Marines does not have its own medical corps: Marines doctors are surgeon lieutenants in the Royal Navy first and then become

Patey seated second from the left during initial Navy training © Ian Patey collection

attached to the UK's amphibious light infantry force. The service can struggle to recruit doctors and priests due to the rigorous standards required to pass the commando course, which are higher for an officer than for an ordinary marine; for instance, the 30-mile march across Dartmoor has to be completed faster. Patey's mountain fitness was outstanding, so passing these tests was not a problem, but he required ingenuity to pass the skiing test in Norway.

Another attractive component of his National Service was that, as the only doctor with 42 Commando, he was his own boss and his judgement was not really challenged. Although his notoriously untidy appearance and habits could have got him into trouble, his ability as a mountaineer and the lack of any senior medical officer to discipline him meant that he was respected and could get away with things others could not. On one occasion, returning to Bickleigh after a weekend's climbing, a fellow officer remarked, 'Good God Patey, you look as if you've been living in a cave,' to which Patey replied, 'That's exactly where I have been.'

As the medic, Patey was not required to instruct mountaineering but was on call in case of any mishaps. Everyone was generally in robust health, and he mostly had to deal with the same afflictions: bruises, sprains, breaks, foot rot, crotch rot and venereal disease. Anything more serious was referred to a hospital, and some of Patey's peers felt his full range of medical skills was not utilised.

The Cliff Assault Wing, which was remote from the main base for lengthy periods, had something of the conviviality of a climbing club, and Patey enjoyed being with like-minded people. The social life was excellent, and in many respects Patey could not have got a better posting. Certain senior officers in administrative roles thought the wing had too much autonomy, but nobody could criticise the quality of the instruction and the calibre of the Marines it turned out.

Although Patey mixed with many Marines of all ranks during his four years of service, he climbed and socialised with four in particular: Mike Banks, Sam Bemrose, Vivian Stevenson and John 'Zeke' Deacon.

Bemrose, who entered as an officer and served from 1954–1977,

Betty eventually moved down to be with Patey and they lived in married quarters accommodation at Yelverton. Their first child, Rona, was born in Devon
© Ian Patey collection

appears in two of Patey's articles about Norway in *One Man's Mountains* (1971), where he was nicknamed the 'Gay Lothario'[1] because he was a bachelor and, as he admitted, 'We all kept our brains between our legs when we were young.' Bemrose was a superb rugby player, turning out for the Navy, Combined Services and London Harlequins. He was on course for an England trial, but a knee injury put paid to that.

Bemrose met Patey for the first time when they travelled together on the train from London to Aviemore. They wore uniforms to make sure they got First Class seats, but as soon as they embarked at Kings Cross, Patey took his jacket, shirt and tie off, revealing a grubby string vest. He reasoned that no one would come near if they saw them dressed like this and they would have the compartment to themselves.

Although Patey was only 25 when he joined the service, Bemrose looked on him as an old man of the mountains, and found him a great companion for his friendliness, intelligence and excellent command of the spoken word. Patey was also a sympathetic listener, if you could get him off the subject of climbing. Being younger, Bemrose became Patey's apprentice, which often entailed lugging the latter's accordion around to various venues.

After the Suez Crisis of 1956, Cold Weather Warfare came under the training auspices of the Cliff Assault Wing, and the Scottish and Norwegian courses began in earnest. The novices' course, based at the old Norwegian Huts at Glenmore in the Cairngorms, taught 40 to 50 officers and men and lasted for about three weeks.[2] During training, Patey was always around in case someone had an accident, but he had quiet periods when he would head into Northern Corries and do a route with one of the instructors.

Despite being incredibly fit, Patey virtually chain-smoked, even

Sam Bemrose, 'The Gay Lothario' (left), and Vivian 'Stevo' Stevenson
© Vivian Stevenson

when attending to patients, and his rough, cracked fingers were ingrained with dirt and tobacco. On one occasion, Bemrose had the opportunity to observe Patey's unconventional approach to medical examinations when a Marine complained of abdominal pain. In the hut, Patey asked the man to lie on the same table they usually dined on. He carried on smoking as he proceeded with his examination, occasionally flicking ash in the patient's belly button, in which he would slot the filter end of the fag when requiring both hands free. If someone complained about blisters, Patey would often show them some even more gruesome examples on his own feet.[3]

Aviemore was a small, sleepy town until the Coire Cas was developed for skiing, but there was a healthy social scene away from the mountains. The main venue was the Aviemore Hotel, although The Struan House Hotel in Carrbridge, run by Karl and Eileen Fuchs, was also popular. This was Scotland's first ski hotel, and complemented the couple's Austrian Ski School.[4] The Fuchs' hospitality was well known, and they allowed after-hours lock-ins in the bar, where Patey would entertain on the accordion, the ash on the end of his fag never seeming to fall off until he allowed it to.

The cosy 'Austrianised' Eidelweiss Bar was the real heart of The Struan. It became very popular with military men, and Karl built up a collection of regimental shields on the walls (which were often donated by visitors), along with skiing and climbing paraphernalia and pictures of mountain scenes. Fuchs also had his own portrait on the wall, in which he was dressed in his war uniform and wearing his Iron Cross. Although the Second World War was still a recent memory, nobody complained, and the decoration garnered respect from military visitors. Patey and his fellow Marines would encourage Karl to sing German war songs such as 'Wir Fahren Gegen Engeland' (We sail to take on the English) and the Nazi anthem 'Horst Wessel Lied', and would accompany him in rousing renditions. Some young Austrian ski instructors would depart the bar in horror as these songs were still banned in their homeland (Brown, 2000).

Patey in Scotland during Royal Marines duties © Vivian Stevenson

Later in the '60s, Patey's preferred watering hole became the Rowanlea in Carrbridge, which was run by the fiddler Jimmy Ross. According to Patey's friends, he rarely had a hangover, despite regularly drinking late into the evening. Moreover, while he was always somewhat slow to rise in the morning, he moved so fast that he always caught up with the others. Bemrose (2014) recalls that, in the mountains, Patey always went uphill at full pelt and he could descend quickly too: 'God, he was good in the mountains, Tom; the best guy I've ever met.'

Although several Marines could usually keep pace with Patey, he excelled on more technical ground. One very fit Marine corporal called Armitage, nicknamed the Animal, wanted to break the Marines' record for the Cairngorm 4,000ers, a circuit of Braeriach, Cairn Toul, Ben Macdui and Cairn Gorm. With Sergeant Ernie Blaber, Armitage covered the distance of around 23 miles in just over eight hours. Patey eventually knocked 20 minutes off this, breaking the winter eight-hour barrier.

Away from the mountains, Patey's domestic habits had a rationale that others found puzzling. One morning, Bemrose was woken by Patey, who was still wearing his pyjamas. A moment later, Patey was in his suit and tie, and Bemrose commented on the quick change. Patey replied that he always wore his pyjamas over his suit to keep it free of all the dirt on his sleeping bag and in the quarters.

Patey often went out to the hills in his suit, which he would also wear when socialising at the local hostelries. Even when he made a special effort, he seemed to be sartorially jinxed. Proudly wearing a new suit for the first time, he stood next to a pot-bellied stove and, to his dismay, burnt a hole in the trousers, which were then crudely patched up.

Keen to make the most of being based in the Cairngorms, Patey was desperate to get on the first-ascent trail again, especially after news he received when he returned to Aberdeen for Christmas leave in 1958. His two younger companions from the first ascent of Scorpion, Nicol and Grassick, had stunned the local climbing community by completing the first winter ascent of Patey and Taylor's Sticil Face on the Shelter Stone Crag, one of the most imposing cliffs in the Cairngorms.

Patey had earlier dismissed its potential as a feasible winter ascent, and Nicol and Grassick had demolished old notions of what was possible. It was bold and exposed, a true mixed route with a technical section just below the top. Moreover, the pair had climbed it in the minimal daylight hours of late December. Patey could only respect and feel envious of this effort by the two young medical students who had once been his apprentices. Grassick observed that:

When he learned about our coup, he was not pleased ... he felt cheated. We had taken his climb and had been secretive about our intentions. He studiously ignored us for months. However, by Easter we were once again the same friendly antagonists we had always been, with an invitation to join him on Zero and Point Five. (Cold Climbs, 1983)[5]

According to Nicol (2014), however, Patey was a bit peeved about their ascent but was not one to hold grudges for long, even when new routes were being poached from him or winter ascents made of his own summer routes.

In January that year, on the neighbouring cliff of Hell's Lum Crag, Patey climbed a route which was technically easier than Sticil Face but also destined to become a Cairngorm winter classic. Deep Cut Chimney (IV,5) follows a rift in the crag, which is deeply recessed at the top. Back-and-footing and a traverse to the outer jaws of the fault are required to quit the final dramatic section, which is capped by large chockstones.

When Patey set out to do the route with instructor Dave Holdroyd, they stopped at Jean's Hut at the bottom of Coire Cas for a drink and, for Patey, a smoke. Patey insisted on having a second fag as the wind and heavy snow would make smoking impossible when they crossed the plateau. They climbed the corrie headwall and descended onto the Loch Avon side, where they found welcome shelter at the base of Hell's Lum Crag, but two feet of fresh snow had been deposited over the icy slabs. Patey led the entire route in the gloom, and about two-thirds of the way up, the chimney-fault cornices collapsed, knocking Holdroyd's ice axe from his grasp. Thankfully, the final technical section was sheltered and excellent hard-packed snow facilitated the three-hour ascent. Holdroyd even recovered his axe from the cliff's base later.

An incident towards the end of the month nearly brought Patey's marriage, and indeed his and Betty's lives, to a premature end. High up in Coire Cas, some of the trainees were testing out circular Canadian tents, which had a central pole and could accommodate up to six people. After pitching the tents in the fresh snow, the occupants enjoyed an idyllic evening ski in powder, then cooked their evening meal while Sergeant 'Happy' Jarvis distributed their daily rum ration. During the night, the wind picked up and they were enveloped in a blizzard. The central pole of Holdroyd's tent began to bend at an alarming angle, and as it began to collapse under copious amounts of snow, the group decided to evacuate and relocate to Jean's Hut at the bottom of Coire Cas. In the driving snow and wind, they spotted the faint outline of Jarvis's tent, whose occupants were also preparing to evacuate. Holdroyd's team squeezed in and, despite the limited space, they got the stove going and made a brew. At 2.00am, the Coire Cas headwall avalanched, trapping the ten men inside the collapsed apex of the six-man tent. One man somehow managed to reach his knife and cut a hole in the tent's canvas, enabling them to struggle out of the tent, where they were met with a surreal sight.

Staggering through the storm towards them were two figures: Patey and Betty. Patey had trousers and a sweater on but was barefooted; Betty, shivering violently, was both trouserless and barefooted. She collapsed onto a pile of equipment, and they bundled her into a sleeping bag as Holdroyd warmed her feet. Someone found some socks for Patey. Betty was partly carried, partly dragged to Jean's Hut, where the occupants of the other collapsed tents were now ensconced. Apparently, the Pateys had turned up, unannounced, late in the evening and pitched their two-man tent just below Holdroyd's. Their tent was in the direct path of the avalanche, and they would certainly have perished if Patey had not spotted torch lights and headed towards them. At Jean's Hut, Captain

'Jungle' Baisley, the officer in charge, was shocked by the pandemonium. Worryingly, one team, led by Gordon Sage, was still missing. Jarvis and Holdroyd, with one Dave Middleton, volunteered to search for the missing team at dawn after a snack and a mug of tea. In the relentless storm, their snow goggles were useless, and they had to use snow shovels as shields to protect their faces from the stinging ice particles. Nearing the tent site area in Coire Cas, Holdroyd spotted the apex of a tent poking out of the snow at an angle. As they approached the tent, a man emerged, had a pee, and then nonchalantly disappeared back inside. Peering inside the tent, they found a relaxed Sage brewing tea, oblivious to the fact there had been an avalanche. No other tents were visible, though they were dug out from under several feet of snow a few days later. For their efforts, Holdroyd, Jarvis and Middleton were all awarded the Commandant General's commendation for courage and initiative when they returned to Bickleigh.

The satisfaction of his success on Deep Cut Chimney soon waned when Patey was told of another major new winter route on Lochnagar, Parallel Gully B, which had been climbed in his absence by Edinburgh raiders Jimmy Marshall and Graham Tiso, who had used crampons rather than tricounis on the photogenic chimney section and the ice scoop above. This was Marshall's first major winter contribution in Scotland.

On the day this significant line fell, Patey was somewhat consoled with the news that the rising star of Scottish and British mountaineering, Robin Smith, had failed high on Patey's own winter route, Eagle Ridge. Even Patey had to admit it had been a fine effort, however, as Smith had no prior acquaintance with the route in summer.

During time off, Patey teamed up with his new friend Joe Brown and headed for Meall Gorm on the Applecross peninsula, which Patey claimed was the Scottish equivalent of the roadside cliffs of Tremadoc in North Wales. The base of Blue Pillar, which Patey had climbed with Nicol in May five years earlier, can be reached in 15 minutes from the road, and at Grade V,6, it was the first winter route on the crag.

Patey on the Girdle, Ben Nevis © Jimmy Marshall

Patey found easy pickings in the Northern Corries during that first course in Scotland in 1958. It seems unbelievable that such an obvious line as Fiacaill Couloir in Coire an t-Sneachda had not yet been climbed, but the absence of an access road back then meant that far more effort was required to reach the venue. In Coire an Lochain, he soloed the technical Central Crack Route (IV,5). When training courses were taking place in the corries, it was not unheard of for Patey to disappear for a short while, though still in sight of the main course, and knock off one of these relatively short routes.

After Patey's first ascent of Zero Gully on Ben Nevis, Point Five Gully was in the sights of most leading climbers in Britain. Eventually, the route was sieged by Ian Clough and party shortly before Patey returned at the end of January 1959. Much ethical debate ensued after Clough's ascent, which had involved 29 hours of climbing spread across several days. Patey wryly referred to it as 'the first seven-day climb in the history of British mountaineering'.

The next locus of attention was the great Orion Face, the 'Scottish Nordwand', but Patey was beaten to this by Robin Smith and Dick Holt. On that weekend, Patey travelled to Fort William from Edinburgh with Jimmy Marshall and George Ritchie, pursued by another group of 'Teutonic tigers' from the same city, including a youthful Dougal Haston, Jimmy Stenhouse, Ronnie Marshall and Graham Tiso. Ahead of them was an Aberdeen team comprising Bill Brooker, Mike Taylor, Ronnie Sellars and Jerry Smith.

The following day, Marshall and Patey made the long tramp up Observatory Gully, intending to follow J.H.B Bell's summer girdle by crossing Observatory Buttress, Point Five Gully, Observatory Ridge, Zero Gully and the Orion Face, and finishing beyond North-East Buttress. It was a great voyage amidst dramatic scenery, and required a strong team for all the traversing it entailed. Patey's account in the *Climbers' Club Journal* (1960) is full of the friendly one-upmanship he enjoyed with Marshall: Aberdeen versus Edinburgh, doctor versus architect, tricounis versus crampons. Patey took the lead initially, excavating footsteps large enough to accommodate his nails. On easier ground, Marshall had the advantage of his axe for balance and wound Patey up by reminding him how good crampons were. Patey's steps were almost superfluous for him, and he was so quick to follow that Patey could not take in the rope quickly enough. One-nil to Marshall.

They took a false line near Point Five, but an abseil allowed them to regain the more amenable route. On the final section into Point Five, Patey removed most of the ice on a particularly tenuous passage, leaving Marshall scraping for holds and Patey gleefully heaving him across on the rope. One-all.

The section from the gully en route to Observatory Ridge involved a very exposed narrow section where any heavy-handed axe work would shatter the thin ice required to unlock the problem. Patey saluted Marshall's lead, which was a textbook example of care and precision. At the stance, Marshall directed Patey to the next section—a blank slab—commenting that it looked ideal for tricounis and that Patey was about to enjoy himself. Marshall's face remained as impassive as Patey's looked forlorn. Despite not being especially adept with ropes and equipment, Patey read the situation quickly and suggested an abseil and diagonal tension traverse, which provided an elegant solution. Following, Marshall, 'the apostle of free climbing', took advantage of the fixed rope, and even accepted an extra pull from Patey to reach the stance. Overall score: Patey, by a whisker.

The route continued more easily across the Orion Face, whose scale is of a level rare in Britain. They gratefully used Smith and Holt's footsteps on one section, crossed the North-East Buttress and concluded their five-hour grand tour by finishing up the Coire Leis face.

Patey had the utmost respect for Smith and Holt's achievement and Marshall's outstanding ascents of Minus Two Gully (V,5), and Smith's Gully (VI,5) on Creag Meagaidh the following month. Marshall was approaching his peak, and when he teamed up with Robin Smith in February 1960, they had an almost mythic week on Ben Nevis, establishing a high water mark for the era. Their ascent of the Orion Face

Brooker and Patey on Hadrian's Wall (West Flank Route) © Jimmy Marshall

Direct put Patey et al.'s Zero Gully in the shade, and set a precedent for pure ice climbing. Patey's mixed climbing legacy in the Cairngorms, though similarly monumental, was not as lauded.

While engaged on the Nevis Girdle, Patey and Marshall had noted a shallow gully on the side of Observatory Ridge, and they wondered about incorporating it into a new route. Marshall's photos of their subsequent first ascent of Hadrian's Wall show Patey in spartan clothing: a sweater, no hat or gaiters, laces tied round the top of his boots, and a waist tie-on. At one point, Patey hammered one of Marshall's pegs in so hard that it was irretrievable. To get his own back, Marshall did the same with one of Patey's favourite ice pitons. Since the creation of the Direct version of Hadrian's Wall in 1971, the lower section of West Flank Route that Patey and Marshall followed that day has become obsolete. Today, climbers favour the direct version up an obvious ice smear which is perfect for front pointing and inclined axes. Patey was in favour of attempting the direct line and naming it 0.25 to express its position between Zero and Point Five Gullies, but there was insufficient ice. Bill Brooker, who was with them that day, recorded in his pocket diary:

Feb 1st, 1959, Perfect day ... Did N. Face Observatory Ridge. Hadrian's Wall. 4½ hours w Tom and Jimmy Marshall—magnificent. Grade IV. Wonderful on top. Down by Càrn Mòr Dearg Arête.

Back at work after this productive weekend away, Patey found time to knock off a couple of new routes in his 'office': the Northern Cairngorms. With officer Vivian North Stevenson, he climbed Ewen Buttress and Milky Way in Coire an Lochain, and Kiwi Slabs on Hell's Lum Crag, opening up the crag's slabby face, which, in optimum conditions, becomes sheeted with ice.

Stevenson was the most prominent among a number of strong and sometimes unruly characters in his officer intake. He was awarded the Sword of Honour, reflecting his outstanding physical endurance and mental resourcefulness, and he should have gone far, but his personality got in the way. At his eulogy in 2013, fellow Royal Marine Nick Vaux celebrated Stevenson's 'reputation for confronting certain issues too positively and ... boisterous behaviour off duty ... If there were pints to be drunk, girls to be chased, or brawls to be settled, then Stevo was your man.' On occasion, this uproarious behaviour had attracted the attention of both the civil and military Constabulary, and it did not pass unnoticed within management. Even Stevenson's second wife, Patsy, translated his initials VNS to Very Naughty Stevenson. He and Patey got on extremely well since neither did things exactly by the book and, like Patey, Stevenson wielded a lot of Irish charm. Climbing and socialising together had fostered a strong bond, and both had a work hard, play hard ethic. Despite being a well-educated, well-spoken officer, Stevenson was 'Very much a free spirit like Tom. Very difficult to control. Did as he liked, when he liked' (Blaber, 2014).

That February, Patey also satisfied his goal of soloing a route in each of the Northern Corries in the same day. The first, Patey's Route, climbs the wide chimney line on the left side of Aladdin's Buttress and is a bold solo at IV,5. In Coire an Lochain, he climbed Western Route, for years given the sandbag grade of III, but now realistically upgraded to IV,6. Patey had climbed this in summer in 1954 when conducting research for Mac Smith's guide, using aid to overcome the crux. On these winter ascents, a buildup of adrenaline likely facilitated the crux moves, but both routes are far from straightforward.

Today, the technical grade of 12 is the current limit for top winter climbers, which is six notches above Patey's hardest lines. Yet even the best can still be humbled by them. A local guide, rightly proud of his mountains and the rich climbing history associated with them, once overheard an internationally famous climber, who was on Patey's Route, making loud, derogatory comments about the conditions and Scottish winter climbing in general. In front of his clients, the guide informed the unfortunate celebrity that he was on a route that had been soloed by Tom Patey, at which point the climber fell off the route—not for the first time that day—uninjured but with bruised pride. Unlike many climbers, Patey could solo at the same level he could climb roped and with a partner.

At that time, the Marines were experimenting with short axes, which were much easier to cut steps with on steep ground and in confined spaces. On Patey's instigation, they had Aschenbrenner axes cut down, and they called this customised model 'The Trotsky'. It was difficult to cut steps in descent with this, but they usually carried both a short and a long axe.

The next noteworthy new winter routes were established at Creag Meagaidh during a busy weekend in February 1960. Lying roughly between the Cairngorms and Ben Nevis, Creag Meagaidh holds on to its snow and benefits from the more settled weather of the East and the freeze/thaw cycles of the west. Coire Ardair is 3km long with four distinct sectors. It is a magnificent sight at any time of year, but in winter it holds ice routes to rival the Ben Nevis classics. On the Post Face lie a series of parallel hoses of ice, only two of which had been climbed at that time, and neither by the direct options.

Patey's partner that weekend was John 'Zeke' Deacon, one of the most significant climbers in the history of the Royal Marines. Zeke had joined the Royal Marines in June 1947, the year before National Service became mandatory. He had begun climbing aged 14, when he made an ascent of a local church steeple in Billesden just outside Leicester.

On a training exercise in the Cairngorms before their foray on Creag Meagaidh, Zeke had woken up with flu symptoms, so the commanding officer asked Patey to check him over. After examining him, Patey advised that Zeke should not go out that day. Zeke protested that, actually, he was feeling a bit better, but Patey was adamant that he should remain in his sleeping bag for the rest of that day and, if necessary, the next, while the others patrolled the Lairig Ghru and Braeriach. Zeke was puzzled at Patey's insistence, but it soon became clear what his motive was:

'You're not well, but not only that, I want you on Saturday.'

'What do you mean "on Saturday"?'

'I've got something in mind: North Post.'

The name meant nothing to Zeke, so he stayed in his pit that day, after which he confirmed he was well enough to climb.

A landrover was organised for Saturday, and George Macleod, Patey's Aberdonian friend who had taken the long tumble from Douglas-Gibson Gully, accompanied them. Macleod was working as an instructor at Glenmore Lodge at the time, and from him, Patey had got wind that someone else had designs on North Post.[6]

They soon reached the crux ice section in the Narrows, and Patey suggested Zeke should lead. The ice was brittle and thin, cracking underneath the front points of Zeke's crampons. After a few metres, he voiced his concern and retreated back to the stance with difficulty. Patey took over and led the long main pitch, showering them with bits of ice: 'He just waltzed up there,' recalled Zeke (2014). On the plateau, Patey was elated. But he was mindful that the route had been on others' hit lists, so he began walking round in ever-widening circles, making sure that nobody had been up there already. Reassured by the absence of footprints, they descended to The Laggan Inn, where Patey treated them both to venison and chips and a glass of Glenfiddich whisky to celebrate.

The next day, Patey and Zeke returned to make the first ascent of the South Pipe Direct (IV,4), which is effectively a more direct and harder version of Staghorn Gully, the original finishing up the parallel North Pipe.

In the same month, Patey and Zeke explored and named the Mess of Pottage, the short, slabby buttress on the left side of the entrance to Coire an t-Sneachda. The name suggests they were less than inspired by the terrain, but they climbed two lines, one on the right-hand side left of Jacob's Ladder, and another diagonal fault on the left-hand section. The latter avoided the steeper terrain above and simply continued via a traverse to escape.[7]

At the hut at Glenmore, Patey and Zeke often had to be reminded that breakfast time was finishing, before which they had to be washed and shaved (Blaber, 2014). The pair usually had breakfast in bed, which consisted of a fag and either a dram or brandy in an enamel mug.

Zeke (2014) recalled that Patey was popular with the rest of the men, always very sociable and entertaining with his accordion. But one thing surprised him: '[Despite] being a doctor, he wasn't particularly hygienic.' Maintaining a meticulous appearance was the norm in the service, but not for Patey.

One event from this time, known as 'The Buggering of Brigadier Billy's Boots', has entered the Royal Marines folklore. A high-ranking officer had come up from Plymouth to see how the men were getting on. He was issued with kit to go on the hill, and he left the unbelievably shiny boots he had arrived in at base. Delayed and disorganised as ever, Patey could not find his own boots, so he donned the nearest pair that fitted. Soon, he caught the others up and began kicking steps in the snow. After a pleasant day with the training groups, the visiting dignitary returned to base and changed out of his hill kit but could not find his boots. A protracted search proved fruitless, and eventually Patey pointed to the now scruffy specimens on his own feet and asked if these could be them. One day on Patey's feet had altered them permanently, and the Brigadier retorted, 'No, mine were really shiny', and departed without his boots.

Even if the Brigadier had discovered the truth, it is unlikely that Patey would have been punished. By then, he had considerable status in the Marines thanks to his mountaineering prowess, and the formidable reputation he had entered the service with would soon become unassailable during a forces expedition to the Karakoram.

1   'Gay' is used in in its original sense, meaning 'lighthearted, free from care'.

2   Those who were satisfactorily competent on skis and able to handle the cold went on to the advanced course in Norway at the Home Guard bases in Dombås and Torpo, where Norwegian officers were instructed in advanced skiing and winter warfare alongside the Brits.

3   Patey was not the only unconventional doctor in the Royal Marines. Barrie Biven recalls his intake jogging along the A38 from Lympstone to Bickleigh on a very hot day, wearing combat uniform and carrying their weapons. Upon reaching Bickleigh compound, they were ordered to march into the camp. Most could barely walk in a straight line, and some were hallucinating. They lined up in the sick bay, expecting to undergo a battery of medical tests. When the Doctor entered, he said none of them needed an examination since, if they had run from Lympstone, they must be in a fine physical condition. He then threw a box of condoms on the floor and told them to help themselves, get down to Plymouth and enjoy themselves, if they had any energy left.

4   Karl had been a member of the Austrian Olympic Ski Team, and was one of the first to qualify with a national ski instructor certificate. His and Eileen's commercial foresight led to Aviemore becoming the centre of Scottish skiing. Despite Karl not being fluent in English (he was dubbed a speaker of 'Scotstrian' by the locals), they were a highly respected and popular couple in the community.

5   Grassick made an error here, as Zero had been climbed earlier that year.

6   Swiss guide Pierre Danelet is also credited as being on the ascent but, when he was interviewed in 2014, Zeke had no recollection of a fourth member of the team.

7   Their start had something in common with the lower sections of subsequently established routes, The Message and The Hybrid. The former was put up in 1986 and marked a resurgence in interest in this sector of the crag. Its accessibility, the shortness of the routes and relative lack of seriousness have created a popular zone in an already heavily used corrie.

09

Figures heading towards the Gendarme. The Monk's Face is to its right at a similar altitude. The summit of Rakaposhi is top left © Richard Brooke collection

After You, Mike

It is usually a good thing for an expedition to have a 'character'. We had Tom Patey.

Mike Banks, *Rakaposhi*

Described by Eric Shipton (1951) as 'the ultimate manifestation of mountain grandeur', Rakaposhi lies in the centre of the Hunza Valley in the Karakoram and dominates the skyline from Aliabad to the north and Gilgit to the south. It spans 20km from east to west and has an uninterrupted drop of 6,000m from summit to base, fully reflecting its translation from the Burushaski language as the 'Shining Wall'.

The peak deflects would-be conquerors by dint of its height (7,788m), its sprawling topography, arduous snow conditions and frequent avalanches. There had been several notable but failed expeditions before 1958. In his SMCJ article, 'Rakaposhi—The Taming of the Shrew' (1959), Patey alludes to the Shakespeare play in which one of the central characters, Katherina—a scolding, bad-tempered woman—is finally tricked and tormented into obedience by her husband, Petruchio. Patey had used an apt metaphor.

In 1947, R. Campbell Secord returned to Rakaposhi after having failed on the North-West Ridge nine years earlier, this time attempting the South-West Spur. With him were the renowned British explorer and climber H.W. Tilman and two Swiss climbers, Hans Gyr and Robert Kappeler. Tilman climbed a huge, imposing blade of snow known as the Gendarme, but became disheartened when he realised it was relatively low down on the route, and that a bigger obstacle lay ahead: the 600m ice face of the Monk's Head. The stoical Tilman was heard to utter, 'Hopeless, hopeless!'

In 1954, George Band, a member of the successful British expedition to Everest, was part of a six-man Cambridge University team attempt led by Alfred Tissieres. They succeeded in scaling the Gendarme then advanced beyond Tilman's high point to ascend the Monk's Face.

In his book, *Road to Rakaposhi* (1955), Band was forthright in his assessment of the Monk's Face: 'In the Alps it would have seemed a serious problem. Had anything like it been tackled in the Himalayas before?'

Although the angle eased after this and the route to the summit was eminently feasible, the team lacked the impetus to progress further.

When Mike Banks's planned expedition to the Muztagh Tower fell through, he had turned his attention to Rakaposhi, which was not only fairly accessible but had been written about extensively. But Banks's first expedition to the mountain in 1956 had only four members, and even with the assistance of porters on the lower section, it was not clear that this would be enough for such a long and arduous route. Although the same sized team had succeeded on the Muztagh Tower that year, its challenges were of an altogether different nature.

Banks did, however, have one member on board who could rival Patey as the strongest all-round mountaineer in Scotland at the time. Hamish MacInnes, then living in New Zealand, was involved in much of the initial planning and recruiting of members. Californians Bob Swift and Dick Irvin completed the quartet.

After many vicissitudes, another heroic attempt ended in failure, but they had now reached a high point 500m short of the summit. Banks had learned two important things from this attempt: he needed more climbers on the mountain, and the top camp had to be established closer to the summit.

Patey had been in the Marines less than a year when he was offered the sweetener of joining Banks on the 1958 British-Pakistani Forces Himalayan Expedition to Rakaposhi. A free trip at the expense of the military was an opportunity almost too good to be true, and participation counted as part of his duties without eating into any holiday leave.

This time, the climbing team was increased from four to ten. With

Banks and Patey was another Marine representative, Dicky Grant, a captain and commando climbing instructor with experience in the Alps, Norway and Canada, who took on the role of expedition treasurer. Completing the Navy contingent was Richard Brooke, a Lieutenant-Commander and one of Banks's closest mountaineering friends. Brooke and Banks had established a lifelong bond during an early British ascent of Route Major on Mont Blanc in 1951.

In charge of the expedition's food was Captain Jimmy Mills of the Royal Army Service Corps, another trusted confidant of Banks. Responsibility for equipment fell to Army Captain Warwick Deacock from the Middlesex Regiment. Completing the British officers was John Sims, a Flight Lieutenant in the RAF. His technical flair was called upon when stoves and cameras were malfunctioning.

Despite the depth and breadth of skills and experience of the personnel, Banks was unequivocal in describing Patey as the 'character' of the team. Although his observations about Patey were given in hindsight, they are perceptive and convey Banks's deep affection and gratitude for a man who had contributed to the success of the expedition and the realisation of his personal goal:

> *Tom is many things; certainly the most gloriously untidy man I have ever camped with: allergic to cooking, but not to eating; a lover and maker of all music: Bach, grand opera, blues; a human dynamo, who somehow contrived to look unhealthy. All of which would combine to make him a very unliveable-with person were it not for his delightful sense of humour. In Tom there is a streak of pure eccentricity, for although he is a most striking person, he does nothing for effect, and is, I am sure, quite oblivious of his impact on people. His energy was, by our standards, superhuman and apparently little affected by altitude. After a gruelling day, he would have a cup of sweet tea and then, while we lay exhausted on our air-beds, would kick snow steps up the next section of mountainside to make our task easier next morning ... We were amused to hear one of the Pakistani members, early in the*

expedition, remark to Tom: 'I shouldn't go above base camp if I were you, doctor; you don't look too strong!' So, despite the fact that the medical kit was strewn between six camps, and one was quite likely to discover the penicillin in a ration box, Tom with his accordion, his humour and his unbounded and trustful energy, his kit always overflowing from his rucksack, was a powerful asset. He was, of course, a Scot—a race very dissimilar to the English. (1959)

The most important of the three Pakistani members, Captain Mohammad Shah Khan of the Northern Scouts, had considerable mountaineering and expedition experience. He had selected six local porters from Hunza whom he knew personally to carry out the high-altitude work. Captain Raja Mohammad Aslam and surveyor Sahib Shah

En route to Rakaposhi, the pinnacle of the expedition's panache.
From Left: Brooke, Mills, Patey, Grant, Banks, Aslam © Ian Patey collection

completed the team.

The mountain showed its mettle early on when Patey and Brooke were caught in a windslab avalanche above Camp I and were forced to retreat gingerly. Fresh snowfalls were an obvious warning for the team, but avalanches were sometimes difficult to predict, and on the day the windslab had given way, Patey was on the firmest snow of the expedition so far. Soon after, a powder avalanche provided a quicker-than-anticipated descent from Camp I for Aslam, Khan and a group of porters. The shrew was testy.

At least Base Camp was now a more sociable place than it had been two years earlier, with entertainment provided by Patey on the accordion and Grant on improvised percussion, lubricated by a crate of whisky, which had proved too tempting to save for the hoped-for summit success. While Patey treated Aslam's malaria at Base Camp, Sims established the route over the Gendarme in waist-deep powder.

Downplaying the Monk's Head, Patey compared it to his first British

Mike Banks enjoying the daily Navy tradition at Base Camp © Ian Patey collection

ascent of the North Face of the Aiguille du Plan with Freddie Malcolm in 1955. The latter was considered TD at the time, and in the Himalaya this was a challenging grade. When it was fixed with ropes, there were 13 climbers and porters on the face at one point—Banks was determined not to skimp on manpower this time.

But progress was always marred by more snowfall, which required the steps on steep sections to be re-established. Above the Monk's Head, they moved Camp IV further across the plateau, from where they could attack the first of three steps higher up.

On the first trek to the new camp, they transported the tents and sleeping bags. On the second, Banks, who was 50m behind Sim, found the latter's footsteps completely concealed by the time he had covered the distance, and in retrospect, he observed that they had committed a cardinal sin by allowing themselves to become separated from their camping equipment. Although Patey did not take any credit for locating the tents in the ensuing white-out, Banks (ibid.) was unequivocal about his contribution:

> *Tom took the lead, working on a hunch, and like a dog on the scent, he plunged unhesitatingly ahead. He must have a highly developed sense of direction because he led us unerringly to the little tent, which would have been so easy to miss in that almost non-existent visibility.*

All those days navigating in the Cairngorms without a compass had attuned Patey's awareness of topography and enabled him to develop a reliable spatial memory map.

Banks chose Patey to accompany him on the summit bid, supported by Grant and Brooke, since all had performed consistently well on the expedition so far. They erected two tents at Camp V as Mills, Deacock and Sims assisted in the ferrying of gear and Patey kicked steps up the slopes they would tackle initially.

The following day dawned clear and sharp but with a chilling wind. Between them, they carried a two-man tent, stove, fuel and enough food for six days to Camp VI at 7,300m. Reaching the camp at 1.00pm, Patey and Grant were tempted to go for the summit there and then. Banks, however, was more cautious and, having got this far, did not want to waste energy on a potentially fruitless effort. At this altitude, distances are deceptive, and it would be nothing less than exhausting.

Squeezing four men into a two-man tent at that height would be uncomfortable and would not allow them vital rest, so Grant and Brooke descended to Camp V with the chance of returning the following day and perhaps pushing on to the summit. During the night, the wind rose dramatically and, despite taking three sleeping pills, Banks remained awake for much of it.

The weather was still hostile in the morning, and the tent, collapsing in the blizzard, now had a snapped guy line. Yet when Banks stuck his head out of the tent during a brief lull in the storm, he glimpsed the summit clear against a cloudless sky. Banks lied, saying he had sledged in similar weather in Greenland, to which Patey replied, no doubt truthfully, that he had climbed in comparable blizzards in the Highlands. Wearing every scrap of clothing, 'hermetically sealed and as bulky as the Michelin Man' (ibid.), they made their summit bid.

Although it stopped snowing, they had to fight through plumes of spindrift whipped up by the ferocious wind. Patey was out in front, 'his typical position for the whole expedition', but his hands were becoming worryingly cold, and, behind his goggles, his face looked haggard. They deliberately avoided donning crampons, concerned that the straps would restrict their circulation. Banks's feet were freezing, but he reckoned losing a toe or two was a fair sacrifice for reaching the summit. Despite their suffering, they battled on doggedly, fuelled by rum fudge and glucose tablets. The orange tent was now barely visible, and with their footprints rapidly disappearing, they knew they would never relocate it if the cloud rolled in once more, and would undoubtedly perish.

Their spirits rose as they emerged onto the final ridge, which curled round to a nearby summit. Banks described the scene:

Patey just below the summit © Mike Banks

With the rocks covered with grey-white snow crystals, and with the hard corrugated snow, the scene was quite Highland; we might have been on Ben Nevis in February.

With only a couple of hundred metres to go, Banks asked Patey for an amphetamine, fully aware of the risks and benefits of taking one. Patey gave him a Dexedrine tablet:

In due course, it provided a supply of energy and I felt my legs become stronger, the slope less steep and the summit nearer. I was careful to delay taking the Dexedrine until the top was really in the bag, for while I consider it usually safe to take these drugs to help the descent, they are potentially dangerous on the ascent when they can easily reduce a man's natural reserve of strength to a perilously low level and induce premature exhaustion. Or, more simply, they enable a man to take more out of himself than is safe.

When Banks peered down the mighty north face to the fields of Hunza almost 6,000m below, he knew they must be close. Just below the top, after five hours of desperate toil, they stopped.

'After you, Tom.'

'No, after you, Mike!'

Patey, displaying the same generosity he had shown Hartog on the Muztagh Tower two years earlier, allowed his leader to reach the summit first.

As Banks laboured up the final steps, Patey created a world record for high-altitude graffiti by scratching the initials of the expedition on a rock. Taking turns to perch on the small summit, Banks was engulfed by relief and wonderment:

> *Storm-lashed though I was, this was a moment of attainment and achievement when my whole heart's desire was just to be there, crouched on the little rock platform with the orchestra of the blizzard loud in my ears.*

Patey's recollection was somewhat less romantic:

> *Ten minutes were sufficient to snatch a few random snapshots and bestow our curses on the landscape; ten minutes of shivering misery as a climax to a year's preparations and six weeks of physical drudgery!*

For Banks (1959), 'The summit of a mountain, particularly a Himalayan giant, is an overwhelmingly emotional place', but, as an officer and a gentleman, he knew it was not the British way to indulge in displays of sentiment. After his and Patey's remarkable achievement, Banks could not even shake hands with his climbing partner due to the state of Patey's fingers.

To make matters worse, as Patey tried to upright the stone he had graffitied, he dropped it onto his hand. Blood seeped through his inner woollen mitts into his down-filled outer ones, which were too tight

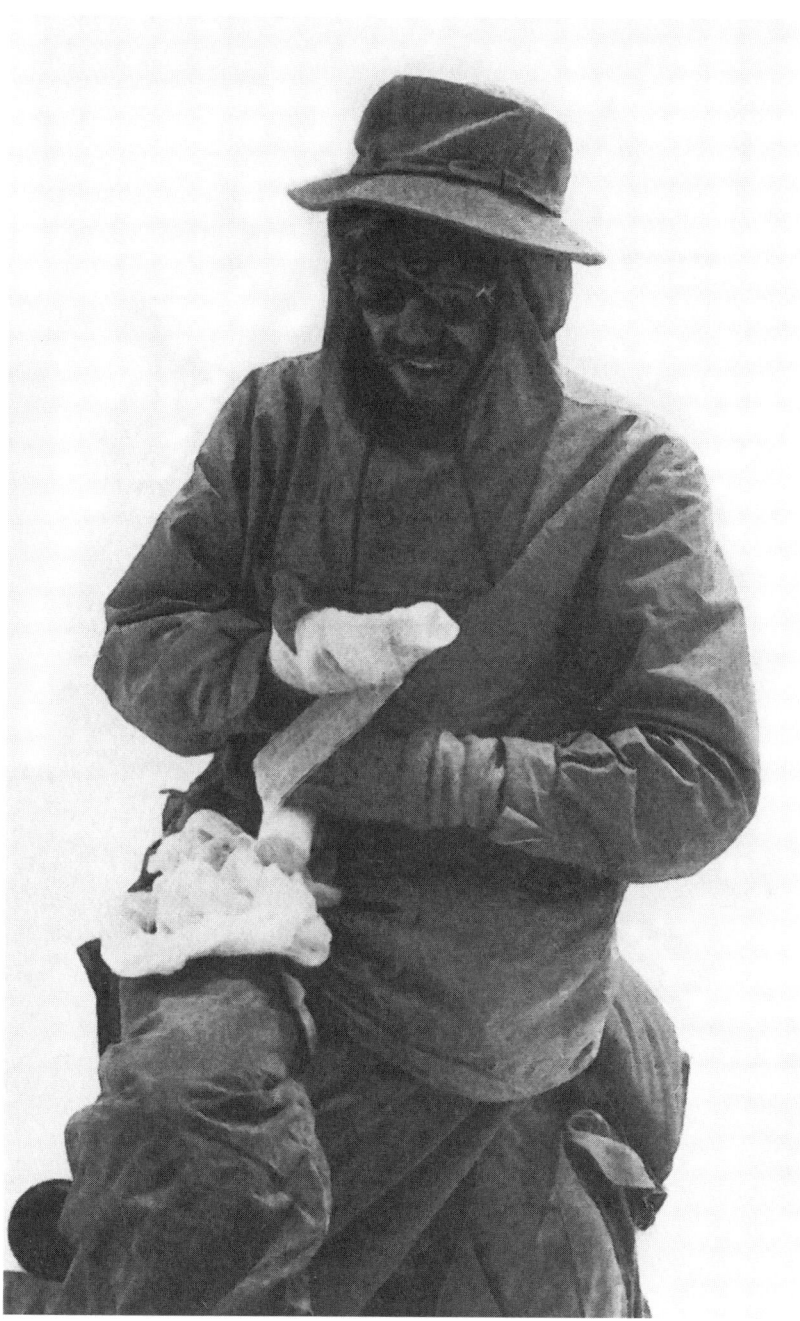
Patey bandaging his frostbitten hand during the descent © Mike Banks

and had left three of his fingers with no sensation. Banks swapped Patey's down mitts for his fur-backed leather gauntlets, one of which was promptly snatched away in a gust of wind. Luckily, he had a spare pair of woollen ones.

As is often the case on a big mountain, reaching the summit is only half the battle and sometimes the crux lies ahead. Patey was eager to descend as quickly as possible due to his frostbite, and Banks had now lost the feeling in his big toes, so they eventually unroped and continued independently to the top camp. The Dexedrine had now worn off, and Banks found the last 100m or so to the camp a real trial. He walked ten paces, half-collapsed over his axe, popped a glucose tablet and repeated this until he reached the partially-buried tent, whose front poles had snapped in their absence. Patey, whose right-hand fingers were bloodless down to the second joint, was careful not to touch the cold primus stove as they sought to rehydrate. Having taken two Priscol tablets, which drives blood to the extremities but also lowers general body temperature, he shook violently as he crept into his sleeping bag. Banks's toes were black at the tips, but he considered himself to be better off than his partner. They consumed several pints of tea and a meagre biscuit before enduring a sleepless, miserable, storm-driven night, made worse by having to share a single air bed after Patey's deflated.

They were delayed the next morning by the continuing tempest. Banks felt exhausted before they even set off, but another night in the tent was unthinkable.

They knew it was essential to exit the snow plateau at the point where a rib of rock offered a guide. Yet again, Patey located the precise spot. The following section, at the foot of the rocks, had no landmarks, and they had to descend a snowfield and vague snow ridge, traverse an expanse peppered with hidden crevasses, drop down a final short, steep slope and cross a wide slot to reach Camp V.

At one point, Patey, who was still out in front, half fell into a crevasse. By now, they were lost and becoming desperate, and spending a night in a crevasse looked like their only option for shelter. 'I remember collapsing in the snow, at the end of my tether. Tom got me to my feet,' recalled Banks (1987). Miraculously, the wind dropped, and suddenly all they needed for a reappraisal was briefly revealed. Patey's instinctive route-finding had saved the day for a third time on the expedition: they were very close to the bump at the top of the final steep slope, a crucial passage between vertical ice cliffs. On reaching the flattened tent, they discovered a note from Brooke informing them they had descended to Camp IV.

Normally, Patey and Banks would have re-erected the tent and spent the night there, but Patey was becoming increasingly concerned about his fingers and wanted to reach the lower camp, which had medical supplies, including Heparin, an anticoagulant. Banks doubted he could go much further, but at Patey's suggestion he took another Dexedrine and managed to continue. Following beautifully crafted steps, which Banks recognised as the work of Brooke, they hailed their companions just above Camp IV. Banks had to be assisted down the final section into the camp.

The priority was treating Patey's fingers, which now looked like drumsticks, three of them potential candidates for partial amputation.

'That would ruin your chances as a surgeon, wouldn't it?' said Banks sympathetically.

'I suppose so, but I was worrying about not being able to play my accordion!' came the reply.

After cleaning his hands, Patey, displaying no sign of being in pain, punctured and drained the blisters with sterile needles, surgical spirit, a hypodermic syringe and cotton wool. By candlelight, he eventually located a vein in his arm, and an intravenous injection of Heparin helped diffuse blood to his bruised, frostbitten digits. Both Banks and Patey took more Priscol, as their feet had been badly constricted in crampons during the descent from the top camp. With little food at Camp IV and the support climbers exhausted, no second summit attempt was launched.

Descent of the snow-covered ice on the Monk's Head would have been perilous had it not been for the fixed ropes. On the final day, they descended all the way from Camp IV to Base Camp, guiding and roping the Hunza porters down sections of insecure, soft snow where the fixed ropes had been removed. At Base Camp, poles had been used to construct a triumphal arch decorated with the British and Pakistani flags, coloured paper, balloons and the words 'WELL DONE — BRAVO'. Banks was touched when, in Pakistani tradition, Raja placed a garland of fragrant mountain flowers around his neck.

They evacuated the mountain at a leisurely pace, with Jagloti porters and donkeys transporting the kit. At the village of Darbar, Patey attended to some unwell locals, but when word got round of free pills being dispensed, the queue of villagers multiplied, with melodramatic clutching of heads and stomachs. One porter, however, was found to have a tumour the size of a grapefruit on his spine. Patey diagnosed it as a symptom of TB, which had crumbled the man's vertebrae. It was a terminal diagnosis, but it had not stopped him from carrying 100lb loads.

The climbing team back at Base Camp minus Warwick Deacock. Back from left: Shah, Grant, Aslam. Front from left: Brooke, Mills, Banks, Khan, Patey, Sim
© Ian Patey collection

Patey and Banks © Ian Patey collection

Since then, Rakaposhi has seen remarkably few ascents, despite its scale and the number of potential new lines. The shrew remains as irascible as ever.

After their success on the mountain, Patey returned to his regular duties with 42 Commando and the Cliff Assault Wing. His key roles in the triumphs of both the Muztagh Tower and Rakaposhi expeditions and his strong performance at altitude meant he would have been an automatic choice on any subsequent British expeditions to the Greater Ranges, but due to his job, family responsibilities, the costs involved and perhaps his diminished desire for that kind of mountaineering experience, these were his only such trips.

At the SMC annual dinner in December 1959, Patey gave an illustrated talk about the Rakaposhi expedition. One unnamed person is recorded as saying:

> *Tom really regarded this expedition as altogether different [from] and much less enjoyable than his previous Himalayan success on the Muztagh Tower, recounted at a Reception three years ago. They were, in fact, lucky to get away with it in the prevailing conditions of avalanchy snow.* (SMCJ, 1960)

Richard Brooke was the only expedition member Patey climbed with in any significant way again, and on Creag Meagaidh and Skye in March 1962, their reconnaissance climbs paved the way later for two of Patey's greatest routes: The Crab Crawl and the Cuillin Ridge in winter.

In 1959, Mike Banks was awarded the MBE, and he would go on to lead a successful all-British attempt on Mount McKinley in 1962. Later in life, Banks (1987) was always generous in his recognition of Patey's involvement in their Himalayan success:

> *Up to that time, I do not think any major Himalayan summit had been climbed in such atrocious weather. For the statistically minded, Rakaposhi was then the sixth-highest mountain in the world to be climbed without oxygen. But this story is not about dull figures. Tom Patey was the sole architect of our success. I could sense his power rising above the blizzard. On the descent, when I was all but finished, he pulled me through. What an experience, what a privilege it was, just to take a free ride in his slipstream.*

Nothing stops the music. Patey back at Base Camp © Mike Banks

10

No Ordinary Skier

Patey on a ski tow while training with the Royal Marines in Norway
© Ian Patey collection

Although the peaks are only 2,000m high, retreat down a route can be long and serious.

Tony Howard, *Walks and Climbs in the Romsdal Valley*

In March 1959, Patey attended his first series of Royal Marines Norwegian courses. These were based at Dombås in the Dovre region, near the dramatic cirque of Snøhetta, the highest Scandinavian summit outside the Jotunheimen.

In 'With Arne Randers Heen on the Romsdalhorn' (1960), Patey sets the scene by admitting his relative ineptitude as a skier. Turning efficiently on skis was something he could not master, and his strategy for achieving the standard for the 10km race was to fall over at each bend, rather than overshoot. In the end, he only just managed to get round the course within the allotted 65 minutes.

Unlike the Scottish courses, it was compulsory for Patey to undertake all the training in snow warfare with the other Marines. Determined to pass the mandatory Norwegian Ski Federation Bronze medal, he planed off all the wax and varnish from his skis before the start of the sprint event, then stood on them so that the planks were clogged up with damp snow. In effect, this created two giant snowshoes, and he ran, rather than skied the course, using his poles to maintain balance on the uphill sections; on the downhill sections, he sat on the poles and glissaded. Despite these unconventional techniques, Patey's superb level of fitness and determination enabled him to complete the course.

These experiences were the inspiration for two unpublished songs about the perils of the activity. 'Ski Patrol Toboggan' gruesomely describes the aftermath of a ski accident:

There was blood upon the bindings
There was brain upon the skis
Intestines were hanging
From the highest of the trees ...

The macabre theme is repeated in 'Skier's Requiem':

Around the curve he lost his nerve
As a tree loomed up ahead,
He was found in Spring when the birdies sing
Both he and the tree were dead.

Pursuing the local women was mischievously referred to as 'she-ing', but the competition in Dombås was fierce so, seeking new pastures and interesting mountaineering objectives during some leave, Patey and the Gay Lothario, Sam Bemrose, headed over to the spectacular Romsdal Valley. They were joined by Henry Berg, a Norwegian ski instructor who lived in Åndalsnes.

From his house, Berg had a tremendous view of the Romsdalhorn, a tapering rock spire with an abrupt flat top and one of Norway's iconic peaks. On the western side of the valley lies the Trolltinder, a continuous ridge of peaks forming an 8km barrier. At its southern end are three great pillars, and beyond the northernmost pillar, above a huge scree-filled corrie, lies the 1,100m Trollveggen or Troll Wall. The highest vertical rock face in Europe, the summit rim overhangs the base by 50m.[1]

On their first day in the valley, the trio made a winter ascent of Store Vengetind, considered one of the most beautiful and shapely peaks in Romsdal. After struggling on the ski approach, Patey was determined to redeem himself on the climbing sections by staying ahead of Berg.

That evening, they visited Arne Randers Heen, the most celebrated mountaineer in Norway. Heen was a tailor in Åndalsnes and an avid collector and curator of mountaineering memorabilia. During the war, he had been a leader in the local resistance movement and had narrowly escaped death at the hands of the occupying Nazis. Heen made most of the significant early first ascents in the area and became known as King of the Romsdalhorn on account of his 233 ascents of that mountain between 1928 and 1985, including the first winter ascent. He was a dynamic personality who had learned four languages, mainly so that he could read world mountaineering literature, and he could burn the midnight oil on the subject of climbing.

When Patey visited Heen, he suggested climbing his favourite mountain. At 5.00am, four hours after consuming the last of the alcohol, they set off for the peak, minus Bemrose, who had dropped out.

En route, they picked up a young tiger, whom the maestro had nicknamed 'The Pupil' and who was to lead them up the route with Heen as the middle man. Patey was unnerved by the style of ascent—The Pupil climbed so quickly that Heen did not have time to belay either him or Patey properly. They were essentially moving together on ground which Patey observed was: 'No worse than Observatory Ridge in foul conditions, but I thought it merited a token respect' (ibid.). Modern climbers would likely be horrified to move together on the lower section of that Ben Nevis classic, even in good conditions, and it is one of the few occasions where Patey's sangfroid was sorely tested. Then, as they were climbing in parallel, sloppy ropework resulted in a spare coil looping around Heen's neck and threatening to strangle him. The only thing the rope seemed to be ensuring was that if one fell, they all would. 'Perhaps it would be safer without the rope,' suggested Patey, which received roars of laughter. As the guest, he felt obliged to grin and bear it, and pray that no one slipped.

Patey found himself in the middle at one point and was nearly torn apart by his partners' ropes pulling in opposite directions. He began to wonder how Heen had managed to survive to such a ripe old age.

There were bolts and fixed ropes already in place on the final difficulty, but The Pupil neglected to use them, perhaps as much a sign of his lack of concern for the party as his climbing ability. Eventually, a relieved Patey arrived at the top, having completed the first non-Norwegian

Patey and his accordion were inseparable. Part of the peak of Snøhetta to the right © Ian Patey collection

winter ascent of the Romsdalhorn, the eighth in total that season.

Proudly pointing out the summit hut and Alpine garden that he had built, Heen was quick to remind Patey that he had been on the other seven too.

Although Heen was a contender for mountaineer with the biggest ego in Patey's poems and articles, Patey, conscious of the man's popularity and reluctant to burn bridges, remained tactful in his descriptions of him while deftly alluding to the great man's self-importance and awareness of his position in Norwegian—and indeed world—mountaineering. Intending to return to Norway after leaving the Marines, he knew that Heen would remain a valuable contact.

On their second spell of leave, Patey and Berg headed for the nearby peak of Snøhetta. Its cirque resembles a grander Lochnagar with steeper rock walls, and they established a new route up the Peder Langdals Top via a couloir between this and the Vest-toppen. On iced rock it was far from straightforward, and Patey graded it Severe. A complete traverse over all the summits in winter remained a major prize, but one which he was not to realise. After these two trips, Patey considered Åndalsnes the finest centre for mountaineering north of Chamonix, especially in winter (SMCJ, 1960).

Patey was respected as a doctor in Norway during this time, and on one occasion, he quickly diagnosed a brain haemorrhage when one of the students complained of a terrible headache. The student's swift evacuation from Snøhetta on a Weasel track vehicle minimised the long-term damage.

Despite his professional standing, however, Patey's dress standards had not improved. When the training courses finished, the Royal Marines contingent would take the return train from Dombås to Oslo, then sail to Newcastle. Although clad in his naval uniform, Patey somehow still managed to look scruffy, and a fellow Marine once remarked: 'Christ, Tom, have you seen the state you're in. You're a Royal Naval officer.' So Patey undid his tie, removed his detachable collar, turned it inside out and put it back on. Although it was admittedly 'whiter', the stitching was now visible (Blaber, 2014).

On another occasion, Bemrose awoke in the room he shared with Patey and could not find his uniform, which should have been on the chair between his and Patey's bunks. Glancing at Patey's grey string vest and other dirty attire lying around, Bemrose asked where his own stuff was. Patey had donned Bemrose's clothes by mistake but would not admit that the grubby items were his. In the end, Bemrose issued a test of identity:

'Mine has a field dressing in a pocket.'
'So has mine.'
'And a couple of morphine capsules.'
'So has mine.'
'But I've got £35 in a pocket.'
'So it has; it must be yours.'

The following March, Patey returned with Bemrose and Vivian Stevenson to find that Heen had breached Trolltinder Wall via two new routes, including the East Pillar of Trollryggen with young hotshot, Per Oybakk, from Oslo. Three decades earlier, Heen had established the Fiva Route with his cousin, Erik Heen. When Patey met up with Heen again, the great man could barely contain his glee that one of his rivals, Arne Næss, had failed on the East Pillar, and that a cow had raided Næss's tent in his absence.

When he had been on the Romsdalhorn the previous Easter, Patey had mused about making a winter ascent of Fiva Route and beating the mighty Heen to a notable first in his back yard. Finishing just below the highest point of the whole wall, Store Trolltind, the 1,600m route follows the longest couloir in Europe.

Seeking leave for the attempt, Patey explained to his Norwegian commandant that the expanse of cliff looked like an ideal place for practising advanced snow warfare, but that he would first have to investigate its potential. Armed with binoculars on a reconnaissance mission, he arrived at the sobering realisation that the route, far from being a continuous snow plod with all summer difficulties banked out,

Henry Berg leading Sam Bemrose on the Fiva Route © Vivian Stevenson

contained several steep ice sections, including a hanging glacier at half height. Beyond that lay a further 650m with an ominous dearth of snow just below the rim. Failure at such a high point would entail a descent of over 1,500m. After consulting Heen about the impassable-looking final section, Patey was heartened to learn of a large hole which the guru implied offered a subterranean passage to salvation by avoiding the difficulties in the main line of the couloir.

Henry Berg was 'a nice man, very straight—as so many Norwegians are' (Bemrose, 2014). He had never climbed on the Trolltinder and had had no intention of doing so, but being the local representative, felt obliged—after several whiskies—to accompany them. This now meant they could tackle the route in two pairs: Patey with Stevenson; Bemrose with Berg.

The initial slabs were not without difficulty, but good-quality snow in a runnel hastened proceedings until they encountered a wall of hard water-ice, whose passage proved time-consuming. This led to the base of the main couloir.

Patey had obtained twelve-point crampons in Oslo, but they had no bindings or straps, and the spikes would not stay on his boots. Berg gave him some ill-fitting nailed boots which were missing crucial tacks on the sole but would have to do. It must have seemed like a return to the early Cairngorm days for Patey, except that with these on, he had to cut steps even on easy-angled ground, which he insisted on doing ahead of the others. Despite the arduousness of this approach, they made excellent initial progress, and after three hours, they were a third of the way up the face.

Heen's summer description of the complex route proved of little help, but an empty beer bottle in a cave confirmed they must be on the right line. Mixed climbing up a 30m corner, a snow arête, then an abseil into a gully led to an enclosed cirque where they had their only stop of the day to consume some glucose tablets. The hanging glacier was accessed by a channel of 60° snow ice. The snow had partially detached from the rock and they had to thrutch upwards inside the cleft. Just before the top of this, Patey spotted an ice cave, which he identified as an ideal spot for a bivouac.

Rock walls overhung the glacier's apex, and the only exit was via a left-hand corner, where a narrow groove marked the start of the final 650m upper gully. Their progress had slowed significantly, and by 2.00pm they were only a little over halfway up the face. The summer route avoided the boulder-choked gully and followed the buttress on the left. However, this was sheathed in ice and, as spindrift rained down on them, their only hope was that hard snow banked out most of the impending chockstone pitches.

In 'The Trolls were Angry' (*Etchachan Club Journal*, 1960), Patey's usual stream of humorous quips about the worrying nature of the situation are noticeable by their absence. After nine hours of effort with only a ten-minute break, Patey was unusually open about the seriousness of their plight, which worsened with height and the dwindling daylight. Tension built as the quartet realised that they were now so far up the route that a failure to complete it would necessitate a night out on the face, 'a harrowing prospect without any bivouac gear' (ibid.).

After a tussle with a chockstone, the gully opened out encouragingly a couple of hundred metres from the top. Stress had frayed the nerves of the normally upbeat Stevenson, who shouted impatiently: 'What does it look like up there?' He had been asking the same question for at least an hour. The true gully was choked by a band of icicles, forcing them onto a vast, exposed 65° snowfield with a vertiginous drop to the valley floor.

Above this, a spur of rock that Patey had spotted the day before interrupted the snow ice in the final section. Remembering the big hole that Heen had described as the exit route, they had to make a crucial decision as there was not enough daylight to try both sides of the spur. In the end, perhaps assuming Berg had some local knowledge of a recent summer ascent, they ceded to his suggestion that they try the left-hand option.

The belays were decidedly inadequate as Patey tackled a difficult rock step, and a fall would have taken the whole team down with him. They were now 'beginning to climb with more desperation than hope' (ibid.). Two long pitches confirmed Patey's worst fears when he was

Patey on the lower slabs of the Fiva Route with the Troll Wall behind
© Vivian Stevenson

confronted with a 40m overhanging chimney with iced-up cracks which were useless for pitons, no escape hole and no decent belay from which to launch. Berg wanted to force the route, but the other three formed a majority for retreat. It was now imperative to find a bivouac site for the night—their clothing was already beginning to freeze.

Patey abandoned his spare axe for a belay and they abseiled to the rock spur, then moved together across the steep snowfield. In a rare moment of lyricism, he described 'the crimson glow tipping the Romsdalshorn' (ibid.). The steps he had cut previously saved precious time. Halfway down the gully, Patey hammered in a piton to abseil down the chockstone pitch. As a precaution, he slid down the pitch on his stomach with one hand on his axe, ready to brake if the peg pinged out. An unamused Stevenson later pulled it out by hand. 'Put it back in and stop shouting,' Patey replied.

Only now did Patey allow a kind of black humour to re-emerge, cheekily referring to Bemrose's excellent night vision as a result of his usual nocturnal activity of 'she-ing'.

They had no head torches but it was more open on the hanging glacier and the light was better. Continuing meant the descent would be shorter in the morning, and at midnight they reached the cave Patey had spied on the way up. With somewhere safe to spend the night, Patey ratcheted up the humour as they sat on their ropes, exhausted, and shivered the hours away.

Patey had worked harder than anybody else, and he had been more adept than the three with crampons on the technical mixed climbing sections. 'Tom was incredibly tired because he was cutting steps all day … literally all day … leading the whole time. He didn't want anybody else to lead, I don't know why' (Bemrose, 2014).

There was still almost 700m to descend the following morning. At noon, after 29 hours, 22 of which had been spent climbing, they reached the valley floor, shattered. Berg had mild frostbite. Royal Marines are indeed a tough breed.[2]

That evening, the team booked into accommodation linked to the local hospital. Bemrose awoke later to hear a seemingly rejuvenated Patey cavorting with one of the local females. Although Patey 'wasn't a big womaniser, he took his chance whenever he could, like everybody else' (ibid.). Even the quintessential party animal Stevenson could not compete with this.

Patey, Bemrose and Stevenson succeeded on other climbs in Romsdal during this period, including the traverse of Kongen and Bispen and the first winter ascent of the East Ridge of Bispen. Patey was impressed by the steepness and exposure on Bispen, a 350m rock route he graded Severe, and he claimed it was as good as any in the Chamonix Aiguilles. A vicious bout of food poisoning curtailed further climbing activity.[3]

Ultimately, though, his most significant outing as a marine in Norway was the failed attempt of the Fiva Route, when his contribution during the ascent and, crucially, his safe execution of the descent epitomised his exceptional stamina and fortitude.

1   Troll Wall would have to wait until 1965 to see the first ascent by a British team led by Tony Howard.

2   The first winter ascent of the Fiva Route was not made until February 1972, when a Polish team took four days to complete it. The route was the subject of a whole book by Gordon Stainforth which was published in 2012. In *Fiva: An Adventure That Went Wrong*, Stainforth describes the epic he and his twin brother John, aged 19, had on the route in the Summer of 1969.

3   Patey sent a summary of his Norwegian activities to the Editor of the *SMCJ*, Geoff Dutton, who was a writer and poet in his own right. Dutton's wit would often raise material above the level of mere information and made the whole journal under his tenure an entertaining and illuminating read. Dutton edited all Patey's later *SMCJ* pieces, which were often 'chaotic and barely legible … hilarious and uncomplicated prose, but requiring much putting in order, often … carrying a plea such as, "do what you can with this!"' (Dutton in Cruikshank, 2006). When he read the edit of 'The Old Man of Stoer', Patey gratefully told Dutton that it was: '… so excellent in fact that I quite enjoyed re-reading the article!' (Dutton in *SMCJ*, 1990).

11

An Admiral and a Christian

Patey on the first ascent
of Ultramontane (HVS)
at Morwell Rocks
© Vivian Stevenson

From 1957 to 1961, the most prominent climbers in Devon were nearly all servicemen ... the most prolific was Tom Patey.

Robert Moulton, *Rock Climbing in Devonshire*

The south-west of England was hardly a convenient place for Patey to pursue the kind of mountaineering he favoured, but when he was not attending Scottish and Norwegian winter courses, he satisfied his thirst for exploration and new routes on the local outcrops near Bickleigh. The most convenient of these is the Dewerstone, a crag long popular with the local Marines.

National Service marine Barrie Biven climbed the classics Central Groove and Climbers' Club Direct at this crag with Patey in late 1957, shortly after the Scot joined the service.[1] Noting that Patey's style was the antithesis of poise and nimble footwork, Biven observed: 'He climbed purposefully but wasn't graceful ... You knew the guy was going to get up, but you wondered if a rock might be pulled down on your head while he led it.' Biven, five years younger, was aware of the difference in rank and ages, and felt that Patey was being dutiful and would rather be climbing with someone else.

Patey climbed several new quality VSs at the Dewerstone (the best of which was Leviathan) and at Vixen Tor on Dartmoor, and more adventurous (aka dangerous) routes on the shale cliffs of Morwell in the River Tamar Valley, which were 'loose, but not desperately so' (Moulton, 1966).

Richard Brooke, Patey's fellow expedition member from Rakaposhi, accompanied him on one occasion and recorded the experience in his diary:

> Spent two days exploring Morwell Rocks, which are extremely steep buttresses up to 200ft on rather untrustworthy looking rock, which

proved sounder than it looked. Tom had done one route solo the weekend before. We repeated it: VS, very exposed and distinctly hard. I would have hated to be on it alone.

Some of Patey's best routes in the south-west include Spider's Web, an elegant spiralling HVS on Lower Raven Buttress at the Dewerstone, which he climbed with Barrie Page and Peter Henry. Page, too, recognised that Patey was not a stylist on rock but even so:

You have to have a certain amount of elegance if you are to go quickly and not fall off … it's not a bull at a gate. On the Dewerstone it was pretty steep, so it was a muscular approach anyway.

The serious Ultramontane (HVS) at Morwell Rocks was climbed with Viv Stevenson and Zeke, and complemented his solo of Salvationist (Severe) on the same cliff.

At Haytor on Dartmoor, the finest of that area's myriad outcrops, Patey added Outward Bound (HVS 4c) with Ernie Blaber, who is not credited in the first ascent list. Despite its relative brevity, they climbed it in two pitches, during which time Blaber witnessed Patey's unconventional techniques at worryingly close hand. At an impasse on the second pitch, Patey enquired about the quality of the belay. Blaber said that it was poor, to which Patey replied, 'Have you got me, because I'm going to jump for it.' Before Blaber could protest, Patey had lunged for the handhold, and he clung on one-handed as he scrabbled for footholds, before clawing his way to the top.

If the outcrops did not provide the same level of adventure as the mountains, then the coastal crags of North Devon went some way towards compensating for this. On the shale cliffs at Cornakey, Patey established Wrecker's Slab (VS), one of his best-known routes from this period, with Zeke and retired Rear Admiral Keith Lawder, a genial and popular custodian of the Count House, the Climbers' Club Hut at Bosigran.

Zeke on Patey's route, Leviathan, at The Dewerstone © Vivian Stevenson

Despite having held down a very senior position in the Navy until his retirement at 55, Lawder's appearance and demeanour were disarming. During a Naval Mountaineering Club meet at the Count House, Lawder was at the sink washing dishes when a young seaman came up to him and said, 'Wotcha Chief, what's this buzz about some bloody admiral coming on this meet?'

'Don't worry. I hear he's not a bad old stick,' replied Lawder with a grin.

Lawder had reconnoitred and recorded the first routes on the Culm coast and knew about the huge slab at Cornakey, the highest in South-West England. Seeking a strong team for an attempt, Lawder called Mike Banks, who suggested Patey and Zeke. Zeke was astounded when he saw the cliff head-on, but Patey reckoned it was doable. From below, Zeke could not see any decent stances, so Patey suggested joining two ropes and climbing it in a single run-out (although even that would not have been long enough).

Zeke had not gotten far up the first pitch when he realised some of the holds slid out like cupboard drawers, which he replaced for the next person. He led a full rope length without any runners, and at a narrow sill hammered a piton into rubble and gingerly took a semi-hanging stance. Patey, who had plenty of experience climbing loose, vegetated rock without protection, climbed through, with just enough rope to finish up a central groove furnished with wobbly flakes and expanding cracks, into which he hammered more pitons of questionable integrity. The modern version is more circuitous, utilising better quality rock.

Arriving at the top, Lawder was elated and thought it a terrific climb. Zeke was less convinced. Even Patey had to tread delicately. Despite this, Patey and Zeke liked the venue, and the trio went on to climb the shorter, parallel VS, Smugglers Slab.

Later, Patey repeated Wrecker's Slab solo, after which he apologised to Lawder for inadvertently removing some crucial holds. The route had a reputation for 'avalanching', and even the young, talented Pat Littlejohn approached it with respect.

Patey also explored the coastal cliffs in opposite directions from Cornakey and put up new routes from Hartland Point to the north, down to Higher Sharpnose Point in Cornwall. These coastal venues would have been a reminder of his early outings at Longhaven near Ellon.

On the limestone cliffs at Chudleigh in Devon, Patey soloed the classic Sarcophagus (VS), which follows an exposed corner with some spectacular moves on large holds. An onlooker saw Patey 'hurling ivy and abuse into the surrounding atmosphere' but obviously enjoying himself. Robin Shaw, who was working at the local Outward Bound School, was also at the crag that day. Shaw had been on the tainted multi-day first ascent of Point Five Gully on Ben Nevis in 1959 with Ian Clough. He also spent some time as a climbing instructor with the Royal Marines, where he had met Patey, and they had crossed paths on various Scottish crags. According to Shaw (2016):

> *As I arrived, Tom had just completed the first ascent of Sarcophagus. It looked an unlikely line, overhanging significantly. He encouraged me to make an ascent. Once I started, it was easier than it looked, and I made good progress. At the top of the climb, capped by an overhang, was a ramp slanting to the left. This narrowed to about a foot at the top and what lay beyond was hidden round the corner. Facing the ramp, I set off and moved upward with difficulty until I was squashed between the overhang and the undercut below. At this point, I found it impossible to retreat, and my right arm could not reach beyond the corner. Stuck! After some time, I heard Tom above me round the corner. He slung the end of a rope towards me, and after several attempts I caught it, tied on, and rolled myself off the ramp into space. Then I managed to get a good hold and climb up to him. When I thanked him, he apologised for not telling me to move up the ramp on my back. We had a good laugh, and when we descended, I repeated the climb successfully. It caused great merriment in the pub afterwards. Tom was a friendly and generous companion.*

Zeke in action at Sennen, Cornwall, in the '50s © John Deacon collection

Vivian Stevenson on Patey's route, Sarcophagus, at Chudleigh © Vivian Stevenson

On another occasion at Chudleigh, Patey turned up late for a climbing session with Dougie Keelan, who recalls that:

> He arrive[d] in a froth for his car had broken down and he had had to run along the dual carriageway for several miles. He had not had time to change out of his Naval Doctor's uniform and looked as though he had just come off a major expedition. We had, for me, an excellent afternoon on the rock, he in his rapidly deteriorating Naval uniform; me learning all sorts of tricks of the trade from the great man.

The preponderance of outcrops in this region inevitably had a positive effect on Patey's climbing. Seven years after climbing Eagle Ridge on Lochnagar with Patey, Tom Weir made a summer ascent of Raven's Gully on Buachaille Etive Mòr with him and noticed a significant improvement in Patey's technique.

One particular spell of rock climbing in August 1960 became the entire subject of one of Patey's articles, 'Over the Sea to Skye' (*Etchachan Club Journal*, 1959).[2] It was the first time he climbed with Chris Bonington, who would go on to become one of Britain's most famous mountaineers.

At the time, Bonington was a mountaineering instructor at the Army Outward Bound School at Tywyn in mid-Wales. He had recently climbed Annapurna II with Patey's fellow expedition members from Rakaposhi, Dicky Grant and Sherpa Ang Nyima.

After plans to climb with Hamish MacInnes fell through, Patey met Bonington on a Euston Station platform and they used their service passes to travel free to the north of Scotland.

Patey knew that Bonington had made some significant winter first ascents in Glen Coe, including Raven's Gully and Agag's Groove with MacInnes in 1953.[3] Bonington had also been on the first British ascent of the South-West Pillar of the Dru and the diretissima on the Cime Grande in the Dolomites. There is no doubt that, on rock, he was a much stronger performer than Patey.

Initially, the pair based themselves at the SMC's Ling Hut in Torridon under the watchful eye of pioneers W. N. Ling and G.T. Glover, whose portrait photo by Tom Weir hangs in the main room. Hidden from view lies Beinn Eighe's spectacular and secluded Coire Mhic Fhearchair. The simple but striking symmetry of its great Triple Buttresses reveals a multi-faceted venue, a playground for climbers in any season.

On previous solo jaunts, Patey had spotted the potential for great rock routes on the Eastern Ramparts, but Robin Smith and Andy Wightman were the first to probe the central area of this impressively steep cliff in 1961, when they established Boggle (E1 5b). It was a further two decades before the corrie's true potential was realised. In both summer and winter, it yielded routes as good as anywhere else in the UK.

The other sector to catch Patey's eye was the phenomenal quartzite east wall of West Buttress, which towers over West Central Gully. This was the main objective when Patey and Bonington left the hut at mid-afternoon on 8 August. Patey had already nicknamed it Wall of the Winds, redeploying the name for the line on Ben Nevis's Carn Dearg Buttress that he had failed to climb. After approaching via Central Buttress then traversing to its base, wet weather foiled an attempt, and they intercepted an overhanging horizontal fault which, with tremendous exposure, led to the West Buttress and escaped up the Ordinary Route finish.[4]

The following day produced an undistinguished route on the quartzite cliffs of the attractive Corbett An Ruadh-stac.

Their third day was one of enforced rest, recorded in the Ling Hut logbook thus:

> *10 August. Patey reported sick with a large carbuncle on the buttock. Bonington attempted some surgery with a razor blade, but only succeeded in causing a minor haemorrhage. Thence to Kinlochewe in search of chemists—nearest one is at Dingwall. Returned to Torridon & located the local doctor (female) who supplied the necessary pills—also offered to lance the carbuncle, but this was graciously refused.*

As a result of Patey's restless night's sleep, they did not leave the hut until noon on the 11th, when they headed back to Coire Mhic Fhearchair for another attempt on Wall of the Winds, below which they had stashed gear. Drizzle thwarted their plans, and instead they tackled the 750m Upper Girdle, the most continuous natural feature in the whole corrie. The sustained, exposed start traverses the Eastern Ramparts, but the most spectacular section is across the east face of West Buttress. Despite being only Severe in standard, the route has never been especially popular, but it is an expedition into some remarkable situations at a reasonable grade.

They soloed most of this giant girdle, and to finish, climbed a new, exposed direct finish to West Buttress. From Bonington's initial protestations that this looked like 'a mere scramble', they had produced a classic which has become unjustifiably neglected. As yet, there has been no single-day complete traverse of the route in winter.

The following day they had to tackle a mountain of unwashed dishes before relocating to A' Chìoch of Sgùrr a' Chaorachain, a dramatic feature in the Applecross peninsula which presents a formidable skyline prow from the head of Loch Kishorn. Following in the footsteps of Glover and Ling, Patey and his student friends had established six summer routes on the mountain in 1952 and 1953. Although none were particularly noteworthy, Patey had hypothesised about a route up the grandest feature of all, which he anticipated would be extremely difficult. Their eventual creation, the Cioch Nose (climbed in the rain after a late start), turned out to be technically easy, the spectacularly exposed third pitch furnished with good holds. The quality of the climbing and situations were of a high order. 'Its exuberant plenitude of excrescences turning a visual XS into a tactile Difficult' led them to pronounce it as 'The Diff to end all Diffs' (*Etchachan Club Journal*, 1959).

The general consensus was that it was harder than V. Diff, and a modern assessment classifies the route more realistically as Severe. Patey was proud of his creation, and he returned several times with old friends and visiting luminaries, including Hamish MacInnes, Tom

Weir and Gwen Moffat, often seeking out variations to the original line. Bonington, too, has repeated it often and in various forms over the years. Content with the original grading, he is adamant that the 'top bit must be one of the most beautiful Diffs in the world' (2017a).

Following the realisation of Patey's eight-year dream and the resultant jubilation, 'Nothing could lower our morale now; not even a night in a youth hostel, for which we paid more than an average B and B.' On arriving, they had no time to cook before 'Lights Out', had to deal with an 'insufferable' warden, and grudgingly undertook morning duties, which was then part of the whole YHA experience. Desperate to leave, 'A faint shout from the hostel brought us to a grinding halt. The warden appeared at the door. "Happy Hostelling!" He shouted, "and remember, chaps—Thumbs Up!"' (SMCJ, 1961a).

The Cioch Nose is one of Patey's most repeated routes, and it became an instant classic. It is unusual in that it can be approached via a descent from the Bealach na Ba, affording a mountaineering air but leaving the route's end close to the departure point. The top of the pass provides a wonderful view of the Isle of Skye, which is where they headed next.

Arriving at Cuillin Cottage at the bottom of Glen Brittle, the pair had to explain to the proprietor, Mrs Campbell, that they had both lost their wallets and would not be able to pay for their stay until they returned home. Patey told Mrs Campbell he was a member of the SMC and, by implication, trustworthy and respectable. 'Maybe so, but you have an honest face, and that is a lot more important,' she replied.

The Upper Cliff of Coireachan Ruadha on Sgùrr Mhic Choinnich is considered by some to be one of the finest cliffs in the Cuillin for its setting and steep lines. It lies on the Coruisk side of the ridge and looks down on that hallowed sanctuary of the Cuillin. As the crow flies, it is close to the sunny aspect of Sron na Ciche and would be much more popular if not for the long approach and the rather austere atmosphere. Patey was following in the new-routing footsteps of his Aberdeen friends, Bill Brooker and Dick Barclay, and Bradford Lad, Mike Dixon, who had become smitten with Skye after his first visit and had written an article in the 1952 *SMCJ* called 'The Forgotten Corrie' about their explorations.

'King Cobra was the best new route we did that summer,' recalled Bonington, and the current SMC guide to the area bestows upon it the plaudit of best E1 in the Skye Cuillin. The crux of the route lies in the corner of pitch two. Bonington struggled on this, and Patey began to wonder about the outcome: 'Will it go?' I asked anxiously, 'or will you?'[5] They split the fourth pitch (which is now done in a single 35m run out), so it fell to Patey to swing across jammed spikes to evade the upper tier of overhangs. Patey was exuberant about the quality of the route, and it was only the second of six times he was involved in the creation of rock climbs in the Extreme category in Scotland.[6] He later described the route as unequalled in the Cuillin 'for technical difficulty and regal splendour' (*SMCJ*, 1961a). Bonington has said it would still be in his choice of Desert Island Climbs, although some believe the route to be overrated.

Rain stopped play for a couple of days, but they were bursting with energy when they returned to one of the most spectacular sections of the Cuillin Ridge—the peak of Am Basteir and its axe-like Basteir Tooth. Patey dismissed the 'three scrappy variants' they climbed, but the King's Cave Wall and Outside Edge combination, especially the section on the spur between King's Cave and Shadbolt's Chimney, is a fine exposed Severe amidst grand scenery at the northern end of the ridge.

Throughout the trip, Bonington, carrying most of the gear, desperately tried to keep up with Patey and persuade him to deploy the rope on technical sections. Bonington would usually lead the hard pitches, but it was a problem persuading Patey to tie on at all: on anything up to HVS, he preferred soloing. When he did lead, he hardly ever put any protection in, and when he did it was badly placed. He 'was not remotely interested in gear' (Bonington, 2017a).

Indeed, Bonington nearly lost his life on the Basteir Tooth. Reaching an awkward, semi-layback move just below the top of the route, he realised there was no point asking for a top rope as the rope was in his rucksack. With one hand on a side-pull and the other on a rounded lump of rock, a foothold broke away. Faced with a 70m drop to the screes, he only just managed to cling on and find another foothold. Topping out, he was greeted by an ashen-faced scrambler who had had a grandstand view of Bonington's near demise.

After the Basteir routes, they traversed along the Cuillin Ridge to the North-West Face of Sgùrr a' Mhadaidh to climb Whispering Wall (V. Diff) on the crag right of Deep Gash Gully. Patey and Bonington eyed up the striking rib on the left-hand side of the gully, but they had run out of time for an attempt of it. In any case, it would not have been a first ascent as Robin Smith had climbed and named it Thunder Rib earlier in the year.

The last day of the holiday took in a new location—the Storr area of the Trotternish Ridge. Don Whillans had already climbed the Old Man of Storr, the highest and most impressive of these tottering rock splinters, which are best admired from a distance. Patey and Bonington chose an adjacent but shorter route, which they named The Cathedral due to its three apertures and resemblance to crumbling masonry. The topmost section looked as if it could be toppled by a human hand. On rock 'no better than porridge', they scrambled 35m then split the remaining 25m into three pitches to reduce the risk of rocks raining down on their unhelmeted heads. Bonington led the final section and was lowered gingerly off the summit spire, Patey feeling no need to reach the very tip. Usually in his element on such terrain, he later said of the route: 'Great care necessary; almost unjustifiable' (*SMCJ*, 1961b), and its current E1 grade reflects its suicidal nature rather than any great technical difficulty.

Thus concluded 'a pure, incredible climbing holiday,' and 'the most magical trip' (Bonington, 2017), which had produced eleven new routes. Patey's personality had contributed significantly to the enjoyment and success.

When Patey returned to Devon, his old friends from Aberdeen, including Graeme Nicol, who was attached to the SAS based in Hereford as part of his National Service, sometimes visited him.

On one occasion, Patey arranged to meet Nicol and Bemrose at the Avon Gorge outside Bristol for a day's climbing. Patey failed to

The Cathedral is the left-hand pinnacle. Photo from Patey's bothy in Ullapool
© Alex Tewnion, Ian Patey collection

turn up, and the strangers were compelled to spend the day together. Bemrose survived a 100-foot fall, arrested by Nicol, who received bad rope burns. Undeterred, Bemrose completed the route, as his anxious girlfriend looked on. She later expressed concern about Nicol's burns, but he said he was proud of them as they would become scars of honour and the basis for an enthralling story. Nicol commended the girl for her choice of partner and offered her a tip: 'If your man falls and carries on, that's alright. If he gives up, then you should have nothing more to do with him.' Bemrose had been introduced to the Teutonic disposition through Patey's commentary and songs, but this was the first time he had met a fully paid-up member of the Munich School's Aberdeen Branch.

Bemrose and the lady later married, and they lived in the same compound in Yelverton as the Pateys, where the rent was subsidised and nobody could afford a mortgage. Ernie Blaber did not even realise

Patey was married to begin with, a telling observation made by others later in the '60s when Patey was a GP in Ullapool.

Betty was a long way from the rest of her family, with a young baby to look after and a second child (Ian), on the way, and Patey spent a lot of time away. Bemrose, who usually became friends with his pals' wives, recalls that 'Betty was a lovely lady ... She was polite, but not hugely communicative. You didn't get involved in deep conversations. She wasn't the same sort of engaging person as Tom.'

Patey had signed up for three years in the Royal Marines, but when he completed his service, he was told he owed several hundred pounds for his accommodation quarters. Technically, this was not his fault because the authorities had not billeted him and they had forgotten to deduct the fee from his salary. Having no spare savings, he was furious at being forced to sign on for another year.

At the end of the last Scottish winter training course before Patey left the service in 1961, the Sergeant Instructor gave a speech thanking him for his medical and mountaineering contributions to the unit, and presented him with a vest and underpants, which the NCOs had dyed black. 'You'll never have to wash them again,' said the Sergeant Instructor. 'He was really pissed off when he opened them because he didn't think he was dirty at all,' recalled Bemrose. This was the only time he ever saw Patey upset.

Despite this, Patey had enjoyed serving in the Marines because, within reason, he could do what he wanted. But he would never become a career officer because he disliked having to defer to authority and be disciplined by people for whom he did not have particular respect. In fact, as a relatively mature officer who had gone through life with a large degree of autonomy, he did not like being disciplined by anyone. As Zeke succinctly put it: 'He was more of a climber than a naval officer.'

After 55 years, Blaber still has a vivid memory of Patey: 'He was a larger-than-life character ... some people you meet in your life have no impact at all.'

1   Biven formed a very effective climbing team with his brother Peter and older industrialist Trevor Peck in the 1950s. Their routes on the main cliff at Bosigran in Cornwall are still respected for their difficulty at the time, but most of all for their enduring quality.

2   The *Etchachan Club Journal* was late that year, and not published until the following year, hence why it contained some 1960 outings. In *One Man's Mountains* it is incorrectly dated as 1962.

3   It had been a fast-track induction for Bonington. The ascent of Crowberry Ridge Direct was the hardest of the trio of routes on Buachaille Etive Mòr and required a peg for aid from MacInnes, who led all the significant pitches. Bonington described seconding Crowberry Ridge Direct as 'a frightening climb'. Bonington showed his own mettle by leading friend John Hammond and the Creagh Dhu apprentice 'Gnomie' up the whole of Agag's Groove, following closely behind the first ascent by MacInnes and partner. Crowberry and Agag's exceeded Patey's own trio of hard mixed routes from the same period by a full grade.

4   The first route on this face did not fall until 1976 when Richard McHardy and B. Chislett climbed Mistral at E1. John Lyall and Andy Nisbet adopted Patey's name Wall of the Winds for their own E1 route in 1990.

5   In 'Skye is the Limit' (*SMCJ*, 2004), Julian Lines reveals the intense existential ruminations he had on this section while soloing it. See also Lines's *Tears of the Dawn* (2013).

6   The others are: Spigolo at South Cove (top-roped); The Cathedral at Storr; The Old Man of Hoy; Knickerbocker Glory at Upper Tollie Crag; and Magic Bow on Sgùrr an Fhidhleir.

12

Patey approaching
the Post Face, Creag
Meagaidh in March 1962
© Richard Brooke

Locum in Limbo

A brilliant storyteller, he held us in fits of laughter with his tales of doughty matrons, inebriate doctors and demanding patients.

Adam Watson, *It's a Fine Day for the Hill*

Following his extended period in National Service, Patey took short-term locum posts in Aberdeen and across the north of the country but, with a wife and two small children, his priority was to secure a permanent medical position in Scotland.

Celebrating his move back into civilian life with Bill Brooker and Mike Dixon, he climbed Twin Chimneys Route (IV,5), a steep line from the fork in Black Spout to the summit of Black Spout Pinnacle on Lochnagar.

New cliffs were also on his radar, and as the winter season of 1961 came to an end, he explored the Fannaichs, the range of mountains from Garve to Braemore Junction. With an Aberdonian team, he climbed Skyscraper Buttress on Sgùrr nan Clach Geala, a vegetated Severe which provides one of the best routes in the area in winter. This was probably not the first route on the cliff, as Jerry Smith and Ronnie Sellers had almost certainly climbed a buttress to the right previously. Sellers was secretary of the Etchachan Club at the time and a leading climber on the Aberdeen scene. In May 1959, he fell to his death from Black Spout Pinnacle when the block he was abseiling from detached. Shortly afterwards, Smith died while abseiling in the Alps.

A fortnight after his ascent of Skyscraper Buttress, Patey returned with R. Harper to repeat and officially record Sellers and Smith's route, naming it Sellers Buttress, 'In memory of an outstanding climber and a staunch friend' (*SMCJ*, 1962). Like its companion route, Sellers Buttress (V. Diff) proved to be a better winter line.

In August, Patey and Harper headed for the magnificent architecture of the North-East Wall of Blà Bheinn on Skye, where they climbed Chock-a-Block Chimney (HS).

They also established the first route at Neist peninsula in the North-West of the island: the prominent pinnacle on the Upper Crag, which they named The Green Lady (HS). At that time, climbers tended to ignore the sea cliffs in favour of the great mountain crags of the Cuillin. Indeed, 16 years would elapse before Mike Geddes and Noel Williams claimed the second route at Neist.

None of his Cairngorm routes from this period was as significant as his 1950s classics, but Patey was glad to be back new-routing with old friends in his early stomping ground.

In October 1961, he had a brief but productive spell of solo exploration on the crags near Loch Carron, where he was locuming. On consecutive days, Patey left his mark on two impressive mountains above Achnashellach: Sgòrr Ruadh and Fuar Tholl.

The best new route of the batch, however, was on the accessible crag on the South Face of Sgùrr a' Chaorachain above the Bealach na Ba road in the Applecross peninsula. With pleasant climbing on immaculate, solid sandstone, Sword of Gideon (VS 4c) became another overnight classic and a worthy companion to his and Bonington's nearby Cioch Nose. It was a route Patey returned to several times, often frightening able climbers from south of the border, who were encouraged to follow him solo in fading daylight on the crux traverse, as he sought to wring as much out of the day as possible. In March 1966, after soloing several other routes with Patey, including the Cioch Nose, 'Bradford Lad' Dennis Gray had a shaky, dry-mouthed twilight experience on the crux. The descent, without a head torch, prolonged the tension. But back in the pub, as the music sessions began, Gray reflected warmly on another memorable adventure. Patey was remembered by locals in the area and treated like royalty in the hostelries they visited there.

On 13 October, Patey did his last new route of the year on another Applecross mountain whose routes are best climbed in winter and in

On the foreground peak of Sgòrr Ruadh, Splintery Edge (V. Diff) climbs the wall left of the prominent right-hand gully. On Fuar Tholl behind, The Nose Direct (VS) lies on the lower crag on the extreme left © Mike Dixon

that season are some of the greatest in the country. Although impressive in summer, Beinn Bhàn is transformed into a phenomenal venue when sheathed in snow and ice, and in the dramatic Coire na Poite, Patey climbed the third summer route: the Upper Connecting Ridge of A' Phoit (Severe), whose three tiers of sandstone lead to the broken upper ridge. The seven-year hiatus before his return to this venue makes one wonder if he visited on a misty day and failed to see the great potential of the five corries.

After this fruitful sortie to the West, Patey returned East for more locum work, but he kept a keen eye on the local climbing competition. Hugh Spencer (2016) recalls:

> *I think it was 23 February 1962, a Friday. I went up to Scott's bothy on my own. There was no one there, but Derek Pyper and Dave Reid dropped in and then left on their way to Corrour. I bedded down, and then at around midnight the door opened, and this guy came in dressed in a suit and tie with highly polished black shoes. He asked me if I had seen anyone that evening and then just climbed into a sleeping bag and bedded down ... and left just as quickly very early in the morning.*
>
> *I learned later [this] was Patey, who was the GP in Braemar at the time and who must have driven up to Derry Lodge that night. The consensus was that he was checking to see if any of his contemporaries like Graeme Nicol et al. were on the move towards Braeriach, where the cherished prize at the time was the first winter ascent of The Great Rift.*

Patey's suspicions were correct, but Nicol, with Jerry Light, would not claim this major prize until three years later.

Perhaps as a result of spending more time with his family after his locum absences, Patey then had one of the longest periods of abstinence from climbing in his mountaineering career.

Respite came at the very end of February 1962, when he and his fellow team member from Rakaposhi, naval officer Richard Brooke, headed for Creag Meagaidh.

When Patey and Brooke approached the Post Face of Coire Ardair, conditions were perfect with hard-packed snow and a heavy frost right down to the loch below the Pinnacle Buttress. Patey was well-versed in the crag's history and was intent on climbing the great central funnel of ice on this sector of the corrie directly. That day the unclimbed pitch on Centre Post was over 30m long and close to vertical. They cramponned up to the base of the pitch with little fuss, and Brooke tied on to a piton belay in the adjacent rocks. Thereafter, Patey took the lead and attacked the icefall. But after 40 arduous minutes, he had only ascended a few metres and had not even reached the steepest section. This was Patey's first climb, and indeed proper exercise, for several months, and he found it extremely demanding cutting steps on such steep, unrelenting terrain, so he retreated and escaped via the traverse taken by Allan and Bell on the first ascent. This was still on vertiginous ice, however, and it took Patey over half an hour to reach easier ground on the right. Even with the bucket hand and footholds that Patey had hewn out of the ice, Brooke struggled to follow the unnerving traverse without the reassurance of a rope above. Patey thought they might break back into the gully higher up, but was thwarted, even though Brooke thought it was within his powers. In a diary entry, Brooke (1962) admitted, 'I'm afraid I wasn't very encouraging, as it was extremely exposed and I had first day-itis with a vengeance.' Leaving a piton and karabiner in place, they took an easier route to the plateau, then descended to The Window, from where gentler slopes lead to the corrie floor.

After supper in the Loch Laggan Hotel, it was off to The Struan Hotel in Carrbridge to enjoy Karl Fuchs's hospitality. Patey's renditions on the accordion won them free drinks and, later, a free doss on a sofa.

The next day, after a complimentary breakfast at the hotel, they returned to the Post Face for a rematch. Given Patey's subpar performance the previous day, they might have plumped for one of the easier unclimbed lines in the Inner Corrie. Instead, they made a girdle traverse of the face. This type of climb has never been particularly fashionable, but Patey was perhaps already prospecting a traverse of the entire corrie via faults across the four adjacent sectors of cliff.

Their Post Horn Gallop linked rising horizontal and diagonal weaknesses in the face. The first, tricky pitch lies left of South Post (which would in its entirety form another new route, Last Post, four days later). After this, snow-plastered turf ledges led to South Post and another awkward pitch to reach the ledge leading round to Centre Post. Here the rope jammed, and when Brooke unroped to untangle it, he dropped two pitons and karabiners into the void. The diagonal line continued to the easy but spectacular balcony crossing above the small upper enclosure of North Post, the first ascent of which Patey had made two years previously. Over 150m of exposed ground led to the upper snow bowl of Staghorn Gully and the top. According to Brooke, it took almost five hours to complete this quality, if unusual, Grade IV, which breaches some impressive ground.

Patey avoiding the Direct pitch of Centre Post © Richard Brooke

Patey walking to Glen Brittle © Richard Brooke

On the plateau, the weather turned, and they were soon immersed in a blizzard. They set off over the high tops in the wrong direction for a while, until Brooke dug out his compass and they picked their way down in encroaching darkness.

Back at the car, they changed, ate a hasty supper, then turned their thoughts to socialising and drove to the Kintail Lodge Hotel at Shiel Bridge. The hotel owner was Norman Tennent, a well-known mountaineer, and the trio chatted and drank whisky into the small hours.[1]

On Saturday, they headed for Skye with the greatest prize in British mountaineering in their sights: a winter traverse of the Cuillin Ridge.

The weather had looked menacing all day, and the car skidded about on a hill on the road to Kyle of Lochalsh. The roads were snowbound from Sligachan, but they managed to reach Carbost, barely able to see through the iced-up windscreen. Brooke leaned out of the door issuing directions, but they had to extract the car out of a ditch several times. Brooke then ran just ahead of the car in what he judged to be the centre of the road, but tripped and sprawled in front of the car and narrowly escaped being run over.

They tried to return to Sligachan but gave up. Patey had once given a girl a lift from Glen Brittle to Carbost, so they went to her home, where they received a friendly reception. 'There were two others (both drunk) taking shelter from the storm. It was a poor household, but [they were] charming people with seven fine sons and daughters. Eventually [we] settled down in their hay barn at about 02.00' (Brooke, 1962).

After a good night's sleep, they breakfasted in their host's house, and in the afternoon walked to Glen Brittle through deep snow in fine weather. In the annexe of Cuillin Cottage, everyone was interested to hear that they had come to attempt one of Scotland's last great challenges. It had become one of the few out-of-season attractions for locals, and the same goal had attracted several parties.

On Sunday, they were away at 5.40am. Brooke (ibid.) described the slog across the moor to Gars bheinn as 'bloody'. Patey did all the trail breaking on the approach as Brooke had a sprained ankle. It was a gruelling five-and-a-half-hour ordeal. 'I felt I might be in the Arctic with the cold, the snow and the stillness, the long slow dawn colours in the sky and the view out over the islands reminding me of Dove Bugt (Greenland).'

Some of the main ridge was clear, but powder smothered all the ledges on the leeward side, and the ice was patchy.

In 'The First Winter Traverse of the Cuillin Ridge' (*SMCJ*, 1965), Patey notes that the pitches were only slightly harder than in summer, and that there was no advantage in wearing crampons. Clearly, this did not meet the criteria for a winter attempt, although Brooke found the Thearlaich-Dubh Gap hard going. King's Chimney was really a rock climb, and at sunset they called a halt at the Inaccessible Pinnacle with just under half of the ridge completed.[2]

Brooke thought that Patey rather regretted not bivouacking and carrying on the next day, but with soaking wet feet and no stove or bivouac gear, it would have been a 'grisly night'. At any rate, they would not have claimed it as the first true winter traverse. Descending from Sgùrr Dearg, Brooke recalled:

> Tom bounding ahead as usual. In fact, my main [memory] of this day was of chasing after Tom and eventually annoyance at always being left behind and going slower than I would have done otherwise ... Having started before dawn, it seemed right to use the last of the gloaming at the other end of the day, [and] I arrived only a few minutes after Tom.

The next morning, they tidied up the annexe and accepted a lift out of the glen, a journey made easier by snow chains. It was then back to the Loch Laggan Hotel for a bath and dinner and, for Brooke, an early night. Patey, however, 'went off to spend a riotous evening at Carrbridge and got back in the small hours—what energy.'[3] Behind the main hotel was a rudimentary bothy where climbers could stay for free. Needless to say, it was very popular and handy for access to Creag Meagaidh. Regulars in the hotel could help themselves to a five-pint bottle of Glenmorangie from the bar and settle up at the end of the night.

On the final day of their holiday, they set off early with 'the usual helter-skelter rush', reaching the crags in just over an hour. They were keen to climb the leftmost fault on the Post Face, the first pitch of which they had climbed as an opener for Post Horn Gallop. Accessing it via the unclimbed Direct start to South Post, they then took a rising traverse across rock, snow and turf to the main line. There lay 70m of steep climbing before the angle eased towards the top. Of all their climbs that week, Brooke enjoyed this the most, and they sauntered back down one of the mountain's south-facing corries in fine weather and contoured back to Aberarder. The Last Post (V) was a fitting end to the trip, by which time an out-of-shape Patey had hit peak form both in the mountains and in late-night socialising.

Patey resumed locum work in the Aberdeen and Deeside areas but returned West for one significant climbing foray. In April, on the first of several solo jaunts there in the '60s, he climbed the second-ever line on

Beinn Dearg near Ullapool, following on from J.H.B. Bell and his wife Pat's 1946 route in the wild Coire Ghranda. Patey's line, The Tower of Babel (V. Diff), was the first on extensive cliffs in Gleann na Sguaib on the north-west flank of the mountain. It climbs a striking corner tower to the right of the wide gully of the Cadha Amadan (Fool's Pass) and is reputed to have some of the best rock on Beinn Dearg, but is another mountain that comes into its own in winter.

April also saw Patey following in the footsteps of Harold Raeburn once more on one of Scotland's finest mountains and a winter venue of untapped potential: Ladhar Bheinn, a majestic, complex mountain in remote, rugged Knoydart. The peak and its subsidiary top, Stob a' Chearcaill, enclose the great Coire Dhorrcail in a wonderful setting next to the sea, above the fjord-like Loch Hourn with views out to the Skye and Rùm Cuillin. Its vegetated schist rock and damp recesses can offer a rich seam of routes in winter, and it has a unique atmosphere among Scottish climbing venues.

In 1897, Raeburn had climbed his eponymous route up the prominent gully in the corrie's headwall with a huge chockstone at half height. The best way of reaching the corrie is by boat and the long approach on foot deters many. Being close to the west coast, the snow can be quickly stripped, but the deeper recesses can be in winter condition while the buttresses are bare.

Sixty-five years after Raeburn's contribution, Patey was joined by his old Aberdeen friends Graeme Nicol and Dick Barclay for a trip to this area, which was an esoteric backwater at the time. It was mid-April after a good winter and Stob a' Chearcaill was liberally coated in snow. Patey applied his imagination to the peak, claiming that it 'remotely resembled' the North Face of the Grandes Jorasses with its soaring buttress and gully lines.

On the walk-in from Kinlochourn to Barrisdale, Nicol recalls carrying an extremely heavy rucksack as Patey sauntered in with next to nothing. 'This was characteristic of Tom; he just manipulated it so that he would do without a sleeping bag and someone else would carry the stove.'

Patey after the first ascent of Last Post. The Cairngorms in the distance © Richard Brooke

From left: Nicol, Barclay and Patey, with Stob a' Chearcaill behind. April 1962
© Ian Patey collection

The trio climbed the central trough-like and most prominent gully on the face in just three hours and named it Gaberlunzie. They had difficulty passing a large chockstone blocking the exit from a cave at about quarter height, but the crux was the final 20m up the right-hand gully wall.

The next day, they set off for the cliffs at the head of the corrie—the finest on the mountain. Here, at 400m, the crags attain their greatest height on a face which Patey named Spider Buttress as he thought it resembled the White Spider on the North Face of the Eiger. The long, narrow gully between this and Raeburn's Gully seemed a plum line, and its upper recesses concealed a succession of steep ice pitches. The team moved efficiently, and it yielded in just two hours. Patey was enthusiastic about the quality of the climb, comparing it to the classic Crowberry Gully on Buachaille Etive Mòr. If it were more accessible, Viking Gully (IV,4) would no doubt receive many more ascents.

After the Knoydart trip, Patey locumed in Ullapool, and stayed in the Argyll Hotel. Exploring mountains further north, he climbed Mild (VS), a bold solo up the left side of the frontal face of Barrel Buttress. This is an impressive prow on Sail Garbh, a constituent peak of Quinag, which towers over the hamlet of Kylesku. Patey's route was the second established line, the first having fallen to the indefatigable Raeburn with Mackay and Ling in 1907.

On days off in June, old Lairig Club friends Nicol, Taylor and Grassick accompanied Patey to the Triple Buttresses of Beinn Eighe, where they climbed The Gash (Severe), a deep chimney above the Broad Terrace on the Eastern Buttress which makes a good introduction to Patey's 1959 solo route, Gnome Wall.

Grassick noted that Patey had retained some of his eccentricities from his student days when the latter arrived at the Ling Hut with only one large packet of sausages, a bottle of whisky and his accordion. Some from Aberdeen have commented that they did not take kindly to being adjuncts to Patey's personal ambition and being expected to provide most of the climbing gear and rations to tackle a climb which he insisted on doing. Despite his meagre contributions to the provisions, however, he enlivened the evenings with entertainment, and he usually cooked breakfast to ensure a speedy departure in the morning.

His two best solos that month were on big, remote crags. Foinaven, in the far north of Sutherland, is a major massif that receives more visitors nowadays due to its status as a Corbett, although its great north-eastern crags see few climbers.

Creag Urbhard, the most extensive and best known of Foinaven's crags, is vast: a kilometre wide and reaching over 300m in height. The intricate structure of the quartzite cliffs requires good route-finding and guile to arrange protection and dodge loose rock and seepage. Easy or middle-grade routes have a committing feel. Occupying the upper part of Strath Dionard and overlooking Loch Dionard, it has a magnificent outlook, and despite its remoteness, it attracted attention as early as 1910, when Ling and Glover established South Ridge (Mod.).

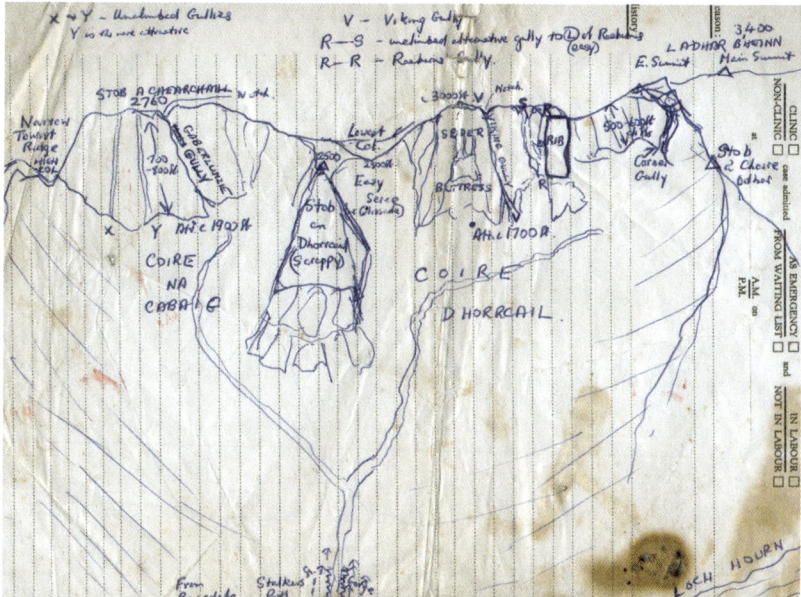

Patey's sketch of the cliffs of Ladhar Bheinn © Ian Patey collection

Patey's route climbs the large area of featureless rock left of the second waterfall. Such a long, lonely solo, with intricate route-finding, ramped up the commitment factor. Although Patey gave Fingal (Severe) a detailed write-up in the *SMCJ*, it has bewildered parties over the years, many of whom have found their own variations to reach the top. Patey carried a short length of rope on these solo climbs, and some pegs and slings for emergencies. This may have been scant solace, but he excelled at judging lines and their difficulty from below and was cautiously confident on such routes.

The other cliff he visited was also off the beaten track, roughly six miles east of the remote Seana Bhraigh. Alladale Wall lies on the North-East Face of An Socach at the head of Glen Alladale, near Strath Carron. The rock here comprises highly polished quartzite slabs, and there are no obvious features to follow, with wrinkles offering meagre options for balancing upon. Protection and belays require cunning—not something the soloist need worry about.

Patey climbed the first route on this crag, a central line on the Central Buttress with immaculate rock on the upper sections. Whigmaleerie was only graded Severe, but at 240m long, it is a committing route: there are few escapes, and the angle steepens towards the crux at an overhanging slanting crack.

In the summer of 1962, a joint British expedition comprising SMC and Alpine Club members was to visit the Pamir Mountains in Central Asia and climb alongside host Russian mountaineers who had visited Britain the year before. Graeme Nicol, who was undertaking National Service at the time, was asked by Malcolm Slesser if he would like to attend the trip in dual capacity as climber and doctor. He declined initially because of the unfavourable impression he had had of Slesser at the CIC Hut during the Zero Gully trip. Iain Smart was offered the place but had to decline. Slesser then recommended Patey for the team to his fellow joint leader Sir John Hunt, citing the following reasons:

> 1. He was and is one of the best climbers ever to come out of Scotland.
> 2. He is a doctor ... and he is likely to be effective at high levels, for he is just so fit and able.
> 3. He is mature, past his prima donna stage.
> 4. He has a certain international acclaim.
> 5. He is a proven high-altitude man. (Cruikshank, 2006)

Patey, in the throes of establishing himself as a full-time GP, could not spare the unpaid time away from his career and family, and he declined the offer but recommended Nicol again, who eventually accepted. 'For one who was obsessed by mountains, [Patey] had an astonishingly ready concern for his friends' (*SMCJ*, 1971). Patey visited Nicol's widowed mother in Aberdeen and assured her that Nicol would be fine as the Pamirs were not particularly dangerous mountains. Nicol did return, but tragically it was the expedition on which Robin Smith and Wilfred Noyce died in a fall while roped together.

Patey's proper break with Aberdeen came in 1962. Although he was about to leave the city for good, he maintained his contacts with friends there, many of whom had tempered their climbing fervour due to the demands of careers and family responsibilities. Patey had these commitments too, but his appetite for climbing was undiminished and it was by no means the only interest he chose to continue pursuing. This meant his lifestyle was extremely busy, and it was difficult to accommodate his wish to climb regularly and at the standard he wanted to maintain.

His periods as a locum in the North-West had afforded him a keen appreciation of the magnificent variety of mountaineering to be had in the region across the seasons. In August, he was awarded the post of Deputy Principal GP in Ullapool. The village would remain his home for the rest of his life.

1   Norman Tennent and his wife, Mona, ran a very welcoming hotel and his personality attracted many Scottish climbers. He took part in several mountain rescues in the Kintail area, Skye and beyond. Like Patey, he was strongly individualist, loved adventure and hated predictability. He was also an engaging conversationalist and writer, but could be rather cutting and acerbic. Tennent valued the people he climbed with as much as the activity itself. Tennent had a cool head, which he had honed during his war service as a submarine commander, and he admitted that his only truly happy time in life was when he was initiating an attack. Although not a leading climber, he was a minor legend in his time and he climbed frequently with SMC members, although he never joined the club, which he said was 'full of old fogies and people in bath chairs, [and] he wasn't quite ready for that.' In Tennent's obituary in the 1993 *SMCJ*, his great friend Malcolm Slesser said of him, 'Norman was a man who flirted with death all his life. He was careless of his welfare and his safety.' In this and other respects, he was much like Patey.

2   This south-north traverse is not the norm in winter, since in the other direction several difficult pitches, such as the long side of the TD Gap, can be abseiled.

3   The Loch Laggan Hotel was run by John and Margaret Small. John Small was introduced to climbing by Patey at the advanced age of 50. When the hotel burnt down later in the '60s, he ran the Inveroykel Lodge, between Lairg and Ledmore Junction, where Patey visited from his home in Ullapool after-hours and provided entertainment with his accordion.

13

Patey with Rona, Betty
with Ian at Michael's
christening at St Mary's
on the Rock, Ellon
© Ian Patey collection

3 West Terrace

A town saturated with tourists in summer and suffering from the overzealous influence of Christianity in all seasons.

Hamish MacInnes, *Look Behind the Ranges*

For a climber with such exploratory drive, the small North-West Highland village of Ullapool was an attractive base, with almost limitless potential for new summer and winter routes. Set against this was its isolation, lack of good climbing partners and, of course, the vagaries of the Scottish weather.

The area was a mountaineering backwater when Patey arrived in the '60s, partly because of its inaccessibility. The road from Inverness to Ullapool was single track and the A9 had no dual carriageway sections, which deterred most from the central belt from visiting at weekends. Some of what are now considered to be the greatest mountaineering arenas in the country, such as Beinn Bhàn in Applecross or the northern corries of Liathach and Triple Buttresses on Beinn Eighe, were still relatively undeveloped. Information was scant and venues deserted outside of holidays. North of Ullapool, it is still not unusual to be the only pair of climbers on one of the great mountain crags.

Initially, Patey ran the GP practice in the village with assistance from the occasional locum. His priority, aside from treating patients, was to get the surgery running efficiently and make sure the records and paperwork were up to date.

The Patey family stayed in the Argyll Hotel before they moved into the surgery accommodation. Betty looked after the house and children, whose number now included Michael, who was born in Aberdeen and baptised at St Mary's on the Rock in Ellon.

It is tempting to think that the life of a rural GP in a cosy backwater like Ullapool was a cushy number with plenty of leisure time. In fact, it was extremely demanding, with one of the largest practice areas in the UK, extending from Achiltibuie down to Dundonnell. The nearest other practices were in Lochinver and Gairloch.

In November 1964, a second doctor, Roger Watters, was appointed to the practice, and this helped reduce Patey's responsibilities. Although Patey's senior by ten years, Watters had only qualified in Medicine in 1961. His wife, Pam, had entered Aberdeen University Medical School a few years before Patey, and when neither doctor was available, she would field calls, issue advice and carry out locum work.

Morning surgery ended at 11.30am and was followed by an afternoon session at 3.00pm. As well as surgery appointments, there were home visits and out-of-hours calls, which required significant travel during the working week. Even with two full-time GPs, it was still a heavy workload. To put it into context, while the population of Ullapool has doubled since Patey's era, it now boasts six doctors.

Watters and Patey had a very good working relationship. Watters was a keen fisherman—a pastime less affected by cloud and drizzle—so their respective hobbies complemented each other. But Patey, adopting a flexi-time approach to work before the term was coined and validated by HR managers, would sometimes leave his partner in the lurch by going away for extended trips.

Having once seen a local teacher sunbathing in his Y-fronts in his garden, Patey was acutely aware that living in the village meant he was highly visible to his patients. To ensure his privacy and professional image he kept a low profile and did his best to avoid being approached in the street and pestered about locals' ailments. Despite this, he would not hesitate to apply his professional skills and knowledge, even if he was off duty.

Local garage owner Macnab Mackenzie remembers Patey as 'always on a mission', with not much time to stop and chat, yet very well regarded. Mackenzie got the impression Patey was shy, which shows just how successful he was in distancing himself and guarding his private life.

Making a long-distance phone call would require an operator to transfer the call, and Patey was cautious about eavesdropping, often travelling outwith the locale to make personal calls. The climber and photographer John Cleare, who became a close friend, recalls that the operator would sometimes tell him where Patey was on his rounds and when he would be back at the surgery.

Despite his sociable nature, Patey could not risk being seen drinking in public by the locals. If friends were visiting, he would retire to their hotel room with a bottle, eschewing the lounge or public bars. When Cleare spent time in the area, the inn at Alltnacealgach was about the closest place they would venture for a meal. Occasionally, though, Patey would attend a local ceilidh and play his accordion.

Robert Scott, a gamekeeper and ghillie in Assynt, described Patey as a 'conscientious and greatly liked doctor in Ullapool'. During the not infrequent periods of bad weather:

> *He would often look after his patients in a lively way by uplifting their weary winter souls with his accordion. He often set Ullapool's or Lochinver's village hall alive with his glorious sounds. Many an Assynt gamekeeper's, shepherd's and fisherman's weather-beaten and sweating face was first kindled by whisky and then stoked by Tom's accordion playing.* (Scott, 2015)

Patey was particularly skilled in his care of children. On one occasion, Aberdeen climber Davie Reid was camping in Ullapool with his family. During the night, one of the children began struggling to breathe and Reid sought out Patey, who came to the campsite and examined the child, but could not figure out the problem. An hour or so later, well after midnight, Patey reappeared and told Reid the matter had been troubling him and he thought that the child might be allergic to the feathers in the sleeping bags. He was proved right, and the crisis was resolved.

GPs are sometimes called upon to be social workers and counsellors, and not all Patey's consultations were of a medical nature. Responding to a call from an anguished crofter, who would not discuss the problem over the phone but said that it was serious, Patey arrived at the man's house to be told that his wife was in bed. When Patey enquired what was wrong, the crofter informed him that she was in bed next door with his neighbour and asked if Patey could sort things out.

His reputation as an excellent and caring GP seems to have pervaded all the communities in which he practised, but everyone has their detractors. Elderly resident Dolly MacLeod lived on a croft near Achiltibuie and was once quizzed by a tourist about making an appointment with a local GP. With a twinkle in her eye, Dolly replied: 'There iss two doctors in Ullapool. One of them iss no use when he is drunk; the other iss no use unless he is drunk' (Biggar, 2020).

Due to a lack of partners, much of Patey's initial climbing was done solo, although old friends would occasionally turn up at weekends or during their holidays. He also commandeered the local Ullapool policeman to join him on gorge explorations in his welly boots, using a wooden stake jammed across narrow sections as a belay.

In the '60s, another policeman, Sgt Donnie Smith, headed up the Ross and Sutherland police rescue team, which was based in Dingwall. The leader for 14 years, he was awarded the British Empire Medal for his services to mountain rescue in 1972.

Smith first met Patey when he attended a mountain rescue to confirm the death of a recovered body. Patey also acted as a volunteer on local rescues and helped Smith with team training sessions. 'Often your closest friends are people you don't take to initially,' said Smith (2013), who at first found Patey to be brusque and off-hand, someone who did not suffer fools gladly and could be brutally frank. Patey would usually leave immediately after a rescue and avoid socialising with the rest of the team, although he maintained his dry sense of humour on even the most gruesome and harrowing rescues.[1] He once saved a mountain rescue team colleague's life after a brain haemorrhage, as he had done for a fellow Marine in Norway. With the nearest A&E Department some distance away, Patey had to think on his feet and try

Sgt Donnie Smith © Donnie Smith collection

to stabilise the patient until he could be transferred to specialised care.

Sometimes when he was on call, Patey would visit an accessible roadside crag, and Betty would drive to the crag and blare the horn if his medical expertise was required. Arriving with Smith at the summit of Beinn Dearg one winter's afternoon after climbing a gully, Patey suddenly uttered a torrent of expletives and announced he had to be back for surgery at 3.00pm, so they ran down the ridge towards Smith's van at Inverlael and got back with five minutes to spare. That afternoon, Patey conducted his surgery in boots, breeches and an old jersey several sizes too big for him.

On another occasion, Patey climbed in black work shoes and a grey suit, and when he returned home the shoes were ruined and his lower trouser legs were in tatters. Betty, very much the doctor's wife, was not pleased. Although Smith was very fond of Patey, he realised he was quite different from other doctors he had met.

Patey and Smith would go out regardless of the weather, but Patey was only interested in doing new routes, and hillwalks were for scouting suitable lines and assessing virgin cliffs.[2]

According to Smith, when Patey did not succeed at what he set out to do, he would be vocal about his disappointment and frustration with himself. He also recalls Patey's tremendous physical and mental endurance. Smith, too, was supremely fit, and at his peak he could reach the summit of Ben Wyvis from the road at Garbat in 40 minutes, but Patey was consistently quicker on the hill. Moreover, he wanted to make use of every possible hour, which, in the summer months, meant that the days could be very long. Winter routes were inevitably completed in darkness.

He was always in a desperate hurry, a feature Smith had noticed in other people who died early, and he would not stop to exchange pleasantries with folk they passed on the hill. After finishing a climb, Smith wanted to relax, enjoy the view and take photographs. Not Patey: he would want to do another route or prospect for one. 'When you look back now, he was hurrying to an untimely end' (ibid.).

Patey also remained a heavy smoker, even when out on the hill, although this did not seem to affect his fitness and energy levels. Reaching the summit of Bidein a' Ghlas Thuil (the highest peak of An Teallach) after a training day with visiting Royal Marines, Patey had already smoked a packet of 10 Capstan Full Strength cigarettes. Flinging his empty packet in the direction of the pristine Fisherfield (then Whitbread) wilderness, he asked if Smith had any smokes left. Food and gear, too, were in short supply in Patey's rucksack, and he would often raid Smith's for both.

This aura of invincibility was combined with a careless, reckless streak. On a difficult mixed pitch on An Teallach in winter, Smith asked for a top rope. When he arrived at the summit, he was alarmed to find that Patey had draped the rope around a shallow nubbin of rock and was pressing an axe head over it to keep it in place. When Smith expressed his concern, Patey insisted that climbing was mostly psychological, and that Smith was too cautious. 'That's where climbing begins,' said Patey,

Patey with axe on a rescue team exercise on Liathach. Chris Brasher to his left. Donnie Smith is third from right © Donnie Smith collection

tapping his head. He said Smith reminded him of Hamish MacInnes, who '[tested] everything twice', and he teased Smith about using screw-gate karabiners. Patey's way of dealing with compromised safety was straightforward: 'You just don't come off' (ibid.).[3]

For Patey, age was all about attitude, and one of his patients exemplified the qualities that he most admired in people. Tom Longstaff (1875-1964) lived in Achiltibuie, and after an establishment education at Eton and Christ Church, Oxford, he trained as a doctor at St Thomas's Hospital in London, though he never practised medicine. Longstaff is best known as a mountaineer and explorer, and the first person to climb a peak over 7,000m: Trisul, in the Himalaya.

Although Longstaff was Patey's patient, their conversation often centred on climbing. Patey was well versed in mountaineering history and was fascinated to meet someone who had begun his Himalayan career at the end of the previous century.

In Longstaff's obituary (*Alpine Journal*, 1964), Patey commented:

Some men never grow old. Age, after all, is no more than a state of mind and cannot be measured in years. My late friend Tom Longstaff was one of the few who proved this argument. At the age of eighty-nine he was younger at heart than many of my contemporaries in their early thirties. The climbing world will remember Longstaff as the greatest mountain explorer of his time ... those of us who knew him more intimately will remember him as one who had discovered the elixir of life. He enjoyed living as few men know how to ... For him, the flame of adventure burned as brightly as it had ever done. Although no longer able to tackle the great peaks, he climbed with us in spirit. Tom Longstaff was never the man to shake his head mournfully over the so-called decadence of modern British mountaineers. Had he been climbing actively today, he would, I'm sure, have joined us on the Eigerwand ... As a friend, I never thought of him as one who was old enough to be my grandfather. Tom was always 'one of the boys'. As his doctor (a position I did not altogether relish), I had to accept the fact that any advice or treatment I gave him had little material effect on the outcome. It was his own vitality and zest for living that kept him going. When eventually the end came, as it had to inevitably, even for the indefatigable Tom, he had no complaints. He would not have wished it otherwise. There were few men less suited to the role of the invalid.

Patey, too, hated the idea of being bedridden, enduring a lingering death or a long period of infirmity. On several occasions, he told Smith that he would prefer to take a pill to end it all.

Patey's only other close friend in the area was Glenn Davies, who had been a Corporal in the Marines and a cliff assault leader with 42 Commando. When Patey returned from Rakaposhi in 1958, he 'was like a god to us', recalled Davies (2013), who vividly described Patey's appearance:

Hands like shovels, orange fingers from the nicotine, cuts and calluses over them, frizzy hair all over the place, boots on, heavy oversized Shetland fisherman's jumper, pasty-faced ... he didn't have the carriage he had in the Marines.

If there was division between the ranks, it was not something Patey attached much significance to, and Davies would not have settled in Ullapool had it not been for Patey and his advocacy for the area. Working in the local quarry, Davies earned three times what he had earned in the Marines, with meals and accommodation thrown in for free. With Davies, Patey could be more relaxed than with any local resident, and they would sandwich in frenetic climbing between Patey's surgeries. Sgùrr an Fhidhleir was a popular destination, and their forays were often exploratory, a means of acquiring information for subsequent ventures. On rock he was 'incredibly quick but erratic, not slow and smooth like MacInnes ... he attacked it. It was the enemy' (ibid.). If there was a spiritual dimension to Patey's appreciation of mountains, it remained unspoken. There were no effusions about the splendours of the scenery during a day out with him: 'He was a matter-of-fact guy. He knew what he wanted, and he went and got it' (ibid.). This epitomised a Marines attitude, although, towards the end of his life, Patey discussed deeper matters with his friend.

Despite his professional standing, Patey retained his mischievous streak, especially around authority figures. He was once pulled over by the Police, who were alarmed by the pill bottles and medication strewn around his car—'a narcotic nightmare' (Boysen, 2013). Seeing the potential for some fun, Patey did not disclose his profession and was arrested and taken to Dingwall Police Station, charged with possession of drugs. He relished the moment when the Chief Inspector greeted him by his Christian name and dismissed the charge, to the embarrassment of the junior officers.

After purchasing his first Skoda, he was committed to replacing it with the same make as dealers were reluctant to take a Skoda in part-exchange. Like its owner, the car was well used and showed signs of wear. Patey was renowned for having neither mechanical aptitude nor interest in technology, and this applied to vehicles as well as climbing equipment. Chris Bonington (1973) remarked, 'It was a replica of its owner: unfashionable, untidy, but very rugged.' Joe Brown recalled running out of petrol with him in the middle of the night on numerous occasions. Even when Betty bought him a five-gallon drum, it usually just prolonged the inevitable.

Although Patey enjoyed driving, he would sometimes relinquish the wheel to others so that he could play his accordion. Composing songs and experimenting with lyrics would be regular ploys to fill the long hours spent travelling. Sometimes journeys were enlivened by novel passenger assessments of the road. On one occasion, Patey was driving Dennis Gray from Fort William to Bradford to deliver a lecture. They were on a tight schedule, and Patey put his foot down. Gray knew the roads well, and as they approached each bend, he would shout out a climbing grade to describe its severity. Racing towards the tight bends at Ingleton Bridge, Dennis optimistically shouted out 'Severe!' rather than 'Extreme!' and they crashed. As oil and water poured onto the road, Patey wondered aloud if it was serious.

Skodas were good rally cars, and they could withstand the unpredictable Scottish weather and Patey's journeys along rough tracks to access crags. Local climber Bob Brown remembered once getting a lift down from the forest edge at the foot of Gleann Sguaib to Inverlael. Back then, the gates were usually left open, but they were locked on this occasion, and Patey went into tank commander mode and drove right through them. Skodas were produced in Czechoslovakia, which was ruled by a Communist regime in the '60s. Nefarious activities in the name of the state were not unknown, and according to one fellow Skoda owner from that era, the user manual contained advice on how to remove bloodstains from the upholstery—rather useful for a car that was sometimes used as a temporary ambulance or hearse.

If Patey's car was strewn with medical accoutrements, climbing gear and empty cigarette packets, his garage was no better. Time was too precious to spend coiling ropes properly or maintaining equipment to any standard, but Patey was a master at disguising his climbing sorties from the locals.

Cleare recalls visiting Patey in 1969 with journalist Peter Gillman to spend a day on the hills for a *Sunday Times Magazine* article on Scottish winter climbing. After morning surgery, Patey, clad in a scruffy, stained suit, trousers held up by his Marine commando belt, drove slowly out of the village, waving to locals and making sure his stethoscope was visible, giving the impression he was heading out on house calls. Cleare and Gillman lay on the back seat under blankets until they left Ullapool and were told to duck down if a car passed them. At the end of the forestry track at the foot of Gleann Sguaib, Patey stripped off his suit and, donning his damp jacket and trousers and odd socks, was ready to climb.

Although he remained guarded in the village, there were still opportunities for discreet fun to be had. Outside the Patey residence was a strip of grass above what is now the town's campsite, with delightful views across Loch Broom to the shapely, isolated peak of Beinn

Patey and Skoda in Applecross. Donnie Smith at the back of the police vehicle
© John Cleare

Dr Patey in Gleann na Sguaib, Beinn
Dearg, just up the road from Ullapool
© John Cleare

Ghobhlach on the Scoraig peninsula. To Patey's irritation, tourists would occasionally picnic here right under his nose, so he devised an effective solution. During his 1965 Alpine holiday, he had purchased some records which were banned at the time and were sold under the counter in brown wrapping. Patey took delight in the scandalised reactions of passersby and picnickers to the marching songs of the Third Reich blaring out from his open window. With the war still a recent memory, most visitors must have been horrified to hear such tracks. For Patey, it was an amusing reminder of a shameful past and a way to shift folk out of view. But he genuinely liked the music, regardless of its associations with evil.

One of the worst things for any local climber is to have a major route poached from under his nose. Shortly after Patey moved to Ullapool, Mike Dixon and Neville Drasdo were on holiday in the North-West when they happened upon Patey in the village. After pleasantries, Patey suggested they try the Direct Nose Route on Sgùrr an Fhidhleir, a superb peak which rears out of the Ben Mor Coigach massif like the prow of an enormous ship.

As far back as 1907, Ling and Sang had attempted it and had succeeded in climbing the lower 200m, which Patey claimed was 'possibly the most audacious exploit in Scottish mountaineering up to that time'. Other luminaries such as Parker, Baird and Young had got so far and retreated, evidenced by the amount of discarded gear. Patey himself had soloed up to the crux. After a late start and in between lulls in dangerous cross winds, Drasdo led Dixon up the entire route, taking the upper edge directly. Walking back in mist and drizzle across the moor in the vague direction of their car, they encountered Patey, who had become worried by their late return. He had left a note written on the back of a prescription sheet under a windscreen wiper, which read: 'I have gone to look for your bloody bodies. Back shortly, Tom.' In the mizzle, the ink had run into a spidery font, like a detail from an Edgar Allen Poe story.

Patey was gracious about their coup and indeed showed no malice to those who beat him to prized routes, of which there was no shortage in the North-West. Patey made the second ascent of Sgùrr an Fhidhleir with Mike Taylor in 1964 via an easier variation of Drasdo's thin, parallel cracks pitch.

Despite his aversion to certain holidaymakers, Patey advertised his home turf to potential climbing partners with zeal. The bothy behind his house became fully functional in 1964 and served its purpose well, providing a cosy socialising venue where Patey could relax in likeminded company in the heart of a watchful community, while remaining totally screened off from it. The concept of closing time there did not exist: Patey hated wasted time, which included hours spent sleeping.

1   In April 1966, An Teallach was the scene of a famous mountain rescue. The mountain was in full winter condition and the snow was bullet hard. Experienced mountaineer Ian Ogilvie became separated from his companions, Charles Handley and Peter Francis, who slipped and fell down a snowslope roped together. Witnessing the fall, Ogilvie downclimbed to a spike of rock, upon which the rope had snagged, but found the pair unconscious. Over many hours spent roping his two inert companions down the slope, Ogilvie himself sustained two falls, but managed to walk out, weak and bleeding. The driver of a passing car refused to help, but Ogilvie eventually managed to contact the rescue services. Patey, ill-clad as ever, arrived on the scene and in the fading daylight dashed into the coire, where he discovered Ogilvie's companions. He lowered the bodies in the dark and they were eventually carried out by the rescue services. For his valiant efforts to rescue his friends, Ogilvie received the MBE. Patey received the Queen's Commendation for Brave Conduct (Thomson, 1993). Patey later confronted and rebuked the driver of the car who had refused to help.

2   Patey did not deem every new route worth recording. One such was on the North-East Face of Sgùrr Mòr Fannaich, the highest peak in the Fannaich Range. The Resurrection (originally Grade V, now III), climbed in March 1980 by John Mackenzie and Dave Butterfield, gained a reputation after being included in *Cold Climbs*. Mackenzie's write-up of the route and its presence on a tick-list guaranteed other climbers would be tempted by it, but those viewing it from a distance were puzzled as to how such a straightforward-looking face could harbour a Grade V route. Repeat ascents confirmed it had been overgraded, and a snowboard descent of the face was the clincher.

3   MacInnes, who was every bit as tough as Patey but more cautious, lived until he was 90.

14

The Ullapool Bothy rules
© Ian Patey collection

The Bothy

THE BOTHY BOOK

① <u>NO SWEARING OR SINGING DURING SURGERY HOURS</u>

② Donations gratefully received
③ All damages to be paid for in full
④ No intoxicating liquor or spirits to be consumed on these premises unless the hut guardian is present. (& participating)
⑤ No Orgies.
⑥ Arrive & Depart inconspicuously.
⑦ Lavatory on right just inside the back door. Do not use during surgery hours
⑧ Records of climbs, constructive suggestions, witty comments welcomed.

Best bothy we've ever encountered. Running H&C and Whisky.

George Rankine and Pete Grant, Bothy Book, 3 July 1966

All bothies and huts owned by mountaineering clubs have rules for use. The bothy behind Patey's house was no different, but the tone was like no other.

Dr Peter Steele, chief medical officer on the International Everest Expedition of 1971 and author of an award-winning biography about Eric Shipton, responded to the rules with the following:

> *19 March 1964. Semi-resident (all orgies committed on a hill out of town) but available daily at coffee and whisky time.*

The bothy, which was basically a garden shed with bunks and a cooking space, was in partial use before a guests' logbook appeared in February 1964. The first entry exemplifies the hospitality offered to some of Patey's old Aberdeen friends, and indeed every visitor:

> *29 February. Arrived at hut 20.00 hrs. Guardian and family very friendly. Drank Glenmorangie with guardian until 02.00 hrs. Dr A.G. Nicol was carried to bed by the guardian and one of the party. Much song. 1 March. The guardian drove the party to Stac Polly* [sic]. *November Grooves. Visited Dr Longstaff. A comfortable and happy bothy. Dep. Aberdeen 20.00.*

Over the years, a collection of photographs and cartoons built up on the walls, many of a humorous nature. There was also a map of the

North of Scotland, highlighting the crags that were worthy of attention for new routes and stars rating them for quality.

As well as Brooker, Taylor, Grassick and Nicol, now respectable members of the SMC, the place attracted the next generation of Aberdeen climbers, including Etchachan Club members Derek Pyper and Jim McArtney, and Robin Ford, one of the leading lights in the University Lairig Club. Mac Smith, 'the Chieftain of Luibeg', visited, as did Dick Barclay of the Kincorth Club.

Guests were usually 'Entertained in the evening by Tom & a bottle of hooch' and, according to Ford, 'Fatigue and foul weather brought out the Hash King element.' This was a reference to the '50s Aberdeen bothy scene when Luibeg and other venues were often frequented by socialisers rather than climbers.

Not all visitors were mountaineers, however. Clive Freshwater was a sailing and canoeing instructor at Glenmore Lodge. During a paddling trip on the north coast with an American girlfriend, their canoe was blown out to sea in a severe gale, never to be seen again. Patey offered them refuge in the bothy, where Freshwater became ill with acute food poisoning after eating two large crabs. Inspired by the incident, Patey composed a brief salutary verse about the perils of gluttony:

His fate is written on the slab,
He died from an overdose of crab.
His fair companion, name unknown,
Now paddles her canoe alone.

Thankfully, Freshwater made a full recovery.

Friends from Patey's National Service days spent time in the area and a few nights in the bothy. The Royal Marine and 'Gay Lothario', Sam Bemrose could not resist friendly banter about Patey's dress sense, approach to safety equipment and role in the community:

24 May–5 June 1964. He is still the immaculate military figure, and to see him in his well-pressed breeches and shirt as he gazes at his beloved hills is a sight to stir the heart. As methodical as ever, it is a joy to see him prepare for the hills. Rucksack packed and checked, I was delighted to see he never left the road without his sleeping bag, map, compass, protractor, torch, whistle, gloves and of course a spare pair of socks. What an example the grand Old Man is to the ramblers of Scotland.

Of course, he still leads a very full life, and on more than one occasion had to leave the hill early to be present at jamborees of the Boy Scout Troop which occupies so much of his great energies. He is loved and respected by the backward natives of the Western Highlands, with whom he has spent a lifetime bringing healing and comfort. And to see them stop and tug their forelock as he strides from cottage to cottage visiting the sick and the old is to get an insight to this great man they lovingly call 'Our Doctor Tom'.

Families were welcome, and Ted Maden's enjoyed their stay:

September 1965. Many thanks to guardian and Betty for hospitality, and their children for sharing [their] swings and tricycles with ours.

Two years after their first ascent of the Direct Nose Route of Sgùrr an Fhidhleir, Mike Dixon and Neville Drasdo returned and added to an earlier humorous cartoon in the Bothy Book which had been drawn by Mike Taylor and which depicted Patey hiding behind a stag's head on the wall, spying and eavesdropping on the bothy residents' conversations for his own comedic repertoire. Dixon and Drasdo suggested that a spare antler they had discovered could be fired from the stag's head to impale the occupant of the bunk bed opposite.

After the dominance of Jimmy Marshall, Robin Smith, Dougal Haston and the Currie Boys, the Edinburgh-based Squirrels Club were in the vanguard of Scottish summer and winter climbing. Members Mike Galbraith, Bill Sproul, Alistair 'Bugs' McKeith, John Porteous and Jim Renny all put in an appearance, and Brian Robertson (who would be involved in two

there is a hidden compartment behind the stag's head thus:—

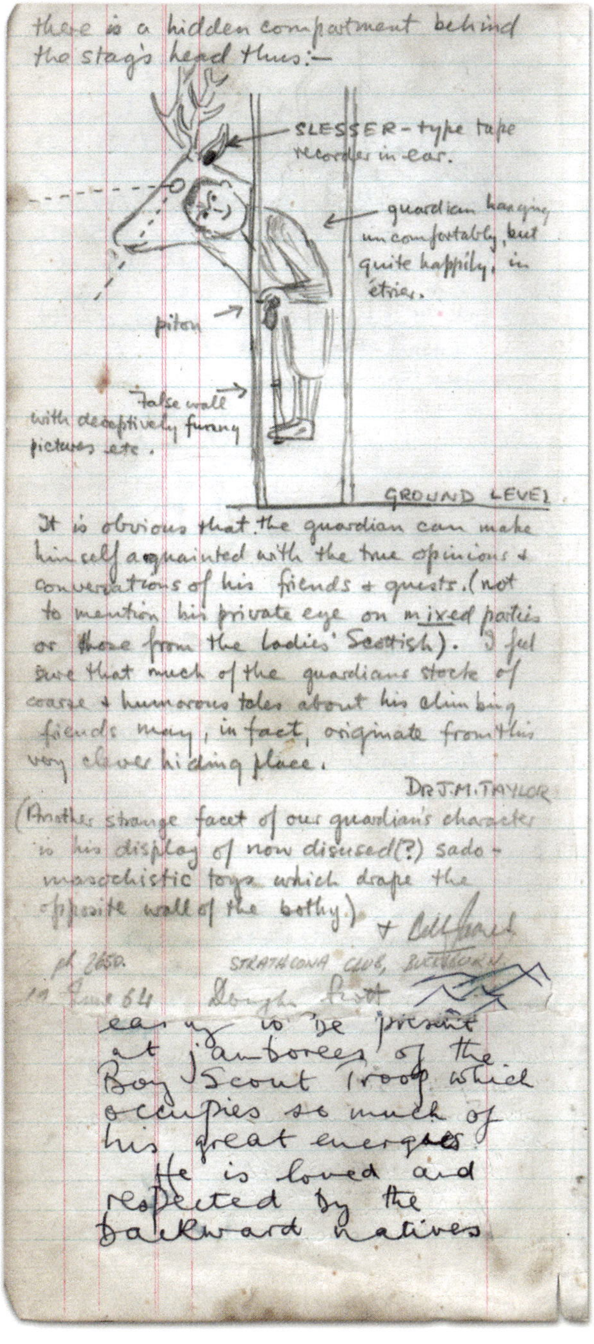

SLESSER-type tape recorder in ear.

guardian hanging uncomfortably but quite happily in étriers.

piton →

False wall with deceptively funny pictures etc.

GROUND LEVEL

It is obvious that the guardian can make himself acquainted with the true opinions & conversations of his friends & guests. (not to mention his private eye on mixed parties or those from the Ladies' Scottish). I feel sure that much of the guardians stock of coarse & humorous tales about his climbing friends may, in fact, originate from this very clever hiding place.

Dr J.M.TAYLOR

(Another strange facet of our guardian's character is his display of now disused(?) sado-masochistic toys which drape the opposite wall of the bothy.) + *illegible*

ph 2650.   STRATHCONA CLUB, SUTHERLAND
19 June 64   *illegible* first
                    easy to be present
                    at jamborees of the
                    Boy Scout Troop which
                    occupies so much of
                    his great energies
                    He is loved and
                    respected by the
                    backward natives

Mike Taylor's sketch
in the Bothy Book
© Ian Patey collection

of Patey's greatest first ascents: the Cuillin Ridge in winter and the Old Man of Stoer), became a frequenter of the bothy. Like Patey, Robertson was partial to the Teutonic dimension in mountaineering, and two of his new routes, The Valkyrie on the Etive Slabs and The Blue Max on Creag an Dubh-loch, were named to reflect this enthusiasm.

New friends, including photographer John Cleare and his wife Vicki, became regulars. Rhodesian Rusty Baillie first stayed just after New Year in 1966, as did American Mary Stewart, whose home outside Glasgow became renowned as a vibrant meeting place for climbers and musicians.

The classic local hills and traverses were common itineraries for visitors. November Grooves on Stac Pollaidh was popular, as was the Direct Nose Route of Sgùrr an Fhidhleir, although not all attempts were successful.

Young climbers from Inverness Mountaineering Club and further afield, seeking information, would turn up unannounced and would be welcomed. When Cambridge University students Geoff Cohen and Rob Collister enquired about route details for the Direct Nose Route, Patey presented them with the relevant page torn from the *Northern Highlands District Guide*, and Cohen (who would go on to compile a volume of the SMC's guidebooks to the Northern Highlands and contribute to another), was shocked at what amounted to the violation of a holy text. In 1967, Cohen, Collister and fellow student Charles Shepherd were also invited to an impromptu ceilidh at the Oykel Bridge Hotel, between Ledmore Junction and Rosehall. It was the nearest 'off the radar' place from Ullapool for such a gathering. As Cohen (2014) recalled, the ceilidh:

> ... had very few people, but that didn't stop Tom playing all night. We three young 'uns drank till 3 or so in the morning then went to doss in a side building, but I think Tom was still playing when we turned in. In the morning, [he] walked in towards Alladale with us for ... maybe an hour, before heading back.

For some, the notion of what constituted real climbing was up for debate. Ian McNaught Davis (Mac), his then-wife Mary and Chris

Bonington stayed at the bothy just before filming a BBC Outside Broadcast of an ascent of the Old Man of Hoy in July 1967. Mac recorded their explorations:

> *Several original methods were devised to avoid climbing. A psychedelic Tyrolean to the top of some guano-covered lump sticking out of the N. Atlantic. Then the old, old excuse of looking for new crags. Eight new routes were done, two almost twenty feet high. Full descriptions will be published in the* Sunday Telegraph *supplement at a future date, hopefully very future.*

The lump in question was the Stack of Handa. In fact, the enormous potential of the area was never fully appreciated in the '60s. Back then, the North-West was seen as a mountaineering venue, but today, it is a cragging and bouldering paradise and definitions as to what constitutes real climbing are wide and inclusive. Beyond Achiltibuie, Reiff is sometimes referred to as 'Stanage by the Sea'.

Poor weather often thwarted plans, however. Llanberis-based artist Anthony 'Ginger' Cain and his wife, Vera, confessed to 'festering'—the art of occupying one's time in inclement weather—over a protracted period:

> *7-9 September 1968. Passing through in retreat from Skye. Enjoyed the hospitalities of the Pateys. Weather indifferent. Did nothing but kill 37 wasps, read the wallpaper and drink.*

But the Patey annexe was not a bad place to be holed up, and it was described as 'the epitome of dosses'.

The following year, Cain returned with Baz Ingle, and recorded their activities in the Bothy Book:

> *17-23 May 1969. We arrived in what may be termed a meteorological rarity in this region, which has persisted for the length of our stay. We have been taken on the renowned 'Tour of the Highlands' by the good*

doctor himself, and introduced to such delights as Quinag (Face Ouest), Tollie Crags (Nordwand) and the Cioch of Applecross. The latter was visited for an evening's climbing, which we found a rather peculiar use of the available daylight hours. In fact, our whole stay has been marked by an inability to start climbing before about 5.00 or 6.00pm and to get back before 2.00 or 3.00am.

Cain elaborated on this 45 years later:

I particularly remember Tom taking us on an evening jaunt to Applecross after he finished his surgery. We got there about 7.00pm and he got us first to do his own route, The Sword of Gideon, which Baz and I climbed roped while Tom soloed alongside (He had done the first ascent of this route solo—very bold). After this we plodded up the corrie to the Cioch of Applecross where he got us to do the direct start that I believe he had done with Hamish MacInnes, and then continue up the length of this long route, then back down the corrie in the semi-darkness, and then [we drove] back to Ullapool. He was an extremely popular GP, and this showed when we called in with him at various hostelries in his catchment area, where we got free drinks pressed on us just for being with Tom.

Patey's love of music attracted one visitor who probably never climbed a mountain in his life. Alex Campbell (1925-1987) was a figure in the British folk revival of the '50s and '60s and one of the first to tour the UK and Europe extensively. A 'melancholic, hard-travelling Glaswegian' (Harper, 2006), he was a charismatic man who beguiled audiences with his singing and storytelling. He could switch from a raucous ballad to the most tender of love songs, and although he did not have the greatest voice or the most accomplished guitar technique, he imbued a song with such emotion that he had audiences hanging off every note. Billy Connolly once said that seeing Campbell in all his wild glory was the reason he became a performer.

Pictures on the wall included portraits of Scottish and Alpine mountains, cliffs, outcrops and sea stacks, and famous climbers. Some had captions added to them
© Ian Patey collection

Campbell, in typical fashion, left an entry about his stay at Patey's:

September 1966. I wis murdered last night, but the guid Doctor's (and his wife Betty's) hospitality put me a' the gether again. I will leave ye now with a new slogan: Alba go brah. *(Gaelic for 'Scotland forever').*

Underneath this, Campbell's wife, Patsy, suggested that he might have been in a far worse state if he had not 'spilled a quarter bottle'. Their companion, the American musician Mary Anne Alburger, wrote:

Ullapool offered solace to several wandering, marauding troubadours last night, of food, drink and maintaining merry. Musical research and documentation was also attempted, gratis. We will return.

For some, it was not the scenery or climbing which made the stay memorable but Patey's personality:

22–25 August 1969. Thanks from me too, Tom, for the shelter from the storm and all the extra favours, but especially for your inspiring company—the songs and tales. I'll be singing your songs in California.

The Pateys' generosity towards people whom they had often met for the first time was noteworthy. A trio of hitchhikers struck lucky when Patey gave them a lift to Ullapool all the way from Gretna Green, a 'Journey enlivened by enlightening tales of mountaineering from the inside.' Patey let them stay in the bothy for a week, and when they were late returning from an attempt to climb An Teallach, 'Tom and wife had the goodness of heart to drive out from Ullapool to pick us up.'

The last picture to go up on the walls was taken by Tony Riley and was of the first main ice pitch on Emerald Gully, which was climbed on 26 March 1970. It accompanied the final entry in the Bothy Book from Paul Nunn, who made the first ascent with Riley and Brian 'Fred the Ted' Fuller:

March 26–29 1970. Grade IV with two 120/30 ice pitches, the first taken direct, the second icicle overhang avoided by a steep traverse right. Convalescence assured by a long stay in Tom's bothy through most of the Easter weekend, emerging occasionally to quaff beer, watch telly and observe the occasional showers. Upon departure we were physically glowing and mind-boggled by our daily ration of hypothetical routes. Magnificent stay—thanks, Tom.

The existence of the bothy reveals Patey's need to get away from the constraints of his job and perhaps also from his more conventional wife. The bothy helped him compartmentalise his life and keep his friends largely separate from his family. It is almost as if he had two distinct personas: the caring doctor and family man, and the wild climber and musician.

Over an eight-year period, the bothy's guardian had become the pre-eminent pioneer of new routes in the North-West Highlands and beyond.

Rusty Baillie in action. The Latin name Pithecanthropus Erectus is also the title of 1956 album by jazz composer and double bassist Charlie Mingus, which the musically eclectic Patey would have known © Ian Patey collection

15

Patey and Brian Robertson at the bivvy spot at Sgùrr na Banachdich during the first winter traverse of the Cuillin Ridge
© Hamish MacInnes

Third Time Lucky

Without doubt the finest winter mountaineering expedition in Britain, the most Alpine in character and yet super-Alpine in length.

Gordon Stainforth, *The Cuillin*

During his Ullapool period, Patey would repeatedly return to reap the harvest on certain cliffs where he had established a climb and assessed other lines. He soloed many of these, and took the opportunity to tackle harder routes when friends were enticed to visit by the huge potential of the area.

In January 1963, Patey began his campaign on the long line of cliffs on Beinn Dearg's Gleann na Sguaib, which was readily accessible from Ullapool. Steep, wet and vegetated terrain is transformed into a superb playground in winter. His opening gambit, Inverlael Gully (II), climbed with old Aberdeen friends Graeme Nicol and Mike Taylor, was followed by a much better route the following March, which Patey recorded in the Ullapool Bothy Book:

> To round off the SMC Easter Meet at Inchnadamph, a Presidential first ascent was made by W.H. Murray with aides de camp Tennent and Patey. This was a 1,000ft ice gully, still in perfect condition (despite the poor winter) … named Penguin Gully from the characteristic attitude of two members of the party throughout most of the climb. Steep cutting on hard ice all the way. 5 hours.
>
> Both senior members had forgotten their crampons and did not, of course, have any rock or ice pitons. The junior member had forgotten his boots, gloves and anorak. Improperly equipped, shod and clad, the party nevertheless forced a passage by sheer SMC grit, classic rock belaying and hewing mighty bucket steps. The inadequacies of cleated

composition soles were vividly illustrated on more than one occasion. 'A thrice royal route in winter.'

Their ascent of Penguin Gully (III,4) was accomplished in a style that would humble modern climbers and which has probably never been repeated with similar techniques and equipment.

Patey returned on two consecutive days in March 1968 to solo four routes. The best of these was Fenian Gully, a sustained Grade IV,4, which he compared to Green Gully on Ben Nevis. Continuing the sectarian theme, he named two of the others Orangeman's Gully and Papist's Passage—a reference to the noticeable Protestant/Catholic divide in the west of Scotland. An earlier route had been named The Reverend Ian Paisley Memorial Gully by a Squirrels team, perhaps in hopeful anticipation of the fiery politician's demise, although he would live for another 47 years.

Not all days resulted in new routes. Retreating from Beinn Dearg's Gleann na Sguaib in January 1966 after Patey was avalanched. From left: Mary Stewart, Rusty Baillie, Patey © John Cleare

Stac Pollaidh's accessibility from Ullapool always drew Patey back. Baird's Pinnacle, an old RAF Kinloss aid route, was one of his more esoteric solo ascents
© Peter Macdonald

The mountains north of Ullapool were obvious targets in Patey's search for new routes. Stac Pollaidh in Assynt is 'a mountain in miniature' with huge charisma thanks to its summit ridge, which bristles with towers and pinnacles. With old Kincorth Club friend Dick Barclay, Patey climbed the strenuous and poorly protected Enigma Grooves on the West Buttress (HVS 5a).

He was also lured back to the imposing prow of Barrel Buttress on Quinag's Sail Garbh, and its Western Cliffs overlooking Lochinver. On Barrel Buttress he added Bitter (VS 4c) with Graeme Nicol, and with The Waste Pipe (II) revealed the winter potential of the Western Cliffs, despite their low altitude and proximity to the sea. In summer this sector appears fractured and vegetated, but Patey uncovered two cleaner, more continuous sections: the Pillar of Assynt (VS 5a), which he climbed with Hamish MacInnes, and Rickety Ridge (also VS), which he soloed.

On the vast, sprawling Foinaven in the far north, he added the opening line on Lord Reay's Seat, a peak on the mountain's main ridge with an attractively steep, quartzite eastern face.

Losing out on the first ascent of the Direct Nose Route of Sgùrr an Fhidhleir to Dixon and Drasdo had not deflected his interest from the further potential on this magnificent peak either, and his eye was caught by the zone of steep slabs to the east of the Nose, which were inlaid with a prominent right-facing corner. In May 1967, the right partner turned up at the bothy in Ullapool in the form of Martin Boysen, one of the most gifted rock climbers of his generation.[1] Patey took time off from his busy day job, and after 500m of soloing with the odd technical move, they roped up for several pitches no harder than VS, before reaching a crux section which Patey took one look at and suggested would better suit Boysen's experience of gritstone cracks. Boysen was afforded little time to savour the situation and technicalities, however:

> The climb was a very fine one and a sense of urgency was with us throughout. The exaggerated time-checking and 'you have only ten minutes to get up this pitch' comments ceased only when I was gripped in

a fierce fight with the final crack. However, much to Tom's satisfaction we made it back to the car 'within five seconds of scheduled time'. A quick change of clothes and the doctor was once again ready for surgery.

In the Bothy Book, Boysen recorded the crux as 'the middle of three short, steep, horrid cracks (XS)', named the route Second Fiddle and graded it VS, the highest in Scotland at the time. XS, meaning Extremely Severe, was then a generic grade used south of the border but there are now many numerical subdivisions, the easiest being E1. The route was subsequently named The Magic Bow and given the modern grade of E1, as the crux 5b and 5a and 4c pitches were much harder than the original appraisal.

Boysen (2013) observed that Patey could have climbed harder on rock. But extreme routes require a cautious, considered approach: hanging on, sorting out protection for the forthcoming difficulties, moving up and down in reconnaissance and preserving strength before committing to extreme moves. All of this would have hampered the speed and flow which Patey so liked about climbing. Nevertheless, sometimes partners who consistently climbed at a much higher standard on rock, such as Joe Brown and Baz Ingle, wanted to rope up when Patey was happy to continue soloing. Indeed, the following year he returned for a bold solo of The Phantom Fiddler, left of The Magic Bow. At HVS, it was close to his technical limit, with or without a rope.

Further afield, Creag Meagaidh saw repeat visits. In 1963 Patey put up three relatively easy routes (Cinderella, The Sash and Will o' the Wisp) in the mountain's Inner Corrie, but none had the significance of the routes he had done on the Post Face with Richard Brooke the year before.

The following February, he and Joe Brown completed the right-hand of two steep parallel icefalls above The Sash, which they named Diadem (IV,4). Two days later, they attempted Centre Post Direct, 'the last great problem' on the mountain, which he had tried unsuccessfully with Brooke. Again, he failed, and it fell to Brian Robertson of the Squirrels the following weekend.[2]

Traverse of A'Chioch, Beinn Bhan. Coire na Feola is on the left, Coire na Poite on the right. The Upper Connecting Ridge lies ahead of the figures. Patey's later route, March Hare's Gully, is the diagonal line on the right © Robert Durran

Brown and Patey tried to climb together in Scotland at least once a year. On Ben Nevis they put up Wendigo (IV,4) on Creag Coire na Ciste, one of Patey's relatively few new routes on that mountain and a fine line combining a lower icefall with a finish up mixed ground.[3] They also climbed Comb Gully Buttress on the same day.

In 1968, Patey and Brown did the first winter route on Beinn Bhàn in Applecross, which has become renowned for its aesthetic beauty and the quality of the routes, several of which are cutting edge. The central two of its six corries are the most impressive: Coire na Poite, whose back wall can be plastered with ice, and Coire nan Fhamhair, with its soaring gully lines and vertiginous face routes. Patey and Brown had designs on The North Gully of A' Chìoch in Coire na Poite, but backed off due to spindrift. Instead, they climbed onto the ridge on the left and, at one point, deviated onto a face above a big drop. The snow disintegrated as Patey, who was leading, kicked into it. Brown insisted they deploy the rope, but Patey had bundled it away without bothering to coil it properly, and it took 20 minutes before he could drop an end down to Brown.

On the summit, a fierce wind blew Brown's balaclava off, but as they were descending, he spotted the item hovering aloft and successfully plucked it out of the air. In calm conditions, the Upper Connecting Ridge of A' Chìoch is a grand excursion in a superb position and, despite only Grade II, a route of quality and atmosphere.

Few new rock routes were recorded in the Cairngorms and the Central Highlands during this period. Fallout Corner, adjacent to Savage Slit in the Northern Cairngorm's Coire an Lochain, is a fine pitch, mild at VS but a testpiece at its grade in winter.

In 1964, Patey climbed it with Robin Ford and Mary Stewart with one point of aid, and soon after, the trio opened up the significant crag Binnein Shuas, whose south-facing granite cliffs lie above the idyllic Lochan na h-Earba. The Fortress (HVS 5a) follows the right arête of a striking central crag of roofs and slabs.

Unusually, Patey appears not to have paid close attention to the potential of the slabs on the crag's eastern sector, which is home to one

Although Patey's preference was for high mountain crags, he dabbled in the abundant outcrop climbing in the area, participating in first ascents on the extensive Tollie Crags at the western end of Loch Maree with Squirrel Club members in 1966. The Hand Rail (Severe), climbed with Mike Galbraith, was a better route than Knickerbocker Glory (E1), which he did with Galbraith and Brian Robertson. Photo from Ullapool Bothy © Ian Patey collection

of Scotland's classic Hard Severes: Ardverikie Wall. Later, he ruefully commented that this was the finest route he walked past, and the honour went to Graeme Hunter and Doug Lang in 1967.

Patey's greatest mountaineering achievement during his time in Ullapool (and arguably his best route anywhere) was undoubtedly the Cuillin Ridge in Winter in 1965. By any standards, this is a world-class expedition in summer but its exposed and sustained six-mile razor-sharp crest is a fantastical undertaking when it is plated in snow and ice. Conditions can be fickle, and before the successful traverse there had been over a dozen attempts, half of which had involved

Cartoon from Patey's bothy depicting the 'Affaire Tiso'. Drawn by Kris Paterson
© Ian Patey collection

Hamish MacInnes. By the '60s, it was the glittering prize of British mountaineering.

In fact, it was MacInnes who contacted Patey with the ultimatum that he drop everything and make his way to Skye. Patey rang Eric Langmuir, the Principal at Glenmore Lodge, who agreed to come over with Graham Tiso. The forecast was excellent, and MacInnes, who had to pull out at the last minute, no doubt regretted suggesting it to Patey. Three was not an ideal number, but by chance Brian Robertson turned up in Ullapool, so the team climbed in two pairs.

Conditions were the best Patey had experienced in 16 years of winter climbing, and their 'hands and feet [worked] like pistons across the iron-hard névé'. Patey (1965) waxed lyrical about the backdrop, which included Sgùrr nan Gillean's Pinnacle Ridge, 'a jagged crescendo of glistening ice-towers, Himalayan in its unaccustomed winter garb,' and quipped that the deserted ridge 'was as empty as the back row of a cinema during the National Anthem.' Wearing rucksacks heavy with bivouac gear, he and Robertson soloed most of the way with two axes and 12-point crampons to hasten speed. They left Langmuir and Tiso to move at a steadier pace and cut out a palatial bivouac for four on Bidein Druim nan Ramh. When the other pair had not appeared by the following morning, they backtracked along the ridge expecting to find two dead bodies, but Langmuir and Tiso had been forced to bivouac near the foot of the Bhasteir Tooth after Tiso had snagged one of his crampons while abseiling off this pinnacle and had neatly flipped upside down, with no way of righting himself. Langmuir had descended the taut rope with a back-up prusik knot and had managed to unhook Tiso, but both men were exhausted by their tribulations.

Thus ended their attempt of the ridge, in frustratingly ideal conditions, but Patey and Robertson returned a few days later with MacInnes and Davie Crabb, who worked at the Glencoe School of Winter Climbing. The organisation was better this time, and local guide Pete Thomas offered to carry their bivouac gear up to Sgùrr na Banachdich. Perhaps due to the prospect of lighter rucksacks, Patey and Robertson imbibed enthusiastically at a ceilidh in Sligachan the night before, several hours after MacInnes and Crabb had gone to bed. The following morning, Robertson had to stop to be sick several times.

Patey's classic article about the traverse has all his signature components: adventure, moments of comedy, vivid characters, witty dialogue, shambolic incidents involving equipment, but above all, an expression of fun and respite from responsibilities. The friendly one-upmanship of MacInnes's banter was tinged with a competitive edge, but Patey gave as good as he got. Soloing on the Cuillin Ridge in winter is not for the incompetent or fainthearted, and there was only one section where, as Patey put it, 'you could have fallen and escaped with your life.' Crabb broke a crampon and needed safeguarding by MacInnes, and there was almost a repeat of the Tiso fiasco when a knot appeared in the rope as Patey abseiled down Naismith's Route on the Bhasteir Tooth. Patey managed to bypass this by hitting it with his peg hammer,

On Sgùrr a' Ghreadaidh, Cuillin Ridge in winter. The Inaccessible Pinnacle is on the far right © Mick Fowler

'Is that all there is?' The team in Glen Brittle the day after the traverse. From left: Robertson, Crabb, MacInnes, Patey
© Hamish MacInnes

but when they tried to pull the rope, the knot would not run through the karabiner attached to the abseil piton, and Patey humbly had to ask MacInnes to free it for him. The one-upmanship continued at the bivouac, with MacInnes extolling the merits of his and Crabb's superior platform and cuisine.

In MacInnes's photos of the traverse, Patey appears unusually well equipped, with a duvet jacket and a pair of Dachstein mitts—although these were not the easiest gloves with which to hold his cigarettes.

Day two began with Patey defrosting himself as the condensation in his plastic survival bag had left his clothing rigid. He soon warmed up, however. Fed up watching MacInnes trying to climb the demanding short side of the Inaccessible Pinnacle, he went for an exploratory solo up the ice-encrusted opposite side. After venturing beyond the point of no return, he was committed to finishing it alone. At the top of this, he threw down a top rope to MacInnes and, in a moment of wavering concentration, inadvertently attended to the handrail rope rather than that which was attached to MacInnes.

Having negotiated this obstacle, the next major impasse was the short side of the notorious Thearlaich-Dubh Gap. They almost abandoned it for a detour down into Coir' a' Ghrunnda until MacInnes, who had such intimate knowledge of the ridge that he knew of a spike at the top of the wall, lassoed this with his first cast. Patey trusted its lodging for a downward pull, and they went on to complete what he described as the 'greatest single adventure in British mountaineering'. Many have to wait years for the right conditions, but when successful, few would disagree with Patey's pronouncement. Despite being super-Alpine in length, its setting and character are uniquely Scottish. No mountaineer could ask for a better first ascent.

1   Boysen's outstanding all-round mountaineering achievements are recorded in his 2014 autobiography, *Hanging On, A Life Inside British Climbing's Golden Age*, published by Vertebrate Publishing Ltd.

2   Centre Post Direct is a huge, sustained pitch which had been on the list of all able climbers operating in Scotland for some time. Using five ice pegs for protection, Robertson led it in four hours and it took a further two hours for his second and third to follow. Knowing that Patey and Brown had got within ten feet of the top of the key section, Robertson could not resist a little one-upmanship at Patey and Brown's expense: 'When we did make an assault on this section, the steps (a great many of them) continued on the right edge of the ice, which we considered a wee bit cheating. Our line was approximately 30ft to the left of that holy ladder, which involved cutting steps on vertical water-ice, but luckily enough it eased off to 80 degrees higher up' (*SMCJ*, 1964).

3   According to the *Scottish Winter Climbs* (2008) guidebook, a wendigo is 'a man-eating monster who haunts the desolate forests and icy wastelands of the northern USA and Canada.' The name is also a reference to Patey and Brown's friend, Wendy Tout.

16

Patey on top of the Old Man of Stoer during a repeat of it, the day before the first ascent of Am Buachaille in 1967
© John Cleare

Lights, Camera, Sea Stacks

They are well travelled today but to climb them for the first time showed real vision and bravery, for these are truly intimidating things.

Simon Richardson

The 1960s were a golden age for British climbing Outside Broadcasts. The dramatic locations, sensational situations and tension-building commentary regularly attracted the armchair audience. Patey starred in two of these, and Joe Brown and Chris Bonington cemented their fame with several performances. Hamish MacInnes's and John Cleare's technical skills were in frequent demand, and Chris Brasher proved an engaging commentator.[1]

In 1966 the venue was Anglesey in North Wales, whose sunny sea cliffs were seeing intense exploration and development after Martin Boysen and Baz Ingle had established the first route, Gogarth, on the Main Cliff in 1964.

Cleare, Brasher and Rusty Baillie headed to the Main Cliff for a recce, but the existing routes were impractical filming locations, so the Red Wall was mooted. Not only was it accessible, it formed the back of a natural amphitheatre, which would be ideal for camera positions.

The next day, Cleare and Baillie abseiled down the wall to the sea, and although the rock was suspect, they reckoned it was climbable. A roof with an aid section would add a bit of variety to what would be called Television Route. This was fully prepared before the transmission, and the belay stances and aid sections were furnished with pitons and bolts.

There would be two climbing pairs. Bonington had pulled out, so Joe Brown stepped in and was partnered with Ian McNaught-Davis (Mac). Brown and Mac, who had climbed together often, were a perfect match. Mac was funny both on and off air and could tailor his bawdier humour to the occasion. Brown could comment knowledgeably on the technicalities as he climbed, which few could do in such a relaxed manner.

Cleare suggested Patey for his intelligent humour and his capacity to behave like a bit of a clown, despite being a very able climber. Royal Robbins, who had been working as an instructor in Switzerland, fitted the role of the straight man and was already a legendary figure in US climbing, having pioneered routes on the granite big walls of Yosemite in California. He had climbed the vast North-West Face of Half Dome and The Salathé Wall on El Capitan. His aid techniques were exemplary,

The Red Wall area, Gogarth: the setting for the 1966 Outside Broadcast. The team abseiled down the broad rib left of Castell Helen and Tyroleaned across a zawn. The top part of the Television Route lies on the upper wall © John Cleare

and his outwardly serious, studious air was the antithesis of Patey's.

Patey's account of the climb, 'The Greatest Show on Earth' (1966), has all his signature features applied to a new environment: a bemused narrator in an alien world of electronics and gadgetry; broken schedules and equipment failures. His thumbnail character sketches are among some of the highlights: Cameraman Cleare was 'aggressively poised in space like a hovering kestrel', capturing all the action while Robbins 'had shorn off his beard … and thus lost some of his Sphinx-like inscrutability'. Peppered with sparse, witty dialogue, it describes another big adventure packed with comic moments which could easily have ended in disaster.

On the final section, a loop of slack rope tangled around Patey's etrier. In the full glare of the camera, he executed a desperate and embarrassing manoeuvre, knowing that climbing friends viewing the broadcast would tease him about it later. When he eventually reached the top of the route, his hands were trashed by the aid section. What follows is one of the greatest exchanges in the Patey canon, told at the author's expense.

Robbins gazed at Patey's bloodied hands:

'Back home in the States,' he remarked, 'they say you can always distinguish a good Aid Man by his hands.'

'Lots of scars?' Patey suggested hopefully.

Robbins shook his head gently. 'No scars,' he said.

At the post-transmission party in a pub in Holyhead, a delighted BBC Director General called and told them to begin thinking about next year.

Patey's family had travelled down with him for the Red Wall broadcast, and afterwards, they met the Brown and Ingle families, and went on a family hillwalk up Tryfan in Snowdonia. Ian Patey (2021) recalls that it was the most challenging climb he and his siblings had done with their parents, and the highest mountain they had summited. The weather was calm and sunny to begin with, but as they scrambled up to the summit, it turned rainy and windy, and after the briefest time in the clouds, they made a hurried descent. This family hillwalk was

Robbins and Patey © John Cleare

the only one the family ever undertook together at that level.

Upon his return from Wales, Patey's new-routing moved away from the mountains towards slender sticks of offshore rock. These mini expeditions had a high adventure quotient, since any routes dictated by tides and requiring abseil descents have an inherent element of danger.

His great sea stack trilogy began with The Old Man of Stoer, a sandstone pillar beyond Lochinver which had been attempted three times before. Slender at the base, it bulges at the centre and tapers to a sharp summit. Like all stacks, it has an alluring aesthetic, and its large, solid holds on fine-grained sandstone provide a route that ranks alongside the finest at that grade anywhere in the country.[2]

Patey on the Tyrolean during the Red Wall Outside Broadcast © John Cleare

Patey's companions were Brian Robertson from the Edinburgh-based Squirrels, Alpha Club member Paul Nunn from Sheffield and Brian 'Killer' Henderson from the North-East of England. Both the Squirrels and the Alpha had some of the most talented climbers in Britain at the time.

On that day in June, four climbers trekking across the approach moor with two ladders must have presented an unusual sight. The ladders were to be the solution to crossing the eight-metre channel to reach the stack, but the original notion of tying them together was rejected as they were too flimsy. With less than an hour before the incoming tide, Patey linked one ladder to a small reef sticking out of the sea, gained the reef and then pulled the ladder across to reach the stack. He set up a Tyrolean for the others but neglected to tension the rope properly, and when a heavily laden Robertson got halfway across, he took an impromptu dip in the Atlantic.

Patey led the first pitch, a traverse across twin cracks which is now technically the crux of the climb and usually damp due to its proximity to the sea. 'To go on was impossible, to retreat unthinkable,' commented Robertson in typical Teutonic style (Patey, 1967).

They fixed another Tyrolean higher up for Nunn and Henderson. Robertson led what was then considered the crux, and in the cave stance above this, both climbers received the welcoming regurgitations of the resident fulmar. Patey set off again and was forced to continue to the top after inadvertently leaving his peg hammer at the previous stance. Later, he mused about the distance he might have fallen:

> *I have a healthy disrespect for the rope, which I regard as a link with tradition and a reasonable assurance against the leader falling alone; the stronger the rope, the better his chances of company.* (ibid.)

The successful summit pair sunned themselves for an hour, admiring the view of the Assynt peaks 'spread out like inverted flowerpots' (ibid.) and oblivious to the yells of Nunn and Henderson, who had decided not to follow them to the top and had instead reversed the

Tyrolean back to the mainland.

As Robertson was abseiling, both ropes jammed and he tried to free them by reascending one rope using Hiebeler clamps (like jumars) after shouting up at Patey to tie the end of the other rope to a piton. In a dangerous lapse in concentration, Patey set about stripping the stance and was about to tap out the crucial piton when Nunn, who was watching events unfold from the mainland, realised what he was doing and yelled out in alarm. For Robertson, the climb confirmed an earlier observation about Patey: 'There's one thing I've been noticing about you,' he said. 'Everything we do turns out to be an epic' (ibid.).

A few months after this first ascent, Patey repeated the Original Route with a contingent of old Aberdeen friends: Bill Brooker, Mike Taylor and Ken Grassick, and Reverend Sydney Wilkinson, who was the minister at Peterhead Prison.[3] They confirmed the quality of the line and it became an instant classic. Patey originally graded it HS, but its current grade of VS is more realistic.

It soon figured on the list of parties visiting Patey's bothy, although there were a few epics.[4] On subsequent attempts, two have died on the Tyrolean traverse after neglecting to tension the rope properly and sagging into the sea.

Six weeks later, Patey, Bonington and Baillie made the first ascent of what would become the most famous stack in Britain—The Old Man of Hoy, off the coast of Orkney. In the interim, Bonington experienced a profound family tragedy when his only son Conrad, aged three, drowned in an accident at Temple Cottage, Mary Stewart's house just outside Glasgow.[5]

Bonington recalled that Patey, 'always compassionate', attempted to forestall debilitating depression by tempting him and his wife, Wendy, away from their home in the Lakes with an engaging distraction.

Despite its relatively lowly height, The Old Man of Hoy stood proud as one of the most impressive unclimbed summits in Britain.[6] Patey had mentioned it to MacInnes back in 1962, and his formidable persuasive powers immediately attracted Bonington, who saw the potential for another photojournalistic essay. Wendy, however, declined the trip and went to recuperate with her parents.

When the weather is clear, the ferry crossing from Scrabster to Stromness on Mainland Orkney offers a fine view of the stack, which appears imminently set to join the collapsed arch that once linked it to the island. But this cannot prepare you for the visual impact of seeing the phenomenally impressive square-cut pencil of sandstone from the headland on Hoy itself.

The first ascensionists climbed the East Face, which has since become the trade route. After a gentle introduction on a pillar furnished with ledges, the second pitch traverses dramatically into an exposed corner and bottomless chimney. This looked as though it would require aid—hardly Bonington's speciality and a form of climbing alien to Patey. Baillie, however, had knowledge of the new gear and techniques that were advancing big wall climbing in Yosemite. He was an accomplished all-round mountaineer who had climbed major Alpine routes, including the North Face of the Eiger with Dougal Haston in 1963. The rock on the Old Man of Hoy is composed of a finer-grained sandstone than its counterpart at Stoer and offers a less secure climbing experience, with the sensation of ball-bearings underfoot. The route was originally graded HVS, but the main pitch is now a more realistic E1 5b, and its scale and atmosphere, amplified by the sea, feel out of proportion to its actual height.

The crucial section occupied Baillie for six hours on the first day and another six hours the next, with Patey taking two hours to follow and strip most of the ironmongery and wedges they had used for aid.

Bonington took dramatic photographs of the first two days of action, including a classic close up of Patey on the main pitch, looking up the crack, preparing to clip a karabiner. The sleeve of his right arm is rolled up and jammed in the wide crack. His waist is festooned with slings; tousled hair clings to a heavily lined forehead; the ubiquitous cigarette is clamped between his lips, a mild grimace on his face: no ballerina, very much the ape.

Aid climbing, when done well, is methodical but sometimes ponderous, and it was anathema to Patey, who liked climbing fast. He later mused wryly that the climb had taken longer than an average ascent of the North Face of the Eiger. Baillie suggested a bivouac and Bonington agreed, but both were persuaded by Patey's preference for a comfortable bed and a bottle of whisky in Rackwick.

On day three, Bonington joined them to finish the route and Patey took over the lead for the third and fourth pitches on terrain more suited to his strengths: off vertical, suspect rock lacquered in moisture and vegetation with scanty protection. This led to the finale, Bonington's pitch: a square corner furnished with good holds which dispelled any suspicions of an anti-climax. Near the top of the corner, an empty slot divides the summit into two tops, and there is plenty of room to savour the truly unique environment.

Unlike the previous day, there were no witnesses on the opposite headland: 'Like the Beatles at an empty London airport, we were already forgotten heroes,' quipped Patey. They built a cairn and lit a brief celebratory fire. Baillie was already talking about coming back to free the aid on the crux crack, but Patey was adamant he would never return. 'And for once, I really meant it,' he said (*Scots Magazine*, 1966).

But after the success of the Gogarth Outside Broadcast and further interest from the BBC, Patey quickly changed his mind, and he was back within the year. In fact, he had first suggested it during the Red Wall broadcast and had presented the BBC with a dossier that underpinned the whole enterprise. The dossier gave no consideration to the cost and the huge engineering obstacles, but Alan Chivers, the BBC's Head of Outside Broadcasts, was impressed with the proposal and put his career on the line by backing the project.

There were two reconnaissance visits before the transmission in July 1967. Cleare brought the cameras and Baillie the ironmongery. They were to climb three-quarters of the way up the stack to take photos (one for the front cover of the *Radio Times*) and gather information about suitable camera positions.

Since the broadcast would extend to the Sunday, Patey felt it would be more likely to appeal to his religious patients in Ullapool if a clergyman was involved, and he invited the Reverend Wilkinson to join them.

Wilkinson's conversion to religion had come about after a life-changing experience on the gritstone outcrop of Laddow in the Peak District. Soloing a long way off the ground, he had reached an impasse. With no option except falling, he had recalled the message: 'Believe and thou shall be saved', which he had spotted while picnicking outside a revivalist meeting venue the previous week. In desperation, he chose to believe, at which point he felt the presence of two angels firmly holding him in place and he completed the climb. This was his epiphany, and he subsequently studied theology and became a minister.

For the Hoy trip, Wilkinson had been given responsibility for the ropes and had taken the lightest reel of rope he could find, which was little more than fishermen's polypropylene carline and unsuitable for absorbing potential climbing falls. Patey took one look at it and said, 'Sydney, where're the fucking angels?' The team had just enough proper ropes for Cleare to get the climbers in position and take the photos. Wilkinson was relegated from a potential climber to sherpa, one of several brought in for this role.

Setting up all the equipment was a major logistical exercise. The BBC engaged a platoon of Scots Guards to transport 16 tonnes of equipment (including a tractor) 450 miles by boat and tank landing craft into Rackwick Bay. The friendly invasion of Hoy began ten days before the transmission, and the locals remarked that the only time they had ever seen so many people on the island was during the war.

Usually during Outside Broadcasts in the '60s, a large vehicle called a scanner was the transmission hub and home to all the electronic equipment. It would receive signals from the cameras, and the Director would select which pictures to transmit to the audience from a bank of TV monitors. Since a scanner could not be taken to the headland, its contents had to be stripped, packed away and then hauled up the hillside from Rackwick Bay using two large tractors. Where the terrain got

Baillie on the second, crux pitch. Patey wrote on the back of the photo: 'The Psychological Belay. Baillie poised on the most precarious move on the climb, Patey unpacking his sandwiches. Communication by the climbers was relayed by Bonington on the cliff opposite, whose signals had been wrongly interpreted.' © Chris Bonington

too steep, the gear was loaded onto sledges and dragged up by a winch. (With relaxed attitudes to the environment back then, there are still scars from this operation to the present day.) The scanner gear was then unpacked and set up in two marquees on the headland. Large cameras had to be positioned on the mainland and on the shore below the stack.

Hamish MacInnes was the ringmaster for the rigging and all the camera work. He adapted a cableway system that had been used on rescues in Glen Coe, and it could lower large amounts of equipment quickly. The real hard work was equipping the stack, as the 'mini cameras' weighed over 30kg each. A rope was fixed from the mainland to halfway up the stack to assist this.

Three routes would be climbed simultaneously. Patey and Bonington would repeat the East Face while Brown and Mac would climb a new route on the South Face. Haston and Crew would tackle the spectacular SE Arête, using aid.

By 1967, the protagonists were known to the wider British public. Bonington had publicity for his Alpine routes, expeditions and lecturing. Brown had recently opened his shop in Llanberis and still had a big reputation as a climber. His route Vector at Tremadog was the Welsh testpiece of the era and he was in the vanguard of the exploration of Gogarth. Haston was a leading Alpinist who had played a pivotal role in the winter ascent of the Eiger Direct, and both he and Crew had a certain cool, pop idol persona. At the cutting-edge of the sport, the taciturn Haston had a European reputation, and the loquacious Crew had been profiled in *The Observer*. Mac and Patey, too, were household names in the British climbing community.

Watching Brown climbing was to witness a master class in control, problem-solving and body positioning; he made everything look easy. Mac would huff and puff on the hard bits and play the Fool to Brown's King. Off-air, he was a master ribald raconteur, very much the soul of any party. Bonington, an enthusiastic leader of men when conquering mountains, represented the Establishment and his received pronunciation accent confirmed that.

The support team was as distinguished as the six main performers. MacInnes and Ian Clough, who worked at the Glencoe School of Winter Mountaineering, would film the East Face and SE Arête routes, Baillie and Cleare the South Face Route. The team of 'sherpas' included Peter and Barrie Biven, the latter of whom Patey had met in the Marines, and Eric Beard, the climber, runner and folk singer.

Journalist Peter Gillman covered the event for *The Sunday Times* and Chris Brasher provided the commentary and conducted interviews with the climbers. The climbers stayed in tents at Rackwick but had use of the schoolhouse where Mac would hold court each evening as Patey led the musical entertainment. Reverend Wilkinson, tiring of the bawdy communal singing, would demonstrate his prowess at karate by chopping pieces of wood in half, a skill which could no doubt be put to good use when dealing with recalcitrant prisoners at Peterhead Prison.

The 'stars' were not required until closer to the transmission, which gave Patey, Bonington and Mac some climbing time in the North-West. They set their sights on the Stack of Handa, which had been summited

Patey and Clough accessing Am Buachaille © John Cleare

in 1876 by Lewis man Donald MacDonald, who had climbed hand over hand across a remarkable early Tyrolean, legs hooked over the rope, with no safety backup.

A massive 100m wedge of rock, tucked away in a small bay and separated from the main island by a narrow channel, it is not the slender feature one normally associates with a stack. Although impressive, the wet, guano-spattered rock did not inspire confidence. Boatman Christopher Macleod steered them expertly through the foaming channel and nosed the craft in close. Patey, using his commando training, leapt from the boat onto a ledge but the others refused to follow.

So they went ashore and up onto the adjoining clifftop, then, with three 50m ropes tied together, linked the stack and the two opposite headlands. Patey used jumars for his crossing and attached himself to the rope as a backup. There was added excitement from seabirds smacking into the rope and, more worryingly, two guillemots on the stack pecking at it.

Despite becoming entangled halfway across, Patey became the second person to visit the summit, but he could not tempt Bonington or Mac, who instead enjoyed the scenery and took photographs.[7]

During the build-up to the Hoy Outside Broadcast, articles and cartoons appeared in the national newspapers, and it became as highly anticipated an event as any major sports fixture.

MacInnes had arranged for a helicopter from RAF Leuchars in Fife to be available in the event of an emergency, but as one of the team wryly observed, 'If anything goes wrong, the only medical equipment we'll need is a spade.'

Before the transmission, Haston and Crew set off on their route, which was pre-equipped with pitons and bolts to save time. Brown and Mac's South Face climb would be a genuine ground-up ascent over two days, with no prior equipping.

Brasher's introduction emphasised the heroic and dramatic elements in gloriously over-the-top language, which Mac mercilessly parodied back at Rackwick.

At the end of the first day, the stack was floodlit to record Brown and Mac bivouacking in the Mouth, a commodious niche on their route. Viewers thinking the pair were in for a miserable night were unaware that they had a bottle of whisky to numb the discomforts.

Haston and Crew occupied a ledge nearby. A hammock was a considerable upgrade from Haston's last bivouac on the Eiger Direct in winter: a step hewn out of the ice and temperatures of -40°.

Sunday saw Patey's entrance on the East Face Route. Bonington led the crux pitch and Patey jumared up, suspended spectacularly in space. While Bonington's commentary was excitedly breathless between difficult moves, Patey sounded unflappable and offered a cogent description of jumars and the penalties of getting them the wrong way round: 'The effect would be rather disastrous, I suppose.' Earlier, he had commented dispassionately to Bonington about the importance of communication: 'If I do it before you're ready, I'll fall 120ft and you'll fall 220ft.' During the actual transmission, he said resignedly, 'Let's hope Chris has fixed that rope well up above,' before launching from a sitting position and swinging across until he was in the line of the rope. 'I'm still here, which is perhaps the most important thing,' he deadpanned as the nylon stretched to capacity (BBC, 1967).

At one point, Brasher persuaded Haston to open up a little, something which was rare in more conventional interview settings: 'You learn the limits of your physical and mental endurance in really difficult situations,' he said (ibid.). But speculating about climbing was something Patey had little appetite for—time spent posturing about its value was better spent doing more climbing or socialising in the pub.

Patey led the final corner pitch and was the first to reach the summit: 'Ah ... magnificent. It's a tremendous feeling of exhilaration up here. It's like being in a little satellite suspended out in space; it's dropping away into nothingness on every side' (ibid.).

The most successful and spectacular Outside Broadcast of all concluded with Bonington being lowered the full length of the stack on a bosun's chair after he refused to abseil, fearing the rope would melt during such a long descent.

The three climbing teams on top of the Old Man of Hoy. Clockwise from left: Patey, Mac, Brown, Crew, Bonington, Peter Biven, Haston © John Cleare

Many years later, Bonington reflected, 'We weren't as good as the climbers of today, but I think we were perhaps more full of character. All that made it something special.'

The BBC was once again delighted, and the broadcast was watched by 15 million people. Brasher promised the biggest booze-up after a celebratory meal in Stromness. At the behest of Chivers, Reverend Wilkinson began to say grace but was interrupted by the secular Biven: 'Fuck off, Sydney.' Brown and MacInnes wrestled; Haston emptied his bladder from the hotel balcony into the street below; MacInnes fell down the stairs; and Baillie took a generous draught from the Orkney Cog, a circular drinking vessel made of wood which contained beer, gin, brandy and whisky. Shortly afterwards, he went missing, and his faithful dog, Puck, led the search party, which found him comatose on a pile of fish boxes in a warehouse near the harbour. Twelve tried to fit on Brasher's bed after failing to find their own hotel rooms.

The next day, the unsteady cast and crew began to strip the stack and pack away all the electrical gear. The Old Man was soon returned to the fulmars and the occasional climbing party. Thereafter, it would become one of the most sought-after summits in Britain.

Some time later, Patey's eight-year-old son, Ian, bought a *Commando* magazine from the newsagent with his pocket money. Inside he found a photograph, captured by Bonington, of his father climbing the Old Man of Hoy in the 'Men Who Dare' series. Despite his son's excitement, Patey was none too pleased that the image had been entered without his permission: 'I had no idea that [Chris] was going to put that in. Wait till I see him; I'll have some words to say to him' (Ian Patey, 2021).

Unclimbed stacks of all sizes were plentiful along the west coast of Scotland, and their scale and visibility proved irresistible to Patey. The next on his horizon was once again in his own back yard.

Sandwood Bay is a serenely beautiful spot in the far north-west of Scotland, five miles south of Cape Wrath. Owned by the John Muir Trust, the exquisite mile-long beach is considered one of the most unspoilt and isolated in Scotland. A series of sand dunes separate the beach from the freshwater Sandwood Loch. At the southern end of the bay lies Am Buachaille, or the Herdsman, a 70m sentinel which stands guard over this idyll. The setting is arguably the finest of Patey's sea stack trilogy, and he first climbed it in July 1967 with Ian Clough and John Cleare, shortly after the Hoy broadcast.

Like its relation at Stoer, Am Buachaille is separated from the mainland by a channel, and swimming across did not appeal due to the strong current and swirling tentacles of dense seaweed.

 Instead, Patey used two aluminium ladders to make the crossing, his feet underwater at the point where the ladders were linked. Clough and Cleare then retrieved the ladders and set up a Tyrolean traverse well above the water level. Using this, they joined Patey and safeguarded the return.

The stack is undercut and resembles a totemic layer cake of red sandstone bedding planes with some unusual holds and features. Their line links up weaknesses with a prominent inset corner about a third of the way up. Patey led the whole route, and the first pitch was initially overhanging but on good, solid holds. Utilising horizontal faults to traverse left and circumvent a steep prow, he reached a generous ledge at the foot of the corner, the incoming tide spurring him on. At the stance was a peg with some rotting line tied through its eye—the abseil point from a previous attempt. Had they been beaten to the prize?

Climbers now treat this as the end of the first pitch, but Patey continued, making the crux moves up the right wall of the corner. These are now graded 5b, and it was one of the few occasions when Patey led moves of this technical difficulty. Above, he followed a series of cracks, but the rock was brittle and the loose holds were coated in fine sand. Eventually, he traversed and belayed on the left arête two-thirds of the way up.

Arriving at the stance, Clough and Cleare witnessed Patey's unique approach to the regurgitating fulmars. Accurate with their foul oily puke at some distance, their multiple stomachs allow them to attack in machine-gun fashion. Patey had become adept at avoiding this, and he quickly walled them in with rocks while he prospected the moves past them. When Clough and Cleare followed, they felt guilty about the avian incarceration and dismantled the prison, only to be hit with gunge from an angry fulmar bent on revenge.

Clough had felt ill all day and he left Patey and Cleare to finish the route. His wife, Nikki, had returned from exploring Sandwood Bay and scrambled down the headland opposite the stack. Preparing a brew for the trio's return, she noticed that the incoming tide had doubled the size of the channel, and she yelled a warning to them.

The final pitch was the least secure, involving wafer-thin overhangs, fragile flutings and snappy holds. At one point, Patey's harness caught on a spike while he was trying to mantleshelf, and he struggled to free himself. Following, Cleare became entangled on the flutings. The top out required kicking steps in a guano-coated headwall where Patey was already preparing to abseil and race the advancing tide.

Before leaving their airy perch, Cleare built a small cairn, confident that those who had abandoned the peg lower down had not got much higher. Tellingly, he felt compelled to improve the belay before abseiling.

Patey the TV pundit © John Cleare

The channel had now widened to around 40m, and Nikki pulled Patey across on the now submerged Tyrolean rope as he dipped beneath the incoming waves. Clough and Cleare stripped off and sent their clothing and cameras across in a polythene bag. This extra care was worth it: Cleare had negotiated a deal with *The Observer* to write an article about the climb, and the following Sunday the photographs and account of the climb were perused by readers all across the country.[8]

Am Buachaille is the least popular of Patey's three stacks, although it is certainly worth climbing. The second ascent was made in the same month by Alpha Club members Paul Nunn, Clive Rowland, Dave Peck and ten others. An alternative easier line was taken to avoid Patey's crux and regain the original line higher up.

In the 1969 *SMCJ*, an anonymous contributor submitted a poem called 'The Ballad of Dr Stack', which included the lines:

> *He's climbed on Rakaposhi*
> *And on the Mustagh Tower*
> *And with a painter's ladder*
> *He climbed the Man of Stoer*
>
> *In the far and distant north*
> *Each ploy he schemes with vision*
> *For the good old SMC*
> *And a fee from Television*
>
> *Faster we must go*
> *We'll climb this new route free*
> *Surgery's at six o'clock*
> *And we didn't start till three*

Three years later, Nunn and Rowland would accompany Patey on another virgin sea stack somewhat further afield.

Patey on Pitch 1 of their route on Am Buachaille, Ian Clough belaying © John Cleare

1   Loud, enthusiastic, self-assured, and at times stubborn and autocratic, Brasher was not short of friends or enemies, but he was very fond of Patey and wrote the foreword to the first edition of *One Man's Mountains*. Both were big personalities who smoked, drank, enjoyed socialising into the small hours and generally burnt the candle at both ends. Brasher was, on the surface, part of The Establishment: Cambridge, Olympic Gold medallist, *The Observer*, the BBC, but a maverick like his friend. He liked Patey's humour: the gentle satirising of sacred cows.

2   In July 1967, the Patey family set off from Ullapool on a family excursion to walk along the coast to the Old Man of Stoer cliffs. This walk was adjacent to the climb that Patey, John Cleare and Ian Clough were undertaking as a rehearsal for Am Buachaille. Ian Patey recalls desperately trying to keep up with the climbing party, equipped with ladders and gear. Either their pace was too fast, or he was politely told to stay with his mother, so he stayed with the spectator's group. On the cliff tops, they sat on the woollen picnic rugs where they had a great view of the Old Man of Stoer and, bored, sang *'Why are we waiting?!'* Ian would later return to the same spot on a family holiday with his three daughters and share this happy memory.

3   Patey first read about Wilkinson in the *Aberdeen Press and Journal* newspaper. The Minister had taken a young boy climbing on Lochnagar and had miraculously survived an epic slide down a snow gully, perhaps thanks to higher intervention. Intrigued by the article, Patey had invited Wilkinson to climb with him and they had become friends.

4   Rob Wood and Steve Smith from California got their money's worth when, on their first attempt, the leader fell off the first pitch into the sea. The following day, they successfully reached the summit. Wood abseiled down overhanging rock without a back-up prusik and was stranded in space with no way of reaching the ledge for the next abseil. He screamed across to a companion who was watching from the mainland, who in turn alerted Smith, who downclimbed to the lip of the overhang to assist. In the process, Smith knocked off a rock, which hit Wood in the face. Eventually, Smith hauled in enough rope for his partner to reach the ledge, where he was greeted with oily, yellow fulmar puke.

5   Bonington's wife, Wendy, had been staying at Mary's with Conrad while she was preparing for her first professional music gig. Both Wendy and Mary had a deep interest in folk music and the environment was a paradise for young children, who could wander and explore freely. During an intense rainfall, the nearby burn was transformed into a swollen torrent. Conrad, who had an adventurous and independent streak, strayed from Mary's four children, fell in and drowned. Wendy discovered her son's body.

6   The first proper route on the stack, The Great Arch, was climbed by MacInnes, Graeme Hunter and Doug Lang in 1969.

7   In 1984, the BBC sought to repeat the success of the original broadcast. Murray Hamilton and Pete Whillance freed the SE Arête, renaming it A Fistful of Dollars, while Joe Brown repeated his own South Face Route with his daughter, Zoe.

8   Others have paid the penalty for failing to complete the route between tides. In 1990, Simon Richardson and Robin Clothier put up a fine E1 named Atlantic Wall on the seaward side of the stack. Cut off by the tide and high waves, they were forced to bivouac before regaining the mainland the following morning.

17

Patey and members of the Pinnacle Club at the Dalmazzi Hut, 1964. Bonington bottom right. Brown above him. Mary Stewart above and left of Brown © Ian Patey collection

With Joe, Don and Bonington

To Don, a spade is just a spade – a simple trenching tool used by gravediggers.

Tom Patey, 'A Short Walk with Whillans'

From 1963 until 1969, Patey regularly drove out to the Alps and Norway in the summer to climb, reacquaint with friends south of the border and meet rising stars on the British scene. 'Holiday' is perhaps a misnomer as the pace on and off the mountains was hardly relaxed.

Back then, the unofficial and unlicensed Biolay campsite in Chamonix was a sort of ghetto for British climbers and somewhere they could stay free of charge. The squalor and lack of facilities were no deterrent. Many sought to avoid paying for anything at all, stealing from the shops and ignoring rescue and hospital bills through lack of accident insurance. Between climbs, dossing, drinking and bullshitting were all part of the scene. Wrestling was a common, high-status leisure pursuit, and Patey often defeated Joe Brown thanks to his determination and formidable upper body strength.

When the gendarmes eventually cleared everyone off the site in 1969, Snell's field a mile or so up the road at Les Praz became the new base for Brits and Eastern Europeans (Porter, 2014). On the Italian side of Mont Blanc, Courmayeur also had an unofficial camping area. At all these sites, 'residents' had to negotiate a minefield of unpleasantness as they wandered ever deeper into the woods to find a fresh toilet spot.

The 1963 season began with Patey's Skoda stuffed to capacity with five climbers and all their gear. Joe Brown was tasked with safeguarding the musical instruments piled onto his lap.

Upon arrival in Chamonix, Patey and Brown led Alpine novices Wendy Tout and Peter Noble up the accessible Frendo Spur on the

Aiguille du Midi as a warm-up. But Patey had not come this far to repeat existing routes, and he meticulously researched new lines and recorded them in his 'black book'. So much the better if they could be tackled in a day from the campsite with an early cable car lift.

Patey's Alpine career included several routes on the Chamonix Aiguilles, which offered a quick fix for someone not overly interested in protracted excursions. Their accessibility allowed him to spend evenings enjoying the vibrant social scene at the campsite. One night, during a raucous sing-song, an angry Ray College told Patey's group of revellers to be quiet as he was getting up early. Patey, who was trying to pack as much into a short holiday as possible, was aghast at someone trying to curtail the general merriment. He seemed to need this kind of release from the more conventional life of a Highland doctor.

On the West Face of the Aiguille du Plan, he and Brown straightened out the Greloz-Roch Route with a direct finish up a superb, sustained

Brian Robertson and Patey enjoying the social side of the Alps © Ian Patey collection

corner system line at a much easier grade than anticipated. Brown led a key section to reach the main feature, which Patey retreated from. Later, unfazed by snow conditions, he unroped and scampered up the final 50m snow couloir. Expecting someone of Brown's calibre to do the same, Patey was surprised to see his partner, unnerved by the snow, plunge his arms in up to his armpits as he cautiously ascended. Today, the West Face of the Plan sees few visitors, despite its accessibility.

During an interlude, Patey took Wendy and Peter over to Zermatt, and they completed a traverse of the Matterhorn in a day, ascending via the Italian Ridge and descending the Hornli Ridge. Peter, suffering from the altitude, overbalanced on the summit ridge and narrowly avoided taking his companions with him on a rapid descent of the North Face, thanks to Patey's diligent attention to the rope.[1]

Thereafter, it was time to attend to another new route with Brown, this time on the Aiguille Sans Nom, a subsidiary peak of the Aiguille Verte. Its North-West Face is an impressive feature overlooking the Nant Blanc Glacier, and it was a completely different experience from the Chamonix Aiguilles. At 1,100m and TD/ED1, it was the length of some of the great mixed routes in the range, and the hardest Patey had done in the Alps.

They shared a pre-ascent bivouac on the Rognon with two Italians who were heading for the West Face of the Dru, and awoke to hear pegs being hammered into their route. The pleasant introductory buttress later gave way to an ice slope with groaning seracs and rotten ice, which denied Patey a direct ascent, but this type of terrain was his forte, and he cut a steep traverse line on more compact ice. The upper buttress and series of overhanging chimneys were choked up, and Brown had to use his hands and aid pegs where modern climbers would place inclined picks. He graded it technically 5b/c, and Patey was annoyed at receiving no warning about its difficulty when it was his turn to follow.

They successfully climbed the face in a day, but a storm was approaching, and by the time they reached the col between the Aiguille Sans Nom and the Aiguille Verte there were fantastic lightning strikes

The Diedre Brown/Patey on the West Face of the Aiguille du Plan © John Cleare

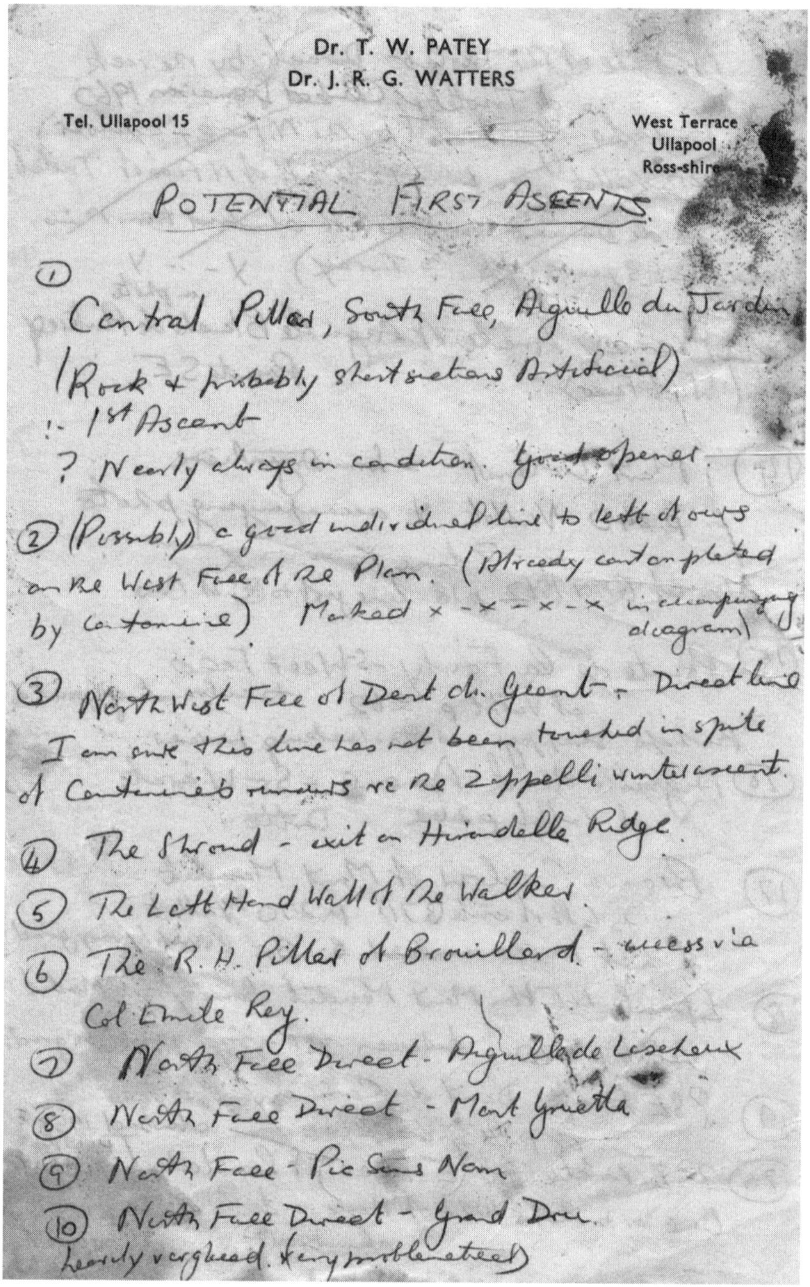

> **Dr. T. W. PATEY**
> **Dr. J. R. G. WATTERS**
>
> Tel. Ullapool 15
>
> West Terrace
> Ullapool
> Ross-shire
>
> **POTENTIAL FIRST ASCENTS**
>
> ① Central Pillar, South Face, Aiguille du Jardin. (Rock + probably short sections Artificial) :- 1st Ascent ? Nearly always in condition. Good opener.
>
> ② (Possibly) a good individual line to left of ours on the West Face of Re Plan. (Already completed by Contamine). Marked x -x -x -x in accompanying diagram)
>
> ③ North West Face of Dent du. Géant - Direct line. I am sure this line has not been touched in spite of Continental rumours re the Zappelli winter ascent.
>
> ④ The Shroud - exit on Hirondelle Ridge.
>
> ⑤ The Left Hand Wall of the Walker.
>
> ⑥ The R.H. Pillar of Brouillard - access via Col Emile Rey.
>
> ⑦ North Face Direct - Aiguille de Leschaux
>
> ⑧ North Face Direct - Mont Gruetta
>
> ⑨ North Face - Pic Sans Nom
>
> ⑩ North Face Direct - Grand Dru. (nearly vergleed. Very problematical)

Patey's potential Alpine new routes in the Chamonix area recorded on NHS stationery © Ian Patey collection

over Mont Blanc. Initially, Patey began descending the couloir solo while Brown abseiled three rope lengths, but eventually the situation became too intense even for Patey, and he humbly asked if he could abseil too.

When they reached the bergshrund, the full impact of the storm hit them, and they were forced to bivouac on the Charpoua Glacier, where they were exposed to the threat of avalanches down the couloir. Brown, propped up against his rucksack, was battered by the driving snow, while Patey, his head in Brown's lap, was slightly more sheltered. Still sleepless at 2.00am, Patey was all for going down, but Brown, erring on the side of caution, persuaded him to wait for daylight.

They had to abseil sections of the steep Charpoua Glacier to reach the hut, where Brown rested for several hours, so fatigued was he after having maintained such a cramped bivouac position throughout the night. Lower down, as they descended the metal ladders to exit the Mer de Glace, they were repeatedly struck by lightning, which '[wasn't] severe but [made] you jump a bit' (Brown, 2013). For Brown, it was yet another 'memorable adventure' with Patey.

Even today, repeat ascentionists describe their route as demanding and of high quality. Simon Richardson (2020) notes that:

> *Significant additions by British climbers to the Alps since the Second World War are relatively rare, so it's a measure of the depth of Patey's creativity that he found and climbed these routes.*

It was during this season that Patey set foot on the most famous and notorious route in the Alps, the North Face of the Eiger, with one of Britain's most celebrated mountaineers, Don Whillans. Many who knew Whillans are keen to point out the better aspects of his personality, which became overshadowed in his bloated and bitter later years. A 'Short Walk with Whillans' (1963) is one of Patey's finest pieces of writing, a superb character study of 'The Villain' (Perrin, 2006) which further mythologised the man as a blunt, droll, practical, wily mountaineer with a gift for killer one-liners. Patey also hints at aspects of

Whillans, such as laziness, sponging and intransigent pronouncements, which would increasingly grate with others who shared his company on expeditions or in the pub.

The Eiger North Face, first climbed in 1938, was the only route anywhere that Patey was interested in making a repeat ascent of.[2] The original line exploits the natural features on the face, and has atmosphere in abundance, a ghoulish history rooted in pre-war Teutonic fanaticism and, above all, embodies a style of climbing that Patey favoured. In fact, it was one of his main ambitions in life, and he described it as 'the greatest mixed route in Europe' (Weir, 1981). Brown, however, thought it 'a big bullshit mountain' and a perilous undertaking due to the threat of stonefall. He had no interest in garnering kudos from its notoriety.

Whillans was in superb shape for the undertaking, having recently returned from Patagonia after the first ascent of the Central Tower of Paine with Bonington. The leader of that expedition, Barrie Page, described Whillans as a 'muscular whippet' who did more than his share of load carrying. (Latterly, he had a reputation for doing very little in this respect, perhaps through inherent selfishness and because he was carrying a lot of weight by then.) According to Page (2014), he was a 'very shrewd bloke; knew what he was doing', and he respected others' knowledge so long as the wool was not being pulled over his eyes. John Cheesmond (2017) observed that, back then, Whillans was 'just bursting with energy', and 'if you could plug a wire into him, you could have lit Manchester for a week'.

In the event, Patey and Whillans bivouacked below the Difficult Crack and reached the Second Icefield the next day, but retreated due to stonefall. Patey's 1963 article described 'the sense of utter isolation that fills this vast face', but the amount of fixed and abandoned gear somehow humanised the place, and he reflected that, as far as the Swallow's Nest bivouac site, they 'could have been climbing the Italian Ridge of the Matterhorn'.

A seasoned suitor of the face (this was his fourth attempt), Whillans knew all the tricks for a rapid and safe return, including an abseil that avoided the Hinterstoisser Traverse, and when he forcefully declared that they should retreat, Patey could hardly object. Whillans often got his own way, partly because he was a superb mountaineer and had survived many serious situations on the higher peaks. At his zenith, he was one of the best all-rounders in the world.

In his article, Patey's tone was jocular and lighthearted, but his true feelings were revealed in a letter home to Betty (Ian Patey, 2014), in which he expressed bitter disappointment about failing. This was compounded by Dougal Haston and Rusty Baillie's successful ascent later that season. If they had sat things out, Patey was sure they could have completed it the next day, when the weather was good. Bonington (2017a), however, praised Whillans's judgement:

> He was ... one of the safest and most sound climbers that I've ever climbed with ... if he judged something, he did a really good risk assessment and wouldn't have gone for the Eiger unless conditions were perfect.

Jim Perrin (2006) highlights the final paragraph in Patey's piece for the 'atmosphere of failure' which seemed to hang around Whillans, despite his major successes. In the event, Whillans never did climb the face, but it would lurk in Patey's mind for the remaining seven years of his life, and it was to be his last big objective.

At the end of October that year, Patey and Whillans combined for a new route together, Gaffer's Groove (Severe), in Coire an Lochain in the Cairngorms. It was scant consolation for the rebuff on the Eiger.

Later that year, Patey delivered an illustrated talk to the Alpine Club headquarters in London about the routes he had done with Brown in the Alps in 1963. He had been climbing with Dennis Gray beforehand and they had to rush to meet the scheduled start time. As he drove through the London rush hour, Patey attempted to change into more formal attire, but his shirt got stuck as he was pulling it over his head, and he narrowly missed hitting a BMW. At last, they reached the clubhouse and

Whillans at his peak © John Cleare

rang the doorbell, but the formidable housekeeper refused them entry, saying they looked too young to be members. Seeking refuge in the Audley Arms across the street, they encountered Anthony Rawlinson, who eventually persuaded the housekeeper to admit them. Patey possessed no slides of the routes, so instead he borrowed Alpine shots from friends and projected them back to front. He spoke so articulately and with such charm, humour and confidence that the disarmed audience was none the wiser.

The following year, 1964, Brown and Patey teamed up again for another Alpine trip, this time accompanied by Bonington and Aberdeen University student Robin Ford. Patey was on a quest for new lines and was not interested in highly technical rock routes or multi-day epics. For him, it was more of a lighthearted holiday, but Bonington liked the planning and preparation aspect of big routes spanning a couple of days. Although he admitted Patey 'was brilliant at seeing a possible route', Bonington (2017a) would rather expend energy on an existing high-calibre route than something new with no guarantee of quality. Moreover, his livelihood now depended on it—the more prestigious the routes the better for lectures, photographs, articles and sponsorship. Patey's approach, consisting of late nights socialising, early starts the following day and frenzied blasts of energy to get up routes and be back in time for the next evening's gatherings, was too carefree for him.

Bonington felt shortchanged by being partnered with Ford. Mismatched in age and experience, they never really hit it off and were frequently following in the footsteps of Brown and Patey. Furthermore, Patey seemed to have all the say in which routes they would tackle. Bonington would go on to record in his diary for this trip that, despite his achievements up until then, he realised how much more effective the other two were in the Alps. They 'bumped my ego and complacency,' he said (2017b).

Nevertheless, the quartet climbed a fine route combining the West Face and South-West Ridge of the Aiguille de Leschaux (D), an attractive, shapely peak off the Leschaux Glacier with the crucible of the Grandes

Jorasses headwall, one of the great north faces of the Alps, nearby. The climb itself was straightforward and only took three hours, but as is often the case in Alpinism, it was combined with a worrying glacial approach and an insecure descent. On the former, they were humbled by the sight of a herd of chamois tackling the glacier's minefield of crevasses and seracs directly and with gay abandon. On the descent, even the shock waves from echoes released loose rock. It was Patey who forged a route through the final section of the now slushy glacier to the sanctuary of the moraine. But even a first ascent was not enough for Bonington, who, with a side glance, could see mighty routes, new and existing, on the monumental North Face of the Grandes Jorasses.[3]

Campsite life followed a regular pattern: Brown would try to match Patey drink for drink, and the following morning he would be hungover and dehydrated, lips stuck to his gums. It was in this state that he set off with the others for the North Spur of Pointe Migot, a minor top in the Chamonix Aiguilles between the Aiguille du Plan and Aiguille du Peigne. Ten days earlier, they had retreated after climbing a mere rope length due to lingering winter ice on the face. This time, Brown was sick on the approach and Patey was suffering from hay fever.

Bonington had abstained from alcohol the previous evening, and he saw his chance to lead from the front for once. He and Ford were actually first on the route, but a rope tangle saw them overtaken. Higher up, Bonington took an alternative line to Brown's and again stole the lead. But to his dismay, Ford was too slow in following, and they fell into second place again. At one point, Patey had to cross a patch of ice to reach a rock ramp which Brown likened to a lengthier version of Longland's Climb on Cloggy in North Wales. However, Patey, having neglected to put his crampons on, fell—luckily without injury. (This was only his second recorded fall after that on the first winter ascent of Mitre Ridge in 1953.) After exchanging expletives with Brown, he saw sense and donned his crampons to complete it cleanly on the second attempt.

Following to the top, Bonington admitted to having enjoyed this final absorbing section on what he considered a mediocre route overall. He

Patey the percussionist. From left: Brown, Bonington, Robin Ford
© Chris Bonington

also relished the added spice of competition, but while Patey was also competitive, Bonington openly showed his emotions when thwarted, which led to others teasing him. In his satirical song, 'Onward Christian Bonington', Patey (1971b) refers to the publicity surrounding his ascents and the financial rewards from them. The first verse ends with the line, 'If you name the mountain, he will name the fee.' In fact, Bonington never did paid guiding work but often had to take any remuneration he could to put food on the table.

The 1964 season was notable for an incident where Patey's professional responsibilities came into play while he was reconnoitring a direct route on the North-East Face of the Aiguille de Leschaux, which he intended to do with Bonington, Brown, Brian Robertson and Mary Stewart. While they were still a long way from the Dalmazzi Hut (also known as the Triolet Hut), an English climber came running towards them—his partner had fallen as they were glissading and was injured and immobile. A trio of Pinnacle Club party members at the scene commended Patey for lying under the casualty on the glacier to insulate him from the cold while others donated clothing. Patey remained in this position until the stretcher arrived: a heavy, old-fashioned type that was difficult to carry, even with eight bearers. A storm broke as they reached the hut in fading daylight, and the injured climber would probably have died if not for their joint efforts and Patey's selflessness in particular.

He was also available for informal medical consultations at the valley campsite. On one occasion, John Cheesmond developed a ferocious boil on his quadricep, so Patey delivered a deep intramuscular penicillin injection via a large needle in his backside. Cheesmond estimated the age of his physician as 'fiftyish' (he was actually about twenty years younger), with 'a kind of ravaged face' that 'no one would have described as boyish' (2017).

The following year, Patey was chosen by the Alpine Club to represent the UK at the International Rassemblement, which was based at the École Nationale de Ski et Alpinisme in Chamonix. He phoned Bonington to enquire about his plans for the forthcoming summer season and suggested they climb together. Bonington prevaricated, citing various other commitments, and Patey replied that this was a pity as he had an offer to attend an international climbing meet in Chamonix with free food, accommodation and all expenses paid. Lamenting that he would have to find another partner, he promptly hung up and let the phone ring repeatedly as Bonington desperately tried to call him back.

With superb cuisine and wine, and free hut and cable car, it was the most opulent climbing holiday either had ever been on. Some attendees did no climbing whatsoever, preferring to indulge in the hospitality and fleshpots, but there were a few prima donnas in the international teams, and competitiveness flourished. Routes were publicly recorded and allotted points according to difficulty. This appealed to Bonington more than Patey, who was still driven by the desire for new routes and relished teaming up with Americans Steve Millar and Lito Tejada-Flores to establish a new line on the West Face of Le Cardinal, an attractive rock spire above the Charpoua Glacier.

With his eye on the tariffs that came with the glittering prizes and therefore an instant rise in the pecking order, Bonington spotted a line in Patey's black book—the unclimbed Right-Hand Pillar of Brouillard, which lies high on Mont Blanc in one of the most wild and beautiful settings in the range. The only problem was that it was a coveted objective for other climbers too, including one of the strongest British climbing partnerships in Chamonix at the time: Pete Crew and Baz Ingle, key members of the Alpha Club, which became the leading club of the next generation.

After Patey discovered the Alphas were planning to attempt the same route, he invited them to join forces. In the event, several factors conspired against them, including unfavourable weather and a lack of peak fitness due to their relatively few achievements on the trip up until then. So the official meet came to an end with a farewell dinner at the École Nationale, after which it was back to the spartan conditions of the campsite at the Biolet.

In 'Days with the Doctor' (1975), John Cleare described climbing with Patey that season. Their first foray began with Cleare, hungover after two hours of sleep, taking the Midi Teleferique with Patey for a one-day blast on the Central Spur on the North Face of the Aiguille du Midi: a parallel route to the Frendo Spur, which Patey had climbed two years earlier. Patey set off solo at a 'breathless pace', demonstrating his genius for route-finding on mixed ground. When he did tie on, it was a safe bet that the ensuing difficulties would be substantial. Mist and snow enveloped the wintry upper section of the route, and the day ended with the usual mad dash to catch the last cable car down.

After that, Bonington disappeared with Tejada-Flores and French climbing legend Lionel Terray for sunny rock climbs in the Vercors (where Terray would be tragically killed a few weeks later). Meanwhile, the heavy partying continued at Biolet. More Alpha Club members turned up, including Paul Nunn and Martin Boysen, as well as the American Gary Hemming and several hard continental climbers.

After a complaint about the noise, two bombastic, sub-machine gun-wielding gendarmes arrived to confiscate Patey's accordion. When Cleare challenged their authority, the owner not being present, one gendarme insulted the Queen. To their surprise, a Scotsman on the campsite endorsed the defamatory comments, and this won over the gendarmes, who instead issued a warning that there was to be no more music. Thereafter, if there was too much pressure from the authorities, Patey would decamp to the Val Veny on the Italian side of the massif, where the nocturnal merriment could continue unrestricted.

Cleare was impressed by Patey's black book of new routes, which was held together with NHS pink surgical plaster and was brimming with photographs, guidebook diagrams and snippets of climbing magazine articles. In places, Patey had drawn potential new lines, and Bonington found this a valuable resource as much of the preparatory work had already been done. On one occasion, Patey was nonplussed to hear that Bonington, back from the Vercors, had teamed up with Tejada-Flores and was already in a position from a bivouac to tackle one of his black

Patey on the rocky terraces and icy gangways leading to the Diedre Brown/Patey on the West Face of the Aiguille du Plan © John Cleare

Patey and Martin Boysen on the West Face of the Aiguille du Plan © John Cleare

book routes on the West Face of the Aiguille du Plan: a rib to the left of the original Greloz-Roch buttress (where Patey had been with Brown two years earlier), terminating at a vertical wall below the summit. The only way to stop Bonington was to get the first cable car up and try to intercept them, so he set off with Cleare, Boysen and Rusty Baillie.

Cleare was concerned about the Pelerins Glacier approach, but Patey did not want to waste time putting on crampons, and they crossed the bergshrund and soloed up the lower section. The rock pitches higher up the route were enjoyable and relatively straightforward, and at last they spotted Bonington and Tejada-Flores engrossed in aiding their way up a formidable chimney on the vertical top wall. This was totally out of character with what had preceded it and deploying the paraphernalia necessary for aid climbing was not Patey's strong suit, so they traversed to find the superb corner system which he had discovered with Brown in 1963. Boysen led the corner, and as he was bringing the others up, Patey unroped and zoomed off up the icy couloir separating them from the summit. Even with crampons, Boysen could only just kick into the slope. It was nightmarishly precarious and he followed gingerly, amazed at Patey's insouciance. Later, Boysen asked why he had not put crampons on and received the reply: 'Didn't have any.'

As usual, Patey was determined to get back down to Chamonix that night, and he descended the Envers du Plan Glacier at breakneck speed. After a brief stop at the Requin Hut for refreshments, it was onto the minefield of crevasses, boulders and moraines of the Mer de Glace. In darkness, with no head torches, an exhausted Baillie praised Patey's spatial memory as he navigated the maze of hazards and led them to the ladders ascending from the glacier. Boysen and Baillie were better technical rock climbers than Patey, but the latter's mountaineering sense was almost peerless.

With the hotel at Montenvers closed, they trudged wearily back to Chamonix in the dark. Patey had run out of fags, and when Boysen kicked a full packet of Gitanes, it seemed like a small miracle and provided the stimulus for them to keep going. Reaching the end of the railway, they encountered a Lancastrian who had twisted his ankle. With his mind on the possibility of campsite entertainment, despite the late hour, Patey carried out a rapid diagnosis and told the man he would be alright and that, if he had gotten that far, he could continue unaided.

The inevitable rush to complete climbs in a day sometimes resulted in errors. On one occasion, Patey headed off with Martin and Maggie Boysen from a campsite in Courmayeur to the Gran Paradiso to climb the shapely, elegant peak of Grivola. This was a typical Patey day out, leaving late and arriving back at the car well after dark. They did indeed climb an attractive, graceful mountain, but they later realised they had ascended the wrong peak: the Herbétet.

In the mid-'60s, several well-known British and American climbers were working at Leysin in Switzerland at The International School of Modern Mountaineering, which had been founded by John Harlin.

When Patey and others paid a social visit, Kris Paterson, a friend of Cleare's who was working at the school, mentioned to Harlin that Patey had written an eponymous song about him. In the tradition of

John Harlin behind Liz Robbins, instructing at Leysin © Ian Patey collection

those early attempts on the North Face of the Eiger, which had claimed several lives, it was a blackly humorous piece about another driven obsessive who meets his end on the notorious Mordwand.

When Harlin asked about the piece, Patey sheepishly tried to downplay it. But Harlin, a large and intimidating figure, insisted, and eventually Patey acquiesced and performed it. 'Very funny, Patey,' said Harlin, without a hint of humour, when he had finished. Patey's song was poignantly prophetic: Harlin later died during a winter ascent of the mountain.

In 1967, Patey broke with tradition and visited Norway with Brown. They met up with Arne Randers Heen, who, though older, was no less interested in modern developments and proud of the international stature his home valley now held.[4]

Patey and Brown climbed on the Romsdalhorn and a 2,300m route to the side of the Troll Wall, a third of which was easy horizontal traversing, much of it scrambling. Leaving at 7.00am, they got a fisherman to

Patey with Arne Randers Heen © Ian Patey collection

Goksøyra © Ian Patey collection

row them across the river to the start, from where they soloed up to just below the top until Brown insisted on roping up on grade III ground. As they summited, they met a group of jubilant French climbers who had just climbed a new Diretissima on the steepest part of the wall. The team, which included the well-known climber Patrick Cordier, had taken 14 days to complete this serious route over a 21-day period. The Frenchmen knew of Brown's prowess and thought that he and Patey had climbed the British Rimmon Route, a major undertaking that had been established two years earlier. They enquired what time Patey and Brown had started, and Brown replied:

'7.00am.'

'Which day?'

'This morning,' said Brown, leaving them speechless as he and Patey walked off.

Patey could not resist a return to the scene of his epic on the Fiva

Patey on the intial slab couloir, Goksøyra © Joe Brown

Route seven years earlier. Starting up the initial 750m, they branched off and took the South-East Ridge of Nordre Trolltind, whose tower at two-thirds height provided a grade V crux.

Their best new route in Norway, however, was in the idyllic area around Lake Eikesdal, a three-hour drive from Åndalsnes, the main town at the bottom of the Romsdal Valley. Here, the highest waterfall in Europe, Mardola, tumbles 600m, and the mountains rise steeply from the lake itself.

Goksøyra is slightly lower than Ben Nevis, but the difficulties start almost from the road, and for once Patey did not object to putting on the rope so early. The North-West Rib took the mountain's Main Wall via an introductory slab couloir, then broke out onto the Valley Buttress before gaining the upper North-West Rib. This is the choicest part of the route with fine, exposed climbing on the edge of the Main Wall, continual technical interest and a finish right at the summit cairn. The time taken, seven hours, led the guidebook writer, Tony Howard, to warn that subsequent ascents might require a bivouac, such was the calibre and speed of the first ascentionists. The route-finding was far from straightforward too, and involved over 1,500m of climbing, at grade VI overall.

Not long after this, word reached them of a fatality on the peak of Bispen on the west side of the Isterdal valley. Liverpudlian Ken Stannard had been climbing with his brother and two friends when the weather deteriorated and he was hit by a falling rock.

In poor visibility, Patey, Brown and several others set off for the peak to find Stannard hanging about 50m up the face. Patey and Brown went up to recover the body, and Patey said they should wrap his face to protect it in case his family should wish to see him. With two paramedics and a fold-up four-handle stretcher, they took turns to help carry the heavy load down the long, steep descent to the col, where there was a shop selling climbing gear. They were soaked to the skin, and the proprietor gave them fresh clothes and offered to send their own gear down when it was clean and dry. Brown never forgot this local generosity, which continued when the son of the owner of the photography shop in Åndalsnes organised the entire funeral. Patey played the piano at the service, the accordion being not quite appropriate.

In 1968, Patey turned his attention back to the Chamonix area and the Italian side of the Mont Blanc massif. He made a first ascent on the Aiguille Rouge de Rochefort (3,109m) with Hamish MacInnes, climbing a combination of the South Wall and South-East Arête. Despite being on a relatively small and unfashionable peak, it was a respectable grade V/VI and 1,000m long.

Patey was now 36. It should be noted that several other British climbers of that era had more impressive Alpine CVs, with big, famous routes in the Western Alps and major rock ascents in the Dolomites. But Patey, for whom there was more to an Alpine jaunt than simply climbing, was confident in his own skin and too much of an individualist to feel the need to acquire prestigious existing routes to impress others. His technical ability had already been demonstrated in Scotland and the Karakoram, and he had the respect of the cream of British mountaineering. He remained committed to seeking out original lines, and his achievements in the winter of 1969 would quash any doubts that he had satisfied his thirst for pioneering significant new routes in Scotland.

1   With Patey, Wendy went on to climb the ordinary route up the Dent du Géant, and the classic traverse of the Meije in the Dauphiné region.

2   The first British ascent had been made by Bonington and Ian Clough the previous year.

3   In fairness, Patey had marked out an ambitious potential line on Point Walker, but he never attempted it. It eventually fell to René Desmaison, Giorgio Bertone and Michel Claret in January 1973 at ED3.

4   The Romsdal Valley became a popular destination for British climbers, despite its annual rainfall exceeding that of Scotland. This was partly due to Tony Howard, John Amatt and Bill Tweedale's ascent of the Troll Wall, the highest rock face in Europe. The route was a quantum leap in difficulty from the original lines which had been established by Arne Randers Heen on this rock curtain.

18

Apollyon Ledge, the second stage of The Crab Crawl, Creag Meagaidh
© John Cleare

The Hare and the Crab

He just buggered off.
Allen Fyffe

A red-letter winter in 1969 saw heavy snow cover and a generous build-up of ice, which led to many new winter routes being recorded in Scotland.

Chris Bonington was planning his forthcoming expedition to the South Face of Annapurna and contemplating the make-up of his team. There was the thorny problem of Don Whillans, with whom Bonington had successfully climbed in the Alps and South America, but who was now drinking heavily.

As a test, Bonington invited Whillans up to Glen Coe in February for a weekend's climbing, not revealing his Annapurna deliberations. They met up with Patey and headed to Garbh Bheinn in Ardgour, where the unclimbed Great Gully was an obvious objective.

Bonington's reservations were justified as Whillans laboured behind on the approach and seconded all the pitches until they reached The Great Cave chimney. Here, they opted for the Left Fork, a 35m vertical chimney high above the cave. Whillans took over for this testing pitch, which was too wide to bridge and was obstructed by ice-encased boulders at the top. Confounding expectations, he led it smoothly, with little fuss and no protection, and the other two followed with difficulty. Whillans commented that, despite a bitterly cold wind, the crux was amenable.[1] But while Whillans had woollen long johns, heavy ski pants, a windproof jacket and goggles, Patey, still blasé about gear, had none of these, and he staggered to the top with stiff legs and eyelids almost frozen shut.

In March, there was a concentrated flurry of activity on Beinn Bhàn in Applecross, where Patey had done the first winter route with Joe Brown the year before.

The base was Glen Cottage, a convenient and private hostel near the foot of Glen Torridon, which was leased from the National Trust and run by Dave Goulder, a keen folk singer. SMC members had the Ling Hut, but Bill Brooker, Syd Wilkinson and Mike Taylor had been to the Ling when it was dirty and neglected and, even though it was free for members, they came down to Glen Cottage instead. In the guest book, Wilkinson thanked Goulder for 'saving us from the squalid horrors of the Ling Hut'.

According to Goulder (2014), Patey first showed up at the cottage in 1968, but he was quiet to begin with:

You never knew he was there; he would never announce himself. Usually there'd be a ceilidh going on; you'd look around and see him standing at the back near the door. He was never up front.

Goulder and other visiting musicians would provide the evening's entertainment:

If you set the scene for [Patey] and he felt comfortable, he'd bring the box in and then start playing ... He wouldn't do it if he didn't know the crowd. He would always arrive with a bottle of whisky. (ibid.)

Usually, Patey would perform amusing songs, but sometimes he would play classical accordion pieces, and Goulder was impressed by his dexterity. On one occasion, Patey accompanied the American musician Mary Anne Alburger on the accordion as she played Mozart's *Eine Kleine Nachtmusik* on the viola. The pair were often spotted together around the Highlands.

That month, Patey and Bonington made the first ascent of March Hare's Gully on the left-hand side of Beinn Bhàn's Coire na Poite.

When in condition, the back wall of this corrie is festooned with ice and approaching it gives the impression of entering a giant frozen cauldron, hence its Gaelic translation of 'pot'. With a succession of interesting, if mostly short ice pitches, it became an instant classic at Grade IV, and it was the first major winter route to be done on this extensive mountain. According to Patey's write-up of the route in the 1970 *SMCJ*, 'The ascent was made without ropes in the dark and occupied 1½ hours.' He compared it to Crowberry Gully in Glen Coe for quality, although it was more sustained.

Hamish MacInnes, who knew of Beinn Bhàn's tremendous potential, had heard his rivals were on the mountain, ready to grab the plum lines, and he turned up at Glen Cottage later that day with his wife, Catherine, and Allen Fyffe, an instructor at his winter climbing school. Although this was the first time Fyffe had met Patey, he had read his articles and knew of his first ascents, and he was rather in awe of him. Routes like Eagle Ridge in winter were still renowned among his peer group.

According to Fyffe (2013), Patey was disgruntled when MacInnes arrived, since they had their eyes on the same two stupendous gully lines in Coire an Fhamair, one of the steepest cliffs on the Scottish mainland. Ice climbing was on the cusp of a revolution to front-point crampons and axes and hammers with inclined picks, but these difficult mixed lines must have looked outrageous at the time.[2]

Bonington and Patey were excited about their new route and had left gear on the mountain in anticipation of a return the following day. There was the usual ceilidh that evening, and early next morning, Goulder heard Bonington whisper agitatedly to Patey that MacInnes was going off to steal their climb, which spurred them on.

'Chris is very competitive; Hamish is fiercely so. It was a really good buzz; it was always electric. Everything was competitive,' said Goulder (2014).

Despite the talent assembled in Torridon that day, little of significance was achieved, as the two sought-after gullies were too lean. With Fyffe, Alburger and Catherine MacInnes, Patey climbed North Gully in

The Wind Pipe, Quinag. Cleare belaying Gillman © Peter Gillman

Coire na Poite, which he had retreated from the year before.

The next day, Patey teamed up with Bonington again and headed for another superlative Scottish mountain: An Teallach. Its northern coire, Glas Tholl, is perhaps not as impressive as the southern Toll an Lochain, with a lesser architecture and aesthetic, but there is much worthwhile climbing, and major challenges remain. (The phenomenal wall above Hayfork Gully is the home of several modern winter desperates.) Checkmate Chimney (IV,5) lies on the extreme right of the coire and is the first good line, although it is rarely in condition. Its real meat is a tricksome 35m icefall about a third of the way up.

Considering the galaxy of ice and mixed routes in the Torridon area, it is surprising that Patey never recorded any new winter routes on

Patey on Eigerwanderer © John Cleare

Liathach or Beinn Eighe's Triple Buttresses, although he investigated both and made some lesser, unrecorded ascents.

The same month, journalist Peter Gillman and John Cleare arrived in Ullapool to shadow Patey for an article for *The Sunday Times* about Scottish winter climbing. By then, Cleare was a close friend of Patey's and a frequent house guest when he was in the area.

On the first day, they visited the Western Cliffs of Quinag and a deep gully at the north end of the line of cliffs. The crux was a 35m chimney, overhanging by five metres, the very top involving bridging round a giant fang of ice. In his route description in the 1970 *SMCJ*, Patey described the pitch as extraordinary and highly technical. Clearing away giant icicles on the crux chimney occupied him for two hours, and he nearly admitted defeat, which was enough for Gillman to reverse the gully and leave the others to complete the ascent.[3]

On the top, a furious easterly gale forced Patey and Cleare to fling themselves to the ground, drive their picks into the snow and try to shield themselves from rocks hurtling by.[4]

The next day, after practice work, they headed up Gleann na Sguaib under Beinn Dearg, where they climbed a diagonal line right of Penguin Gully. They named it Eigerwanderer, in a nod to Patey's ongoing preoccupation with his great objective, six years after his retreat with Whillans.

Five days later, on Sunday, 23 March, Patey's focus turned to the spectacular Coire Ardair on Creag Meagaidh in the Central Highlands. Patey, Cleare and Gillman were joined by Fyffe, Jim McArtney and his girlfriend, Mary Ann Hudson, who would act as models for the photo-shoot for *The Sunday Times* article. Gillman, an inexperienced winter mountaineer, would be a non-climbing observer collecting written material.

Fyffe and McArtney instructed at MacInnes's Glencoe School of Winter Climbing and represented the vanguard of Scottish winter climbers, having repeated some of the hardest routes of the previous decade while starting to pepper the first ascent lists with their own. It was Patey who had recommended McArtney to MacInnes (during a typical 2.00am

From left: Fyffe, Patey, McArtney
and Cleare heading for Coire Ardair
© John Cleare

phone call) after meeting him through mutual Etchachan Club friends. McArtney turned out to be a superb instructor and was universally liked. Despite his easygoing manner, he was 'safe; he wouldn't take any chances' (Fyffe, 1971). Cleare (1971) commented that 'You would never have an epic with Jim ... if ever there was trouble, Jim would get you out of it.' Indeed, Patey had trusted McArtney to take his son, Ian, up Stac Pollaidh in Assynt, a mountain in miniature which nevertheless commands respect when traversing its ridge to attain the true summit.

Hudson had been at RAF Kinloss and had attended a course that McArtney was running. She then became an outdoor activities instructor at the Benmore Outdoor Centre near Dunoon, and was a regular at Glen Cottage in Torridon. A keen amateur musician, she played the guitar, sang and wrote her own songs, interests she shared with Patey.

Patey, the oldest and most experienced member of the party, was now 37 years old and was neither the tidiest nor healthiest looking of them. His craggy, lantern-jawed face was topped by a tousle of dark curls. Bonington (1973) described his visage as 'that of a man who had seen life—the perfect Raymond Chandler, tired-and-battered-private-eye face—grey, creased, hard-worn, yet somehow compassionate.' His fingers were nicotine-stained, and although he moved quickly, he had a hacking cough.

It was a dazzling day with the snow shining like coruscating jewels, and there was much friendly banter on the walk-in. Having left late, it was midday by the time they started—no time to tackle a major route comfortably.

The team decided to climb The Scene, on the left-hand sector of the corrie, Bellevue Buttress. Immediately after the initial steps rightwards, it follows a narrow and spectacular sloping ledge, which that day was banked out with snow for 300m. It was an exhilarating position but technically straightforward, and Patey casually announced that he would solo ahead for a bit as five tied together would be too slow. They could get photos of him, and he would wait for them further on. Fyffe (2013) recalls that one minute he was with them, and the next, 'He just buggered off.'

But there was nothing casual or random about what Patey had in mind for the rest of the day—a vast, horizontal odyssey across the phenomenally exposed series of cliffs that make up the corrie. Patey had previously suggested this girdle traverse to Whillans, who was dismissive of the venture: 'This isn't a climb, it's a bloody crab-crawl!' (Patey, 1970). It was why they had ended up instead on Garbh Bheinn's Great Gully with Bonington the month before, but the idea had been simmering since.

Patey swiftly began side-stepping, using his ice axes for balance. He completed The Scene in half an hour, despite encountering patches of windslab and black ice. He crossed Raeburn's Gully, but instead of finishing up to the top of the cliffs, he continued traversing. The next section, a ledge crossing Pinnacle Buttress, is no harder than The Scene, but the situation is even more sensational. Several hundred metres high, the buttress is roughly akin to a parallelogram and tapers to a pointed summit. It bulges outward and is undercut in places with three obvious horizontal ledges and little else to break the verticality. Apollyon Ledge, the middle of these weaknesses, is a reference to the angel of the bottomless pit in the Book of Revelation, and in one place is a mere slit across a holdless wall.

The climbing was far from repetitive, and Patey stealthed across snow and ice of varied quality and thickness. At times he encountered frozen vegetation, a reassuring medium for his sharp points to penetrate. Sometimes he would kick in directly, at other times place his feet sideways, intensely focused on the next move and trying to ignore the yawning drop below him; the rational part of his brain, which would be screaming out under normal circumstances, quietened.

At one point, the ledge[5] crossed Smith's Gully, one of the hardest routes in Scotland at the time, and when Patey looked up and down this formidable line, he felt he was trespassing.

He could briefly relax when he reached Easy Gully, but next up was the most technical section of the Girdle, The Post Horn Gallop, the first ascent of which he had made seven years earlier with Richard Brooke.

Patey in Coire Ardair before The Crab Crawl. He never cared for gaiters, and his right boot had a hole in the toe. The only item of equipment that might be described as fashionable was his rucksack, the Whillans Alpinist, designed by his friend © John Cleare

Then, it had taken them five hours, and conditions had been perfect. Today, they were variable. He could have called it a day here and met up with the others. But he had tallied the guidebook times for the four sections of the Girdle as 15 hours and, despite the late start, he had only been on the route for an hour and a half and was moving swiftly.

It must have taken significant resolve to set off again from benign ground into a serious position. The Post Face consists of a series of parallel vertical faults filled with snow and ice alternating with steep pillar-like buttresses, each one of which must be traversed. Of the four main Posts, Patey had been on the first ascents of two of them, and had added a direct start to another.

The start of Last Post is formidably steep, and he traversed from higher up Easy Gully. The ice was a metallic consistency, and he was forced to cut steps, a taxing process at the best of times, and especially when moving sideways. He could not weight his left-hand axe, lest the straight pick pop out. Gingerly, he used it for balance, his right hand scything the ice where his right foot would be placed when the step was substantial enough.

Soloing is all about speed, rhythm and flow, and recalcitrant ice is disruptive. Musings about one's situation and fate must be relegated to the back of the mind while one's whole existence reduces to the immediate surroundings. His absorption was broken when he encountered other climbers on the South and Centre Posts. Their safety equipment perhaps reminded him of his vulnerability.

The leader on Centre Post offered Patey the chance of climbing through, but only if he led the pitch for them. It was no doubt strange to be tied on after so long being unencumbered, but Patey made use of the three ice pegs already in place and added one of his own. (He carried two ice screws, a rock peg with a ring through its end and a short length

While Patey was engrossed in the later stages of The Crab Crawl, Fyffe belayed McArtney as he cut steps up South Post Direct. Patey had made the first ascent with Richard Brooke seven years previously © John Cleare

of rope.) After bringing one of the team up, he untied and continued, at once experiencing the seriousness of his lonely undertaking again.

The gully opened out on a ledge under a huge canopy of rock: he had arrived at North Post. He had been here twice before for the Post itself and the Post Horn Gallop.

From North Post branch two diagonal slabby weaknesses, which are the key to easier territory beyond. Here, he made a navigational error, realising he was off route when the fault he was descending petered out and did not link with the ledges beyond. His first attempt at climbing back up was unsuccessful. On the second, the snow overlaying the slab sheared off in a mini avalanche. Desperate, he dug his crampon points into a thin veneer of verglas, to no avail. Fortuitously, his right hand had jammed behind the roots of some frozen vegetation—the only thing preventing him from falling. Ascending was no longer an option. For once, his spare gear was not in his rucksack, and he fumbled in a pocket for a ring peg, placed it in the only crack he could see and hammered it in, one-handed. Below him lay most of the faultline of North Post, and the ant-like figure of Gillman by the frozen loch.

Despite his best efforts, he could not drive the peg in to the hilt, so he tied it off close to the rock to reduce the chance of it pinging out if it was loaded. With his jammed right hand rapidly weakening, he carefully untied his rope with his teeth and his left hand and threaded it through the highly dubious piton—his only option. Wrapping the rope around his leg and across his shoulder, he gingerly embarked on a 20-foot abseil, trying to avoid any jerky movement. To complicate matters, the abseil was diagonal, and he had to land on the ledge on the far side of the gully without swinging back and dangling in space with no means of jumaring up the rope. On such an inhospitable and remote part of the cliff, there would be no hope of a speedy rescue.

Miraculously, the shoogly peg held, and when he hit the ledge, he dug in frantically with his hands and feet. It had been some of the most exciting few metres of his life. Shaking with adrenaline, he pulled the rope through, and in the process dropped another ice screw from his waist. All he had now was his rope.

He was now entering the Inner Coire, which is hidden during the approach walk from the road but is a significant crag in its own right. Reaching the snow bowl near the top of Staghorn Gully, he could have been on the plateau in a few easy minutes. But he was now only one section off the full Girdle, a route that Dennis Gray (Patey, 1970) had predicted would require three days and two bivouacs to complete. He traversed into his own route, The Sash, parallel icefalls looming overhead, the right hand of which, Diadem, he had climbed with Joe Brown in 1964. And so it continued.

Passing Cinderella Gully, he made another error, descending too far and finding himself below rather than above the crux ice pitch in Crescent Gully. Although he was virtually home free, he knew that he could not claim the complete Girdle if he skipped the Quasimodo Traverse, the 'sting in the tail' of The Last Lap. So he had to reascend 100m to the starting point of the ledge, an obvious feature across the vertical right wall of the gully, but which ended abruptly. The continuation involved a system of good holds, but the convexity above made it precarious. Hunched over like the route's namesake, he turned a corner to get established on another horizontal ledge, so off-balance that he had to take off his rucksack and tie one end of his rope to it; once on easier ground, he pulled the sack across.

Hoping the difficulties were over, he encountered a second sting: another long and exposed traverse. Positively 64th Street (named by Bugs McKeith, who had done the first winter ascents of three sections of the Girdle) was certainly a stylish, classy finish to a mighty traverse, ensuring the journey ended with a bang rather than a whimper. He was now amongst broken ground and scree, not far above the Window col, which marks the end.

Five hours after embarking on his odyssey and 20 years after his first new route, he had completed one of his greatest climbing achievements. He had come a long way from Crab's Wall on the north-east coast to The Crab Crawl, 3,000m longer and a mountain route as individualistic as

The Post Horn Gallop section of The Crab Crawl, crossing North Post
© John Cleare

the man himself. His vision and ability shattered preconceptions and redefined what was possible, and his cumulative achievements meant that he would forever be recognised as one of Britain's greatest mountaineers. Simon Richardson (2020), himself a productive creator and chronicler of new routes, considers Patey as one of the true greats of Scottish winter climbing, alongside Harold Raeburn, Jimmy Marshall and Andy Nisbet. With approximately 200 new routes in Scotland, Patey exceeded the prolific Raeburn and Dr J.H.B. Bell. Hamish MacInnes and Jimmy Marshall each made around 100 first ascents. In terms of sheer output, his closest rival was Ian Clough, but even he established

After The Crab Crawl, the team headed north to Achnashellach. Before walking up into Coire Lair, they affected a mock Victorian pose for the camera. Front from left: McArtney, Fyffe. Middle from left: Hudson, Patey, Alburger. Back: Gillman
© John Cleare

very few routes of comparable quality and significance.

Reunited with the others by the frozen loch at the base of the corrie, Patey 'wore the widest grin his friends had seen for years' (Gillman, 1969), although he felt some guilt that McArtney, whom he liked immensely, had not been with him. His friends congratulated him without envy; they all knew he had achieved something really significant.

With thoughts turned to celebratory drinks, they strolled off the hill amid much banter—golden moments of shared experiences and friendship which would soon be cut brutally short. Within ten months of Patey's mighty excursion, McArtney and Hudson were dead after being caught in an avalanche on Ben Nevis.

At Easter, Patey and John Cunningham of the Creagh Dhu mountaineering club took part in a film about ice climbing, which was shot in Coire an Lochain in the Cairngorms. Cleare and a crew of technicians from London Weekend Television were to record the action. The climbers had not reckoned with the obduracy of the members of ACTT, the film technicians' trade union. To begin with, their accommodation in Aviemore was unlicensed, so time was wasted finding an acceptable alternative during the busy Easter holidays. When they eventually got on the hill and prepared to ascend the long snow slope to reach The Vent, Patey joked that if they fell off on this, they would probably end up in the lochain. Unamused, the technicians plonked themselves down on the snow and demanded that the producer immediately return to Aviemore and negotiate 'danger money'. Cleare muttered that he hoped they would get piles from sitting in the cold. Eventually, the extra money was granted and filming could commence.

Cunningham led up the Left Hand Branch of Y Gully, which Patey, Graeme Nicol and Andy Wedderburn had made the first ascent of in 1952. In *Creagh Dhu Climber* (Connor, 1999), Cleare notes the stark differences between the two climbers:

> *Johnny was so neat, competent and meticulous in his climbing; Tom would go for it, punching holes, forcing it with his head-down style.*

Johnny, of course, was always immaculately turned out, too, always with the latest climbing wear while Tom would invariably have odd socks on. But they obviously got on very well together.

Later in the year, Patey's adventurous streak took him to the chalk cliffs of Beachy Head on the south coast of England. In 1894, Aleister Crowley (1875-1947), the occultist and mountaineer, used ice axes to establish the first climbs there: Etheldreda's Pinnacle and the Devil's Chimney. Crowley (SMCJ, 1895) was evangelical about the attractions of chalk climbing: 'Your reward shall be joy unspeakable in the glorious divinity of sun-glistening altitude and towering whiteness.'

The soft rock is prone to collapse, and when Patey and Cleare approached the Pinnacle, its summit profile had changed since Crowley's ascent. The upper section of Devil's Chimney had fallen into the sea. They did not even reach Castor and Pollux, the chimneys which lead up to the gap separating the Pinnacle from the main cliff. The initial traverse on a 50° grassy slope unnerved them enough to warrant a retreat. They would have been better off with axes and crampons, as Mick Fowler and friends would later discover.

For his Alpine holiday that year, Patey was in Chamonix again with MacInnes. He was drawn to the Mont Rouge de Peuterey, one of the armrests of the huge armchair formed by the Aiguille Noire de Peuterey and its two satellite peaks, Mont Rouge and Mont Noir. The South-East Face (1,200m, grade V/V1) follows a shallow spur between enormous overhangs dominating Val Veny. It had been first climbed by Joe Brown and Pete Crew in 10 ½ hours the previous year. The Scots repeated it in 4 ½ hours, soloing in tandem.

By the end of 1969, Patey's climbing fame was assured, and his target for next year's Alpine season was a solo of the North Face of the Eiger, a feat only achieved thus far by the Swiss Guide Michel Darbellay in 1963. His prestigious climbing record in Britain, the Alps and the Karakoram was recognised later that year when he was elected President of the Alpine Climbing Group, the elite branch of the Alpine Club.

Patey on Left Hand Branch of Y Gully © John Cleare

Patey weighing up the dodgy traverse to
Etheldreda's Pinnacle © John Cleare

1   On the basis of this pitch alone, Bonington offered Whillans a place on the Annapurna South Face expedition the following year. The rest is history.

2   They did not succumb until the '80s, when weekend commuter Mick Fowler and partners claimed two of Scotland's greatest lines: Great Overhanging Gully (VI,7) and Gully of the Gods (VI,6).

3   The Wind Pipe was really a hybrid route and given the dual grade of II and VS in the *SMCJ*, as the chimney was only 'lightly iced and otherwise dry'. It is graded II/VS in the current SMC guidebook.

4   On that same day, in a force nine gale and 20m-high waves, the Siberian ship *Irene* radioed for help off the Eastern side of the Orkney Islands. The Longhope lifeboat was launched in response to the mayday call, but in one of the worst tragedies in British lifeboat history, it capsized with the loss of all eight crew.

5   Fourteen years later, Mick Fowler would pause for breath on this ledge before he continued upwards to create one of the most sought-after ice routes in the country: The Fly Direct. Fowler, who would be recognised as one of Britain's most significant all-round mountaineers, was influenced by Patey's adventurous deeds and his descriptions of them in his articles.

19

Burning the Candle

Approaching the Post Face with little daylight left, January 1965. From left: Boysen, Bonington, Patey © John Cleare

He was just greedy for experience ... I don't think he could stop himself. He just had to keep going.

Paul Nunn

A central theme of Patey's story is how much he packed into his short life and how he sustained his frenetic lifestyle. Paul Nunn (1994), who came to know Patey well, remarked on his lust for life:

> The thing about him was his vast appetite for experience, whether it was climbing, people, amusement [or] seeing the odd and quirky sides of things.

His propensity to burn the candle at both ends was taken to a new level when he moved to Ullapool. As the local GP, he could not freely socialise, and he would travel long distances just for an evening's entertainment.

After finishing work on a Friday, he would visit his ever-widening circle of friends at weekends. This would entail a 12-hour drive if he was going to visit Joe Brown or Baz and Pat Ingle in North Wales. Patey also gave lectures to University Clubs as far away as Durham, Manchester and Cambridge, combining these with visits to other friends down south.

The social scene in North Wales was very different from the bothy culture Patey had experienced in the Cairngorms the previous decade. The sex, drugs and rock and roll lifestyle was in full swing, including within the local climbing community, although it was not really Patey's style.

Weekends were hectic, with a day's climbing on Saturday, followed by late-night socialising then more activity on Sunday before the long journey home. Patey invariably did all the driving, on roads that were significantly inferior to today, and with fewer refreshment stops along the way. Set against this, there was less traffic back then and few speed checks. Val, Joe Brown's wife, once commented on the great distances Patey covered for climbing and socialising. She told him she did not know how he could be bothered to do it, nor how he had the energy. Patey's reply was: 'If you lived in Ullapool, you'd do it.'

Dennis Gray, who lived in Edinburgh, recalled that it was not unusual to receive a phone call from Patey at 3.00am in winter asking to meet at dawn for a day's climbing on Ben Nevis, Creag Meagaidh or in the Cairngorms.

In February 1964, he and Patey were guests at the women-only Pinnacle Club dinner in North Wales, so they drove down from Scotland and arrived late on Saturday evening. The event was at the Pen y Gwryd Hotel, and Gray made the after-dinner speech before Patey sang and

Alpha Club members Pete Crew and Paul Nunn in the Padarn Lake Hotel, Llanberis in the '60s © John Cleare

Dennis Gray © John Cleare

played his accordion. In *The Pinnacle Club: A History of Women Climbing* (1988), Shirley Angell records one Helen Goodburn, on her first meet, committing the faux pas of inviting Patey and Gray back to the club hut in Cwm Dyli after a long evening of drinking and carousing. Gray (1993) recalls that:

> *We opened the door and strode boldly inside, an action which caused something akin to an earthquake ... One burly female, smoking a clay pipe, rounded on us ... 'Get out! Get out! No men are allowed in here!' And we were physically bundled out by arms more powerful than ours, to watch the door slammed in our faces ...*

Evicted into a foul February night, Patey and Gray spent an uncomfortable few hours dozing in the car until daylight, before attempting Slanting Gully on Lliwedd. Conditions were terrible, however, and they only managed 25m before retreating. In typical Patey fashion, they had had nothing to eat or drink, so they went back to the Pen y Gwyrd Hotel. As they were breakfasting, Patey announced that he had rung a friend in Aberdeen and heard that conditions were great on Lochnagar. So they headed north again, via Leeds, where Gray, also a keen performer, had several friends in the local folk scene. They arrived at the folk club at about 8.00pm on Sunday night and played three or four songs before setting off again. By the time they reached Edinburgh, Patey having driven the whole way, Gray had had enough. He was absolutely shattered and wondered how Patey could sustain this kind of schedule.

Don Whillans, too, commented that:

> *Some of [Patey's] driving marathons were absolutely staggering. He'd think nothing of driving 80 miles for a pint. I was never actually with him in the car on these drives, I was usually at the other end waiting for him. One [time], I was leaving on an expedition to the Himalayas and it was a farewell party. This would be a minor drive for Tom. He drove from Ullapool nonstop down to Manchester ... and he arrived at*

about [1.30am], played his accordion for about 2½ hours, produced a bottle of whisky from out of his pocket ... and then drove off to Derby, saying he ... was only going to stay [there] overnight and [then] drive back [home] again. (1971)

Patey's mother and half-brother, Maurice, had moved to the Derby area. After a brief visit to see them, he was back home in Ullapool that night.

Still a regular at The Struan in Carrbridge, Patey would play from an extensive repertoire, including Scottish country dance, continental folk music and bothy ballads. Richard Brown, who worked there as a domestic, observed that Patey knew all the songs that others sang or suggested, and even when someone hummed a snippet of a tune, he could develop it into a full piece. Even as a non-climber, Brown was entranced by the soft-spoken Patey and his impressive musical ability: during a lull in his domestic duties one day, Brown put on a record of Beethoven's Eighth Symphony, which Patey played along to, note perfect.

Residents at The Struan needed to have a relaxed attitude towards sleep: two sets of boisterous eightsome reels would often take place in the tiny bar, and Patey would patrol the corridors of the hotel, serenading on his accordion those who had retired to bed early. Influenced by Patey, the proprietor, Karl Fuchs, acquired his own accordion and would perform Austrian songs with a decidedly inferior technique, interspersed with bursts of yodelling. The following morning, Fuchs would mischievously wake up the residents at 4.00am to depart for the ski slopes with a cry of, 'In bus, please!'

All this revelry took its toll, and Eileen Fuchs (Brown, 2000) recalled that, during one season in the '60s:

Tom ended up in hospital with nervous exhaustion and totally lost his voice, while I moved in a daze for weeks after sitting up night after night, cooking in the morning and skiing for the rest of the day.[1]

This milieu was not for everyone, but when the establishment's reputation spread, the guests became self-selecting. Richard Brown (ibid.) summarised its attraction:

Many ... deeply want to be frivolous, or ... would love to indulge in extravagant display, but ... are constrained by inhibitions. With its rare atmosphere of freedom, The Struan seemed to take away the worries about looking silly. It was totally acceptable to [be] outrageous.

Occasionally, Patey's medical expertise would be called upon here, too. One of the Austrian ski instructors had a party trick which involved draining his beer glass and then biting chunks out of it until all that was left was the stem and base. After each bite, he would methodically munch the glass into small shards before swallowing, leaving onlookers stunned. Patey had previously reassured him that, as long as he chewed thoroughly, there should be no harmful effects (ibid.).

In the early '60s, when Joe Brown was working as an instructor at the Whitehall Centre in Derbyshire, he came north to run a canoeing course down the Great Glen. Patey drove from Ullapool and picked him up near Inverness for an extended evening in The Struan. Brown rarely got drunk, but with Patey, whose normal bedtime was about 2.00am, it was hard not to, for alcohol did not seem to affect him and 'he never seemed to have a hangover'. Brown (2013) left the pub 'cross-eyed'. As Patey was driving him back to Inverness, they noticed a police car tailing them and pulled over. Inside the car smelled like a micro-distillery, so Patey stepped out smartly and announced confidently: 'I'm Dr Patey from Ullapool and this is a friend, who I'm taking home.' Despite Patey being well over the legal limit for driving, and Brown barely able to give his name, the police told them to 'take care', and off they went (ibid.).

Patey's favourite haunt of the later '60s was the Rowanlea, also in Carrbridge, where he would play duets with the landlord, Jimmy Ross, who was a fine fiddler. Patey's reputation preceded him: when he first

Jimmy Ross at the Rowanlea © James Ross collection

arrived at the Rowanlea, Ross placed a bottle of whisky on the table, anticipating an extended session. Lock-ins were the norm.

The Rowanlea had a reputation for more serious music sessions than The Struan—woe betide anyone who talked when a performance was in full flow. Fag in mouth, Patey would play Tyrolean and Scottish tunes on his accordion as others sang. Ross would join in and play jazz on the fiddle. Clive Freshwater (2014), who had introduced Patey to the establishment, recalls the skill with which he played: 'It just fell out of the machine. He moved from one thing to the other. He was brilliant.'

For anyone interested in the cross fertilisation between the domains of mountaineering and music, Temple Cottage at Balmore outside Glasgow was one of the crucibles of the '60s. The home of American Mary Stewart, herself a keen musician, it was the sometime home and party venue for a remarkable cast list of musicians and climbers, including Eric Beard, Rusty Baillie, Kris Patterson and the Boningtons.[2] Patey met Mary through her then husband Stan, who was a member of the SMC, and thanks to their mutual love of music, they hit it off instantly. She also introduced Patey to John Cleare.

Joe and Val Brown visited, too, and on one occasion, Patey brought Don Whillans to a big party at the cottage. Friends of Mary, June and Ian, were staying in one of the rooms upstairs and June went to bed early. When Whillans had finished partying, he went in search of a bed and, finding one with a woman in it, climbed in beside her. June's screams brought the merriment downstairs to a halt. Ian threatened to kill Whillans and a fight broke out. Patey rushed upstairs to separate them and escorted Whillans off to a nearby hotel. Unsurprisingly, this was Whillans's only visit (Stewart, 2014).

Big names from across the Atlantic included Gary Hemming and John Harlin. Royal Robbins also stayed there with his wife before climbing in Glen Coe with Patey, whom he already knew from the BBC's 1966 Gogarth, Red Wall Outside Broadcast. After the Robbins arrived in Glasgow, which 'seemed not a gay city', Patey met them and took them to Temple Cottage:

> We awakened to a life which one occasionally reads about in books, but rarely sees in reality, at least in the sedate American sort of reality to which we were accustomed. There were about half a dozen children, robust youngsters, beaming with superb health. Their frontier dress gave a hint of their wild, free-spirited nature. The older ones cared for the younger, the strong for the weak. And there were the animals ... dogs and cats, goats, a horse and ... a lamb ... Scattered about the house were individuals of widely varying sorts, folk-singers, do-wells and ne'er-do-wells, even a climber or two. All had come to Mary Stewart's pad for a bit of comfort and relaxation, and to escape the cares of the world. (Robbins, 1969)

One of these individuals was the renowned folk singer Hamish Imlach. Patey and Imlach got on well and Patey took him out to the Alps one summer, not that mountaineering was a common interest. Imlach was a ferocious eater and drinker whose motto was, 'When I die, I want everything to be knackered!' (Imlach and McVicar, 1992). Patey's own lifestyle might be considered unintentionally synchronous with Imlach's goal.

At Hogmanay in 1965, Chris and Wendy Bonington, Martin and Maggie Boysen, John Cleare and Eric Beard were all staying at the cottage. On New Year's Day, Mary Stewart, who was relatively inexperienced, followed Bonington up the West Fork of Crowberry Gully on Buachaille Etive Mòr in Glen Coe and was left exhausted by its demands. That evening, they met the Boysens and Patey in the Clachaig Inn, and after closing time, drove round to the bothy attached to the Laggan Hotel with the intention of climbing on Creag Meagaidh the following day.

After a leisurely breakfast, they only began walking in at midday, breaking trail through snow that was knee-deep in places.

At 3.00pm, they perused the Post Face for something to climb. Bonington and Boysen went for the South Post, after Patey optimistically told them they could do it in an hour if they moved quickly. Floundering in the soft snow, they did not even reach the bottom. Eventually, they

Mary Stewart © John Cleare

followed the others, who had gone to do Staghorn Gully, an easier route on the right of the imposing Post Face. At the top of the entry ramp, they saw Patey engaged in the upper gully pitches with Stewart. When Bonington finally emerged on the plateau, after a gruelling step-cutting session, the lead pair had gone. Bonington brought up Boysen, then Beard and Cleare, who had tied on to their rope. It was now nearly pitch dark.

Stewart, who had now endured two demanding days in the mountains, was shattered, and Patey realised he had to get her down off the mountain quickly, so he set off without the others. Although he knew the topography of the corrie, it is a notoriously tricky place to navigate off in poor visibility, and he strayed worrying close to the edge before finding the correct descent gully.

But either Patey did not know, or had forgotten, that none of the others had a map, and Patey's footsteps, which they followed initially, soon filled in with snow. Fortunately, Beard had a compass, a torch and

Hamish Imlach in partying mode. Pinned under his right knee is Billy Connolly, under his left fiddler Aly Bain. Connolly turned up at Temple Cottage one Christmas Day morning with a present of a guitar for one of Mary Stewart's children © Fiona Imlach

some meagre supplies of food, but nobody was equipped to bivouac, and Boysen was recovering from flu. All four were still tied on the rope, and at one point, Bonington and Boysen realised they were standing on a huge cornice and rapidly retraced their steps. Warily, they skirted the corrie edge, consulting their vague compass bearing as the torch battery faded. Persevering out of necessity, they reached the col known as The Window, from where the descent is more straightforward. Even then they were uncertain, however, and they negotiated the steep ground with trepidation. The prospect of hitting a barrier of cliffs and having to reascend, or walking over them in the gloom, meant there was no respite from the tension.

Meanwhile, Patey and Stewart were enduring more arduous trail-breaking on the walkout. Even Patey was struggling, 'flaking out' beside Stewart (1965). He too was recovering from flu, had had little sleep and had eaten nothing since breakfast:

I think he was hypoglycaemic, for he gradually lost all his energy and just wanted to stop, especially when deep in a drift. I had to keep egging him on. At one point, I remember him saying, 'You go on and save yourself, I'll be alright here.' I don't think he ever told anyone about that. (ibid.)

Stewart tried to ease his burden by setting off in front, but disappeared up to her waist in a burn of icy water when the snow covering it collapsed. Fearing she would succumb to hypothermia, Patey was spurred on to keep up with her. Eventually they reached the road, whereupon Patey drove Stewart to the hotel, before returning to meet the others as they walked out. The occasion could so easily have ended with the demise of some of the cream of British mountaineering. According to Stewart (ibid.), 'Chris was furious with Tom; said he'd *never* climb with him again. But, of course, he did forgive him, for he loved Tom, as everyone did.'

In 1967, Dennis Gray organised an anniversary Muztagh Tower

lecture series with Patey and Joe Brown as the main speakers. Brown had just moved to Llanberis to establish his first climbing shop, and he welcomed the idea of some extra cash for the enterprise. In Manchester, Liverpool and Bradford, two legendary figures in British mountaineering entertained and enthralled their audiences. Although Brown had never lectured before and Patey had never performed in such large venues, it was extremely successful: the first two nights sold out and the third, in a hall that could hold almost two thousand, was nearly full.

After the first show, Patey, Gray and several local climbers were taken by Ronnie Cummaford, an original Rock and Ice Club member, to the Riverboat Club, a nightclub in Salford. Unbeknown to them, a strip tease competition was underway, and against a backdrop of suspender belts, rotating tassels and flying bras, Patey was heard to proclaim, 'Nothing like this ever takes place in Ullapool!'

Before the Bradford show in St George's Hall, Gray encountered Patey playing the first movement of Grieg's piano concerto on the Steinway grand piano in the empty auditorium. It was a genre of music Gray had never heard him perform before, and although Patey was obviously out of practice, it was a reminder of how much all music meant to him, and that he could have easily taken a different career path. The same could perhaps be said of writing, although he never wrote anything unconnected with mountaineering.

These jaunts away threw into stark relief how conservative life was in Patey's home village. He wanted to maintain his wide social and climbing network and enjoy a sense of freedom, and he seemed to need the stimulation of activity and company away from home. Friends in Ullapool noticed the way his careful approach to soloing routes seemed to be at odds with a lack of restraint in other aspects of his life. Sgt Donnie Smith (2013) was struck by how 'He was driven by some unforeseen force'; Glenn Davies (2013) said that there was 'something burning inside him'. Davies thought there was a touch of pathos about Patey, and ultimately something rather sad.

Patey knew that his father's heart problem likely had a genetic basis, which might affect him later in life too. Davies (ibid.) remembered that 'He would get quite morose at times ... about his health and family medical history. He would never waste time, never waste a day.' But if he was concerned about his health, he seemed to be doing everything he could to worsen it.

Even decades after his death, Patey's capacity for epic days climbing fast and socialising late, often punctuated by long drives, is legendary. This all had to compete with the demands of being a GP. It is part of mountaineering folklore that his recreations were sustained by the use of amphetamines,[3] although much of this is hearsay and it is one of the more contentious areas in Patey's life.

The stimulant effect of amphetamine and its ability to dampen hunger and fatigue led to its widespread use as Benzedrine by the British military in the Second World War (Kamienski, 2016). One of the best-known examples of a mountaineering achievement facilitated by stimulants is Herman Buhl's solo ascent of Nanga Parbat in 1953, when he took the methamphetamine Pervitin (Tabin and McIntosh, 2001).

Documentation of amphetamines being used in a mountaineering context can be found in Mike Banks's book about the 1958 Rakapsohi expedition, where both climbers and sherpas took them. At one point, Patey and Richard Brooke safeguarded the route above Camp I by fixing ropes, 'having taken Dexedrine tablets to counter the fatigue by slogging through deep snow at 19,000 feet' (Banks, 1959). Banks, too, used them during his own summit push and descent.

Until 1956, many amphetamine-based drugs could be bought over the counter in a chemist without a prescription, and it was commonly used as a tonic by those who felt low or needed an energy boost, such as long-distance lorry drivers. Some even used it as a slimming aid (Medline Plus, 2022). With regular use of amphetamines, however, the body eventually crashes, unable to sustain any more activity. Extended binges have the most serious effects, placing heavy strain on the heart and leaving the user gaunt, malnourished and at risk of depression (ibid.). By 1964, unauthorised possession of amphetamines was banned in the UK.

Joe Brown (1987) confirmed that Patey 'used to take amphetamines to stay awake when he was driving'. In *The Ordinary Route*, Harold Drasdo (1997, p102) said, 'I've mentioned the use of Benzedrine to keep going. Some Alpinists of the sixties, notably Tom Patey, took narcotics for a good bivouac followed by stimulants for a busy day.' Drasdo does not elaborate or reveal his sources. Neither does he confirm seeing Patey actually taking them.

Patey also gave them to his friends for other purposes. After socialising with Patey in Carrbridge one evening, Sam Bemrose left early in his car for Glenmore. Despite having to walk the 14 miles in the dark back to the Norwegian Huts with his accordion, Patey was awake early the next day, extolling the splendid weather and seemingly eager to go climbing. Bemrose was hungover, so Patey offered him a pill to get him going. It was only after drawing the curtains back that Bemrose realised the weather was, in fact, appalling, but he was now wide awake and too revved up to catch up on precious sleep until the effects of the drug had worn off. Patey, having got his revenge from being left to walk home the previous evening, retired to his bed with a grin (Bemrose, 2014).

Joe Brown (1987), too, recalled, 'He gave me one as a cure for the usual hangover after a Rock and Ice dinner, and I never stopped talking for 20 hours. But after that, I felt really depressed for the first time in my life.' Brown never took another amphetamine again.

Lakeland climber Paul Ross, who was also a folk singer in a group, remembered that Patey would arrive at The Cairngorm Hotel in Aviemore at about 10.00pm, just as they were finishing performing, and would coax them into going to the Rowanlea for more festivities, handing out pink pills beforehand. At the end of the evening, Patey would suggest meeting in the car park a few hours later to go climbing. During a week with Jim McArtney, they were in the Rowanlea every night. Despite retiring earlier than Patey, McArtney told Ross that, from the moment they left the car park until they arrived at the day's climbing venue, Patey was a mere speck in the distance (Ross, 2019).

In 'The Past is a Foreign Country' (*Alpine Journal*, 2010), Peter

Gillman reminisced about the memorable time in Patey's company in the Rowanlea era, where Jimmy Ross would lock them in and they would listen to Patey singing his irreverent mountain songs until close to dawn:

> *Drinking and singing would continue into the wee small hours. Finally, it would occur to Tom that he had to be in Ullapool for morning surgery. He'd gulp a handful of amphetamines and hit the road, leaving himself just enough time to change his shirt and don a tie, and so present the face of respectability to his patients.*[4]

Amphetamines perhaps gave Patey the energy to sustain his frenetic lifestyle and long days out climbing. They could also partly explain his increasingly haggard looks: several friends observed that Patey seemed to eat very little, if anything, when out climbing. Alan Will, Patey's old friend from Aberdeen, saw him in the late '60s in the Kingshouse Hotel in Glen Coe and was struck by how much he had aged.

Despite Patey's endorsement of stimulants, Joe Brown (1987) recalled an argument at Temple Cottage where '[Patey] was violently against [cannabis and LSD], which were becoming popular at the time. I think he realised the harm they did because he'd become a bit hooked.' After Patey's death, Brown (2013) claimed he had sometimes been taking several amphetamines a day, along with sleeping pills.

There is often payback for such a full and complicated lifestyle, and things came to a head in early 1970, when Patey entered one of the darkest periods in his life.

1   No other details are known about Patey's hospitalisation.

2   Members of the 'psychedelic folk' group The Incredible String Band lived there at one time, and Mary's children appeared on the front cover of their album, entitled *The Hangman's Beautiful Daughter*.

3   Amphetamine is a strong stimulant that acts on the central nervous system, speeding up the heart rate and increasing blood pressure. Bypassing all the body's normal capacities for creating energy, the drug increases feelings of alertness and power but it can also make users feel agitated and aggressive. Amphetamines are addictive, and regular users quickly build up a tolerance and require higher doses to achieve the same effect. This, of course, increases the associated risks. The 'comedown', which can last several days, can affect concentration and make users feel lethargic and depressed (Medline Plus, 2022).

4   This entry did not go down well with certain older SMC members. To quote Gillman, 'All hell broke loose.' So much so, that when Gillman was scheduled to be the guest speaker at the SMC dinner in Fort William in 2013, some members contacted the SMC President, concerned at the potential content of his talk. Gillman subsequently chose the safe topic of George Mallory's early climbs on Ben Nevis.

20

Patey on the gabbro cliffs of Hirta near Dun channel, St Kilda © John Cleare

Shades of Black

We were all numbed by the death of Jim and his friends, and probably Tom was the worst affected.

Hamish MacInnes, *They Sought the Summits*

The last five months of Patey's life are significant for a tragic event that affected him profoundly. In January 1970, Jim McArtney, his girlfriend Mary Ann Hudson, John Grieve and Fergus Mitchell were on the Italian Climb on Ben Nevis when the upper slopes avalanched. Grieve, a keen climber, mountain rescue team member and teacher in Kinlochleven, was the sole survivor, having been outwith the path of the slide.

The following year, the radio documentary *They Sought the Summits* (BBC, 1971) paid tribute to McArtney, Patey and Ian Clough, all of whom had now perished in climbing accidents. In it, Grieve described events on the Italian Climb:

> *Because of the very high winds, there was a tremendous amount of new snow ... accumulating ... over the crest of the ridge.*
>
> *We'd just finished climbing a difficult pitch, which was not on the route but off on unexplored territory, which Jim McArtney had led. The climb continued ... round a corner, skirting an overhanging rock onto a large snow basin, which led easily to the crest of the ridge at the end of the climb.*
>
> *The other three were round the corner, and I was climbing up to join them. The rope ... tied to my waist was snagged lower down ... the easiest way to unsnag [it] was [to untie]. I was in the process of flicking the rope round a spike of rock encrusted with ice when there was a roar. ... straight away, I cowered underneath the rock overhang, dug my ice axe in and waited ...*

It's difficult to describe one's reactions at the time because they're mixed up with great feelings of grief when you realise what's happened. And then an indescribable sense of relief ... that you are still alive, albeit in a very dangerous position situation ... [there] was still dust, powder snow in the air; everything was quiet; the wind had stopped ... I shouted 'Jim, Jim'. I was not expecting an answer ... you somehow push all these things aside; they become something that you think about later, something that's got to be faced in the future.

I was still a few hundred feet from the top. My first thought was the snow above, which was no longer held by anything below ... So I traversed right across ... right up against the rock where the snow was [shallower] and ... I could get secure handholds on the rock. I carried on this way to the top of the ridge, and that night I spent a lot of time trying to get up, trying to get down. Most of the night I sat thinking, and this was the worst part: ... comprehend[ing] what had happened. I'd had accidents and friends had been killed before, but three people in one go ... [and] McArtney a particularly close friend ...

The alarm was raised when Grieve failed to turn up for work on Monday morning. Via radio messages from Ian Sutherland, deputy leader of the Lochaber Mountain Rescue Team, Hamish MacInnes heard that a lone figure had been spotted on Tower Ridge, calling for help. With Ian Clough, he headed up to the CIC Hut, where they could see the stranded figure. Patey was due in Glen Coe that evening for a ceilidh, but when he heard about the rescue, he too headed up to the hut.

Despite his protracted ordeal, Grieve arrived at the hut in good shape, having been assisted down the lower section of Tower Ridge by the rescue party. After a warm drink, he was escorted down to the road.

The first body was discovered amongst the avalanche debris, following an hour of exhausting digging by headtorch. Finally, at 3.00am, they found McArtney, buried head-first. From their injuries, MacInnes believed that the three victims would have died instantly.

The bodies were brought down late Tuesday morning and evacuated by helicopter about half a mile below the hut. McArtney's father was waiting at the landing strip, already planning the funeral. He wanted either Patey or MacInnes to give the eulogy.

Having initially declined the request, Patey was eventually persuaded by MacInnes, and he gave a fine speech at the emotional service in Aberdeen. 'The Wild Rover' was sung in place of a conventional hymn.

Like many others, Patey had been drawn to McArtney's warm personality and joie de vivre, believing him to be 'the most accomplished winter mountaineer of his generation, [whose] horizons were only beginning to open' (Patey in *SMCJ*, 1970). In McArtney's obituary (ibid.), Patey described him as:

> *An athletic, ruddy-faced lad, as large as life ... radiating enthusiasm like an open furnace ... Life was one long hearty laugh, and everyone laughed with him. You do not often meet folk like that ... For him, the climbing scene was more than just the mountains; it was also the people who went to the mountains, and the great evenings we had at Luibeg, Corrour and Geldie.*
>
> *Jim was not just a friend to us all, he was a symbol. Over two hundred climbers attended the funeral. They came from all parts of Britain and in all age groups, and they were not men given to making token appearances at graveyards. Few of them could find anything to say to each other.*
>
> *No doubt the shadows will eventually lift and during a rip-roaring evening, we will be able to remember Jim and what he stood for, in the way he would have had us remember him.*

Mary Ann Hudson was buried in the graveyard in Glen Nevis, and Fergus Mitchell's ashes were scattered in the River Coe.

In the interim between the accident and the funerals, Grieve, still in shock, was interviewed at Kinlochleven Police Station, where he suffered an intense grilling lasting hours by two detectives:

Jim McArtney © Diane Thom

... who did not know the difference between crampons and tampons. They asked the same, to me stupid, questions time after time. I now know that Tom, highly distraught [at] the death of Jim, [had] contacted the Procurator Fiscal at Fort William and suggested that more than a simple accident had taken place. Tom could not accept that I had survived and Jim had not. In his tribute to Jim in the [SMC] Journal, he wrote, 'most of us find the whole thing difficult to accept'. What Tom really thought had taken place I do not know. Part of what [he] could not stomach was witnessing my return to the CIC Hut in what ... might have [been] construed as good spirits. My mind had been on the rack the whole time I was stranded on Tower Ridge. The enormity of the loss had filled my head for twenty-four hours. Now, having reached safety, I was only certain of two things: Our sport was a ridiculous, criminal pastime, and I was bloody well glad to be alive. Amidst the

sheer anger at the stupid waste of three great friends must have been mixed a little euphoria. (Grieve, 1982)

Unsurprisingly, there was no evidence of foul play or negligence. Grieve was baffled by Patey's reaction to the accident,[1] but to his great credit, he understood the grief Patey must have felt over the deaths and bore no grudge; indeed, he praised the speech Patey gave at McArtney's funeral. They crossed paths just once more, when Grieve attended a Mynydd Mountaineering Club dinner in the Lake District with Ian Clough. Patey and MacInnes were at another club dinner in Borrowdale. The encounter resulted in little more than an acknowledgement, and Patey offered no apology.

Despite his obvious fondness for McArtney, it is difficult to understand Patey's response to this tragedy, but it must be viewed in the wider context of his life at that time. At a meeting in the Lake District in 1969 for Bonington's forthcoming expedition to the South Face of Annapurna, Martin Boysen (2013) observed that Patey was unusually quiet: 'Towards the end ... he seemed to be having a few big downers; ... he seem[ed] a bit depressed.'

Rusty Baillie (2015) noticed that, by now, Patey's home life was strained: 'Betty was socially ambitious and never appreciated Tom as a dirtbag climber ... Tom maintained an uneasy peace in his household.'

Although Ullapool was remote, the bothy was a magnet, and Patey was often drawn away from the family by younger friends with a much more carefree existence, their world revolving around the next climb, just as it once had for him. Patey 'was selfish, but I thought all climbers were selfish then,' observed Gillman (2015).

During Patey's trips away Betty was left to tend to domestic and family duties single-handed. Frustrations sometimes spilt over, and Cleare (Hedgecoe, 2007) recalls Betty, who was far away from her family and friends in Aberdeen, once tipping the evening meal over Patey's head when they returned late after climbing. 'Marriage could not have been very easy for his wife Betty, for a climbing genius is not the most restful man to live with' (Weir, 1981).

Patey was able to compartmentalise his life, and his persona could revert from married doctor and father to that more akin to a student or single man on jaunts away. His old climbing friends from Aberdeen seemed to have accepted their adult responsibilities and that the intensity of their early climbing years was over. They still got out, but at a level that was insufficient for Patey. Having had a lot of autonomy as a boy and as a student, fulfilling the roles of father, husband and busy doctor whilst maintaining his time-consuming interests was an impossible balancing act, and he clutched at precious moments of freedom.

Spending time away to avoid tension at home no doubt compounded the problem. Glenn Davies (2013), Patey's friend from Ullapool, thought Betty had given up trying to curtail Patey's climbing and socialising. 'I shudder to think what the atmosphere would have been like in the house ... He had this double life.'

After McArtney's death, Davies (ibid.) noted that: 'All the energy seemed to have gone out of him ... [He was] as flat as a pancake.'

Simon Thompson, author of *Unjustifiable Risk? The Story of British Climbing* (2010), observes that:

> *Much of [Patey's] life was characterised by spontaneous, manic outpourings of energy, a wild, devil-may-care gaiety, but in the years leading up to his death on The Maiden sea stack in 1970, there were also signs of depression in the long gaps between the intense experience of extreme climbing.*

Bonington, too, has admitted to experiencing lows after the highs of a successful trip, although these were not pronounced enough to warrant a clinical diagnosis. But it is doubtful whether Patey would have sought professional help for depression.[2] Even today, doctors can find it difficult to get appropriate help due to the stigma associated with mental illness (Carpenter, 2014), perhaps fearing that admitting depression or addiction will negatively affect their careers. Half a century ago, these

Chris Brasher and Patey on the first St Kilda recce © Hamish MacInnes

attitudes were no doubt more prevalent.

MacInnes (BBC, 1971) said that Patey stopped climbing for a while after the Italian Climb accident. Patey was also grieving the loss of his friend Eric Beard, a master fell runner, climber, singer and performer, who had died in a car accident the year before.

In February, Patey took the opportunity to spend recuperative time away with friends on the spectacular archipelago of St Kilda, 50 miles west of the Outer Hebrides, with nothing but sea beyond it until North America. Some of the earliest rock climbing in Britain had taken place on the cliffs on the main island of Hirta and the nearby sea stacks, not for its own sake but to collect sea birds, which were an important element of the St Kildans' diet. Feathers were sold on the mainland to pay for their rent; fulmar oil provided fuel for lighting their lamps.[3]

Patey had been to St Kilda once before with MacInnes, Chris Brasher and Alan Chivers, the BBC's Outside Broadcast supremo, in search of another spectacular filming location. MacInnes had permission from Morton Boyd, Chairman of the Nature Conservancy Council for Scotland, to make the first visit, and there was the advantage of a ready-built road on Hirta, west of Conachair, the cliff they were prospecting.

Conachair is the highest sea cliff in Scotland, and their initial explorations were on slopes that allowed for no casual slip. Mist concealed the full drop to the sea, but the combined sound of singing seals and rhythmic pounding of the waves were a constant reminder of its presence. Inspection by boat confirmed the unsuitability of the cliff for an ascent: it is mostly precipitous hillside with intermittent rock, the kind that, when frozen, would yield favourably to crampons and axes.

They did, however, spy an impressive cliff round the corner from Conachair and closer to Village Bay on Hirta. The next day, using a pair of Zodiac rigid inflatable boats, and with the assistance of the Nature Conservancy warden and the army, they gained a shelf at the base of the cliff. This could have served as a stance for the cameras, but they would have had to be attached to mobile platforms, and the top of the cliff was too far away for the scanner to pick up a signal. Moreover, it would involve transporting a large vehicle over highly complex terrain.

The cliff was festooned with overhangs and loose rock, and although Patey was optimistic about its potential, he wished Joe Brown was with them to cast his eye over the venue and its likelihood of yielding an Outside Broadcast. There were too many negatives for Alan Chivers, who gave the project the thumbs down.

To commemorate their visit, Patey, assisted by the others, wrote a song entitled 'Village Bay' or 'The Horny Ornithologists Blues'. Sung to the tune of 'Galway Bay', its bawdy words and imagery are like nothing else in *One Man's Mountains*, which is why it never appeared in that volume.

One of the milder verses below gives a flavour of the piece:

There's going to be some wildlife on St Kilda,
Around the second week in May;
'Cos we're bringing proper birds out to St Kilda,
Aboard a floating brothel in the bay.

Chivers was eventually persuaded to reconsider the venue, and on the second recce, Patey was joined by Cleare, Crew and, crucially, Brown. Patey and Cleare arrived early on Benbecula, where a supply boat would ferry them over to Hirta when the others arrived. In the interim, they had a fantastic day on Beinn Mhòr and its satellite peaks, Ben Corrodale and Hecla on South Uist.

There was little snow, but the ground was encased in a creaking frost, and Cleare proclaimed the circuit as one of the finest in the country. They were fortunate to get a lift down to their starting point but then had a long trek back on single-track roads to return to their temporary base. To pass the time, they conducted an informal survey: counting the number of discarded whisky and beer bottles lying in the ditches. The tally reached several hundred—recycling was unheard of amongst the thirsty locals in the Western Isles in 1970.

When Brown and Crew joined them on Benbecula, they went out in an army minesweeper at night, arriving at Village Bay at about midnight.

Cleare and Patey © John Cleare

With no jetty back then, they began to unload onto the open beach in force-eight winds and a blizzard. Halfway through, the skipper abandoned them and left for Oban.

Their original plan was to spend three days there, but continual bad weather stranded them for nearly three weeks. Despite the remote location, they observed military etiquette, and because of their National Service ranks, Patey and Cleare were housed in separate officers' mess and quarters, although everyone ate together.

The hillsides above the sea on St Kilda are so steep in places that they had to wear crampons as they inspected the 250m North Atlantic Wall. Brown and Crew abseiled down one arête, Patey and Cleare down the other. Between them, an enormous, concave face resembling the North Face of the Eiger plunged from a peaked summit straight into the sea. As a setting for a climbing spectacular, it had undoubted charisma, especially for the armchair layman.

Crew and Brown descended to sea level and scrutinised the bottom of the cliff, which comprised overhanging basalts and gneisses, amid yawning caves and a huge swell. It was seriously overhanging for about 100m, and beyond that was a 200m zone of featureless slabs, capped by a band of roofs, whose only weaknesses were loose grooves and chimneys. 'Aye, well, it's a gripping place,' muttered the usually imperturbable Brown (Cleare and Collomb, 1973). Given the technical difficulties involved, he concluded that a climbing broadcast was not feasible, but nobody would come to pick them up in the poor weather conditions. Day after day, the shipping forecast predicted storm force 10 winds for Rockall and the Hebrides; even a passing Russian trawler could not make it into the bay. There was, however, radio contact with Benbecula, and Patey was able to contact Betty, who had to frantically arrange locum cover for him.

Patey and Brown prospecting on the south coast of Hirta © John Cleare

North Atlantic Wall © John Cleare

It was now a month since the avalanche on the Italian Climb, and in a photograph taken by Cleare, Patey looks pensive as he is standing next to Brown. Haggard and lined, he could pass for Brown's father; in fact, he was two years younger.

'He was very troubled,' recalls Cleare (2014). 'He would get up in the middle of the night and go for a walk. I would say to him, "Hey Tom ... what the hell's going on?"'

'Jim shouldn't have died; Mary Ann shouldn't have died,' an anguished Patey had replied, admitting that he blamed Grieve for not getting off the mountain quicker and alerting the rescue team, even though MacInnes was certain that they would have died instantly.

Cleare (in Hedgecoe, 2007) remembers: 'We started to get philosophical, as one does in the middle of the night, and I said, "You push too hard, you know. You're always on the go. Why don't you relax?" And he said, "Well, I haven't got too long." I said, "What do you mean?" and he said, "My father died ... quite young ... I'm not going to live to an old age. My prognosis is probably early fifties, something like that.

Patey on Hirta, sensibly wearing crampons as he strides up a ridge near the top of Conachair. Stac Lee and Boreray are in the background © John Cleare

There's a lot I want to do.'"

Finally, during a weather window, a fisherman from Harris picked them up in his lobster boat. The waves en route back to Lochmaddy were enormous, and Brown likened the journey to scaling and descending mountains. Near the Sound of Harris, the experience was more like surfing, but they still managed to drink whisky and eat lobster.

The last verse of 'Village Bay' captured the mood of the trip perfectly:

So there's not a lot to see upon St Kilda,
Two dozen empty bothies and a wall,
It's a dreary little dot of desolation,
One hundred miles due west of bugger all.

Patey later reflected on the climbing potential of the archipelago:

Climbing was not an easy task, for during the nesting months many of the cliffs were plastered knee-deep in excrement; hence the quality of the underlying rock is a purely academic point. In winter, when the rocks are clean, it's too rough to land at the bottom. Anything really good (less than you might think) is too steep to provide any major free climbs. Pitoners would find a lot to do. Remember to take crampons and an axe if you go. Getting to any of the routes would probably involve traversing short-cropped grass at an enormous angle. No wonder the original St Kildans had prehensile, divergent toes! (Skye and the Hebrides Volume 2, 1996).[4]

Upon his return to Ullapool, Patey had no visitors to the bothy until Easter, when Paul Nunn, Brian Fuller and Tony Riley stayed and established Emerald Gully (IV,4) on Beinn Dearg. It must have seemed like a very long winter.

In Spring, Hamish Brown, the first person to complete a continuous circuit of the Munros, spotted Patey on his own in Aviemore. They did not speak, but Brown was struck by Patey's lined, gaunt appearance. 'There was a face of death,' Brown noted portentously in his logbook.

1   Grieve later became leader of the Glencoe Mountain Rescue Team, after MacInnes stood down. Now retired, he has given over 50 years of service and saved many lives.

2   According to research cited in the 2011 *Journal of Mental Health*, 10–20% of doctors become depressed at some point in their careers and have a higher risk of suicide than the general population. A survey of members of the UK-based Doctors Support Network found that 68% of the 116 doctors who took part had a diagnosis of depression; others reported diagnoses of bipolar disorder, anxiety, eating disorders and addictions (Carpenter, 2014).

3   Climbing trips by non-residents were rare. In 1883, Charles Barrington, who had been in the first ascent team of the Eiger, climbed Stac an Biorach. The landing was the most technical aspect of the ascent.

4   The North Atlantic Wall on the North-East Face of Conachair was finally breached in 1987 when Pete Whillance, with the permission of the National Trust for Scotland and the sponsorship of Independent Television News, was joined by a team of climbers, including Chris Bonington and Brian Hall. Whillance was a talented and bold climber who had put up high grade, classic rock routes all over the Highlands. They climbed around 20 routes on several of the cliffs of Hirta, mostly Extremes, including the E6, The Edge of the World, on the North Atlantic Wall (*SMCJ*, 1998).

Patey, Crew and Brown by a cleit on Hirta
© John Cleare

21

Death and the Maiden

Patey leading the last pitch of The Maiden, eastern stack © Paul Nunn

I hate having to trust a rope.
Tom Patey

A week before his death, Patey stayed up late talking with Tom Weir, who had come to visit him in Ullapool. They continued their conversation the following day as they sat in a car in Applecross, waiting for the rain and sleet to abate so that they could climb the Cioch Nose.

> Tom was in a serious mood ... and told me things I don't think he ever told anyone else ... It was a kind of philosophical review of his beliefs. He had never spoken to me about religion, although he was a son of the manse. He explained to me his own belief, not in any particular religion, but in an all-seeing God, which made possible the good in man to live on. (Weir, 1987)

After the traumatic period at the beginning of the year, Patey was perhaps reflecting on the worth of his life's deeds.

He had had a similarly rare conversation with ex-marine friend Glenn Davies on the immortality of the soul and man's capacity for beauty, love, generosity and sublime creativity, as well as appalling atrocities. For Patey, it was crucial for the good to outweigh the bad, and to influence future generations in a positive way. This was the only time he discussed such issues with Davies, and there is no spiritual dimension evident in his writings. Davies (2013) felt that Patey saw the mountains as an enemy to be conquered, rather than appreciating them in any sort of wistful way.

Patey told Weir that his happiest times had been exploring the

Cairngorms with his friends when he was a student. 'He thought something simple and joyous had been lost' with the advent of the '60s (Weir, 1987). Mountaineering was becoming more commercial and organised, and its equipment more sophisticated. Spontaneity and freedom, which he valued highly, seemed in short supply, and reputations amongst leading climbers had, in his opinion, led to a more serious, ruthless approach at the expense of carefree fun. The outdoors were also increasingly being used as a medium for character building in young people, a trend that he was sceptical of.

Moreover, the popularity of folk music was on the wane, and psychedelia was infusing the culture. Who would want to listen to Jimmy Shand on the accordion when there was Jimi Hendrix and his electric guitar virtuosity?

Despite these lamentations, Patey had perhaps gained a different perspective and discovered new satisfaction in his professional life:

I'd rather be a good doctor any day. Climbing is not a reason for living. Providing a good medical service to a remote region like Ullapool and the North-West is as important to me as any climbing. I've worked hard to build up that practice, and I've enjoyed it, though I'd like more time for climbing. (Weir, 1981)

Compared with earlier in the year, he was in an optimistic mood. He talked of his plan to solo the North Face of the Eiger that summer and had bought a new pair of crampons for the climb. He still believed it was the greatest mixed route in Europe and said it was one of the few he would happily repeat, 'Because it has every problem in climbing, heaped on top of each other' (Weir, 1981). But he was aware of the objective dangers such as stonefall from his attempt with Whillans, and he wanted to complete the route as quickly as possible: 'Every day you are up there lessens your chance of staying alive. And I want to live' (ibid.). Bonington (2017a) was in no doubt about Patey's suitability for the challenge: 'The Eiger was perfect for him ... mixed climbing ...

he could have soloed it ... definitely.'

Patey was also looking forward to meeting publisher Livia Gollancz to finalise a forthcoming book of his collected writings: 'I've worked damned hard on these pieces, and I need the money now,' he said.

The elements relented enough for Patey and Weir to climb the Cioch Nose that day, although they were soaked to the skin by the time they finished, so they opted to abseil down the route rather than walk off. Weir set up a belay, and as he was about to descend, he looked at the 'battered visage' of Patey and commented that his friend must be loving the escapade.

'I don't. I hate having to trust a rope,' came the reply.

A couple of days later, Patey dropped in to see Davies, who noticed that he seemed to have perked up since the Italian Climb accident. Although not his old bubbly self, he was nevertheless quite chatty.

During the Whit holiday at the end of May, it became a tradition for Alpha Club members to spend time in the North-West of Scotland with family and friends. Paul Nunn was the main organiser of these trips. Despite being based in Sheffield, Nunn was inspired by the new route potential in the area and motivated by Patey's zeal.

Whit week in 1970 saw Nunn and fellow climbers Brian 'Fred the Ted' Fuller, Clive Rowland, and 20-year-old Dave 'Spud' Goodwin, among others, ensconced at Sheigra, beyond the village of Kinlochbervie. From the great mountain crags of Foinaven to the accessible nearby sea cliffs and the idyllic gneiss outcrops, the scale of unclimbed rock in the area was vast. And, of course, there were sea stacks. Patey generously shared information about new routes, and he suggested a first ascent of The Maiden, off Whiten Head.

There was much excitement when Patey arrived in his ramshackle Skoda. Fuller had a big tent with an extended flysheet, and everyone crowded into it for a sing-song as Patey played the accordion and bottles of Glenmorangie whisky were passed around. It was the first time Goodwin had met Patey, and he was rather in awe of him, having heard and read a lot about his exploits. Gill Canon, Fuller's girlfriend, thought

Clive Rowland and Patey en route to Whiten Head © Paul Nunn

him 'fantastic, a lovely bloke'. Di Cundy, also in her 20s, recalled that, at 38, Patey seemed like an old man compared with the others.

The stack was trickier to reach than any of the others Patey had climbed, and its distance from the mainland required a boat for access. Fuller had been tasked with organising the open craft boat, which took them across Loch Eriboll and to Whiten Head.

The Maiden is, in fact, a pair of quartzite columns, and the team had set their sights on the eastern one, which has a cave puncturing its base and sits on a plinth surrounded by deep water. As the boatman nosed in, Patey, keen as ever, was the first to leap off the bow.

Their intended line of ascent lay on the northern aspect of the stack. Patey and Nunn swung leads over three pitches (it is now usually done in two), with the inexperienced Goodwin, wearing big boots, in the middle. Rowland and Fuller followed as a pair. Although the climbing is technically VS, it is graded HVS to reflect the overall seriousness of the undertaking. The experience was an eye-opener for Goodwin, and the prospect of an intimidating abseil and a leap back into the boat added spice to the adventure. Patey was in a playful mood and bantered with Canon, Cundy and Clive's wife, Stephanie, who were spectating in the boat far below him, flinging vegetation down in their direction.

They constructed the abseil by hammering two solid pegs vertically into cracks in the summit block and linking these together before threading the abseil ropes through. A backup sling over the block would take the load in the unlikely event that the pegs failed.

In the gathering wind, the ropes blew across their descent line and snagged on flakes of rock, so they weighted the ends with surplus climbing gear to ensure they reached the foot of the stack. Nunn went down first, swinging free from the rock for the last half. Goodwin, in a waist harness and without a figure of eight device, was concerned about abseiling with only a karabiner on his harness and the rope wrapped over one shoulder, so Patey attached him to another line, which he paid out as the young man abseiled cautiously.

Patey was the last to descend, using an old, skinny figure of eight clipped via a karabiner into his harness. Back then, it was less common for climbers to attach prusik loops to the rope when abseiling, and none of them had used this safety backup.

Patey approaching his final summit © Clive Rowland

Nunn (BBC, 1971) would later recount what happened next:

The others were just getting their abseil loops off and putting their bits of climbing gear away, standing [under an overhang] to get out of the way [of] any loose stones or anything else that might be coming down. And as Tom set off down, I looked ... up at his spectacular position, just dangling over the end of the stack in this very strong wind. He descended for about 15 feet quite steadily, and then briefly, very briefly, he just stopped. And I assumed he was just adjusting his abseil a little bit. I glanced away and then glanced back and saw that he was ... attempting ... to take some of his weight on one of his arms on the rope. I ... was horrified to see him just fall straight off the rope ... without any sign of a last-minute grab or anything. It was so sudden. And he fell straight onto the plinth about halfway between me and the base of the stack ... about 100 feet... straight onto bedrock. I was the first one to get across to him, and he was lying face upwards, absolutely still, [with] very little visible injury. It seemed to me immediately that he was dead.

Patey was wearing a thin red cagoule, and it seems that either this or his jumper had jammed in the figure of eight. In trying to free it, the karabiner attached to his harness had most likely unclipped from the device. Crucially, in his typical careless fashion, he was not using a screwgate.

There was a dull thud as Patey landed at Rowland's feet. He had suffered catastrophic injuries on impact, and one of his rock shoes had flown off. The only movement was his hair, flecked with grey, fluttering gently in the wind.

The occupants of the boat did not understand what had happened at first. Canon recalled, 'I think it was Di [who] said someone's fallen. Then they said, It's Tom.' Their fears were confirmed when Nunn turned to look at them, and with arms outstretched and palms up like a supplicant, slowly shook his head.

The boatman was absolutely knocked for six ... We girls had been around climbers; we kn[e]w that [tragic] things happen. The boatman ... didn't know what to do. We had to actually say, Look, you've got to get the boat in ... Then, of course, he did a brilliant job, because the weather was pretty rough ... He was a good seaman, but for about half a minute he went completely cold. (Canon, 2014)

Everyone was in varying degrees of shock, but the weather was worsening, and they needed a practical solution immediately. They attached Patey's body to the plinth using pegs as anchors, and Rowland, ever calm in a crisis,[1] covered his face to prevent the birds from pecking at his eyes. The ropes had to be abandoned because Patey's figure of eight was still attached to them.

The boat lurched perilously as the climbers jumped onto it, and a strong north-westerly whipped up the waves on the way back, battering the boat broadside. Nunn, in an effort to keep the shaken Goodwin occupied, tasked him with bailing out the water with a bilge pump as the boatman steered grimly on. Nobody wore lifejackets.

Nunn and Rowland were very experienced and had encountered tragedies in climbing, but Goodwin (2014) recalls that: 'It was the first time I'd ever actually seen the[ir] vulnerability.'

They eventually fought their way back, and the weather eased as they reached the landing point and disembarked. After informing the Police, they made their way back to the campsite and broke the news to the others. Cundy (2014) felt the poignancy of seeing Patey's accordion in his tent, but recalled that they 'never did speak about the event much' afterwards.

When Betty heard about the accident, she immediately contacted Patey's Aberdeen friends, and Mike Taylor drove Adam Watson and his father, a solicitor, across to Ullapool that night. Hamish MacInnes travelled up from Glencoe and later collected Patey's car from the Kylesku Ferry.

The following day, Nunn, Rowland and Fuller set off to retrieve the body in a sturdier boat with some policemen from Sutherland. The sea was as rough as it had been the previous day, and the leap onto the plinth

The Maiden, Eastern stack © John Cleare

perilous. They wrapped Patey in a sea rescue corset, and it took all of them to transfer him to the boat, which had only a tiny wheelhouse. Most of the sombre party were drenched on the return journey.

Not long after the accident, Bill March and John Cunningham took a boat out to The Maiden. They retrieved the rope and figure of eight, and took the opportunity to climb another harder route on the stack. Both were instructors at Glenmore Lodge at the time, and they tried to work out how Patey could have fallen. Testing out various hypotheses back at Glenmore, they confirmed that a snaplink karabiner could unclip from the figure of eight that he had used. MacInnes, who had been climbing with Patey recently, had given him the old Pierre Allain karabiner and a sling, as Patey had lost his belt, but had stressed that it was only to be used for something like sack hauling and not for actual climbing. The model was later recalled due to safety concerns (Hedgecoe, 2007).

Word of Patey's death spread quickly through the British climbing community. He would no doubt have smiled at how his old Eiger rope-mate summarised his demise. When Whillans was asked what had happened, he replied in his typical laconic style: 'He went splat.'

It had been a bleak five months for British mountaineering, with Jim McArtney, Mary Ann Hudson, Fergus Mitchell, Gunn Clark,[2] and now Patey, all dead. Ian Clough was killed five days later on Annapurna. Nunn, who would lose his life in the Karakoram some years later, reflected on the impact of Patey's death in the immediate aftermath:

> I'd seen accidents before, but never [involving] people I liked as much as Tom or [had] come to feel relatively close to. It was a sort of coming of age ... it took part of the golden glow away ... there was a joyfulness ... which just wasn't there when [Tom had] gone.

The funeral was held at St Andrew's Cathedral in Aberdeen and was attended by a huge congregation comprising many well-known British mountaineers. A strong contingent of Scottish climbers was joined by Joe Brown, Chris Brasher, Ian McNaught-Davis, Chris Bonington and Baz Ingle, as well as Patey's companions from The Maiden trip, Paul Nunn, Brian Fuller and Gill Canon. Maurice, Patey's half-brother, acted as a pallbearer with Adam Watson, Hamish MacInnes and Mike Taylor. The burial took place at St Mary's on the Rock, Patey's father's church in Ellon; the grave inscription bore little testimony to such a rich and accomplished life.

The Patey family moved back to Aberdeen soon after, to make way for the new village doctor. There was little money paid out from life insurance, and a memorial fund based on donations was set up to support them, and advertised in the climbing press. Betty rose to the challenge of bringing up a family single-handed, and she retrained as a religious education teacher. Rona followed in her father's footsteps to Medical School and subsequently became a consultant anaesthetist. She is an Honorary Professor and Lead for the Institute of Education for Medical and Dental Sciences at Aberdeen University. Both Ian and Michael worked for oil-related companies in Aberdeen.

Ian Patey remembers the kindness of three people in particular in the years following his father's death. Joe Brown invited the Patey family down to his home in Llanberis for holidays and would stop off to visit them in Aberdeen when he ventured north on fishing and climbing trips. Hamish MacInnes regularly sent postcards from his expeditions and filming assignments all over the world. Mike Taylor, an executor of Patey's will, was generous with gifts at Christmas and other occasions. But Betty, who had never been part of Patey's climbing scene when they moved to Ullapool, maintained no close contact with his mountaineering friends.

Patey was an irreplaceable friend and climbing companion. The loss of their good doctor shook the Ullapool community, too—even today, older residents, 'broken-hearted at his passing' (Beattie, 2022), rue the tragedy. His far-reaching influence and the impact of his death were perhaps perfectly expressed by Paul Nunn (1978):

> *From a climbing point of view, it was the end of an era. Tom had exercised an unchallenged hegemony over the North-West, and his going left a void in his fief which could never [again] be so adroitly filled.*

1   Joe Brown had been on trips to the Himalaya and Alaska with Rowland and found him to be a very good companion in a big mountain situation. Along with Mo Anthoine, Rowland almost certainly saved the lives of Doug Scott and Chris Bonington in 1977 when Scott broke both legs and Bonington broke ribs during an epic descent from The Ogre in the Karakoram.

2   Gunn Clark made the first British ascent of the Walker Spur with the late Robin Smith, and the first British ascent of the Brandler-Hasse route on the Cima Grande with Chris Bonington. These achievements did a great deal to open up the hard Dolomite routes for other British climbers. At the age of 32, Clark was killed while climbing a gully on Buachaille Etive Mòr when a party above him dislodged an avalanche (*Alpine Journal*, 2022).

Tom Patey, 1932– 1970 © Pete Crew

Ian Patey's Memories

In 1966, when I was 6, I went up Ben Mor Coigach with my father, my sister Rona, my brother Michael, and Douglas and David Beattie, sons of the local minister. It was a sunny, clear morning and our curiosity for the summit inspired us to race each other to the top, my father following closely behind. This was our first big hillwalk with him, and he was so impressed at how fast we completed it. He hoped to take us up Suilven when we were a wee bit older, and although this didn't happen, I completed it myself many years later on the back of that memory. I waited for a summer's day with a clear forecast and left Aberdeenshire at 2.00am, returning that same day, having had a terrific time. This inspired me to hillwalk regularly with my wife, Jennifer, and daughters Rachel, Megan and Emma on the west coast, where we have made some wonderful memories.

Singing was something both our parents were known for, and on one occasion, after reaching the top of Ullapool Hill, my father sang as we proudly showed him the natural stone 'slide' we had found. (Rona inherited this talent for singing and would successfully compete in the local Gaelic Mod for Ullapool Primary School. She also inherited an adventurous streak, taking part in expeditions to the Himalaya as the Team Doctor.)

We would also walk to the beach with him to look for crabs and crustaceans under the rocks, enjoying scrambling on the small rocky outcrops. My father would reassuringly guide us to the top, making sure we searched for good holds. He said we all showed promise as climbers, but this was not going to happen, as Michael and I had other interests. (Michael became a great darts player and regularly attended Pub League darts for the Kirkgate Bar. He also played football for Summerhill Spurs in local cup tournaments.)

After discovering that Michael and I were keen footballers and loved playing with him, my father inserted goalposts strung together with netting found on the beach and mowed a football pitch in the back garden at 3 West Terrace. He was none too pleased, however, when we were able to nutmeg him.

My father would often reiterate the importance of practice, and he encouraged us to play with very skilled players. One year, concerned for my wellbeing, he gave me advice on how to run the Primary School Cross Country Race. He said I must walk, then run, at my own pace. I was small in stature at the time, but when I found myself at the back of the pack, I bolted to catch up and found, to my surprise, that I was able to pass the field of runners. The leader and I sprinted to the finish, tripping on rabbit holes. When we were neck and neck, my rival fell down a large hole, and I crossed the finish line as the winner. My father could not believe I had won! But he seemed rather proud of my disregard for his advice and my opponent's fate, and of what I had achieved.

Sometimes my father would take me with him on medical rounds to places like Achiltibuie and Dundonnell. During these adventurous excursions, he would race his Skoda along the winding single-track roads, while I attempted to remain sitting in the front seat. Sometimes, we would leave the road temporarily, or he would abruptly jam on the brakes. Despite often feeling nauseous, I thoroughly enjoyed these times with him.

At some stage, one of the Royal Navy Frigates my father had served on visited Ullapool. These Battleships always created a buzz when they harboured at the old Ullapool pier. My father was invited as a guest, and we were thrilled to hear we had all been granted permission to board her. He would tell us in detail about his connection to the Royal Navy, praising his ancestors' bravery during events dating back to the late 18th century.

A good life is not measured by any biblical span.

Ernest Hemingway, *For Whom the Bell Tolls*

Even if Tom Patey were better known for his writing than for pioneering new routes, he would remain a substantial figure in British mountaineering history. Indeed, 'A Short Walk with Whillans' alone would have guaranteed him a significant footnote in mountaineering literature.

Patey's work was initially published in the journals of the SMC, Etchachan Club, Climbers' Club and Alpine Club. His songs were performed informally all over the country, sometimes by others, but they only became widely known when they appeared in *One Man's Mountains*, which was published posthumously in 1971.

Largely thanks to *One Man's Mountains*, he remains the favourite mountaineering writer of many British climbers, for the simple reason that he offers some of the funniest material written about the sport and, crucially, he writes with humanity and warmth.

According to Dave Roberts (1974), himself a leading practitioner of climbing literature:

> *One Man's Mountains may well be the most entertaining climbing book ever written. By fusing the British tradition of intelligent, whimsically self-deprecating mountain writing (in the vein of Shipton, Tilman, Longstaff and Murray at their best) with the fierce and rowdy iconoclasm of the Creagh Dhu and the Rock and Ice clubs, Patey discovered a jocular voice all of his own. His accomplishment emerges as all the more remarkable when one reflects that he milked all his best effects out of what really amounts to a single conceit: the climber as Don Quixote, tilting at Nordwandes.*

The equally respected author Jim Perrin (1987) observes that every piece has the stamp of Patey's character upon it, and that 'There are perhaps half-a-dozen fully-finished, fully-polished items which rank as masterpieces within the genre of the climbing essay.'

Patey's writing deviates from much modern mountaineering literature that describes not only the act of climbing but presents an inner dialogue about its meaning or how it fits in with broader social responsibilities. Success is often equated with some form of insight and self-awareness. There is not a whiff of this in Patey's writing. That he loved the mountains is clear, but nowhere does he refer to any mystical experience they might give rise to. Indeed, Patey rejoices in the ridiculousness of the whole endeavour, and avoids seeking any meaning or trying to justify it. Climbing was important to him, but he could always stand back and see it for what it was. What comes across in all his accounts is someone having enormous fun, whether it be a tussle with the technical problems of a route or delighting in banter with his companions. His essays are a celebration of the absurdities of what is regarded by the layman as a serious and dangerous game.

'Apes or Ballerinas?' (1969) is probably the closest Patey came to a serious discussion and is a kind of statement of his general philosophy of mountaineering. It also satirises those who see climbing as a taught activity with an emphasis on kinaesthetic finesse and balletic agility. Patey preferred functional efficiency, reflecting his own inelegant but practical style:

The sort of climber I like to watch is the man who knows where he's going and wastes no time getting there. A latent power and driving force carr[y] him up pitches where no amount of dynamic posturing would do any good.

He ends the piece by berating the self-glorifying metaphors which climbers attach to themselves:

Climbers are conceited characters when you pause to think about it. They liken themselves in print to Gods, Goddesses, and Gladiators; tigers, eagles and chamois; craftsmen, gardeners and ballet dancers; and even, in one case at least, to computers!

Patey's prose may seem undemanding and uncomplicated, but it was carefully crafted and is harder to replicate than might first appear. Nothing escaped his eye, and he would often observe people and proceedings from a distance for a while before joining in (Goulder, 2014). He is at his most effective when he deftly slips humour into the narrative in a subtle and unexpected way, exploiting the comic potential of the situation and the characters of those involved, including himself. Once he had honed his style, he hit on a winning formula: things failing to go smoothly due to technicalities, conditions and cock-ups; a supporting cast of unforgettable characters; an ear for amusing quips; and self-deprecation. All this was infused with the gentlest brand of satire.

The personnel and friendly one-upmanship inherent in climbing are key to the success of Patey's writing. 'If Nicol, MacInnes, Grassick, Bonington, Whillans had never done anything other than appear in Patey's essays, they would still live on in our consciousness,' said Perrin (1982).

Paul Nunn (1972) commented that 'egos fall like flies' in Patey's work, but this seems too harsh. He only gives them a light swat, and the flies are soon buzzing again. Patey 'essentially was a warm character and ... because of that, [it] was a fun, joyous satire ...' says Chris Bonington (2017a). Of course, his character portraits are exaggerated for effect, but they are affectionate and without malice.

Patey also deployed imagination and artistic license to craft his pieces into the pleasing end products they are. Did a stone really fall and hit the ash off his fag on the Eiger, thus providing the decisive reason for a retreat? Highly unlikely, but it is a beautifully-timed plot device. The dialogue in his articles is embellished for effect, but it remains authentic.

Not all his satirical pieces were successful, however, and he has attracted criticism from Perrin (1982) and reviewers such as Robin

Campbell (*SMCJ*, 1972). Some of his lyrics were pure doggerel, and were designed to be sung to keen audiences, where their inferior quality could be masked through live performance and mischievous ad-libbing.[1]

Indeed, Patey had the 'tragicomic gift of the balladeer' (Roberts, 1974). The sober subject matter of 'Annapurna', or 'Twenty Frozen Fingers', where Patey describes the appalling consequences of frostbite and primitive amputation techniques, is intentionally set to the jaunty, bouncy, upbeat tune of 'Twenty Tiny Fingers'.

Probably his most famous and popular tune, 'Onward Christian Bonington', set to the familiar 'Onward Christian Soldiers' gently mocks his friend's supposed quest for fame and fortune. But although he poked fun at his friends in his writing, there was a line he would never cross. At Temple Cottage, for example, he refused to sing 'The John Harlin Song' to a company including Royal Robbins and his wife as it seemed in bad taste after the demise of the song's subject. Despite his carefree approach to many aspects of life, Patey was polite and knew the boundaries of decorum.

When he was considering submitting an early version of the 'Alpine Club Song', which lampooned the private school and upper echelon social networks that permeated that venerable institution, he wrote a letter to Geoff Dutton, then Editor of the *SMCJ*:

> *I really am very dubious about printing the A.C. Song. I cannot imagine Sir John being able to enjoy a laugh at his [own] expense. Slesser and everyone else I have sung it to also disapprove of publishing it. If you do print it, you had better not put my name to it ...*[2]

Patey has never really fallen out of fashion. His writing retains a healthy pulse in mountaineering literature, and he crosses oceans well, appealing to those who may never have set foot in Scotland or the other places he describes. His longevity is telling, and his appeal spans a wide demographic, from hillwalkers to climbers at the cutting edge.

While climbing the Mazeno Ridge[3] on Nanga Parbat with Rick Allen in 2012, Scot Sandy Allan recalls digging an emergency bivouac in a coffin-like snow cave. Crawling into his sleeping bag, he observed the sweat on his skin begin to freeze in the sub-zero night air. Despite the extremity of the situation, Allan was determinedly positive about his circumstances as he mumbled a verse from Patey's 'The Last of the Grand Old Masters':

> *I'm the Last of the Grand Old Masters*
> *But now I am old and grey,*
> *When the sweat on my neck turns to verglas*
> *You will find I have passed away.*

Allan is emphatic about the author of that verse: 'I love Tom Patey!' He repeated the original British route on the Muztagh Tower in 1984, and has shared the adventure of Patey's great Scottish routes in his role as a mountain guide.

Aberdeen-based climber Guy Robertson, who remains at the forefront of climbing in Scotland, has been directly inspired by Patey's writing and adventurous approach. Patey pioneered many of Scotland's best routes, most of which Robertson has repeated:

> *Classics like Eagle Ridge and Parallel Buttress on Lochnagar, and Vertigo Wall on the Dubh-loch ... these will always remain as some of the finest climbs anywhere in Scotland. Then there was his persona and his style—always irreverent, humorous and fun. We loved the fact that he never seemed to take any of it that seriously, but just enjoyed going on mad adventures. This was so evocatively captured by his writing. I just really relate to the guy, and the idea that you can still climb ... great, interesting routes without necessarily being a full-time or professional climber. Climbing to me has always been nothing more than a fun escape and a great way to meet new friends and go to new places—everything Patey did and said epitomised that.* (2020)

Callum Johnson, who in his 20s is creating some of the hardest new winter lines in Scotland, became aware of Patey early on in his climbing career when he was still an undergraduate:

Serving my trad apprenticeship on the Aberdeen coast, it would have been difficult not to have been influenced by Patey's new routes, his character and his antics. The history section of the local guidebook alluded to the adventures and misadventures of Patey new-routing on the coast. I followed his lead, cycling from the city to the coast, escaping the bustle of people and cars, free from the burden of university, lectures, ropes and gear. My sticky rubber climbing shoes where his nailed boots once passed. Cruising back to the city on my bike, I felt re-energised. These midweek adventures on the coast kept the fire burning until the next weekend's escape to the mountains. (2020)

Johnson recalls 'lucking out' and finding a copy of *One Man's Mountains* in his local charity shop:

I read it cover to cover, then re-read several sections. Humble in his achievements, Patey acknowledged the work of his predecessors; those early routes inspired everything that followed. His [own] accomplishments inspire[d] every successive generation ... every short story [is] injected with anecdotes and banter. (ibid.)

Former President of the SMC, Simon Richardson, who is also based in the north-east of Scotland, reflects on Patey's imagination:

He was not content to follow the conventional path and his early ascents are far more about exploration and raw adventure than the pursuit of technical difficulty. The Crab Crawl and Cuillin Ridge Winter Traverse spring to mind, but perhaps the best examples are his sea stack ascents. With Hoy, Stoer and Am Buachaille he left a wonderful legacy of adventure routes ... All this has had an influence on my own climbing ... I enjoy looking round new corners, whether it is on a Scottish winter cliff, finding an unclimbed sea stack, or climbing a previously overlooked feature in the Alps or further afield. In a world where the pursuit of technical excellence is king, Patey's adventurous approach legitimises these styles of climbing. (2020)

Of course, Scottish mountaineering has changed dramatically since Patey's time. The Cairngorms climbing scene no longer revolves around the network of bothies, something Patey lamented when he opened his heart to Tom Weir shortly before his death. With increased affluence and acquisition of private transport, day hits from Aberdeen are the norm; mountain bikes have reduced the long approaches. Patey personified the adventure, freedom, fun and the social dimension of mountaineering, which some modern climbers have perhaps lost sight of.

Patey was attractive company not least because he hated negativity and apathy (Nunn, 1972). The great American big wall climber Royal Robbins (1969) said, 'His enthusiasm ... was so infectious as to be virulent ... I had long admired him as one of those rare persons who have so much life that it rubs off on those around them.' This endeared him to both the climbing establishment and its counter-culture, and he could socialise effortlessly with members of both.

John Cleare and Robin Collomb (1973), too, have referred to his pluralistic social network:

His style was also coupled with an ability to mix and harmonise with the extremes of other movements and personalities in mountaineering. None more so than those flourishing south of the border. His companions were often English and parties frequently travelled several hundred miles to join him in his exploits.

If he were alive today, Patey would no doubt still be attending SMC dinners and breathing life into these restrained social occasions composed mainly of attendees in possession of free bus passes. The subjects of his humour might have included: the erstwhile stuffiness of the SMC in its reluctance to admit women; the popularity of lycra in the '80s; sport climbing and artificial walls; rehearsed moves and serious training; climbing as a means of self-realisation; the obsession with ticking off hills or routes.

Summarising the previous 25 years of Scottish mountaineering in the 1964 *SMCJ*, W.H. Murray observed that:

> *History is made by individual men, small in number, who have ideas and the vigour to carry them into effect, often in defiance of mass opinion. So it is too in mountaineering ... Throughout the period reviewed, all the advances in the technique of summer rock have come into Scotland from England. That was true before the war, and has been true since. The distinctive contribution made by Scotland to British climbing is on ice and on snow—and ice-bound rock. The leading part in that work has been taken by our own members. The men who have done most to shape the recent history of Scottish climbing have been Tom Patey, Jimmy Marshall, and Robin Smith, not only for the climbs they've done themselves, but the great influence they have had on others.*

Murray's closing comment resonates as much today as it did back then.

But against all these virtues, it must be acknowledged that Patey, like everyone else, had his faults. People who are talented and driven by their own agendas can strain their relations with others, especially those closest to them.

Some were privately disappointed about aspects of Patey's later life and his sometimes insensitive treatment of his wife. For many of his friends, however, this was eclipsed by his merits.

Rusty Baillie (2015) observes that Patey was one of the rare few whose presence and memory transcend what he was ostensibly famous for:

> *Either you can be slow, meticulous and careful, or you can cruise through on a wild blast of energy ... Tom climbed with such intuition*

and confidence that it seemed magical—his ability to get up steep ground didn't seem to depend on textbook techniques or tool placements but on the mystical cliché of 'being one with the mountain'. He didn't wait around to have to deal with technicalities but moved up before that became necessary.

As well as holding Patey in high regard as a mountaineer, Baillie believes that, as a songwriter, Patey is up there with Bob Dylan:

Tom was bard and minstrel combined. Back in that age, we were privileged to enjoy the sublime pleasure of singing powerful songs together: a beer or two, a bottle of vino and the songs took us off to stirring adventures with emotions hot and our atavistic energies rampant. But it wasn't just the music ... He was mischievous and took great glee in mocking our self-importance, but I never heard him sing, or say, a vindictive word about anyone. His piss-taking was actually a subtle pat on the back, occasionally a kick in the butt, but never spiteful.

Of Patey's lust for life, Baillie says:

Tom's legendary willingness to travel countless hours to meet, mingle and carouse left many feeling they had been blessed by his company and his music. Was all this fuelled by more than mince and tatties? Who cares! He used his talents to contribute happiness to this world of travail; he had no pretensions, and he lived life to the full. Salut! It was an honour to have served with you.

In that conversation with Tom Weir just before his death, Patey pondered the good people do and its continuation beyond their mortal lives. Patey's great routes, the style in which he achieved them and his accounts of them remain an integral part of British mountaineering culture and history. Half a century after his death, his legacy endures.

1   During a week camping in Chamonix in August 1963, Peter Noble borrowed Patey's handwritten songbook and copied the lyrics from it. It contained thirty-four songs, mostly Patey compositions, only five of which ('Onward Christian Bonington', 'The Joe Brown Song', 'Aiguilles des Cairngorms', 'Two Tiny Figures' and 'Twenty Frozen Fingers') appeared in *One Man's Mountains*. Recurring themes included gruesome accidents and the perils of drink.

2   Patey was already performing the complete version to an enthusiastic audience. Modern readers would be surprised at Patey's concern as the humour is so light and good-natured.

3   At 10km, this is the longest route up the ninth highest peak in the world, and indeed up any of the 8,000m peaks. Ten expeditions had failed previously. The pair took eleven days to reach the summit. They were rewarded with the Piolet d'Or for their historic effort.

Acknowledgements

Firstly, thanks to Rob Lovell and the Scottish Mountaineering Press for their support throughout this process, and to the Scottish Mountaineering Trust for awarding a grant for the research. Deziree Wilson has been a most conscientious editor, and the whole editing process was an enjoyable, collaborative experience. Gino Di Meo has applied his skills to the design of the book. Special thanks must go to Peter Biggar for selflessly looking at the whole manuscript, cutting it significantly and offering pertinent comments and suggestions so that it could be submitted to a publisher.

Ian Patey has been very generous in his enormous effort to share the huge archive related to his father. The following interviewees also provided invaluable information (which will eventually be housed in the SMC archive) to supplement existing written material: Sam Bemrose, Barrie Biven, Ernie Blaber, Chris Bonington, Duncan Boston, Martin Boysen, Maggie Boysen, Richard Brooke, Joe Brown, Val Brown, Paddy Buckley, John Cheesmond, John Cleare, Di Cundy, Glenn Davies, John 'Zeke' Deacon, Harold Drasdo, Neville Drasdo, May Forbes, Clive Freshwater, Brian Fuller, Gill Fuller, Allen Fyffe, Peter Gillman, Dave Goodwin, Dave Goulder, Dennis Gray, John Grieve, Dick Hardie, Baz Ingle, Pat Ingle, Gordon 'Goggs' Leslie, Ted Maden, Freddie Malcolm, Richard McHardy, Graeme Nicol, Barrie Page, Paul Ross, Clive Rowland, Donnie Smith, Mary Stewart, Wendy Tout-Hughes and Alan Will. Sam and Noni Bemrose, Barrie and Lucy Biven, Ernie and Ann Blaber, Duncan Boston and Zeke Deacon kindly put me up at their homes during visits. Face-to-face conversations with Sandy Allan, Hamish Brown, Pete Crew, John Hay, Guy Hedgecoe, Dave Peck and Tony Riley were illuminating. Others corresponded their thoughts or memories of meeting Patey by email: Rusty Baillie, Geoff Cohen, Mike Galbraith, Callum Johnson, MacNab Mackenzie, Simon Richardson, Alf Robertson, Guy Robertson, Robin Shaw, Hugh Spencer and Alex 'Sticker' Thom.

John Barry, Mark Bentinck, Dougie Keelan, James Mann, Bob Moulton, Iain Peters and Guy Sheridan provided Royal Marines-related information and contacts. James Mann generously collated and scanned Marines-related pictures from Vivian Stevenson's widow, Patsy.

Greg Strange was immensely helpful in answering (often very obscure) questions concerning Cairngorm climbing history, of which he has an encyclopaedic knowledge. He also provided archive material, and supplied images from his own extensive photographic collection and contact details for Patey associates from the early days. Greg also gave feedback on the edited chapters, as did Geoff Cohen, Peter Gillman and Peter Macdonald.

The following helped locate the necessary books and articles, or loaned me their own copies: Peter Biggar, Dave Broadhead, Robin Forrest, Lisa Hutchison, Derek Pyper, Roger Robb, Alison Robertson and Greg Strange. Arthur Bennett generously gifted me a large number of SMC *Journals* which made my research a lot easier. Ewen MacNiven loaned me the music of various folk singers from the period, and Peter Noble shared his collection of Patey songs.

Thanks to all the credited photographers for taking the trouble to scan old slides and submit digital images from their own collections. John Cleare provided access to his superb picture library, while James Mann and Grahame Nicoll helped trace and provide modern photographs of Patey routes and related crags. Adam Watson identified personnel in archive Patey Cairngorm pictures, and Watson's daughter, Jenny Aitchison, supplied pictures from her father's archive. Graeme Hunter provided pictures from Hamish MacInnes's archive and helped with the preparation of digital images.

David Nightingale checked pictures in the archive of the late Douglas Scott. Iain Brooker allowed me access to his father Bill's pocket diaries and photo albums.

From the SMC, John Fowler (when Secretary), David Stone (Image archivist) and Robin Campbell (Archivist) all provided me with important material. Archivists David Medcalf (Climbers' Club), Glyn Hughes (Alpine Club) and Chris Sherwin (Fell and Rock Climbing Club), Amy Adams (Archives Collections Team Manager, National Museum, Royal Navy), George Gelder, Lt Col RM [Retd] (Royal Marines Historian, Naval Historical Branch, Portsmouth: archives), Lee Cullen of the *Globe and Laurel* magazine, Kelda Roe (Collections Manager, Mountain Heritage Trust) and Mick Tighe (Scottish Mountain Heritage Collection) answered various queries and provided information. The following also provided information, photographs and advice: Dick Balharry, Jon Barton, Colin Beechey, Paul Brian, Zoe Brown, Jim Brumfitt, John Burns, Rob Collister, Ken Crocket, Jimmy Cruickshank, Bob Davidson, Brian Duthie, Roger Everett, Helene Fuchs-Fraser, Glacier Books of Pitlochry, Alan Halewood, Jas Hepburn, Dave Holdroyd, Tony Howard, Andrew and Louise James, Susan Jensen, Bob and Rosemary Jones, Sean Kelly, Dave Kerr, Peter Langhorne, John Lyall, Robert McMurray, Peter Macdonald, Sarah Mackenzie, Mari Mander, Jimmy Marshall, Tony Martin, John Porter, Ali Rose, Stephen Reid, Brian Robertson, Raymond Simpson, Tony Smythe, Ian Sutherland, Phil Swainson, Ian Sykes, Ian Taylor, Henning Wackerhage, Kirk Watson, Mike Watson, Gavin Watters, Colin Wells and Noel Williams. Hugh Spencer was extremely helpful with a range of enquiries concerning the early years period. Ken McKinlay provided valuable assistance with any IT issues.

I'm grateful to Mick Fowler for writing the foreword to a book about one of his personal heroes.

Finally, thanks to Jim Perrin for encouraging me to take on this biography in the first place and to Andrew Greig for similar encouragement after the first draft was completed but there was still a very long way to go.

ACKNOWLEDGEMENTS

Bibliography and References

Allan, S., 2015. *In Some Lost Place*. Sheffield: Vertebrate Publishing.

Almond, H.H., 1893. 'Ben-y-Gloe on Christmas Day', *Scottish Mountaineering Club Journal (SMCJ)*, vol.2, no.5, pp.235–39.

'In Memoriam: J.F.G. Clark', *Alpine Journal*, 1970. pp.331–32.

Alvarez, A., 1965. 'The Edge of the Impossible', *Observer Magazine*. In Press. 22 August.

Angell, S., 1988. *Pinnacle Club: A History of Women Climbing*. UK: Pinnacle Club.

Baillie, R., 2015. Personal communication by email. 17 April.

Band, G., 1955. *The Road to Rakaposhi*. London: Hodder & Stoughton.

Banks, M., 1959. *Rakaposhi*. London: Secker and Warburg.

Banks, M., 1987. 'The Incomparable Dr. Patey', *Climber Magazine*, May.

Beattie, A., 2022. Facebook. June 27.

Bemrose, S., 2014. Interview with M. Dixon on 14 July. Chilton, Polden.

Bentinck, M., 2008. *Vertical Assault: The Story of the Royal Marines Mountain Leaders' Branch*. Royal Marines Historical Society Special Publications 34.

Biggar, P., 2020. Personal communication by email. 2 December.

Biven, B., 2014. Interview with M. Dixon on 17 October. Wilsford.

Blaber, E., 2014. Interview with M. Dixon on 18 July. Midsomer Norton.

Bonington, C., 1973. *The Next Horizon*. London: Victor Gollancz.

Bonington, C., 2017a. Interview with M. Dixon on 18 July. Nether Row.

Bonington, C., 2017b. *Ascent: A life spent climbing on the edge*. London: Simon & Schuster UK.

Boston, Duncan., 2021. Telephone interview with M. Dixon on 15 December.

Boysen, M., 2013. Interview with M. Dixon on 30 December. Hale.

Boysen, M., 2014. *Hanging On: A Life Inside British Climbing's Golden Age*. Sheffield: Vertebrate Publishing.

Brasher, C., 1986. 'We'll Take the High Road: The New Highlanders', *Observer Magazine*, 18 August.

Brebner, A., 2017. *Beyond The Secret Howff*. Edinburgh: Luath Press.

Brooke, R., 1962. Diary entries from 27 February–6 March.

Brooker, B., 1971. *They Sought the Summits*. London: BBC Radio.

Brooker, W.D. et al., 1971. 'In Memoriam: Thomas Walton Patey', *SMCJ*, vol.29, no.162, pp.433–38.

Brooke, B., 2001. 'Mitre Ridge in Winter', *SMCJ*, vol.37, no.192, pp.555–59.

Brown, J., 1967. *The Hard Years*. London: Victor Gollancz.

Brown, J., 1987. 'The Incomparable Dr. Patey', *Climber Magazine*, May.

Brown, J., 2013. Interview with M. Dixon on 6 August. Llanberis.

Brown, R., 2000. *Struan: The Extraordinary Story of Karl and Eileen Fuchs*. St. Albans: Right Words.

Campbell, R., 1972. 'One Man's Mountains Review', *SMCJ*, vol.30, no.163, p.108.

Canon (Fuller), G., 2014. Interview with M. Dixon on 7 July. Brampton.

Carpenter, L., 2014. 'Why Doctors Hide Their Own Illnesses', *The Guardian*, 16 May.

Cheesmond, J., 2017. Interview with M. Dixon on 2 July. Edinburgh.

Chorley, R., 1987. 'In Memoriam: John Hartog', *Alpine Journal*, pp.301–2.

Cleare, J., 1971. *They Sought the Summits*. London: BBC Radio.

Cleare, J., 1975. *How we climbed Am Buachaille* in *Mountains*. London and Basingstoke: Macmillan London Ltd.

Cleare, J., 1975. *Days with the Doctor, Exploits at Chamonix* in *Mountains*. London and Basingstoke: Macmillan London Ltd.

Cleare, J., 2014. Interview with M. Dixon on 15 April. Fonthill Gifford.

Cleare, J. and Collomb, R., 1973. *Sea Cliff Climbing in Britain*. London: Constable.

Cohen, G., 2014. Personal communication by email. 24 February.

Connor, J., 1999. *Creagh Dhu Climber: The Life and Times of John Cunningham*. Glasgow: The Ernest Press.

Craig, D., 2001. *First and Last Climbs* in *The Way to Cold Mountain: A Scottish Mountains Anthology*. Edinburgh: Polygon.

Crocket, K. and Richardson, S., 2009. *Ben Nevis: Britain's Highest Mountain*. 2nd ed. UK: Scottish Mountaineering Trust.

Crowley, A., 1895. 'Chalk Climbing on Beachy Head', *SMCJ*, vol.3, pp.288–94.

Cruickshank, J., 2006. *High Endeavours: The Life and Legend of Robin Smith*. Edinburgh: Canongate Books.

Cundy, D., 2014. Interview with M. Dixon on 14 August. Hilton, Cumbria.

Davies, G., 2013. Interview with M. Dixon on 13 November. Ullapool.

Deacon, J., 2014. Interview with M. Dixon on 16 July. Sennen.

Dixon, C.M., 1952. 'The Forgotten Corrie', *SMCJ*, vol.25, no.143, pp.2–13.

Doric Columns, 2021. *The Aberdeen Mittwoch Blitz* [online]. Available at: https://doriccolumns.wordpress.com/ww2-1939-45/ [Accessed 29 November 2021].

Drasdo, H., 1997. *The Ordinary Route*. Glasgow: The Ernest Press.

Drasdo, N., 2009. 'My Recollection of the First Ascent of the Direct Nose Route on Sgùrr an Fhidhleir', *Miscellaneous Notes*, vol.40, no.200, pp.492–93.

Dutton, G., 1990. 'Editor the Tenth', *SMCJ*, vol.34, no.181, pp.374–79.

Dutton, G., in Cruickshank, J., 2006. *High Endeavours: The Life and Legend of Robin Smith*. p.145. Edinburgh: Canongate Books.

Forbes, M., 2014. Interview with M. Dixon on 20 June. Ellon.

Freshwater, C., 2014. Interview with M. Dixon on 4 May. Loch Insh.

Fyffe, A., 1971. *They Sought the Summits*. London: BBC Radio.

Fyffe, A. 2013. Interview with M. Dixon on 27 November. Aviemore.

Gillman, P., 1967. 'TV Circus Goes Up the *Old Man of Hoy*', *The Sunday Times Magazine*, reprinted in author's *In Balance, Twenty years of Mountaineering Journalism* (1989). London: Hodder & Stoughton.

Gillman, P., 1969. 'Cold, Hard, Dangerous — and fun', *The Sunday Times Magazine*, reprinted in the author's *In Balance, Twenty years of Mountaineering Journalism* (1989). London: Hodder & Stoughton.

Gillman, P., 1989. 'Review of One Man's Mountains', *The Sunday Times Magazine*, reprinted in the author's *In Balance, Twenty years of Mountaineering Journalism* (1989). London: Hodder & Stoughton.

Gillman, P., 2010/11. 'The Past is a Foreign Country', *Alpine Journal*, pp.159–67.

Gillman, P., 2015. Interview with M. Dixon on 5 December. Carrbridge.

Gillman, P. and L., 2015. *Extreme Eiger: Triumph and Tragedy on the North Face*. London: Simon & Schuster.

Goodwin, D., 2014. Interview with M. Dixon on 15 October. Derbyshire.

Goodwin, S., 2013. 'Mike Banks Obituary', *The Independent*, 20 February.

Goulder, D., 2014. Interview with M. Dixon on 25 January. Rosehall.

Grassick, K., 1983. 'Sticil Face' in Wilson, K., Alcock, D. and Barry, J., *Cold Climbs*. London: Diadem Books.

Gray, D., 1993. *Tight Rope! The Fun of climbing*. Glasgow: The Ernest Press.

Gray, D., 2007. 'The Last of the Grand Old Masters', *SMCJ*, vol.40, no.198, pp.463–70.

Gray, D., 2014. Interview with M. Dixon on 6 April. Leeds.

Gray, D., 2016. Personal communication by email. 1 October.

Greig, A., 1985. *Summit Fever*. London: Hutchinson & Co.

Grieve, J., 1982. 'Nowhere to Fall but Off', *SMCJ*, vol.32, no.173, pp.246–50.

Grieve, J., 1971. *They Sought the Summits*. London: BBC Radio.

Hardie, D., 2016. Interview with M. Dixon on 30 October. Aberdeen.

Harper, C., 2006. *Dazzling Stranger: Bert Jansch and the British Folk and Blues Revival*. London: Bloomsbury.

Hartog, J., 1956. 'The Climbing of the Muztagh Tower', *Alpine Journal*, pp.253–70.

Hay, J., 2016. 'Not a Sunset Song', *SMCJ*, vol.44, no.207, pp.107–10.

Hedgecoe, G., 2007. 'Tom Patey: The Tiger of Yesterday', *Rock and Ice Magazine*.

Holdroyd, D. *Halcyon Days*. Unpublished manuscript.

Howard, T., 1970. *Walks and Climbs in the Romsdal Valley*. Manchester: Cicerone Press.

Imlach, H. and McVicar, E., 1992. *Cod Liver Oil and The Orange Juice: Reminiscences of a Fat Folksinger*. Edinburgh: Mainstream Publishing.

Irving, R.L.G., 1935. *The Romance of Mountaineering*. London: J.M. Dent & Sons.

Johnson, C., 2020. Personal communication by email. 22 May.

Kamienski, L., 2017. *Shooting Up: A History of Drugs and Warfare*. London: C. Hurst & Co.

Land, D., 1969. 'Eagle Ridge of Lochnagar in Winter', *SMCJ*, vol.29, no.160, pp.163–64.

Lates, M., 2011. *Skye The Cuillin*. UK: Scottish Mountaineering Trust.

Leslie, G., 2014. Interview with M. Dixon on 14 January. Inchmarlo.

Lines, J., 2004. 'Skye is the Limit', SMCJ, vol.39, no.195, pp.555–61.

Lines, J., 2013. *Tears of the Dawn*. Aboyne: Shelterstone Ltd.

Ludwig, C., 1933. 'The Douglas Gully, Lochnagar', SMCJ, vol.20, no.116, p.154.

MacInnes, H., 1971. 'Tom Patey obituary', SMCJ, vol.29, no.162, pp.38–439.

MacInnes, H., 1971. *They Sought the Summits*. London: BBC Radio.

MacInnes, H., 1973. *Call Out*. London: Hodder & Stoughton.

MacInnes, H., 1979. *Look Behind the Ranges*. London: Hodder & Stoughton.

Malcolm, F.R., 1954. 'Aiguille du Peigne', *Etchachan Club Journal*, vol.2, no.2, pp.15–21.

Malcolm, F., 2013. Interview with M. Dixon on 3 December. Aberdeen.

Marshall, J.R., 1961. 'The Orion Face', SMCJ, vol.25, no.152, pp.112–15.

McNaught-Davis, I., 1956. *The Mustagh Tower Diary*. Keswick: Mountain Heritage Trust.

Medline Plus, 2022. *Substance use—amphetamines*. [Online]. Available at: https://medlineplus.gov/ency/patientinstructions/000792.htm [Accessed 30 May, 2022].

Moulton, R.D., 1966. 'Rock Climbing in Devonshire', Her Majesty's Naval Service (Royal Navy & Royal Marines Mountaineering Club).

Murray, W.H., 1947. *Mountaineering in Scotland*. London: J.M. Dent & Sons.

Murray, W.H., 1964. 'The Last Twenty-Five Years', SMCJ, vol.28, no.155, p.5.

Murray, W.H., 1971. 'Tom Patey obituary', *Alpine Journal*.

Murray, W.H., 1987. 'In Memoriam: John Hartog', SMCJ, vol.33, no.178, pp.536–37.

Nicol, G., 1971. *They Sought the Summits*. London: BBC radio.

Nicol, G., 2014. Interview with M. Dixon on 14 January. Aberdeen.

Nisbet, A., Anderson, R. and Richardson, S., 2008. *Scottish Winter Climbs*. UK: Scottish Mountaineering Trust.

Nunn, P., 1970. 'Tom Patey is Dead: A Eulogy', *Mountain*, 10 July, p.10.

Nunn, P., 1971. *They Sought the Summits*. London: BBC Radio.

Nunn, P., 1972. 'Review of One Man's Mountains', *Mountain*, 19.

Nunn, P., 1978. 'Foinaven Saga: The Cnoc and the Maiden', *Mountain*, 62.

Nunn, P., 1988. *At the Sharp End*. London: Unwin Hyman.

Nunn, P., 1994. *The Edge: One Hundred Years of Scottish Mountaineering*. London: BBC.

Old Man of Hoy Outside Broadcast, 1967. London: BBC.

Page, B., 2014. Interview with M. Dixon on 17 October. Nottingham.

Patey, I., 2021. Personal communication by email. 3 October.

Patey, T., 1953. 'Parallel Gully "B"', Lochnagar', SMCJ, vol.25, no.144, pp.115–20.

Patey, T., 1954. 'Aiguilles des Cairngorms' in *One Man's Mountains* (1971). London: Victor Gollancz.

Patey, T., 1955. 'Accident in the Aiguilles', Etchachan Club Journal, vol.2, no.3, pp.84–91.

Patey, T., 1956. 'Appointment with Scorpion', *Etchachan Club Journal*, vol.2, no.4, pp.145–51.

Patey, T., 1957. 'The Mustagh Tower', SMCJ, vol.26, no.148, pp.101–14.

Patey, T., 1958. 'The Zero Gully Affair', SMCJ, vol.26, no.149, pp.205–16.

Patey, T., 1959. 'Rakaposhi— The Taming of the Shrew', *SMCJ*, vol.26, no.150, pp.343–55.

Patey, T., 1959. 'Over the Sea to Skye', *Etchachan Club Journal*, vol.3, no.1, pp.21–41.

Patey, T., 1960. 'The Trolls were Angry', *Etchachan Club Journal*, vol.3, no.2, pp.71–93.

Patey, T., 1960. 'The Girdle Traverse of Ben Nevis in Winter', *Climbers' Club Journal*, vol.13, no.1, no.85, pp.75–80.

Patey, T.W., 1960. 'With Arne Randers Heen on the Romsdalhorn', *SMCJ*, vol.27, no.151, pp.6–12.

Patey, T., 1962. 'Cairngorm Commentary', *SMCJ*, vol.27, no.153, pp.207–20.

Patey, T., 1963. 'A Short Walk with Whillans' in *One Man's Mountains*. London: Victor Gollancz.

Patey, T., 1964. 'In Memoriam: T.G. Longstaff', *Alpine Journal*, vol.69, no.309, pp.325–26.

Patey, T., 1965. 'The First Winter Traverse of the Cuillin Ridge', *SMCJ*, vol.28, no.156, pp.69–87.

Patey, T., 1966. 'The Greatest Show on Earth', *Climbers' Club Journal*, vol.15, no.1 (new series), no.91, pp.70–86.

Patey, T., 1966. 'Climbing the Old Man of Hoy', *Scots Magazine*, December.

Patey, T., 1967. 'The Old Man of Stoer', *SMCJ*, vol.28, no.158, pp.261–67.

Patey, T., 1969. 'Apes or Ballerinas?', *Mountain*, 3.

Patey, T., 1970. 'Creag Meaghaidh Crab-Crawl', *SMCJ*, vol.29, no.161, pp.231–38.

Patey, T., 1970. 'In Memoriam: James McAtney', *SMCJ*, vol.29, no.161, pp.330–31.

Patey, T., 1971. *They Sought the Summits*. London: BBC Radio.

Patey, T., 1971. *One Man's Mountains: Essays and Verses*. London: Victor Gollancz.

Perrin, J., 1982. 'The Ice Climbers: A Literary Discourse', *Climber & Rambler*.

Perrin, J., 1987. 'The Incomparable Dr. Patey', *Climber Magazine*, May.

Perrin, J., 2006. *The Villain: The Life of Don Whillans*. London: Arrow Books.

Porter, J., 2014. *One Day as a Tiger: Alex MacIntyre and the Birth of Light and Fast Alpinism*. Sheffield: Vertebrate Publishing Ltd.

Pyper, D., 2001. 'The Way Things Were', *SMCJ*, vol.37, no.192, pp.525–32.

Roberts, D., 1974. 'Patey Agonistes or A look at Climbing Autobiographies', *Ascent*, 2/2, pp.86–91.

Robertson, G., 2020. Personal communication by email. 9 April.

Robertson, G. and Crofton, A., 2014. *The Great Mountain Crags of Scotland*. Sheffield: Vertebrate Publishing Ltd.

Richardson, S., 2020. Personal communication by email. 18 August.

Robbins, R., 1969. 'An Excursion in Scotland', *SMCJ*, vol.29, no.160, pp.139–44.

Roch, A., 1949. *Climbs of my Youth*. London: Lindsay Drummond.

Ross, P., 2019. Interview with M. Dixon on 30 July. Keswick

Scott, B., 1971. *They Sought the Summits*. London: BBC Radio.

Scott, R. and Nicol, G., 2015. *Of Bens, Glens and Rambling Auld Men*. Market Harborough: Matador.

Scottish Episcopal Church, 2021. *Who we are: Introduction* [online]. Available at: https://www.scotland.anglican.org/who-we-are/about-us/introduction/ [Accessed 29 November 2021].

Shaw, R., 2016. Personal communication by email. 30 March.

Shepherd, N., 1977. *The Living Mountain*. Aberdeen: Aberdeen University Press.

Shipton, E., 1951. *The Mountains of Tartary*. London, Hodder & Stoughton.

Skye and the Hebrides, Rock and Ice Climbs. Volume 2. 1996. UK: Scottish Mountaineering Trust.

Slesser, M., 1993. 'In Memoriam Norman Sinclair Tennent', *SMCJ*, vol.35, no.184, pp.341–42.

SMCJ, May 1960. Proceedings of the Club, Reception. Vol.27, no.151, p.92.

SMCJ, 1960. 'SMC and JMCS Abroad', Norway, p.103.

SMCJ, 1961a. Notes (King Cobra, Cioch Nose). Vol.27, no.152, pp.171–72.

SMCJ, 1961b. New Climbs (Storr). Vol.27, no.152, p.159.

SMCJ, 1962. Vol.27, No.153. p.274.

SMCJ, 1964. Central Highland Notes. Vol.28, no.155, pp.41–42.

SMCJ, 1969. 'The Ballad of Dr. Stack' (Anon.), and Miscellaneous Notes. Vol.29, no.160, p.205.

SMCJ, 1970. New Climbs. Vol.29, no.161, p.286.

SMCJ, 1971. 'In Memoriam Thomas Walton Patey', vol.29, no.162 pp.433–38.

SMCJ, 1998. New Climbs, St Kilda. Vol.36, no.189, pp.572–77.

SMCJ, 2012. *In Memoriam: William Dixon Brooker*. Vol.42, no.203, p.275.

Smith, D., 2013. Interview with M. Dixon on 2 October. Dingwall.

Smith, J., 1957. 'Sestogradists in Scotland', *Climbers' Club Journal*, vol.12, no.1, no.82, pp.51–58.

Smith, M., 1961. *SMC Climbers' Guide to the Cairngorms Area, Vol.1*.

Smith, M., 1962a. *SMC Climbers' Guide to the Cairngorms Area, Vol.2*.

Smith, M., 1962b. *The Etchachan Club*. SMCJ, vol. 27, no.153, pp.250–53.

Smith, R., 1960. 'The Bat and the Wicked', *SMCJ*, vol.27, no.151, pp.12–20.

Spencer, H., 2016. Personal communication by email. 12 December.

Stainforth, G., 2012. *Fiva: An Adventure That Went Wrong*. UK: Golden Arrow Books.

Stainforth, G., 1994. *The Cuillin: Great Mountain Ridge of Skye*. London: Constable.

Stewart, M., 2014. Interview with M. Dixon on 19 January. Temple Cottage, Balmore.

Stewart, M., Jan 1965. *Creag Meagaidh*. Unpublished.

Strange, G., 1976. 'The Winter Mitre', *SMCJ*, vol.31, no.167, pp.30–35.

Strange, G., 2010. *The Cairngorms: 100 Years of Mountaineering*. Edinburgh: Scottish Mountaineering Trust.

Tabin, G., and McIntosh, S., 2001. 'Mountain medicine, performance-enhancing drugs and climbing', *American Alpine Journal*.

Thom, A., 2013. Personal communication by email. 10 December.

Thompson, S., 2010. *Unjustifiable Risk? The Story of British Climbing*. Milnthorpe: Cicerone Press.

Thomson, I.D.S., 1993. *The Black Cloud: Scottish Mountain Misadventures 1928–1966*. Glasgow: The Ernest Press.

Various. Ullapool Bothy Book. 29 February 1964 to 29 March 1970, pp.1–36.

Watson, A., 2005. 'In Memoriam, Malcolm Stirton Smith', *SMCJ*, vol.39, no.196, p.210.

Watson, A., 2011. *It's a Fine Day for the Hill*. Trowbridge: Paragon Publishing.

Weir, T., 1981. 'Remembering Tom Patey' in *Weir's Way*. Edinburgh: Gordon Wright Publishing Ltd.

Weir, T., 1987. 'The Incomparable Dr. Patey', *Climber Magazine*, May.

Weir, T., 1994. 'Harum-Scarum Days' in *Weir's World*. Edinburgh: Canongate Books Ltd.

Whillans, D., 1971. *They Sought the Summits*. London: BBC Radio.

Will, A., 2013. Interview with M. Dixon on 3 December. Aberdeen.

Wilson, Ken., 1974. *Hard Rock*. London: Hart-Davis, MacGibbon.

Wilson, K., Alcock, D. and Barry, J., 1983. *Cold Climbs*. London: Diadem Books.

Index

Aberdeen 20, 26–27, 29, 31, 33–35, 69, 89, 90, 98–100, 120, 165, 236–39, 260, 264–66, 282–83, 404, 406–7, 428–29, 432
   and climbing 41–42, 81–103, 118–19, 137, 148, 163–64, 177, 182, 244, 257, 385, 438–40
   and medical work 117, 156, 244
   and university 29–30, 38–40, 60–61, 74–77, 81–103, 117
Aiguille du Peigne
   Papillons Arête 109
   West-North-West Face 110
Aiguille du Plan
   Greloz-Roch Route 335
   North Face 111–13
   Ryan-Lochmatter 115
   West Face 335–36, 349
Aitken, Donald 51–52, 106–7
Aladdin's Buttress (Coire an t-Sneachda) 92
Alburger, Mary Anne 289, 361
Alladale Wall (An Socach) 259
Alligator Crawl (Long Haven) 50
Alpha Club 315, 329, 347, 422
Alpine Climbing Group 77, 133, 376
Alpine Club 77, 259, 341, 346, 376, 434
Alps, The 104–27
Am Buachaille 326–30
Amphetamines 100, 201, 395–98
An Socach 259
   Alladale Wall 259
   Whigmaleerie 259
An Teallach 270
   Checkmate Chimney 364
Åndalsnes 213–16, 355–56
Aviemore 26, 120–21, 173, 175, 190, 375, 396, 415

Baillie, Rusty 310–26, 349–50, 406, 441–42
Baltoro Glacier 134, 139
Banks, Mike 133, 153, 170, 195–208, 395
Barclay, Dick 254, 297
Barrel Buttress (Quinag) 257, 297
BBC Outside Broadcast 310–31, 409–12
Beard, Eric 322, 389–93, 409
Beinn a' Bhùird 42, 74, 85
Beinn Bhàn 248, 300, 361–62
Beinn Dearg
   Eigerwanderer 365
   Fenian Gully 295
   Inverlael Gully 294
   Orangeman's Gully 295
   Papist's Passage 295
   Penguin Gully 294–95
   Tower of Babel, The 254
Beinn Eighe
   Gash, The 257
   Gnome Wall 257
   Triple Buttresses 234, 257, 264, 365
   Upper Girdle 235
   Wall of the Winds 234–35
   West Buttress 234–35
Bell, J.H.B. 67, 90, 122–24, 161, 182, 249, 254
Bell's Route (Lochnagar) 99
Bemrose, Sam 172–77, 213–23, 238–40, 283–84, 396
Ben Macdui 26, 177
Ben Mor Coigach 277, 432
Ben Nevis
   Castle Ridge 44
   Cresta 159
   Gardyloo Gully 44
   Hadrian's Wall Direct 185

INDEX

Italian Climb *402–6*
Little Brenva Face, The *158*
Nevis Girdle *182–85*
North Castle Gully *44*
Observatory Ridge *161*
Orion Direct *71*
Point Five Gully *71*
Sassenach *75, 76*
Tower Ridge *44, 403, 405*
Wendigo *300*
Zero Gully *160–62*
Ben Vorlich *156*
Bennachie *27, 40*
Bhasteir Tooth *303, 304*
Bickleigh *170–72, 180, 190, 226*
Biolay campsite *334*
Bispen *222, 355*
Bitter (Quinag) *297*
Biven, Barrie *190, 226, 241, 322–25*
Blaber, Ernie *177, 227, 239–40*
Black Spout Buttress (Lochnagar) *62*
Black Tower, The (Coire Sputan Dearg) *51*
Bonington, Chris *35, 135, 273, 325*
    and the Alps *343–49, 357*
    and bothies *287*
    and Glencoe *68, 241, 360*
    and the Himalaya *360, 379*
    and North-West Scotland *361–62, 364*
    and Outside Broadcasts *287, 310*
    and sea stacks *316–25*
    and Skye *233–38*
Bonington, Wendy *316, 331*
Bourdillon, Tom *77–78*
Boysen, Martin *297–98, 347–50, 390–93*
Braemar *33–34, 42, 48, 64, 85–86, 100, 248*
Brasher, Chris *310, 322–26, 331, 408–9*
Brooke, Richard *196–208, 248–55, 298, 395*
Brooker, Bill *283*
    and the Alps *106*
    and Ben Nevis *68, 75, 182, 185*
    and bothies *32–33*
    and the Cairngorms *32–33, 39, 52–53, 67, 69–71, 76, 79, 103, 120, 123–27, 244*
    and music or socialising *57, 165*
    and North-West Scotland *316*

Brown, Joe *13, 111, 115, 273–74, 382*
    and the Alps *334–45, 376*
    and Ben Nevis *76, 300*
    and bothies *55*
    and Creag Meagaidh *298, 307*
    and Tom Patey's death *428–30*
    and the Himalaya *133–153, 394*
    and music or socialising *175, 344, 387, 389*
    and North-West Scotland *180*
    and Norway *352–55*
    and Outside Broadcasts *310–12, 321–25, 331, 410–14*
    and sea stacks *321–25*
    and stimulants *396–97*
Buachaille Etive Mòr *29*
    Raven's Gully *68, 233*

Cairn Gorm *26, 177*
Cairngorm Club Journal *46*
Cairngorm Hotel, The *120–21, 396*
Cairngorms, The
    climbing and socialising *38–103, 168–191*
    formative years *38–103*
    Patey's childhood *20–35*
Campbell, Alex *288–89*
Canon, Gill *422–29*
Cardinal, The
    South-East Face *108*
Carn Etchachan
    Crevasse Route *117*
    Route Major *156–57*
    Scorpion *62–65, 93*
Carrbridge *175–77, 249, 253, 386–89, 396*
Castle Ridge (Ben Nevis) *44*
Cathedral, The (Storr) *165, 238, 428*
Central Crack Route (Coire an Lochain) *182*
Central Groove (Dewerstone) *226*
Centre Post (Creag Meagaidh) *249*
Centre Post Direct (Creag Meagaidh) *298*
Chamonix *79, 106–17, 334–36, 344–50, 356, 376, 443*
Charlet, Armand *111–12, 127*
Charmoz-Grépon Traverse *106*
Checkmate Chimney (An Teallach) *364*
Chivers, Alan *318, 409–10*
Chock-a-Block Chimney (Blà Bheinn) *245*

CIC Hut *44, 158–62, 403–5*
Cinderella (Creag Meagaidh) *298*
Cioch Nose (Sgùrr a' Chaorachain) *235–36*
Clam, The (Lochnagar) *93–94*
Cleare, John *266, 376, 406, 440*
    and the Alps *347–49*
    and bothies *286*
    and the Cairngorms *375*
    and Creag Meagaidh *365, 391*
    and Tom Patey's death *413*
    and music or socialising *389–90*
    and North-West Scotland *389–90*
    and Outside Broadcasts *310–12, 318–19, 322, 410–11*
    and sea stacks *318–19, 322, 326–29*
Climbers' Club Direct (Dewerstone) *226*
Climbers' Club Journal 123, 182
Climbers' Guide to the Cairngorms (SMC) *39, 156*
Clough, Ian *182, 322–31, 402–3, 428*
Coire an Lochain
    Central Crack Route *182*
    Ewen Buttress *185*
    Fallout Corner *300*
    Gaffer's Groove *341*
    Milky Way *185*
    Western Route *92, 186*
    Y Gully Left Branch *60, 375*
Coire an t-Sneachda *182, 188*
    Aladdin's Buttress *92*
    Patey's Route *186*
Coire Ardair (Creag Meagaidh) *187, 249, 365*
Coire Mhic Fhearchair (Beinn Eighe) *234–35*
Coire na Poite *248, 361, 364*
    March Hare's Gully *361*
    North Gully of A' Chioch *300, 363*
    Upper Connecting Ridge of A' Chioch *300*
    Upper Connecting Ridge of A' Phoit *248*
Comb Gully Buttress (Ben Nevis) *300*
Conachair *409*
Corrour Bothy *93, 248, 404*
Coutts, Maurice *29, 41, 57*
Crab Crawl, The (Creag Meagaidh) *365–75*
Crabb, Davie *303–6*
Crab's Wall (Collieston) *41*

Creag an Dubh-loch
    False Gully *53*
    Labyrinth Direct *101*
    Sabre Cut *156*
    Sabre Edge *53, 120*
    Vertigo Wall *96–97, 120*
Creag Meagaidh *187–88, 248–51, 298, 365, 390–93*
    Centre Post *249*
    Centre Post Direct *298*
    Cinderella *298*
    Coire Ardair *187, 249, 365*
    Crab Crawl, The *365–75*
    Diadem *298*
    Last Post *253*
    North Post *188*
    Post Horn Gallop *248–51*
    Sash, The *298*
    Scene, The *367*
    South Pipe Direct *188*
    South Post *253*
Creagan a' Choire Etchachan *42, 100*
    Dagger, The *118*
    Djibangi *164*
    Original Route *86*
Creagh Dhu Club *159*
Cresta (Ben Nevis) *159*
Crevasse Route (Carn Etchachan) *117*
Crew, Pete *347, 410–12*
Crumbling Cranny (Lochnagar) *44*
Crystal Ridge (Coire Sputan Dearg) *33, 86*
Cuillin, The (Skye)
    climbing *236–38, 251–54*
    First Winter Traverse *292–307*
    formative years *44, 75*
Cundy, Di *423–26*
Cunningham, John *159–60, 375–76, 428*

Dagger, The (Creagan a' Choire Etchachan) *118*
Davies, Glenn *272, 394–95, 407, 420–22*
Davidson, Betty *see* Patey, Betty
Deacon, John 'Zeke' *187–90, 227–31*
Deep Cut Chimney (Hell's Lum Crag) *178*
Deeside *26–27, 39, 41, 89, 111, 253*
Derry Lodge *26, 42, 62, 248*
Dewerstone, The
    Central Groove *226*
    Climbers' Club Direct *226*

Leviathan *226*
Spider's Web *227*
Diadem (Creag Meagaidh) *298*
Diagonal Crack (Long Haven) *50*
Direct Nose Route (Sgùrr an Fhidhleir) *277*
Dixon, Mike (C.M.) *50–53, 277–78, 284*
Djibangi (Creagan a' Choire Etchachan) *164*
Dombås *190, 212–16,*
Douglas-Gibson Gully (Lochnagar) *44–48*
Dutton, Geoff *223, 437*

Eagle Ridge (Lochnagar) *62–68, 76–78, 180, 438*
Eiger, The *339–41, 376, 421*
Eigerwanderer (Beinn Dearg) *365*
Ellon *20–34, 41–42, 98–99, 120, 264, 429*
Enigma Grooves (Stac Pollaidh) *297*
Escalator (Hell's Lum Crag) *120*
Etchachan Club *32–33, 82–84, 100, 162, 244, 283, 367, 434*
Etchachan Club Journal 66, 71, 115
Ewen Buttress (Coire an Lochain) *185*

Fallout Corner (Coire an Lochain) *300*
False Gully (Creag an Dubh-loch) *53*
Fannaichs, The *244, 279*
Fenian Gully (Beinn Dearg) *295*
Fife Arms, The *33, 48, 85–86*
Fingal (Foinaven) *259*
Fiva Route (Store Trolltind) *217–22*
Foinaven *258, 297*
Fortress, The (Binnein Shuas) *300*
Fowler, Mick *379*
Frendo Spur (Aiguille du Midi) *334*
Freshwater, Clive *283, 389*
Fuchs, Eileen *175, 190, 386*
Fuchs, Karl *175, 190, 386*
Fyffe, Allen *158, 362–67*

Gaberlunzie (Ladhar Bheinn) *257*
Gaffer's Groove (Coire an Lochain) *341*
Gardenstown *25*
Gardyloo Gully (Ben Nevis) *44*
Gash, The (Beinn Eighe) *257*
Gelder Shiel *46, 56*
Gillman, Peter *274, 371, 396–98*
Glen Brittle *33, 236, 251–52*

Glen Coe *29, 33, 68, 321, 360, 390, 397, 403–4*
Glen Cottage *361–62*
Glenmore *60, 174, 188–89, 428*
Gnome Wall (Beinn Eighe) *257*
Gogarth *310–18*
Goksøyra (North-West Rib) *355*
Gray, Dennis *57, 245, 273–74, 383–85, 393–94*
Great Diedre (Long Haven) *50*
Great Gully, The (Garbh Bheinn) *360, 368*
Green Lady, The (Neist) *245*
Greloz-Roch Route (Aiguille du Plan) *335*
Grieve, John *402–6, 413, 416*
Gutter, The (Lochnagar) *99*

Hadrian's Wall Direct (Ben Nevis) *185*
Hallelujah Staircase (Long Haven) *50*
Handa, Stack of *287, 322–23*
Hanging Dyke (Coire Sputan Dearg) *86*
Hardie, Dick *24, 27, 42*
Harlin, John *350–52, 437*
Hartog, John *130–34, 140, 145, 150–51*
Haston, Dougal *31, 321–25*
Hay, John *118–22, 127, 145, 153*
Haytor *227*
Hell's Lum Crag
    Deep Cut Chimney *178*
    Escalator *120*
    Kiwi Slabs *185*
Horrible Hielanders *31–32*
Hudson, Mary Ann *365–67, 375, 402, 404*
Hutchison Memorial Hut *92–93*

Imlach, Hamish *390–92*
Inaccessible Pinnacle (Skye Cuillin) *252, 306*
Ingle, Baz *287, 298, 310, 347, 428*
Inverlael Gully (Beinn Dearg) *294*
Italian Climb (Ben Nevis) *402–6*
It's a Fine Day for the Hill 89

Karakoram
    Muztagh Tower *128–53*
    Rakaposhi *192–209*
Kincorth Mountaineering Club *84*
King Cobra (Sgùrr Mhic Choinnich) *237*
King's Cave Wall/Outside Edge combination (Am Basteir) *237*

Kiwi Slabs (Hell's Lum Crag) *185*
Knickerbocker Glory (Tollie Crags) *301*

Ladhar Bheinn *254*
   Gaberlunzie *257*
   Viking Gully *257*
Lairig Club *41, 42, 44, 50, 52, 60, 76, 82, 84, 257, 283*
Lairig Ghru *27, 120*
Lake District *90*
Langmuir, Eric *303*
Last Post (Creag Meagaidh) *253*
Leslie, Gordon 'Goggs' *29–30, 42–44, 46–49, 57, 85, 101, 106*
Leviathan (Dewerstone) *226*
Ling Hut *234–35, 257, 361*
Little Brenva Face, The (Ben Nevis) *158*
Loch Avon *26, 62, 117*
Lochend Bothy *61, 63, 94, 126*
Lochnagar *42, 126, 145, 164*
   Bell's Route *99*
   Black Spout Buttress *62*
   Clam, The *93–94*
   Crumbling Cranny *44*
   Douglas-Gibson Gully *44–48*
   Eagle Ridge *62–68, 76–78, 180, 438*
   Gutter, The *99*
   Parallel Buttress *51, 122–24, 438*
   Parallel Gully B *52–53, 74, 164, 180*
   Polyphemus Gully *66, 164*
   Raeburn's Gully *44, 93, 99*
   Route 1 *126*
   Route 2 *68, 164*
   Shylock's Chimney *164*
   Stack, The *51, 62*
   Tough-Brown Traverse *51–52*
   Twin Chimneys Route *244*
Longstaff, Tom *271, 434*
Lovat, Len *113–16, 121–22, 158–59*
Luibeg Bothy *30–31, 34, 54, 62, 92–93, 283, 404*

MacInnes, Hamish *72, 271, 272, 279, 406, 408*
   and the Alps *356, 376*
   and Ben Nevis *159–63, 403–4, 409, 413*
   and Tom Patey's death *426–29*
   and Glencoe *68, 72, 233, 241, 416*
   and the Himalaya *133, 195*
   and North-West Scotland *235, 288, 297, 362*

   and Outside Broadcasts *310, 321–25, 331, 409*
   and sea stacks *316-25*
   and Skye *303–6*
Macleod, George *45–46, 94–97, 188*
Magic Bow, The (Sgùrr an Fhidhleir) *297–98*
Maiden, The *407, 422–28*
Malcolm, Freddie *84, 89, 93–97, 103, 108–13, 156*
March Hare's Gully (Coire na Poite) *361*
Marshall, Jimmy *71–72, 162–64, 180–85*
Matterhorn, The *106, 336*
McCartney, Jim *283*
   and Creag Meagaidh *365–67*
   and Tom Patey's death *375, 402–7, 428*
   and music or socialising *396*
   and North-West Scotland *367*
McNaught-Davis, Ian 'Mac' *182, 286, 310, 428*
Milky Way (Coire an Lochain) *185*
Mitre Ridge (Garbh Choire) *42, 69–71*
Mont Rouge de Peuterey *376*
Morrison, Charlie *29, 41, 52–54*
Morwell Rocks *226–27*
   Salvationist *227*
   Ultramontane *227*
Murray, W.H. *13, 50, 62, 79, 90, 112, 122–24, 132, 151, 159, 294, 434, 441*
Muztagh Tower *128–53*

National Service *23, 164–65, 170–72, 226*
Nevis Girdle (Ben Nevis) *182–85*
Newburgh *25–26*
Nicol, Graeme *84, 98–99, 102, 283*
   and the Alps *108–110*
   and Ben Nevis *158–62, 167*
   and bothies *62*
   and the Cairngorms *60–66, 74, 85, 120, 177, 248*
   and the Himalaya *259–60*
   and music or socialising *86, 89, 282*
   and North-West Scotland *257, 294, 297*
   and university *60*
Nisbet, Andy *57, 103, 241*
No 5 Buttress Gully (Sgòr Gaoith) *122*
North Castle Gully (Ben Nevis) *44*
North Face (Aiguille du Midi) *347*

North Face (Aiguille du Plan) *111–13*
North Face (Eiger) *339–41, 376, 421*
North Face (Muztagh Tower) *143, 146*
North Face (Pain de Sucre) *113*
North Gully of A' Chìoch (Coire na Phoit) *300, 363*
North Post (Creag Meagaidh) *188*
North-East Arête de la République (Aiguille des Grands Charmoz) *108*
North-West Face (Aiguille Sans Nom) *336–39*
Norway *210–23, 352–56*
Nunn, Paul *382*
    and Tom Patey's death *425–29*
    and North-West Scotland *290, 315–16, 329, 422–28*
    and sea stacks *315–16, 329, 422–28*

Observatory Ridge (Ben Nevis) *161*
Old Man of Hoy, The *316–26*
Old Man of Stoer, The *313–16*
One Man's Mountains *72, 173, 410, 434*
Orangeman's Gully (Beinn Dearg) *295*
Original Route (Creagan a' Choire Etchachan) *86*
Orion Direct (Ben Nevis) *71*
Outward Bound (Haytor) *227*

Papillons Arête (Aiguille du Peigne) *109*
Papist's Passage (Beinn Dearg) *295*
Parallel Buttress (Lochnagar) *51, 122–24, 438*
Parallel Gully B (Lochnagar) *52–53, 74, 164, 180*
Patey, Betty (nee Davidson) *120*
    and bothies *89, 92, 164, 284, 289, 341, 406–7*
    and the Cairngorms *74, 89, 92, 122, 126, 164*
    and Tom Patey's death *426, 429*
    and marriage *93, 156, 165, 179, 240, 264, 269*
    and music or socialising *89, 120*
Patey, Audrey *20–25, 27*
Patey, Ian *14, 240, 262, 312, 326, 331, 367, 429, 432–33*
Patey, Maurice *20–24, 127, 165, 386, 429*
Patey, Michael *264, 429, 432–33*
Patey, Reverend Thomas Maurice *20, 23–24, 27, 34–35, 90, 120, 127*
Patey, Rona *102, 429, 432*

Patey, Tom
    and the Alps *39, 50, 69, 106–17, 152, 334–41, 343–52, 356, 376*
    and Ben Nevis *44, 68, 75, 135–36, 158–62, 182–85, 300*
    and bothies *30–34, 42, 48, 54–55, 68–69, 85–86, 89, 93–94, 126, 164, 248, 253, 278, 282–90, 406*
    and the Cairngorms *26, 29, 30–34, 39–56, 60–77, 82–89, 92–97, 99–101, 117–18, 120–24, 156–57, 164–65, 177–80, 182, 185–88, 244, 300, 341, 375*
    and Creag Meagaidh *187–88, 208, 248–50, 298, 365–74 390–93*
    death of *395, 413, 425–30*
    and Glencoe *29, 34, 233*
    and the Himalaya *130–52, 195–208*
    and marriage *93, 156, 165, 179, 240, 264, 269*
    and medical work *20, 23, 98, 102, 116, 133, 170–72, 189, 205, 216, 253, 257, 259–60, 264–67, 271, 290, 345–46, 355, 407, 421, 433*
    and music or socialising *28–29, 48, 54–55, 61–62, 69, 76, 86, 89, 93, 101, 126, 175, 253, 282–90, 361, 382–90, 394, 396–97*
    and North-West Scotland *234–36, 254, 257–59, 264, 269–70, 274, 294–98, 300, 313–16, 326–29, 361–65, 420, 422–26*
    and Norway *173, 212–22, 352–56*
    and Outside Broadcasts *310–12, 318–26, 409–12*
    and the Royal Marines *23, 165, 170–77, 187, 189, 212, 216, 226, 240, 270, 272–73*
    and school *24–25, 29*
    and sea stacks *313–29, 423–28*
    and Skye *44, 75, 233, 236–38, 245, 251–53, 303–6*
    and stimulants *100, 201, 205, 395–97*
    and university *30, 34, 38–39, 40–41, 48, 60, 76, 98, 101–2*
Patey's Route (Coire an t-Sneachda) *186*
Penguin Gully (Beinn Dearg) *294–95*
Peterhead *40–41*
Phantom Fiddler, The (Sgùrr an Fhidhleir) *298*

Pillar of Assynt (Quinag) *297*
Pirrit, Jock *44*
Point Five Gully (Ben Nevis) *71*
Polyphemus Gully (Lochnagar) *66, 164*
Post Horn Gallop (Creag Meagaidh) *248–51*

Quinag *257, 288, 297, 365*
  Barrel Buttress *257, 297*
  Bitter *297*
  Pillar of Assynt *297*
  Rickety Ridge *297*
  Waste Pipe, The *297*

Raeburn, Harold *45, 57, 254, 257*
Raeburn's Gully (Lochnagar) *44, 93, 99*
Rakaposhi *192–209*
Ramsden, John 'Ram' *115–17*
Randers Heen, Arne *212–20, 352*
Raven's Gully (Buachaille Etive Mòr) *68, 233*
Red Wall (Gogarth) *310–18*
Rettie, Ian *42*
Richardson, Simon *339, 374, 439*
Rickety Ridge (Quinag) *297*
Robbins, Royal *311–12, 389–90, 437, 440*
Robert Gordon's College *29–30*
Robertson, Brian *284–86, 303–4, 307, 315–16*
Roch, Andre *115*
Rock and Ice Club *115, 135, 394*
Romsdalhorn *213–16*
Ross, Jimmy *387–89, 397*
Route 1 (Lochnagar) *126*
Route 2 (Lochnagar) *68, 164*
Route Major (Carn Etchachan) *156–57*
Rowanlea, The *387–89, 396–97*
Royal Marines, The *23, 165, 170–77, 186–90, 212–17, 222, 226, 240, 270–74, 283*
Ryan-Lochmatter (Aiguille du Plan) *115*

Sabre Cut (Creag an Dubh-loch) *156*
Sabre Edge (Creag an Dubh-loch) *53, 120*
Salvationist (Morwell Rocks) *227*
Sarcophagus (Chudleigh) *230*
Sash, The (Creag Meagaidh) *298*
Sassenach (Ben Nevis) *75, 76*
Scene, The (Creag Meagaidh) *367*
Scorpion (Carn Etchachan) *62–65, 93*
Scott, Bob *30–34*

Scottish Mountaineering Club (SMC) *45, 84, 97, 151, 162, 207, 236, 259, 294, 361, 434*
Second World War *26–27, 38, 131, 175, 339, 395*
Secret Howff *85, 103*
Sellers, Ronnie *244*
Sgùrr a' Chaorachain
  Cioch Nose *235–36*
  Sword of Gideon *245, 288*
Sgùrr an Fhidhleir
  Direct Nose Route *277*
  Magic Bow, The *297–98*
  Phantom Fiddler, The *298*
Shelter Stone Crag *62, 73*
Shylock's Chimney (Lochnagar) *164*
Skye *see* Cuillin
Skyscraper Buttress (Sgùrr nan Clach Geala) *244*
Sligachan *251–52, 304*
Slugain Bothy *85, 103*
Smith, Donnie *267–72, 394*
Smith, Jerry *118–20, 123–26, 182–83, 244*
Smith, Malcolm 'Mac' *32–33, 39, 82–83, 97–98, 100, 156–57*
Smith, Robin *171, 75, 183, 234, 238, 260*
Smuggler's Slab (Cornakey) *229*
South Pipe Direct (Creag Meagaidh) *188*
South Post (Creag Meagaidh) *253*
South Wall and South-East Arête combination (Aiguille Rouge de Rochefort) *356*
South-East Face (The Cardinal) *108*
South-East Ridge *139, 143*
Spider's Web (Dewerstone) *227*
Squareface (Garbh Choire) *74*
Squirrels *284, 295, 298, 315*
Stack, The (Lochanagar) *51, 62*
Stag Rocks
  Diagonal Gully *117*
  Relay Climb *118*
Stevenson, Vivian *172, 185–86, 217–22*
Stewart, Mary *286, 389–93*
Sticil Face, The (Shelter Stone Crag) *73, 177*
Stob a' Chearcaill *254*
Stob Coire nan Lochain *29*
Store Trolltind *217*
Struan *175, 249, 386–89*
Sword of Gideon (Sgùrr a' Chaorachain) *245, 288*

Taylor, Mike 97, 283
   and the Alps 106–7
   and Ben Nevis 68, 75, 182
   and bothies 93, 283–84, 361
   and the Cairngorms 40, 44, 51–53, 62–64, 67–68, 73–74, 76–77, 82, 85, 92–93, 126
   and Tom Patey's death 426, 429
   and medical work 98
   and music or socialising 93, 283
   and North-West Scotland 257, 278, 294
   and sea stacks 316
   and Skye 75
   and university 40–41, 98, 101
Temple Cottage 316, 389–92, 397, 437
Thearlaich-Dubh Gap (Skye Cuillin) 306
Thom, Alex 'Sticker' 84, 89, 93, 103, 108–10
Tiso, Graham 180, 302–4
Torridon 361–67
Tough-Brown Traverse (Lochanagar) 51–52
Tower of Babel, The (Beinn Dearg) 254
Tower Ridge (Ben Nevis) 44, 403, 405
Triple Buttresses (Beinn Eighe) 234, 257, 264, 365
Troll Wall (Store Trolltind) 213, 352
Tryfan 312
Twin Chimneys Route (Lochanagar) 244

Ullapool 12–13, 240, 264–66, 382–87, 394, 420–21, 432–33
   and the Bothy 280–91, 406–7
   and climbing 254, 267–71, 273–77, 294–97, 301–3, 365, 415
   and medical work 257, 260, 272, 397, 429
Ultramontane (Morwell Rocks) 227
Upper Connecting Ridge of A' Chìoch (Coire na Poite) 300
Upper Connecting Ridge of A' Phoit (Coire na Poite) 248
Upper Girdle (Beinn Eighe) 235

Vertigo Wall (Creag an Dubh-loch) 96–97, 120
Viking Gully (Ladhar Bheinn) 257

Wall of the Winds (Beinn Eighe) 234–35
Waste Pipe, The (Quinag) 297

Watson, Adam 83, 90, 97, 99
   and bothies 34, 86, 89, 93
   and the Cairngorms 34, 76, 82, 86, 89, 92–94
   and Tom Patey's death 426, 429
   and music or socialising 85–86, 89, 93, 101
   and university 76
Weir, Tom 84, 97, 407, 421
   and the Cairngorms 76–77, 122
   and Tom Patey's death 420–21, 440, 442
   and Glencoe 233
   and music or socialising 98–99, 121
   and North-West Scotland 235, 420–22
   and stimulants 98
   and university 76
Wendigo (Ben Nevis) 300
West Buttress (Beinn Eighe) 234–35
West Face (Aiguille du Plan) 335–36, 349
West-North-West Face (the 'Chamonix Face') (Aiguille du Peigne) 110
Western Cliffs (Quinag) 297, 365
Western Route (Coire an Lochain) 92, 186
Whigmaleerie (An Socach) 259
Whillans, Don 115
   and the Alps 135, 339–41
   and Ben Nevis 76, 135, 153
   and Creag Meagaidh 368
   and Tom Patey's death 428
   and Glencoe 360
   and the Himalaya 379
   and music or socialising 385–86, 389
   and North-West Scotland 238
   and stimulants 360
Whispering Wall (Sgùrr a' Mhadaidh) 238
Will, Alan 45–46, 94–101, 126, 397
Wrecker's Slab (Cornakey) 227, 229

Y Gully Left Branch (Coire an Lochain) 60, 375

Zero Gully (Ben Nevis) 160–62

All profits from Scottish Mountaineering Press books go to help fund the Scottish Mountaineering Trust, a Scottish charity that provides grants to projects and organisations that promote recreation, knowledge and safety in the mountains, especially the mountains of Scotland.

www.thesmt.org.uk